VOLUME ONE
BY
SONNY STRAIT

D0103435

HAMBURG // LONDON // LOS ANGELES // TOKYO

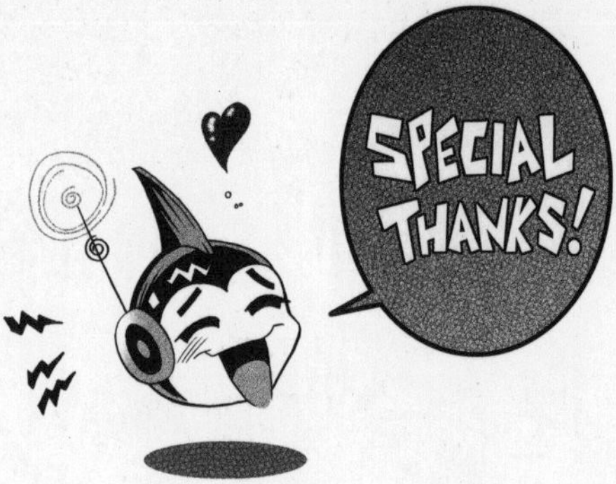
SPECIAL THANKS!

For...

Gayla, Savannah, Mary, Velma,
Lenore, Melinda, Ashleigh, Taylor, Tonya,
Sue, Avis, Andy, Bea, Mary Elizabeth,
Leanne, Karen, Michelle, Darlene, Thelma,
Rosemary, Davina, Susie, Janet, Alicia,
Jessica (the "real" Goat), Ramona, Cris,
Kate, Bethany, Colleen, Laura, Lois,
Linda, Bella and Wendy.

You ladies have made a profound impact
on my life and helped make me the man
I am today.

Thank you.
- Sonny

CONTENTS

FOREWORD
BY *ELFQUEST* CREATOR WENDY PINI

COME ON. YOU DON'T REALLY EXPECT ME TO BE ABLE TO TELL YOU WHAT THE HELL IS GOING ON IN THIS MANGA, DO YOU? I'M THE QUEEN OF ELVES AND STRAIGHT-UP ELF ENERGY IS WAY, WAY DIFF FROM WACKO FAERIE ENERGY. SONNY AND I FOUND THAT OUT WHEN I SHOWED HIM HIS FIRST REAL, LIVE FOREST. HE DIDN'T GO FOR THE TALL REDWOODS WITH THEIR BUILT-IN THRONES. HE WENT STRAIGHT FOR THE CRAZY, TANGLED BOWERS AND SAID HE FELT RIGHT AT HOME. NATURALLY. HE'S A FAERIE GLAMMED UP TO LIVE SORT OF--BUT NOT QUITE--A HUMAN LIFE.

BY THE WAY, THAT IS "FAERIE" WITH AN "AE," WHICH INDICATES FULL, ELDER POWER--NOT TO BE CONFUSED WITH THE DILUTE DESIGNATION: "FAIRY," WHICH APPROPRIATELY REFLECTS THE LETHARGY THAT DESCENDED ON THE FAERIE REALM WITH THE HUMAN INVENTION OF THE BULLET. ONCE HUMANS COULD KILL EACH OTHER WITH IRON (AND WITHOUT HAVING TO LOOK INTO EACH OTHER'S EYES), THE INDUSTRIAL REVOLUTION TOOK HOLD AND THE REIGNING "AE" GOT HUMBLED INTO THE SUBSERVIENT "AI." TODAY, IN MANY HUMAN QUARTERS THE WORD "FAIRY" IS, UNFORTUNATELY, SYNONYMOUS WITH FRAILTY AND EFFEMINACY.

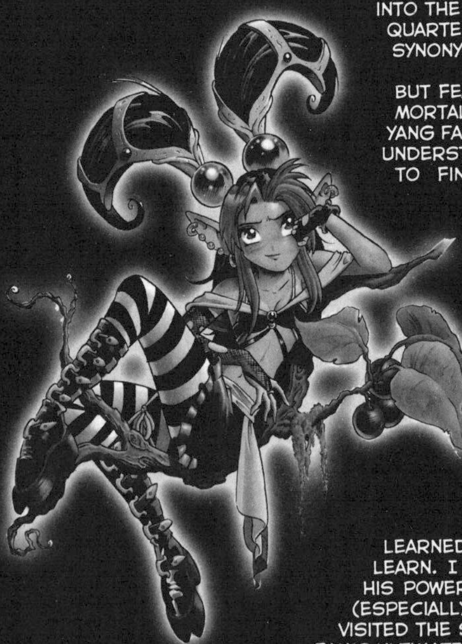

BUT FEAR NOT! SONNY'S HERE TO REINTRODUCE MORTALS, IN EASY-TO-TAKE DOSES, TO FULL YIN/YANG FAERIE POWER. BEING FAE, HIMSELF, I DON'T UNDERSTAND WHERE HE FINDS THE DISCIPLINE TO FINISH ANYTHING. BUT NO MATTER WHAT GEEKY FORM OF SELF-EXPRESSION HE CHOOSES--AND HE GOES FROM ONE TO ANOTHER WITH SUCH INSANE RAPIDITY IT'S IMPOSSIBLE TO SAY WHAT HE REALLY DOES FOR A LIVING--HE BRINGS TO IT A PROFOUNDLY TWISTED BUT UPBEAT ENERGY THAT ORIGINATES IN PURE LOVE. IN OTHER WORDS, EVEN THOUGH MANY DESERVE IT, HIS INTENT IS NOT TO SCARE THE CRAP OUT OF HUMANS.

WHEN SONNY WAS MY BELOVED ASSISTANT ON *ELFQUEST*, HE ABSOLUTELY PLUGGED IN TO MY CREATED UNIVERSE AND, WITH GREAT RESPECT AND SELF-CONTROL, LEARNED WHAT HE WANTED AND NEEDED TO LEARN. I WAS AWARE OF HOW HE SIMMERED DOWN HIS POWER, THOUGH AT TIMES IT EXPLODED FORTH (ESPECIALLY WHEN SEAN SCHEMMEL, VOICE OF GOKU, VISITED THE STUDIO AND I LIVED EVERY *DRAGON BALL Z* FAN'S ULTIMATE DREAM OF HAVING MY HAIR BLASTED BACK BY FULL-THROATED KAMEHAMEHAS).

IN *WE SHADOWS*, SONNY STRAIT DOESN'T HOLD ONE KINETIC BIT OF WACKINESS BACK. WHICH IS NOT TO SAY PARTS OF IT AREN'T DISTURBING--THEY ARE...BUT NOT FOR LONG. HIS METHOD OF STORYTELLING IS SIMPLY TOO TRIPPY FOR COLOR TV. AND YET, YOU'RE GOING TO LOVE THE RELUCTANT HEROINE GOAT, WHO STRIKES A CHORD OF SYMPATHY AND RECOGNITION.

ENTER, NOW, THE TANGLED BOWER OF FAERIE WHERE NOTHING GOES IN THE DIRECTION YOU EXPECT IT TO OR FLUTTERS BEFORE YOUR EYES FOR MORE THAN AN INSTANT. YOU MAY END UP WISHING *WE SHADOWS* WERE MERELY SURREAL, LIKE *ALICE IN WONDERLAND*. NO SUCH LUCK. SONNY REALLY IS MESSING WITH YOUR MIND. BUT GIVE HIM YOUR HANDS, IF YE BE FRIENDS, AND LIKE THE TRUE PUCK, HE'LL "RESTORE AMENDS."

- WENDY PINI

1 Faerie

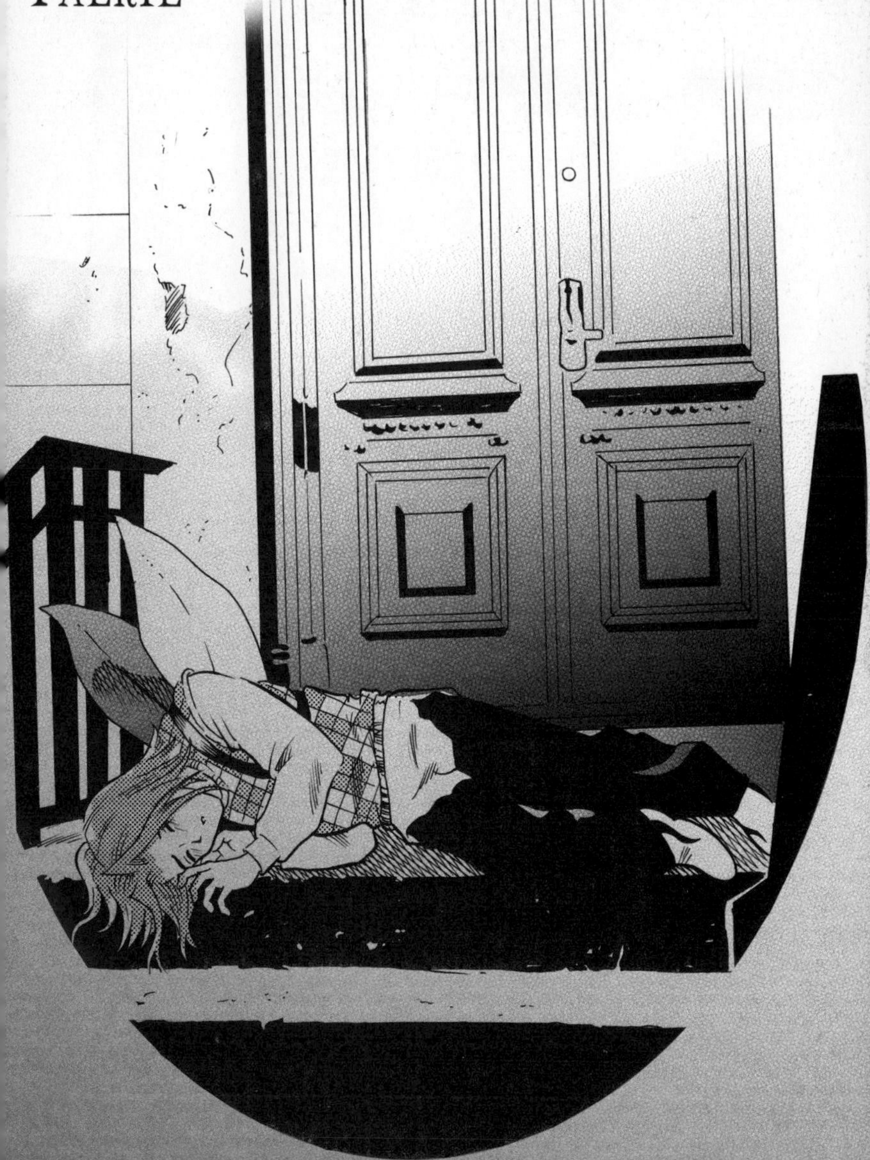

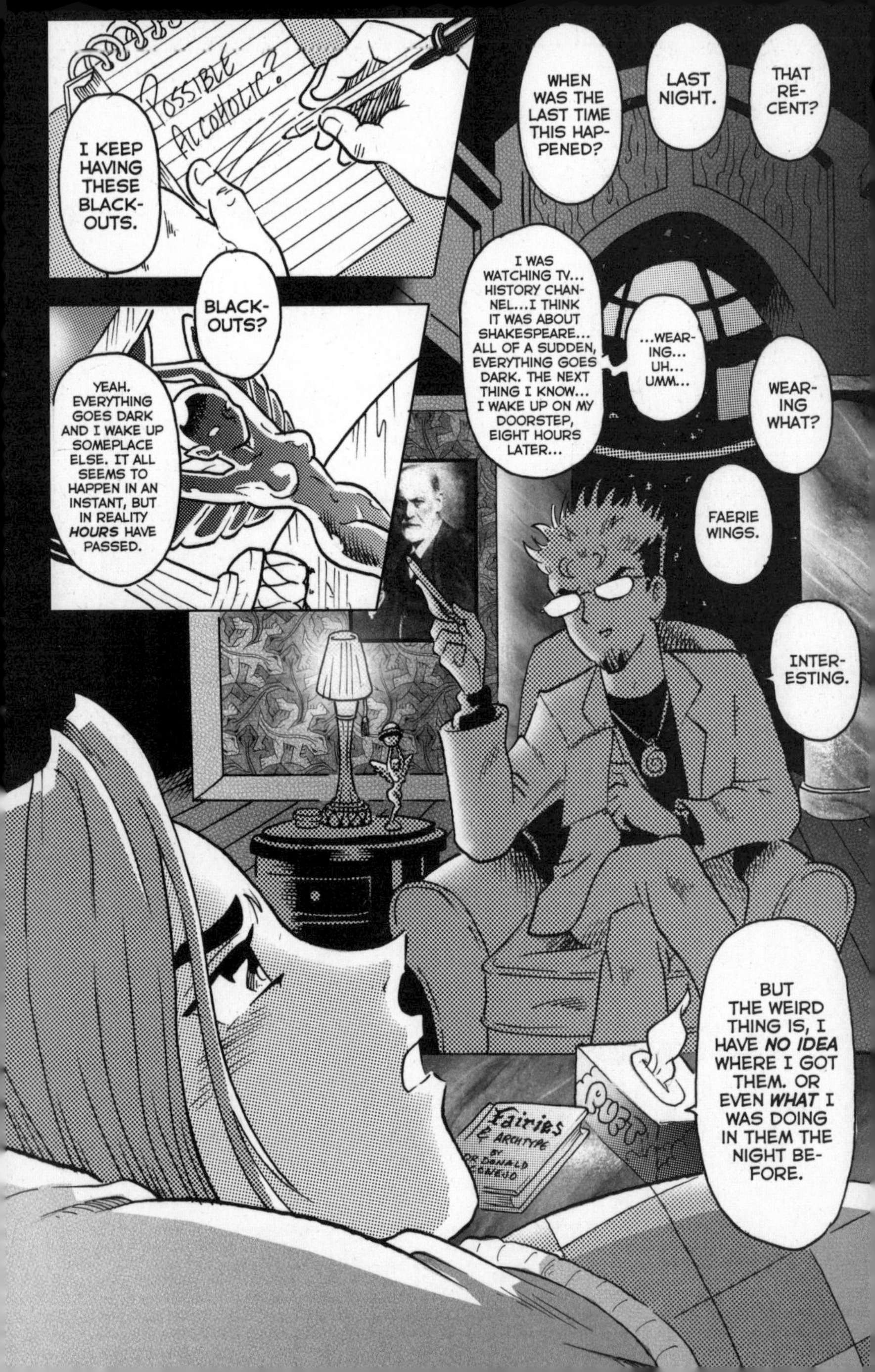
POSSIBLE ALCOHOLIC?
I KEEP HAVING THESE BLACK-OUTS.
WHEN WAS THE LAST TIME THIS HAP-PENED?
LAST NIGHT.
THAT RE-CENT?
BLACK-OUTS?
YEAH. EVERYTHING GOES DARK AND I WAKE UP SOMEPLACE ELSE. IT ALL SEEMS TO HAPPEN IN AN INSTANT, BUT IN REALITY *HOURS* HAVE PASSED.
I WAS WATCHING TV... HISTORY CHAN-NEL...I THINK IT WAS ABOUT SHAKESPEARE... ALL OF A SUDDEN, EVERYTHING GOES DARK. THE NEXT THING I KNOW... I WAKE UP ON MY DOORSTEP, EIGHT HOURS LATER...
...WEAR-ING... UH... UMM...
WEAR-ING WHAT?
FAERIE WINGS.
INTER-ESTING.
BUT THE WEIRD THING IS, I HAVE *NO IDEA* WHERE I GOT THEM. OR EVEN *WHAT* I WAS DOING IN THEM THE NIGHT BE-FORE.
Fairies & ARCHETYPE BY DR DONALD CONEJO

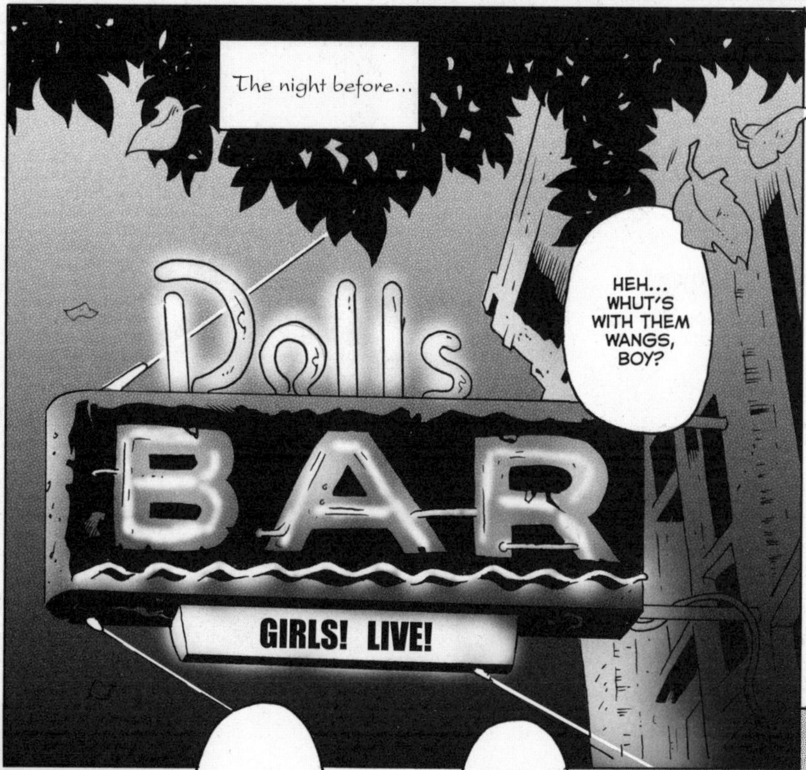
The night before...
Dolls
BAR
GIRLS! LIVE!
HEH... WHUT'S WITH THEM WANGS, BOY?
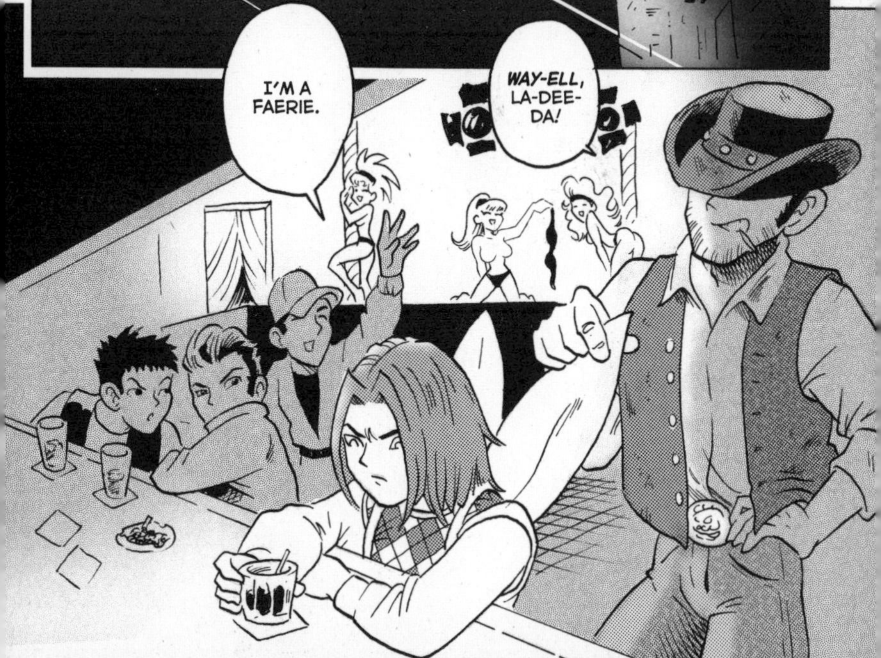
I'M A FAERIE.
WAY-ELL, LA-DEE-DA!

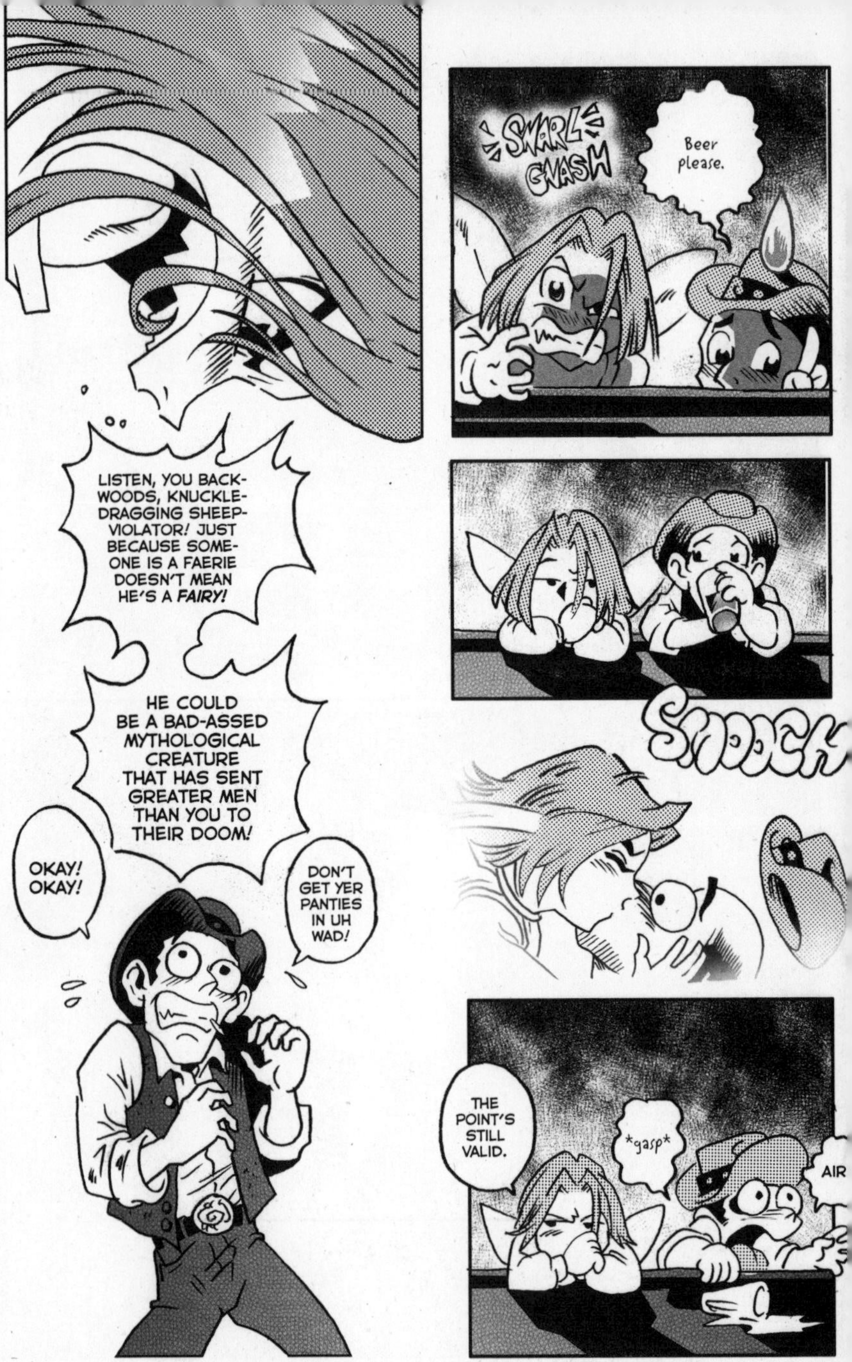
LISTEN, YOU BACK-WOODS, KNUCKLE-DRAGGING SHEEP-VIOLATOR! JUST BECAUSE SOME-ONE IS A FAERIE DOESN'T MEAN HE'S A *FAIRY!*
HE COULD BE A BAD-ASSED MYTHOLOGICAL CREATURE THAT HAS SENT GREATER MEN THAN YOU TO THEIR DOOM!
OKAY! OKAY!
DON'T GET YER PANTIES IN UH WAD!
SNARL GNASH
Beer please.
SMOOCH
THE POINT'S STILL VALID.
gasp
AIR

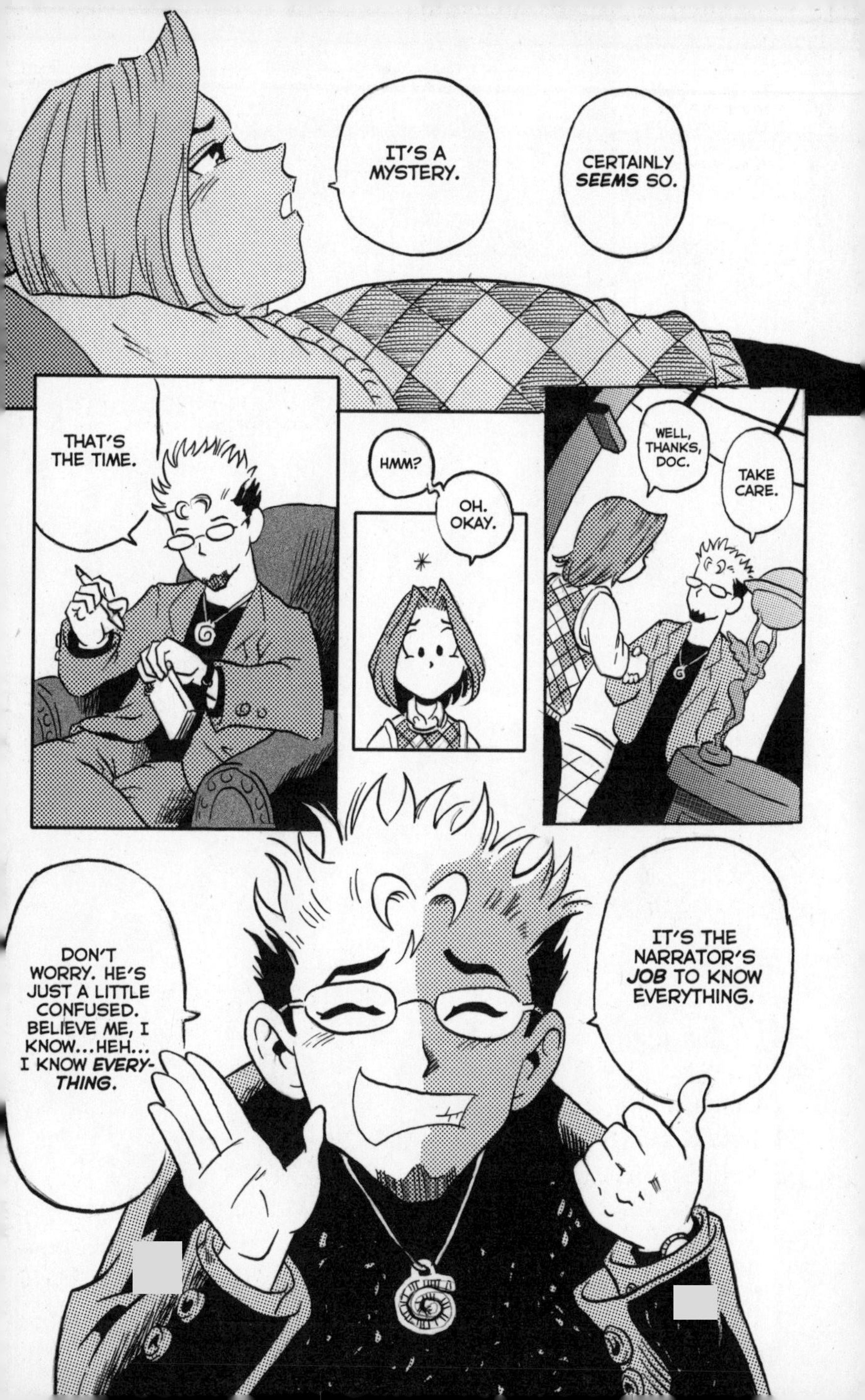
IT'S A MYSTERY.
CERTAINLY *SEEMS* SO.
THAT'S THE TIME.
HMM?
OH. OKAY.
WELL, THANKS, DOC.
TAKE CARE.
DON'T WORRY. HE'S JUST A LITTLE CONFUSED. BELIEVE ME, I KNOW...HEH... I KNOW *EVERYTHING*.
IT'S THE NARRATOR'S *JOB* TO KNOW EVERYTHING.

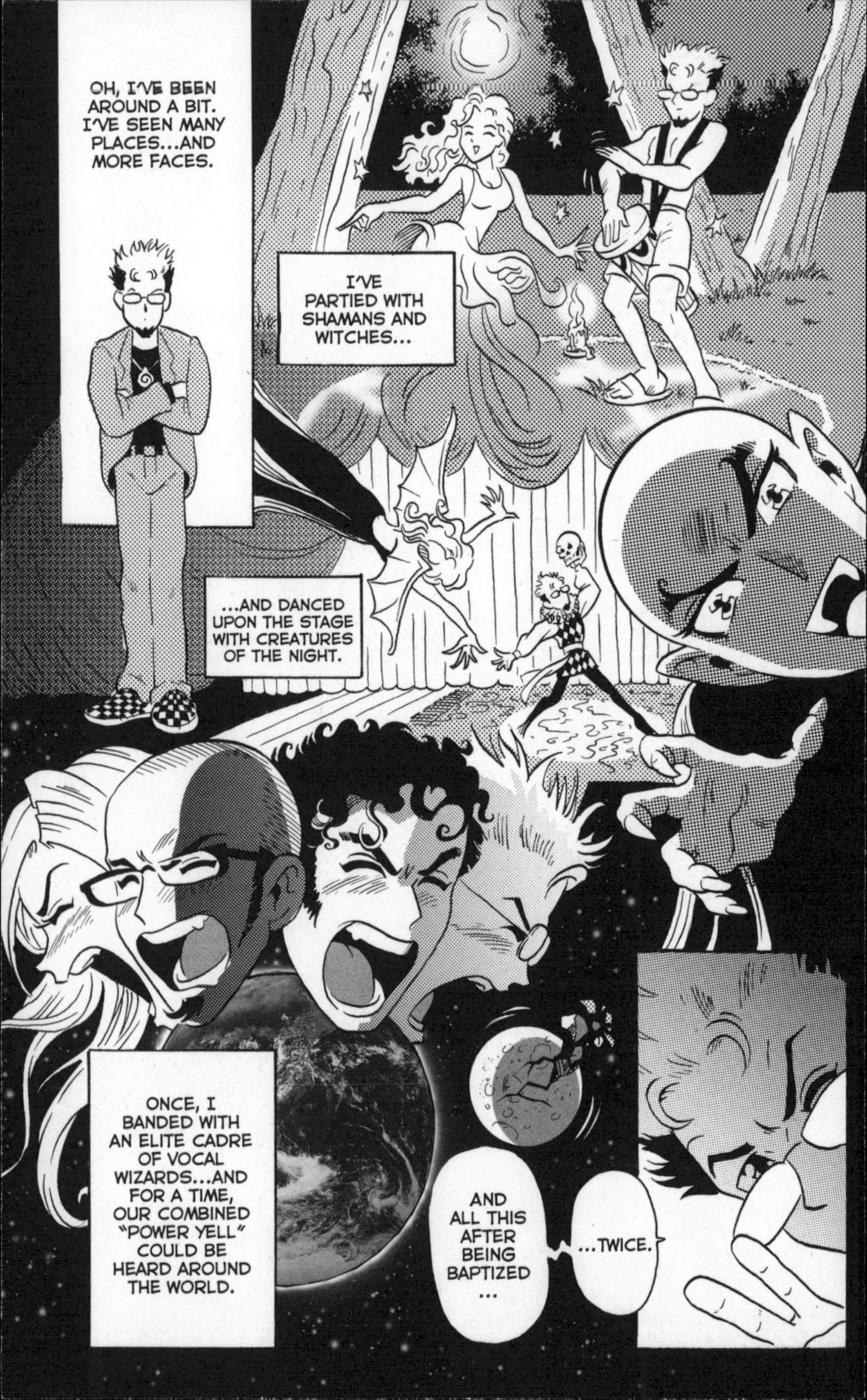
OH, I'VE BEEN AROUND A BIT. I'VE SEEN MANY PLACES...AND MORE FACES.
I'VE PARTIED WITH SHAMANS AND WITCHES...
...AND DANCED UPON THE STAGE WITH CREATURES OF THE NIGHT.
ONCE, I BANDED WITH AN ELITE CADRE OF VOCAL WIZARDS...AND FOR A TIME, OUR COMBINED "POWER YELL" COULD BE HEARD AROUND THE WORLD.
AND ALL THIS AFTER BEING BAPTIZED ...
...TWICE.

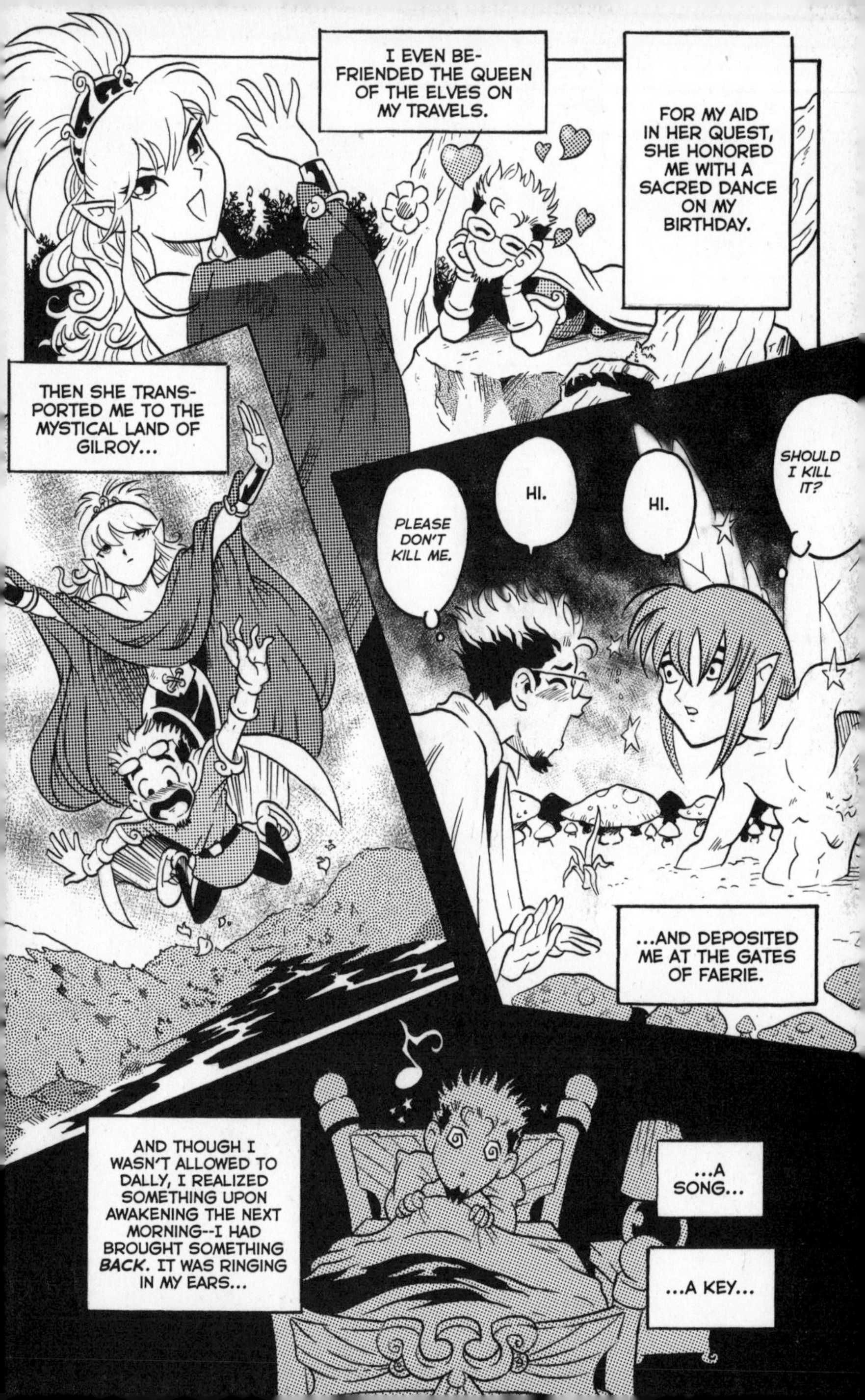

I EVEN BE-FRIENDED THE QUEEN OF THE ELVES ON MY TRAVELS.
FOR MY AID IN HER QUEST, SHE HONORED ME WITH A SACRED DANCE ON MY BIRTHDAY.
THEN SHE TRANS-PORTED ME TO THE MYSTICAL LAND OF GILROY...
PLEASE DON'T KILL ME.
HI.
HI.
SHOULD I KILL IT?
...AND DEPOSITED ME AT THE GATES OF FAERIE.
AND THOUGH I WASN'T ALLOWED TO DALLY, I REALIZED SOMETHING UPON AWAKENING THE NEXT MORNING--I HAD BROUGHT SOMETHING *BACK*. IT WAS RINGING IN MY EARS...
...A SONG...
...A KEY...

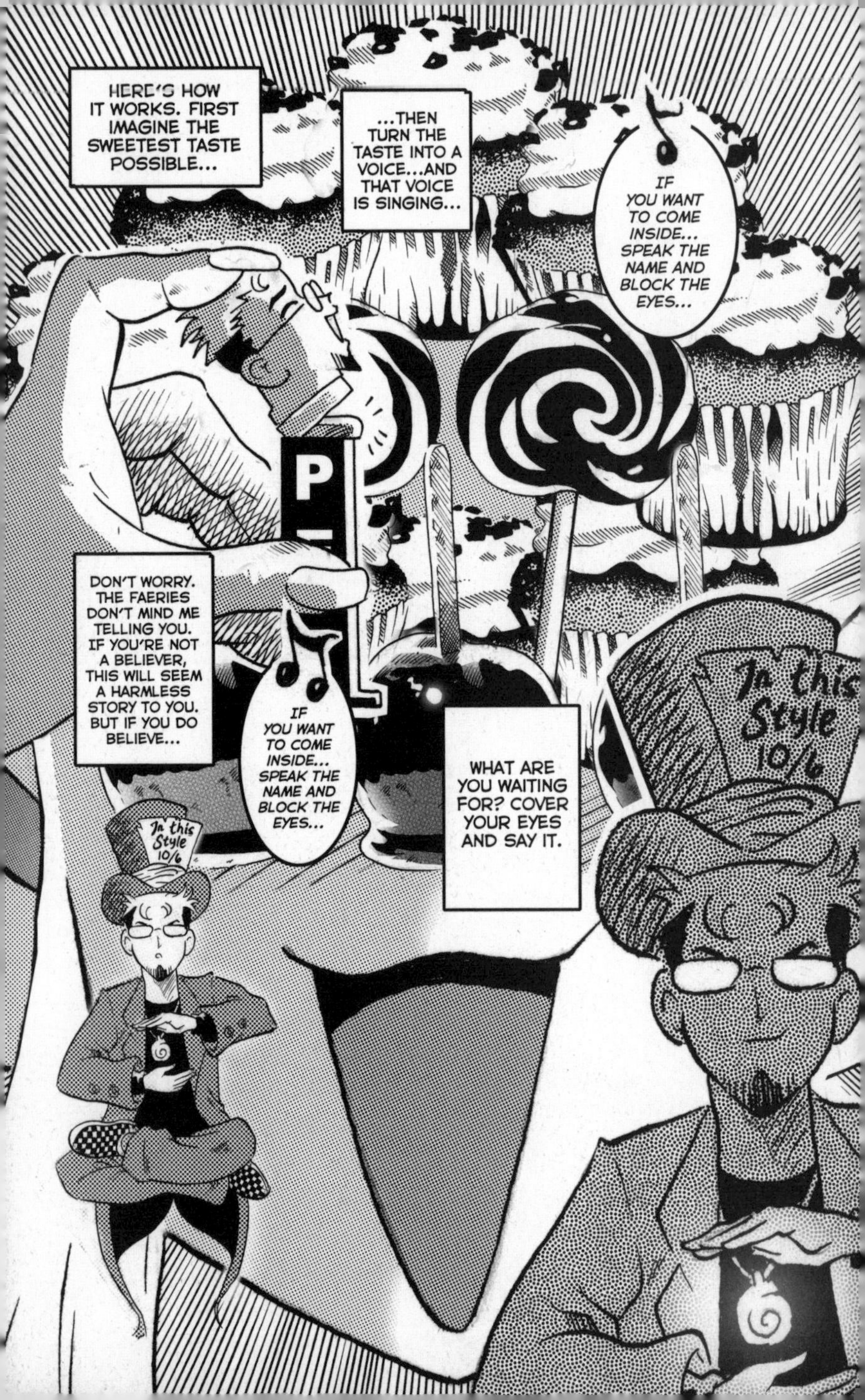
HERE'S HOW IT WORKS. FIRST IMAGINE THE SWEETEST TASTE POSSIBLE...
...THEN TURN THE TASTE INTO A VOICE...AND THAT VOICE IS SINGING...
IF YOU WANT TO COME INSIDE... SPEAK THE NAME AND BLOCK THE EYES...
P
DON'T WORRY. THE FAERIES DON'T MIND ME TELLING YOU. IF YOU'RE NOT A BELIEVER, THIS WILL SEEM A HARMLESS STORY TO YOU. BUT IF YOU DO BELIEVE...
IF YOU WANT TO COME INSIDE... SPEAK THE NAME AND BLOCK THE EYES...
In this Style 10/6
WHAT ARE YOU WAITING FOR? COVER YOUR EYES AND SAY IT.
In this Style 10/6

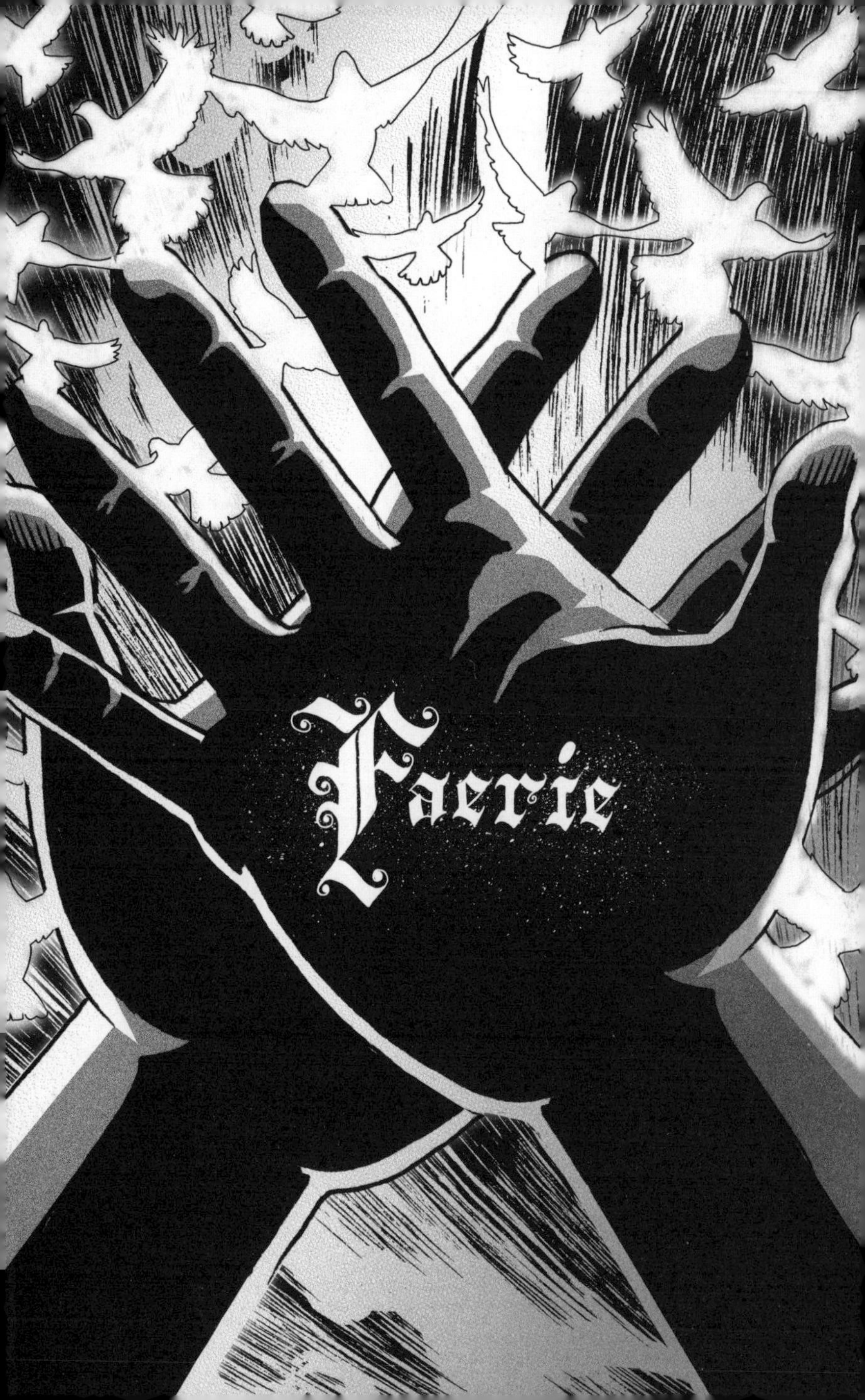
Faerie

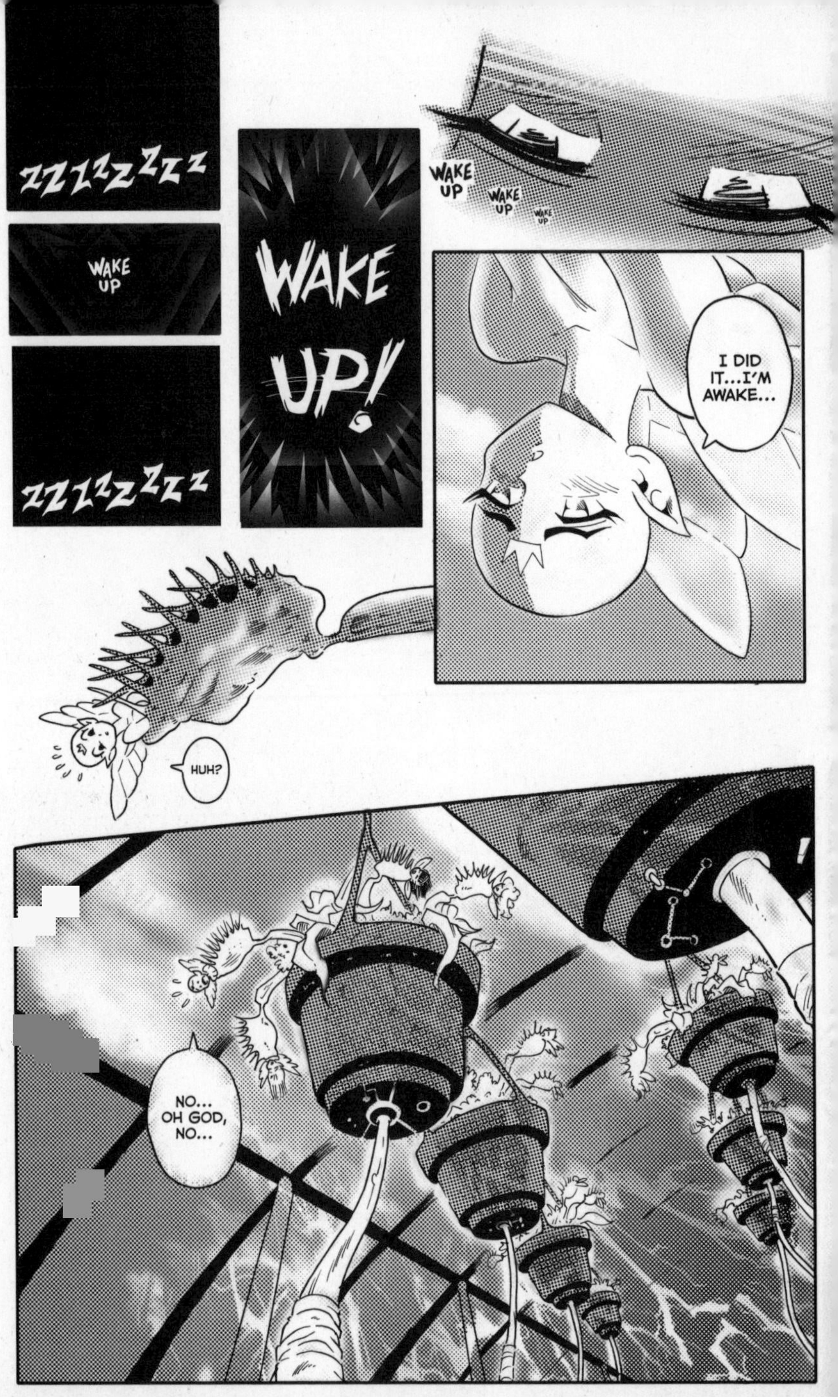
ZZZZZZZZZ
WAKE UP
ZZZZZZZZZ
WAKE UP!
WAKE UP
WAKE UP
WAKE UP
I DID IT...I'M AWAKE...
HUH?
NO... OH GOD, NO...

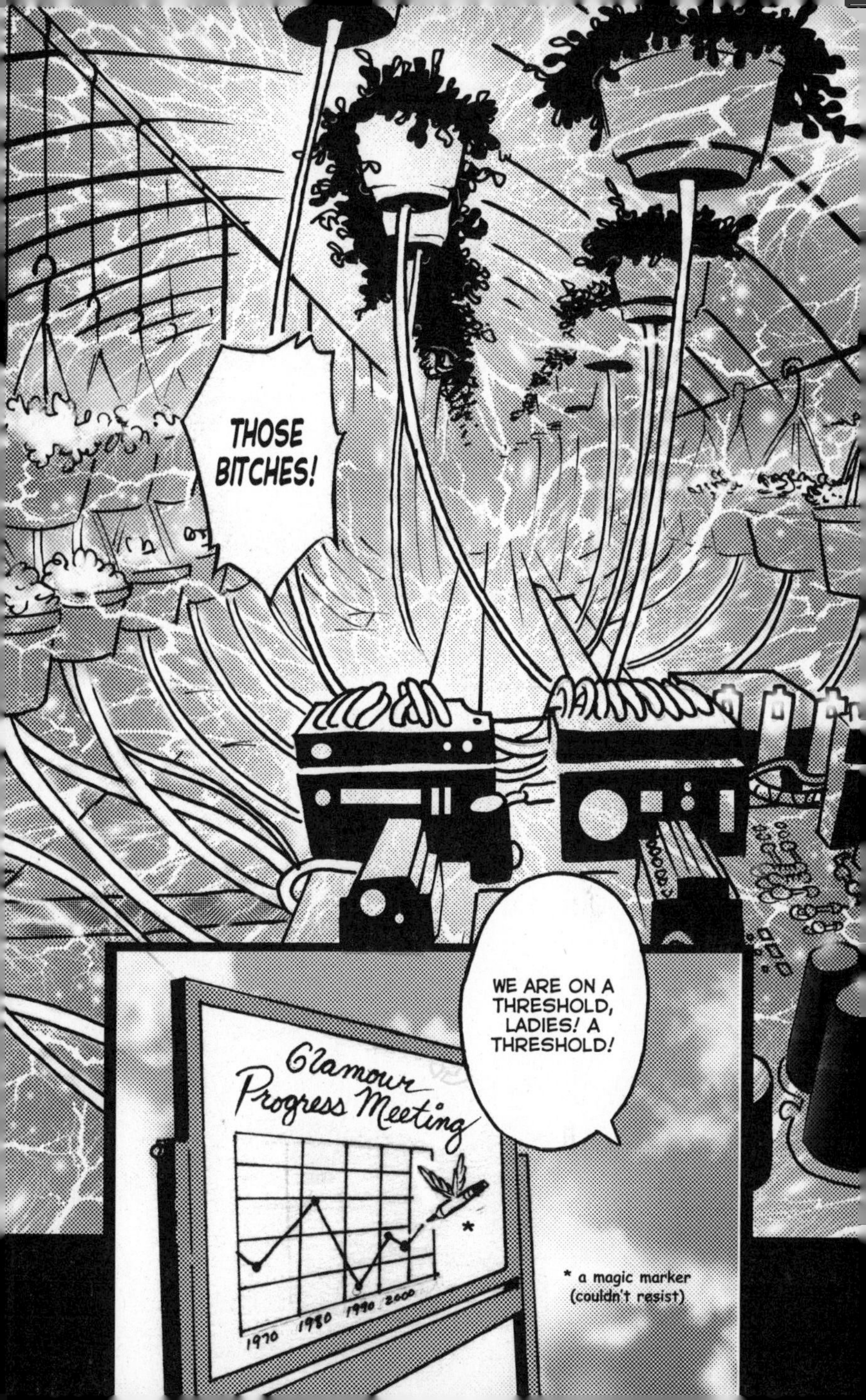
THOSE BITCHES!
WE ARE ON A THRESHOLD, LADIES! A THRESHOLD!
Glamour Progress Meeting
1970 1980 1990 2000
*
* a magic marker (couldn't resist)

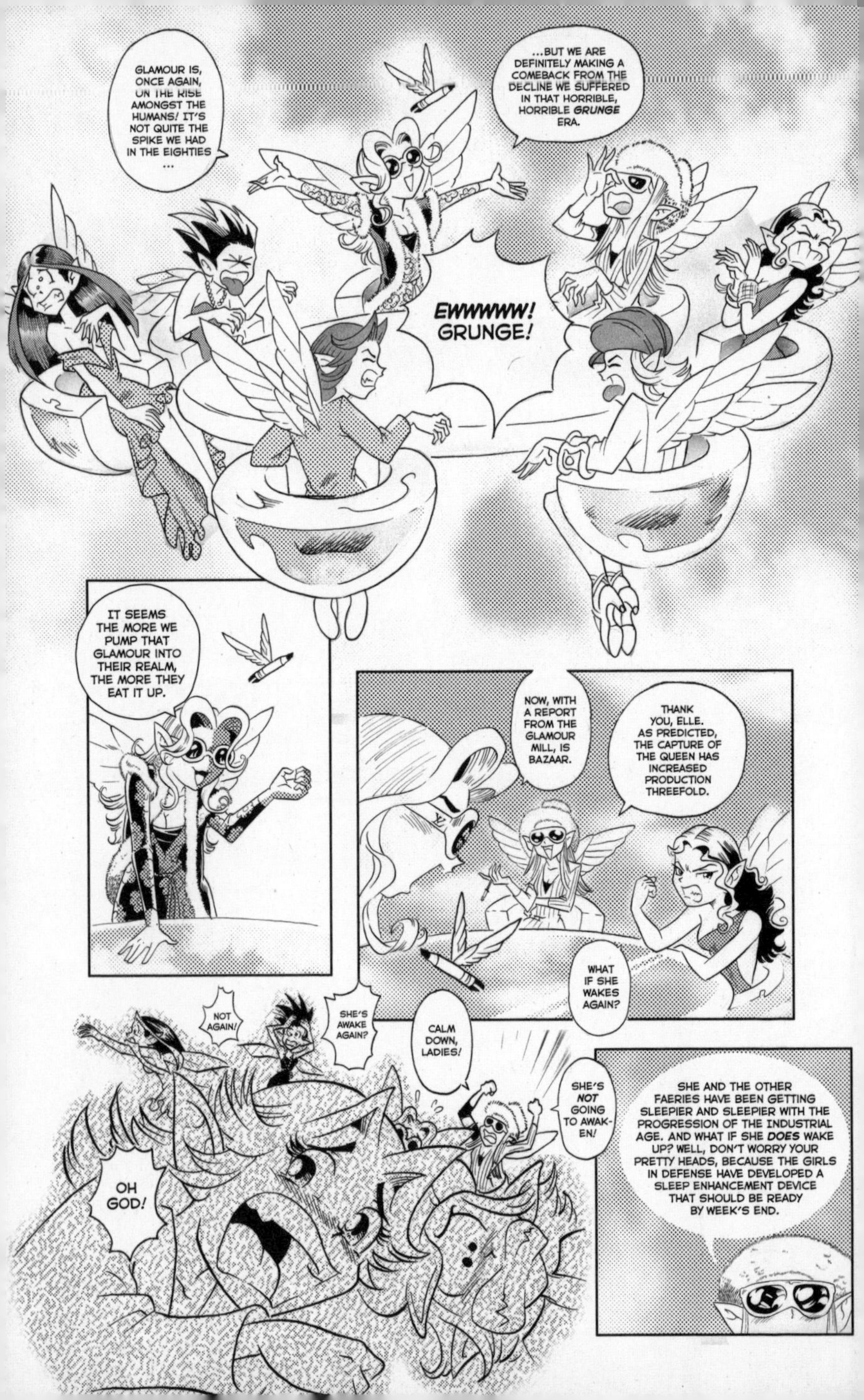
GLAMOUR IS, ONCE AGAIN, ON THE RISE AMONGST THE HUMANS! IT'S NOT QUITE THE SPIKE WE HAD IN THE EIGHTIES ...
...BUT WE ARE DEFINITELY MAKING A COMEBACK FROM THE DECLINE WE SUFFERED IN THAT HORRIBLE, HORRIBLE GRUNGE ERA.
EWWWWW! GRUNGE!
IT SEEMS THE MORE WE PUMP THAT GLAMOUR INTO THEIR REALM, THE MORE THEY EAT IT UP.
NOW, WITH A REPORT FROM THE GLAMOUR MILL, IS BAZAAR.
THANK YOU, ELLE. AS PREDICTED, THE CAPTURE OF THE QUEEN HAS INCREASED PRODUCTION THREEFOLD.
WHAT IF SHE WAKES AGAIN?
NOT AGAIN!
SHE'S AWAKE AGAIN?
CALM DOWN, LADIES!
SHE'S NOT GOING TO AWAKEN!
OH GOD!
SHE AND THE OTHER FAERIES HAVE BEEN GETTING SLEEPIER AND SLEEPIER WITH THE PROGRESSION OF THE INDUSTRIAL AGE. AND WHAT IF SHE DOES WAKE UP? WELL, DON'T WORRY YOUR PRETTY HEADS, BECAUSE THE GIRLS IN DEFENSE HAVE DEVELOPED A SLEEP ENHANCEMENT DEVICE THAT SHOULD BE READY BY WEEK'S END.

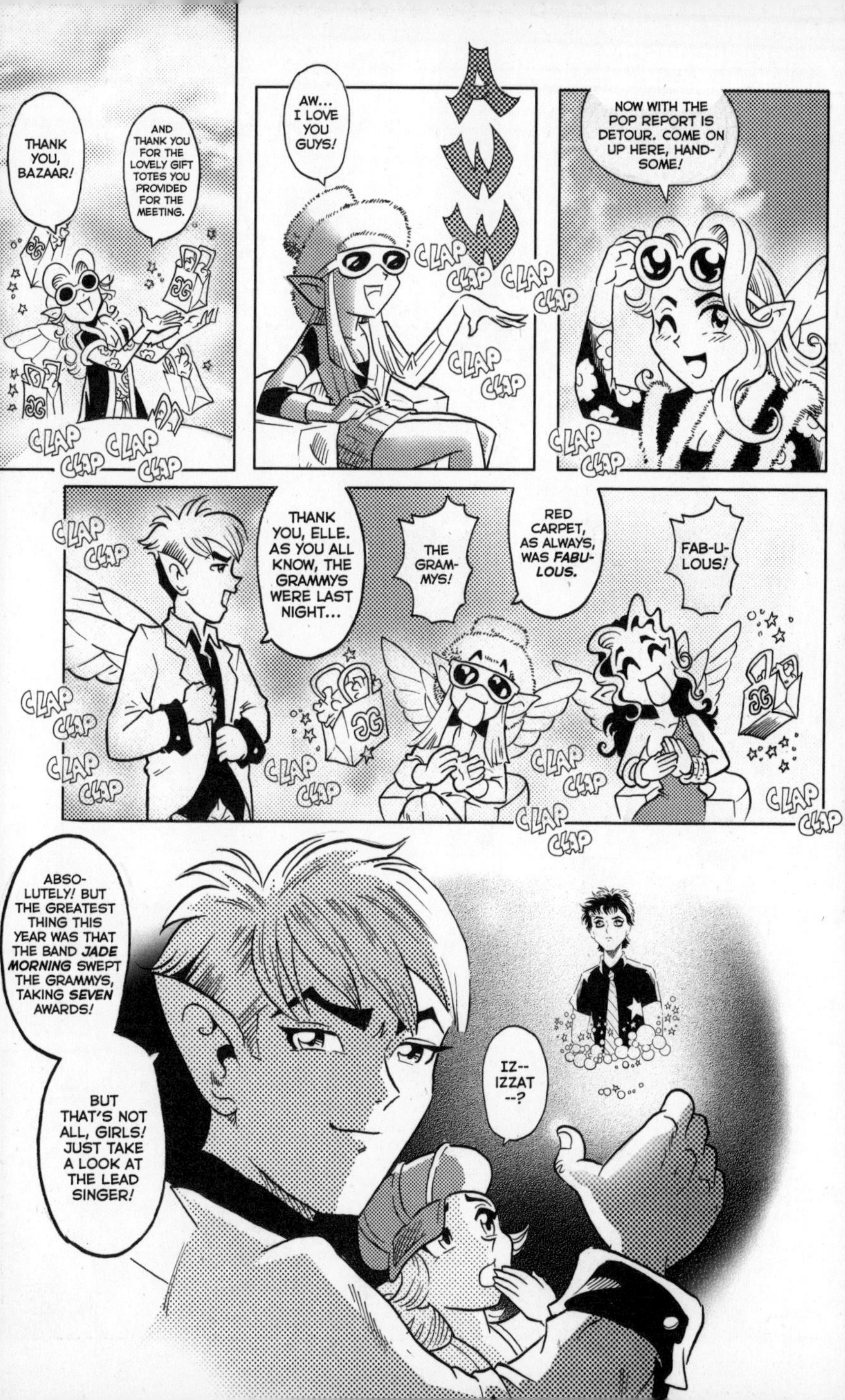
THANK YOU, BAZAAR!
AND THANK YOU FOR THE LOVELY GIFT TOTES YOU PROVIDED FOR THE MEETING.
CLAP CLAP CLAP CLAP
AW... I LOVE YOU GUYS!
AWW
CLAP CLAP CLAP CLAP
CLAP CLAP
NOW WITH THE POP REPORT IS DETOUR. COME ON UP HERE, HAND-SOME!
CLAP CLAP
CLAP CLAP
THANK YOU, ELLE. AS YOU ALL KNOW, THE GRAMMYS WERE LAST NIGHT...
THE GRAM-MYS!
RED CARPET, AS ALWAYS, WAS *FABU-LOUS.*
FAB-U-LOUS!
CLAP CLAP
CLAP CLAP
CLAP CLAP
CLAP CLAP
CLAP CLAP
CLAP CLAP
ABSO-LUTELY! BUT THE GREATEST THING THIS YEAR WAS THAT THE BAND *JADE MORNING* SWEPT THE GRAMMYS, TAKING *SEVEN* AWARDS!
BUT THAT'S NOT ALL, GIRLS! JUST TAKE A LOOK AT THE LEAD SINGER!
IZ-- IZZAT --?

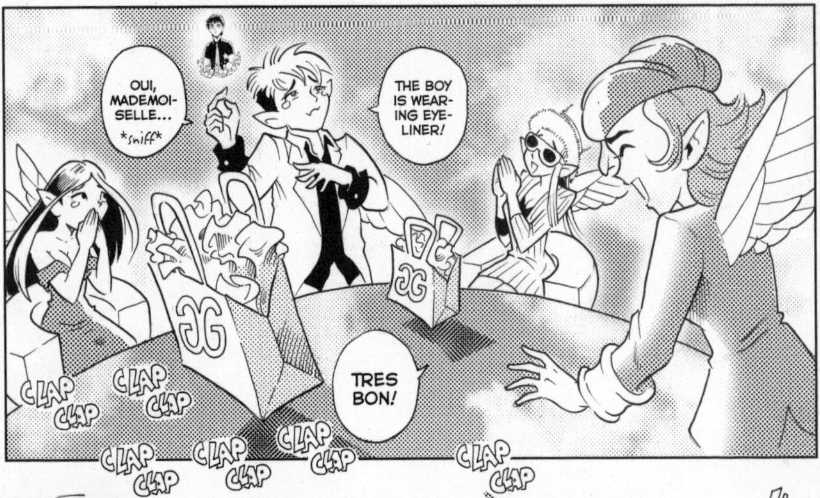
OUI, MADEMOISELLE... *sniff*
THE BOY IS WEARING EYELINER!
CLAP CLAP
CLAP CLAP
TRES BON!
CLAP CLAP
CLAP CLAP
CLAP CLAP
CLAP CLAP
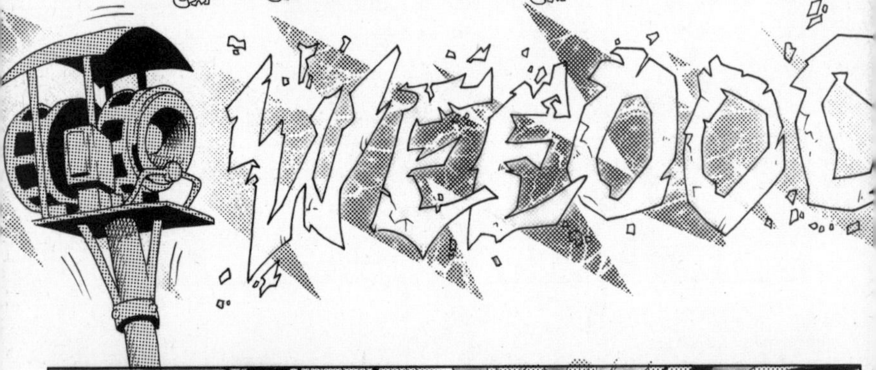
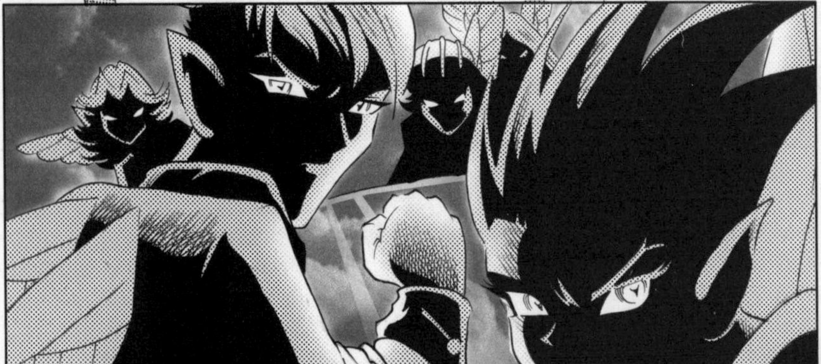

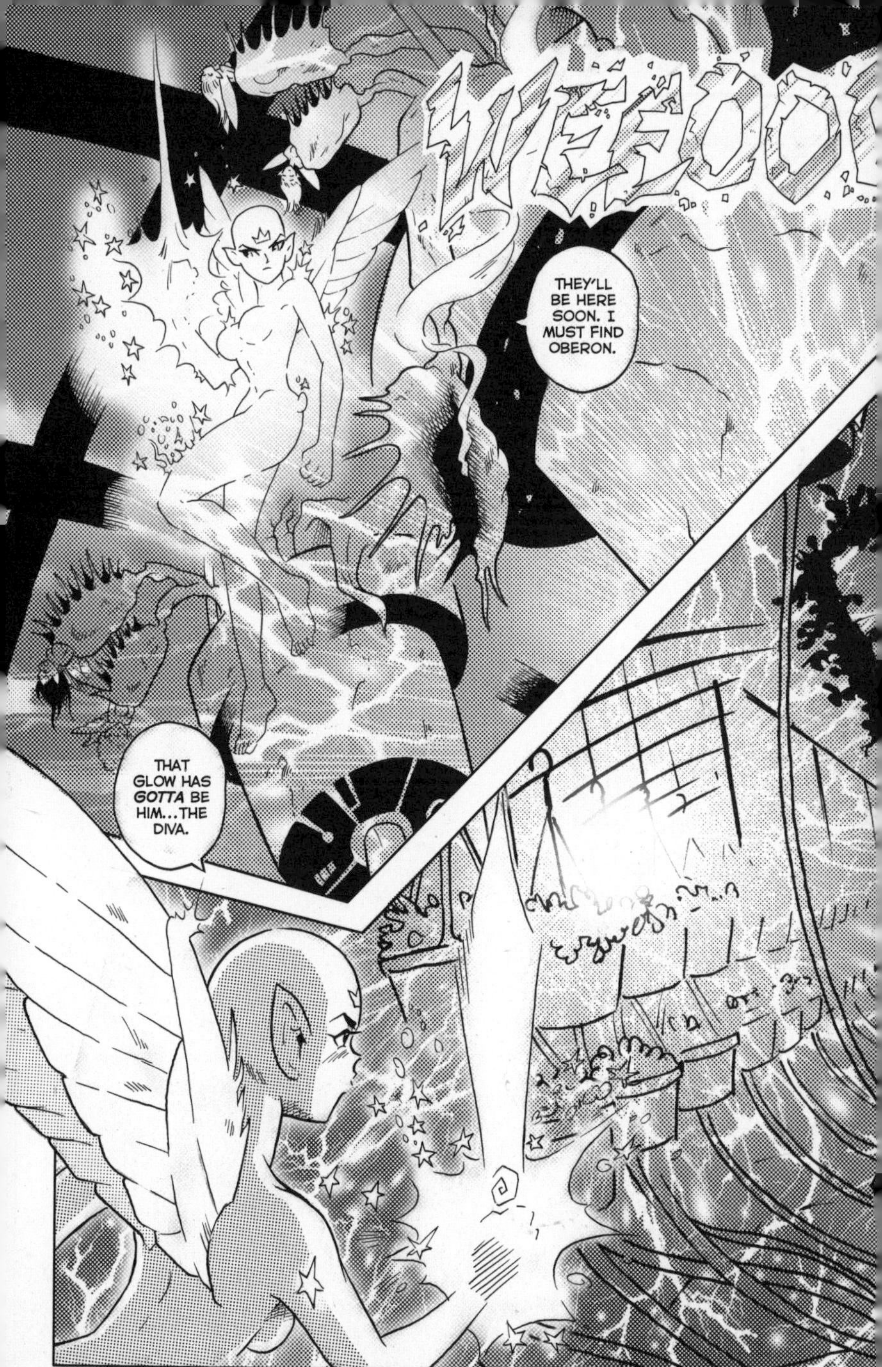
THEY'LL BE HERE SOON. I MUST FIND OBERON.
THAT GLOW HAS *GOTTA* BE HIM...THE DIVA.

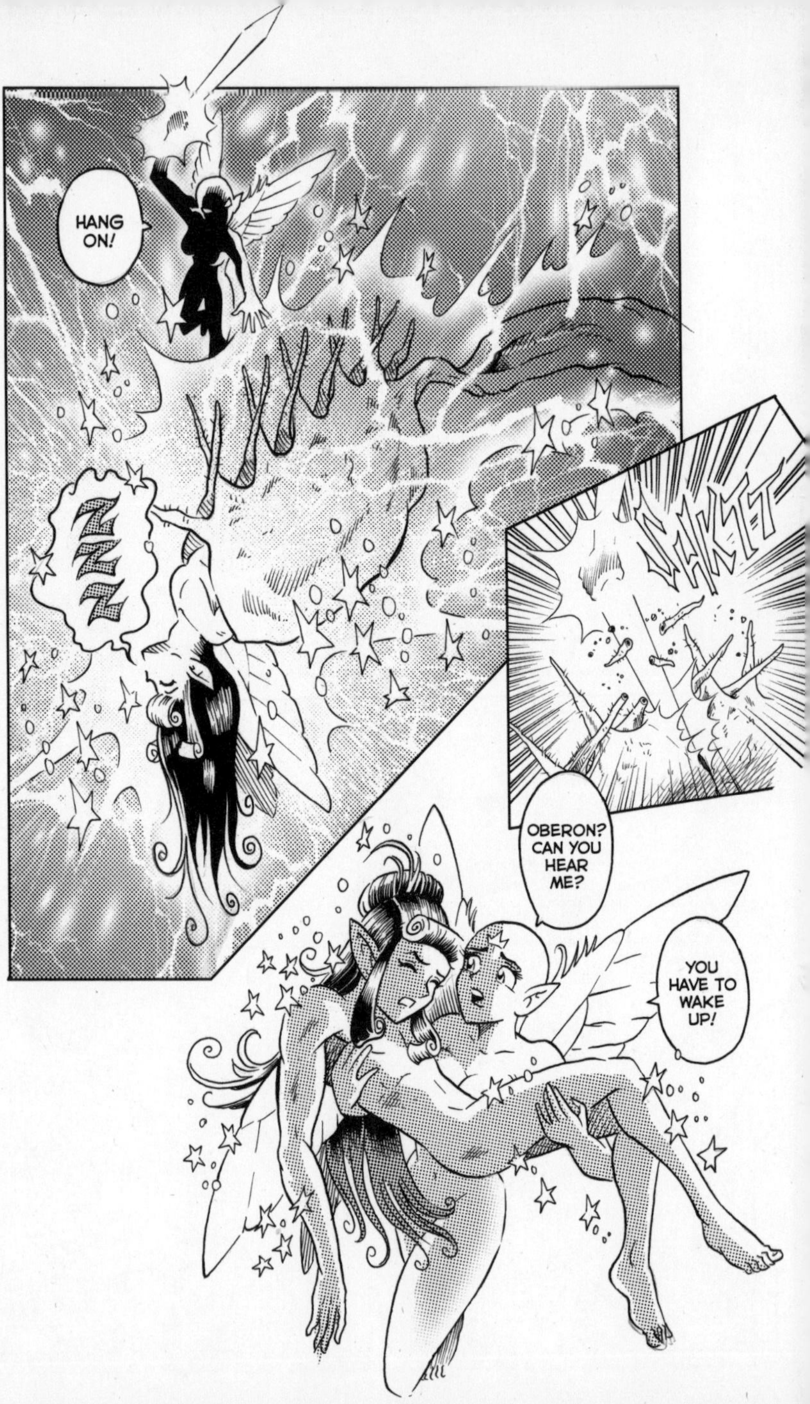
HANG ON!
OBERON? CAN YOU HEAR ME?
YOU HAVE TO WAKE UP!

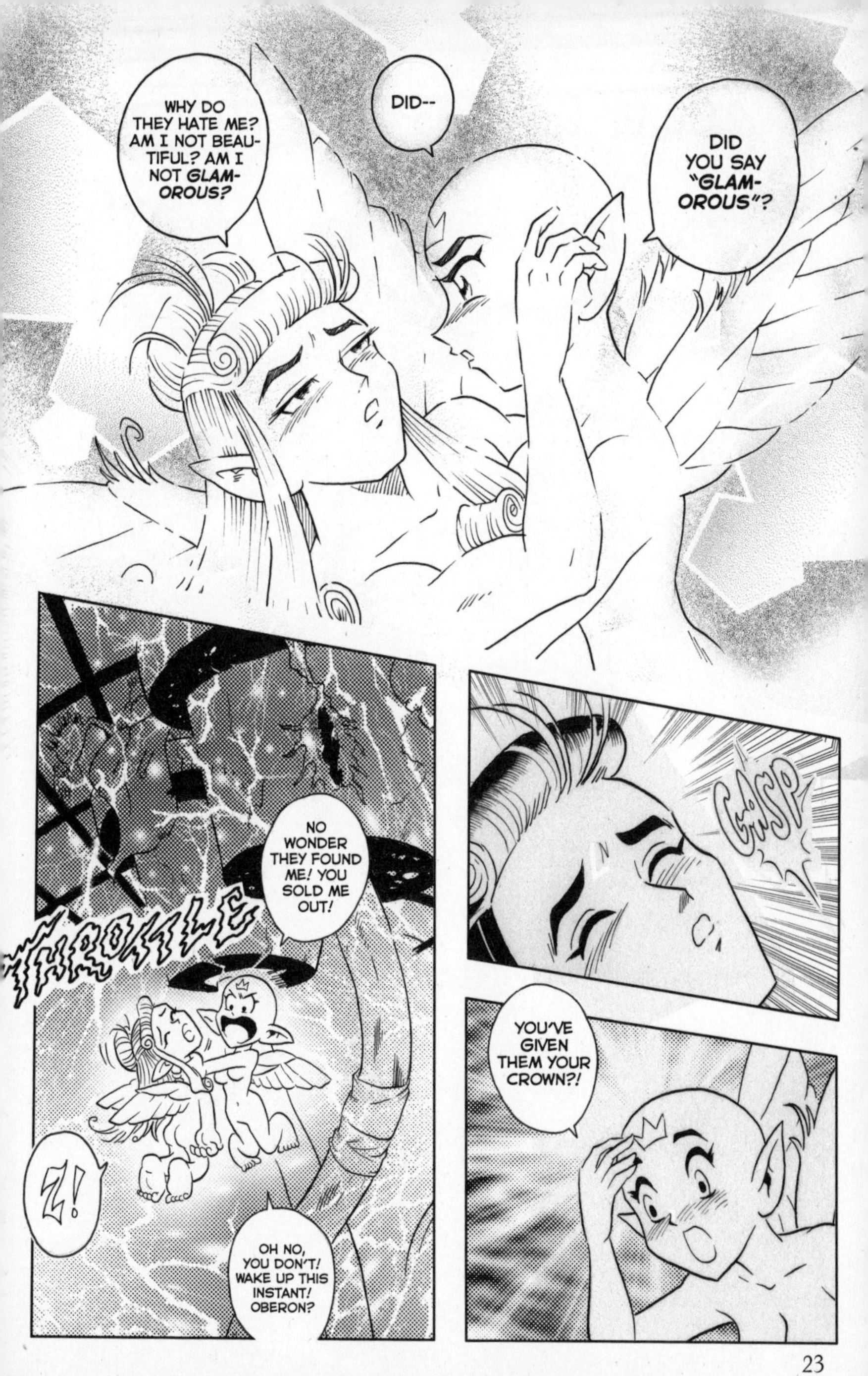
WHY DO THEY HATE ME? AM I NOT BEAUTIFUL? AM I NOT GLAMOROUS?
DID--
DID YOU SAY "GLAMOROUS"?
NO WONDER THEY FOUND ME! YOU SOLD ME OUT!
THROTTLE
Z!
OH NO, YOU DON'T! WAKE UP THIS INSTANT! OBERON?
GASP
YOU'VE GIVEN THEM YOUR CROWN?!

2 Goat Dreams

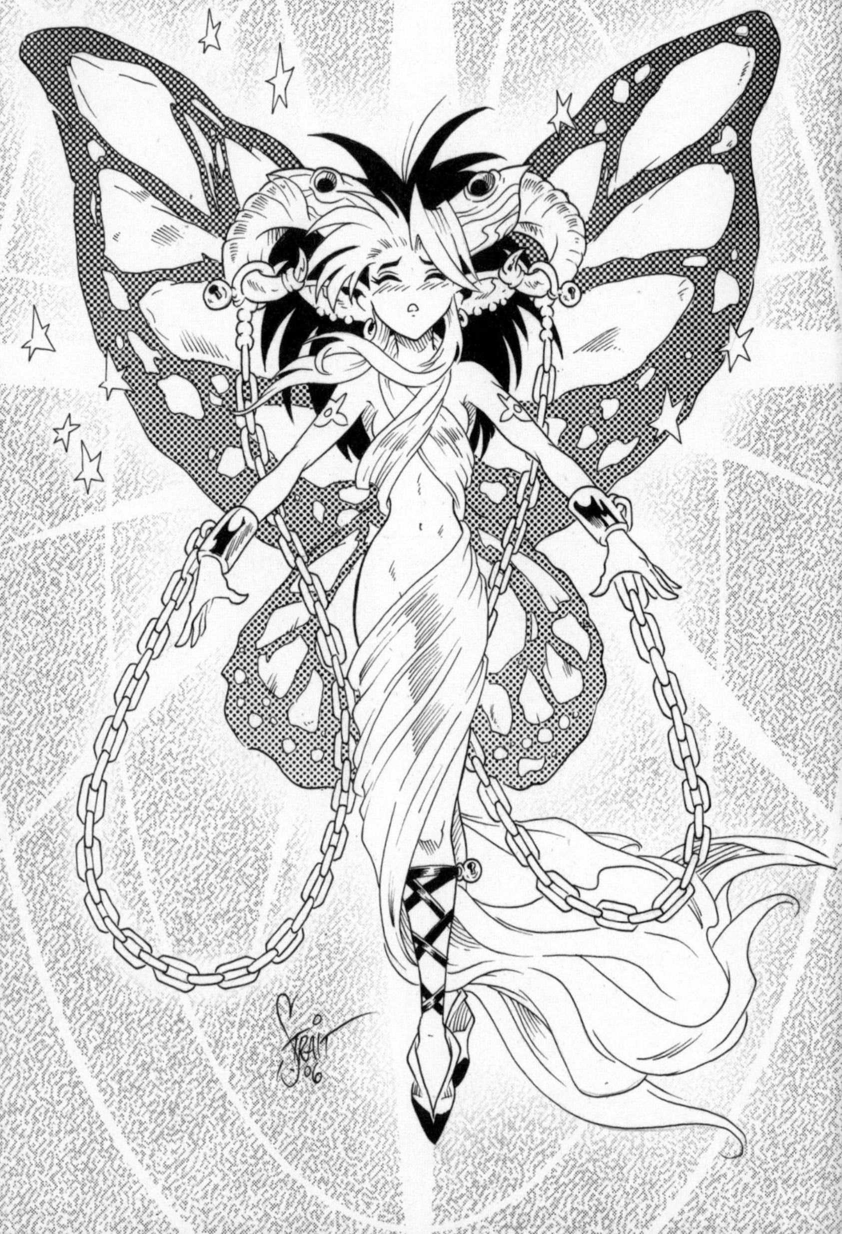

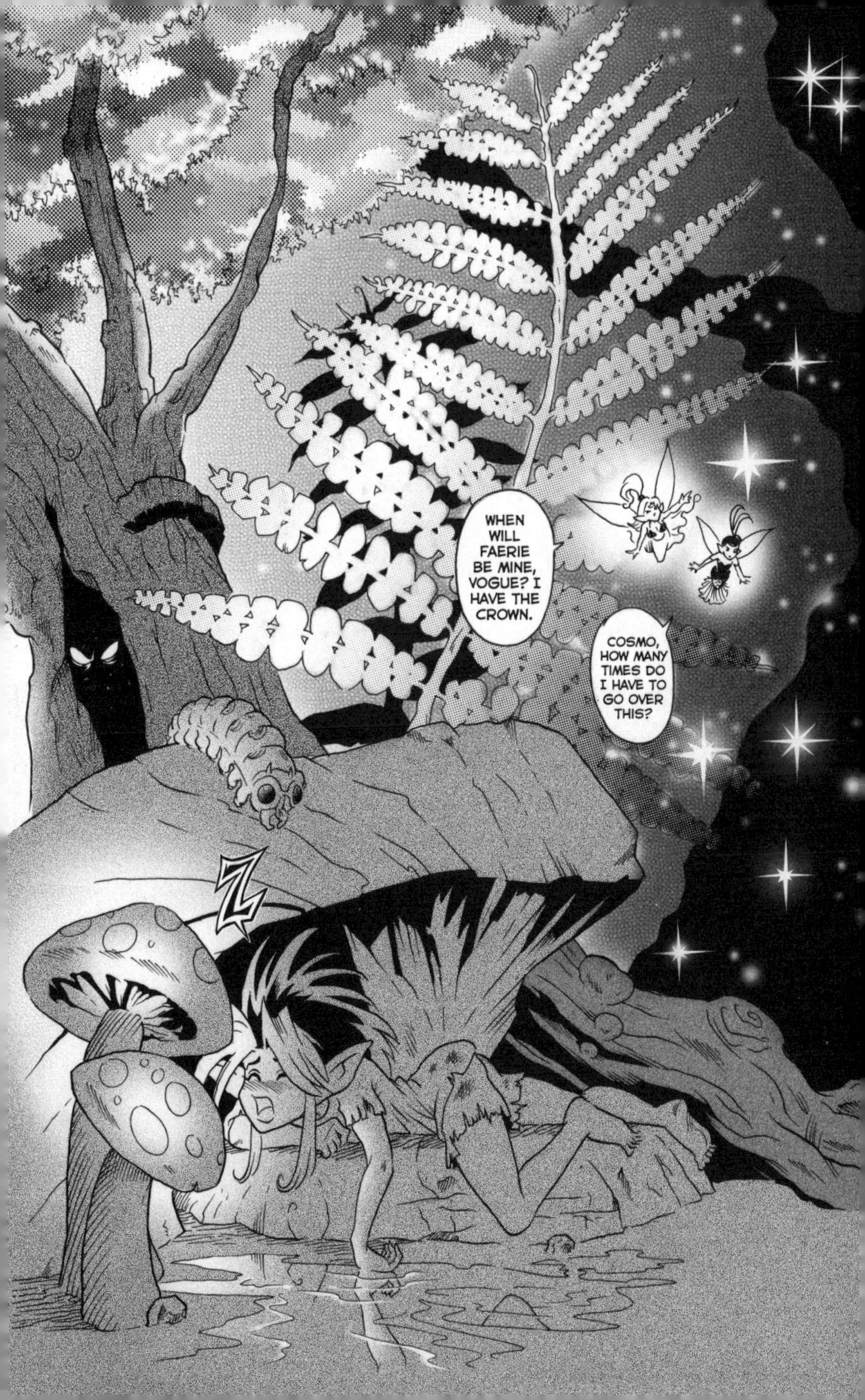
WHEN WILL FAERIE BE MINE, VOGUE? I HAVE THE CROWN.
COSMO, HOW MANY TIMES DO I HAVE TO GO OVER THIS?
Z

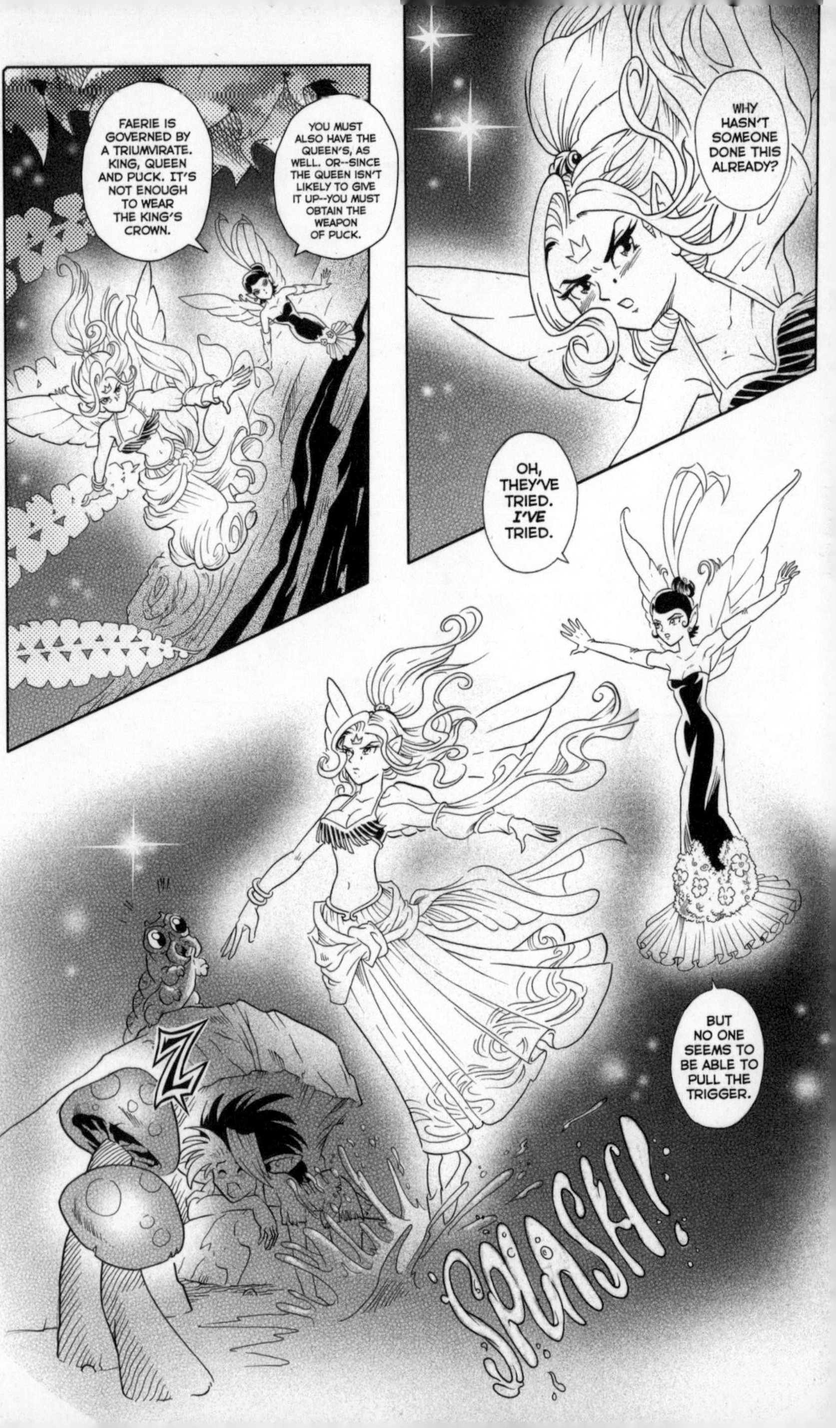
FAERIE IS GOVERNED BY A TRIUMVIRATE. KING, QUEEN AND PUCK. IT'S NOT ENOUGH TO WEAR THE KING'S CROWN.
YOU MUST ALSO HAVE THE QUEEN'S, AS WELL. OR--SINCE THE QUEEN ISN'T LIKELY TO GIVE IT UP--YOU MUST OBTAIN THE WEAPON OF PUCK.
WHY HASN'T SOMEONE DONE THIS ALREADY?
OH, THEY'VE TRIED. *I'VE* TRIED.
Z
BUT NO ONE SEEMS TO BE ABLE TO PULL THE TRIGGER.
SPLASH!

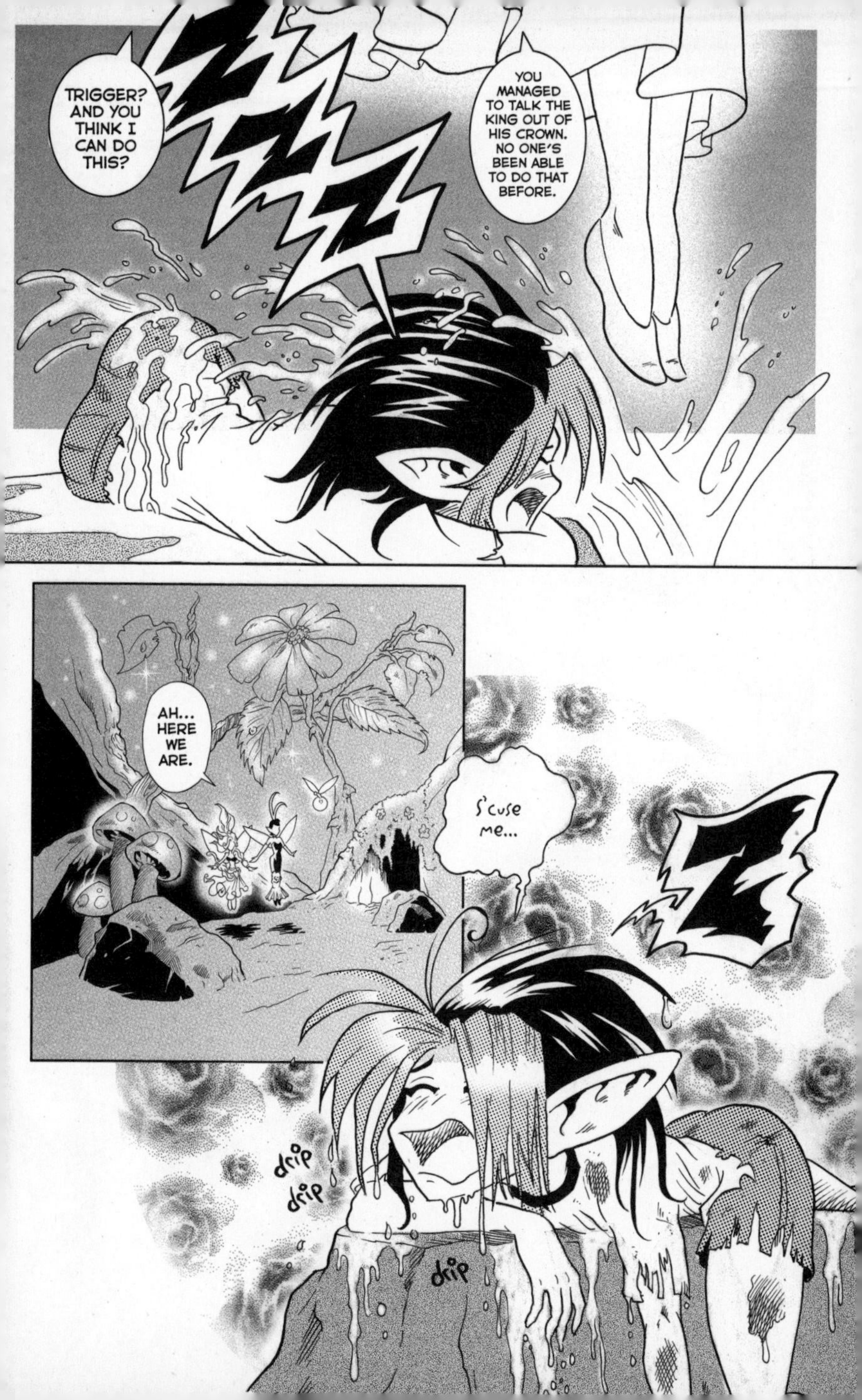
TRIGGER? AND YOU THINK I CAN DO THIS?
YOU MANAGED TO TALK THE KING OUT OF HIS CROWN. NO ONE'S BEEN ABLE TO DO THAT BEFORE.
AH... HERE WE ARE.
S'cuse me...
drip
drip
drip

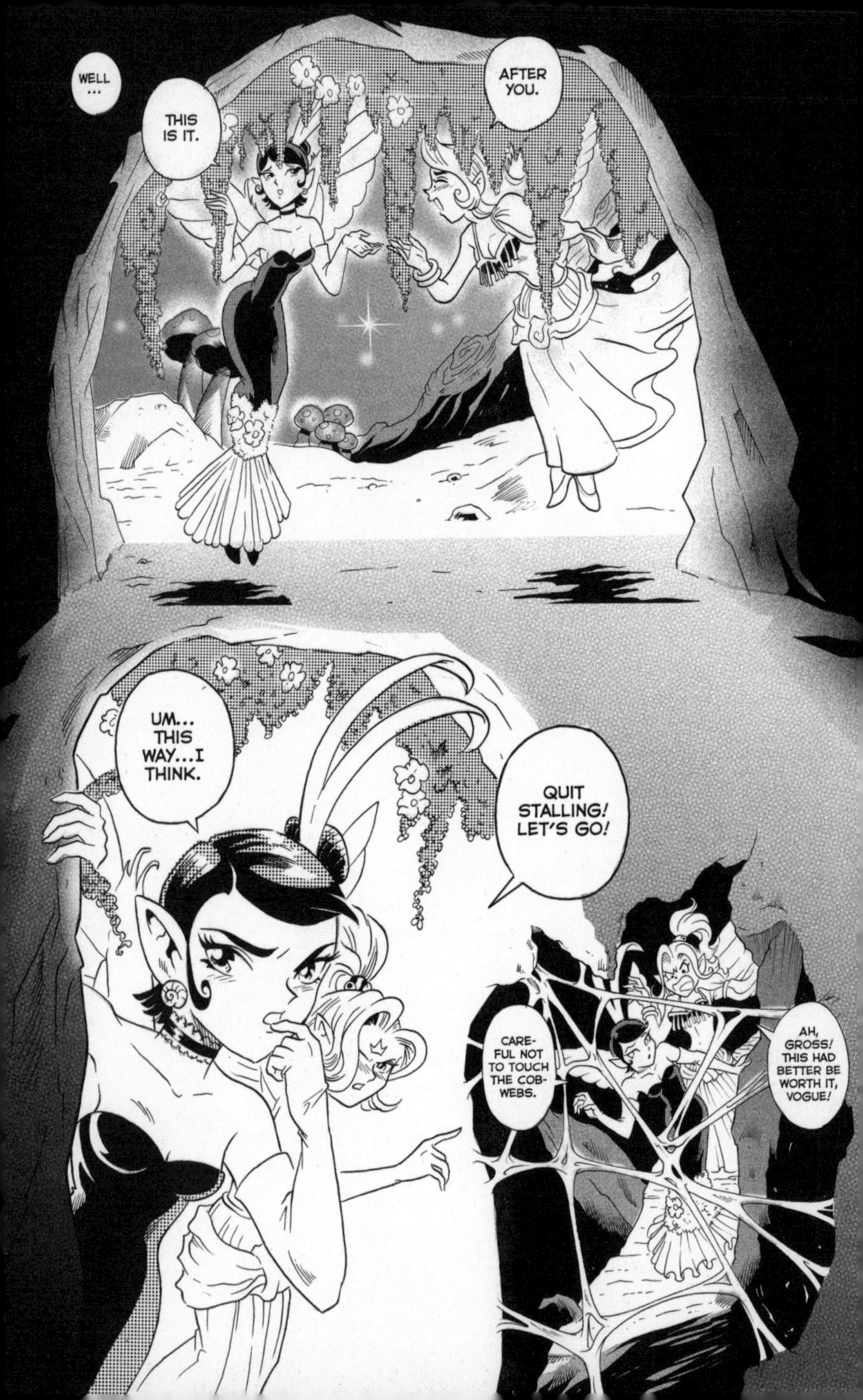
WELL ...
THIS IS IT.
AFTER YOU.
UM... THIS WAY...I THINK.
QUIT STALLING! LET'S GO!
CARE-FUL NOT TO TOUCH THE COB-WEBS.
AH, GROSS! THIS HAD BETTER BE WORTH IT, VOGUE!

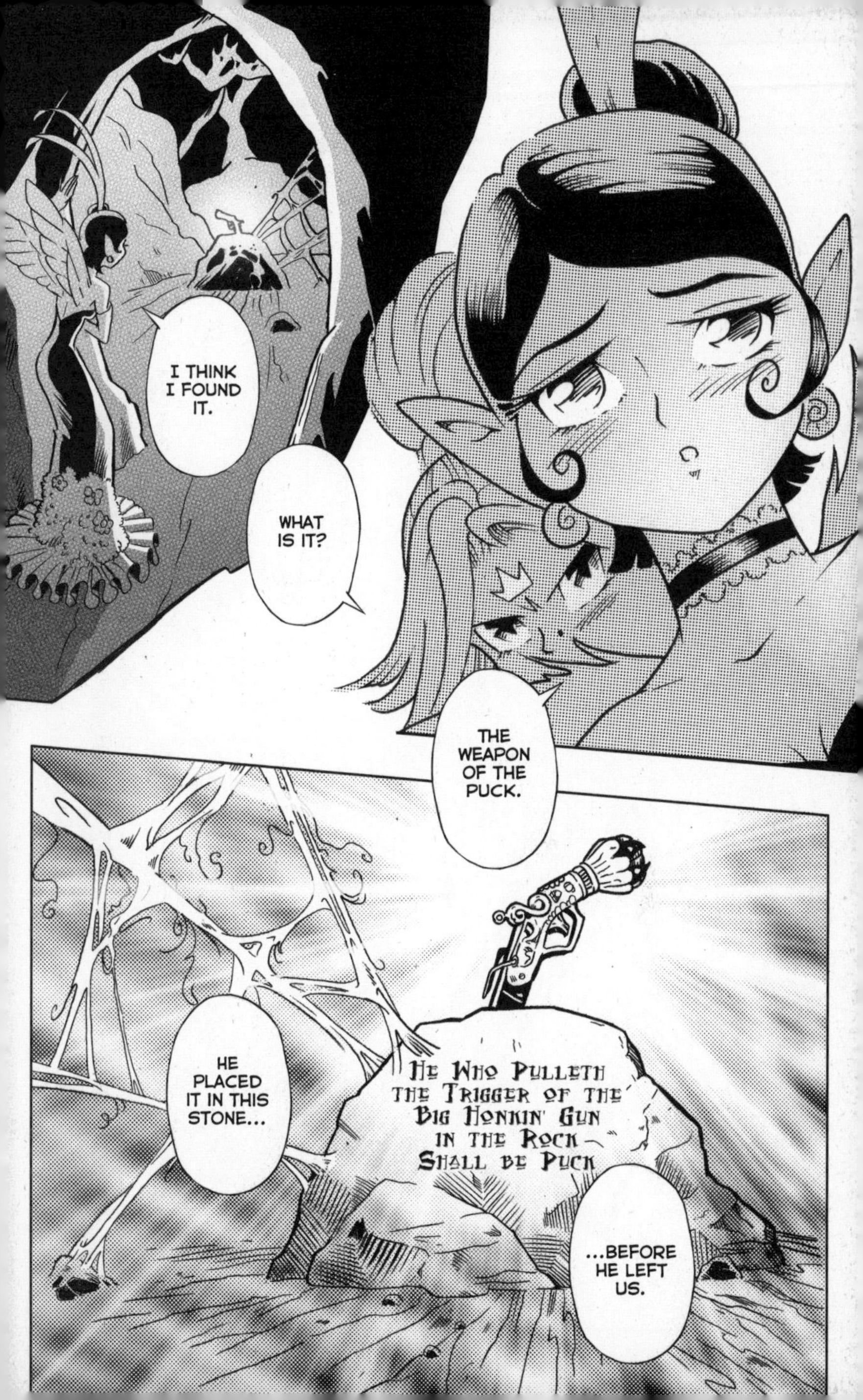
I THINK I FOUND IT.
WHAT IS IT?
THE WEAPON OF THE PUCK.
HE PLACED IT IN THIS STONE...
HE WHO PULLETH THE TRIGGER OF THE BIG HONKIN' GUN IN THE ROCK SHALL BE PUCK
...BEFORE HE LEFT US.

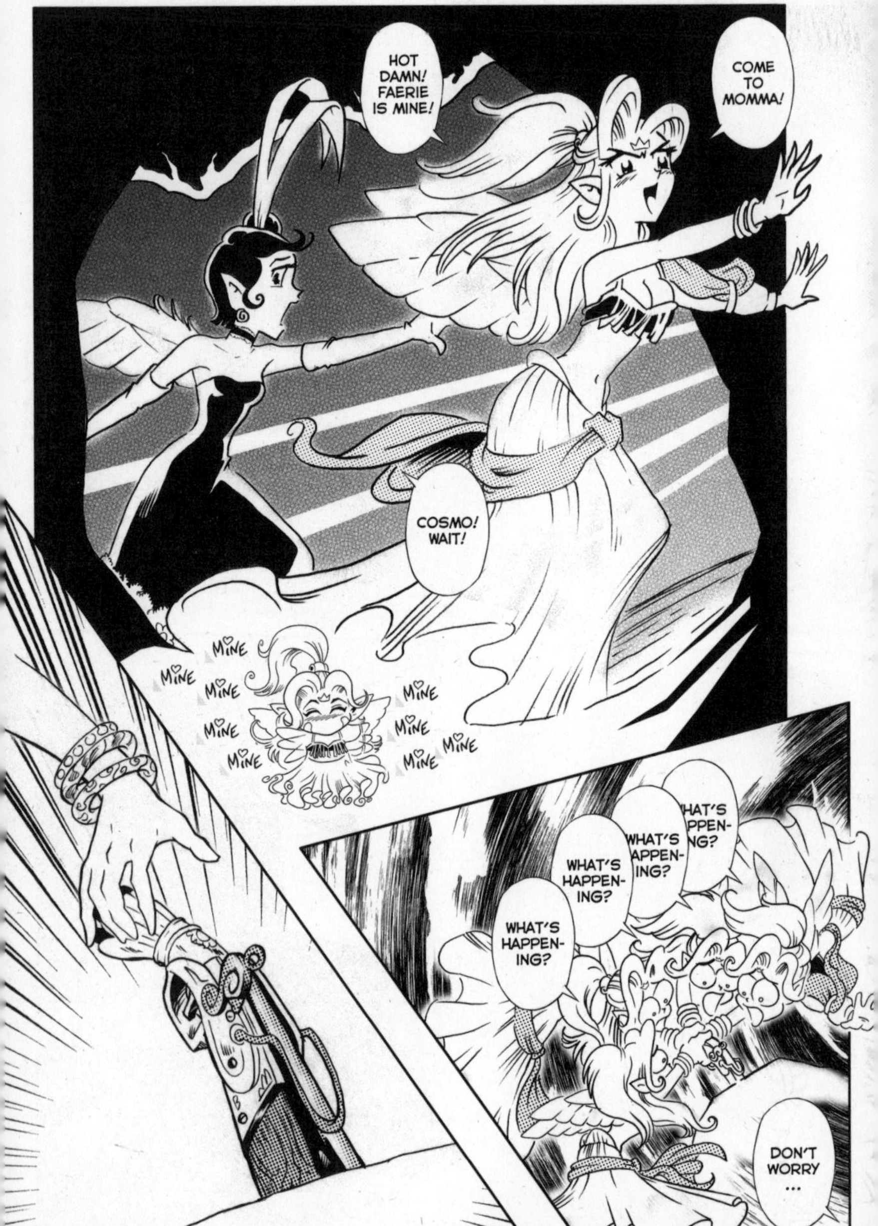
HOT DAMN! FAERIE IS MINE!
COME TO MOMMA!
COSMO! WAIT!
MINE MINE MINE MINE MINE MINE MINE MINE MINE
WHAT'S HAPPENING?
WHAT'S HAPPENING?
WHAT'S HAPPENING?
WHAT'S HAPPENING?
DON'T WORRY ...

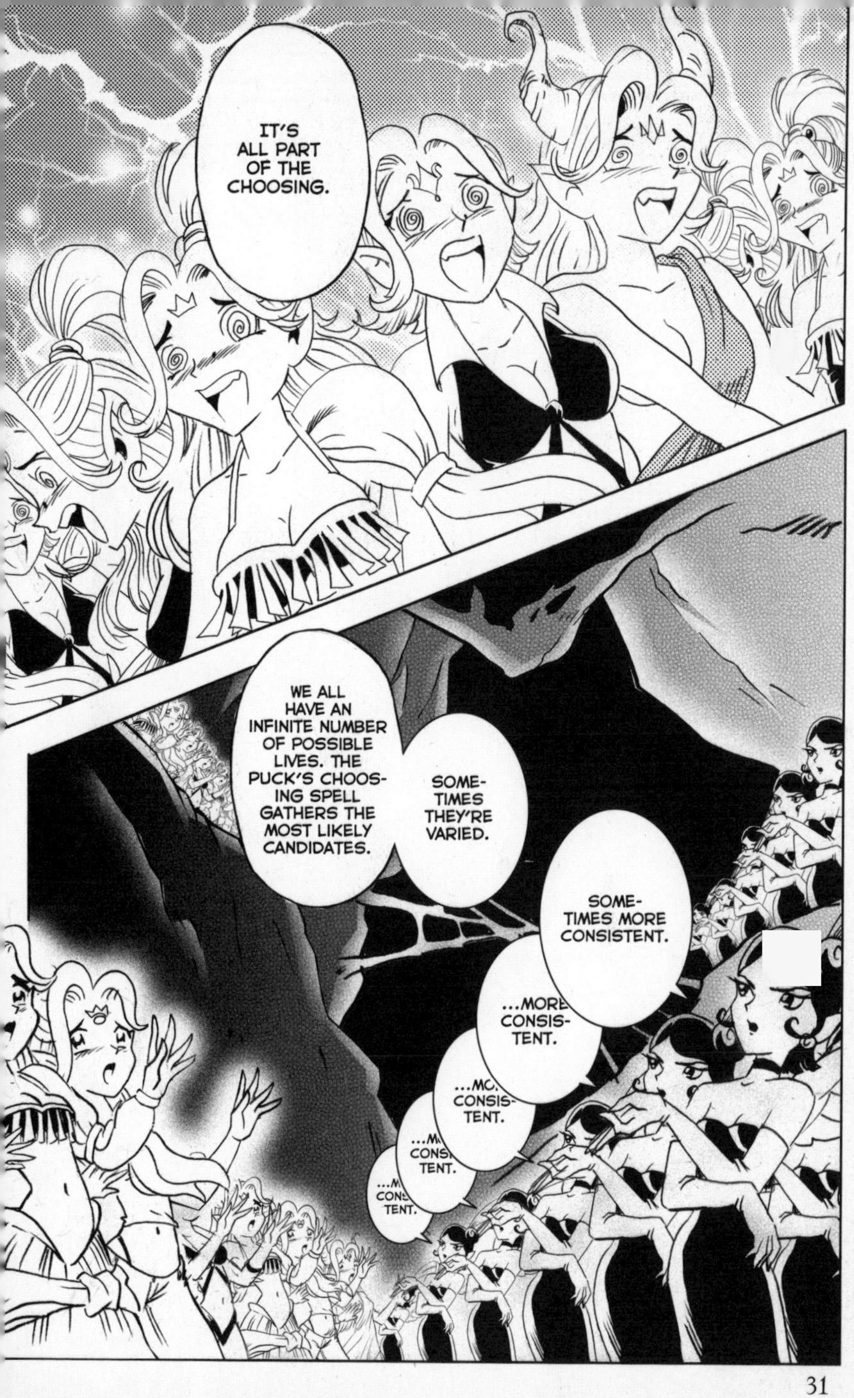
IT'S ALL PART OF THE CHOOSING.
WE ALL HAVE AN INFINITE NUMBER OF POSSIBLE LIVES. THE PUCK'S CHOOSING SPELL GATHERS THE MOST LIKELY CANDIDATES.
SOME-TIMES THEY'RE VARIED.
SOME-TIMES MORE CONSISTENT.
...MORE CONSIS-TENT.
...MO CONSIS-TENT.
...M CONSI TENT.
...M CONS TENT.

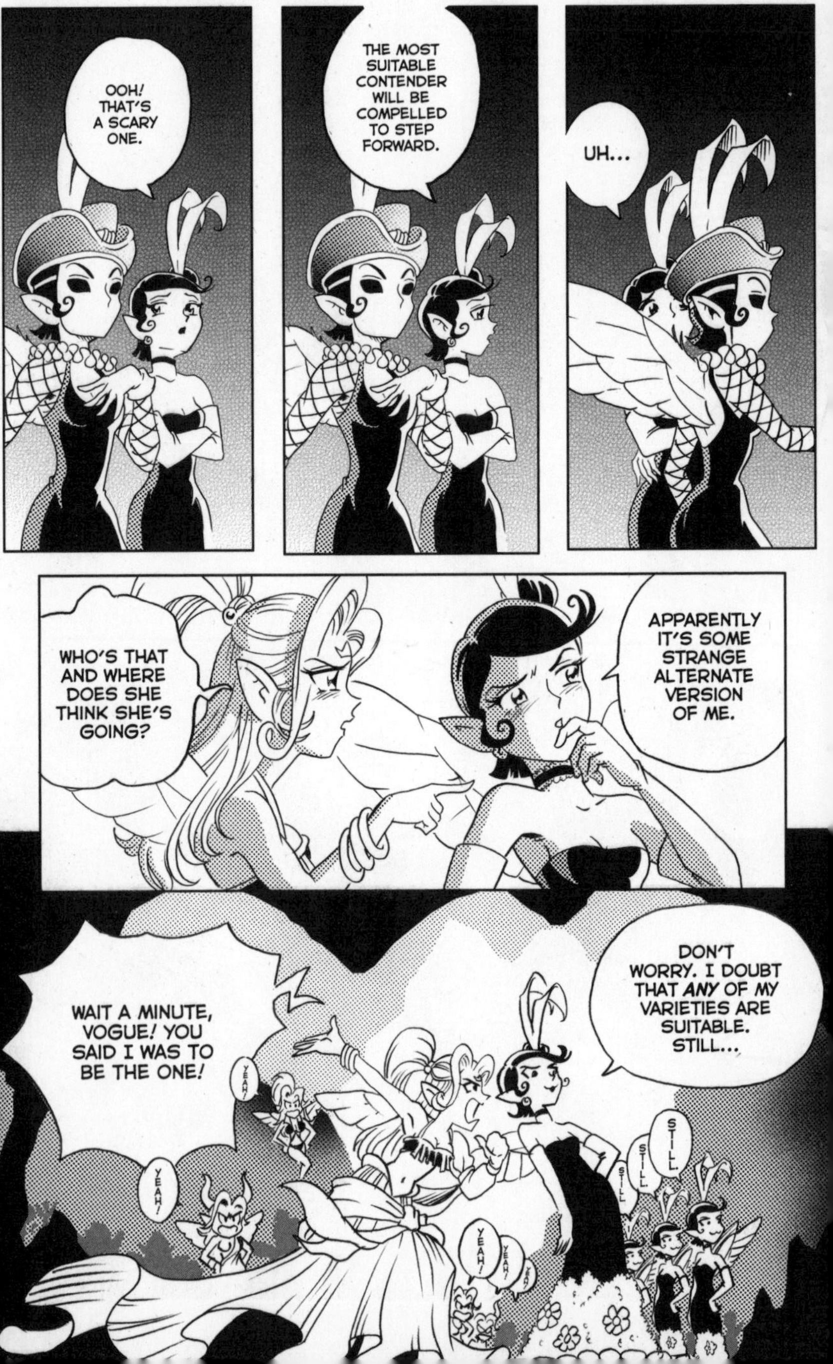
OOH! THAT'S A SCARY ONE.
THE MOST SUITABLE CONTENDER WILL BE COMPELLED TO STEP FORWARD.
UH...
WHO'S THAT AND WHERE DOES SHE THINK SHE'S GOING?
APPARENTLY IT'S SOME STRANGE ALTERNATE VERSION OF ME.
WAIT A MINUTE, VOGUE! YOU SAID I WAS TO BE THE ONE!
DON'T WORRY. I DOUBT THAT *ANY* OF MY VARIETIES ARE SUITABLE. STILL...
YEAH!
YEAH!
STILL.
STILL.
YEAH!
YEAH!

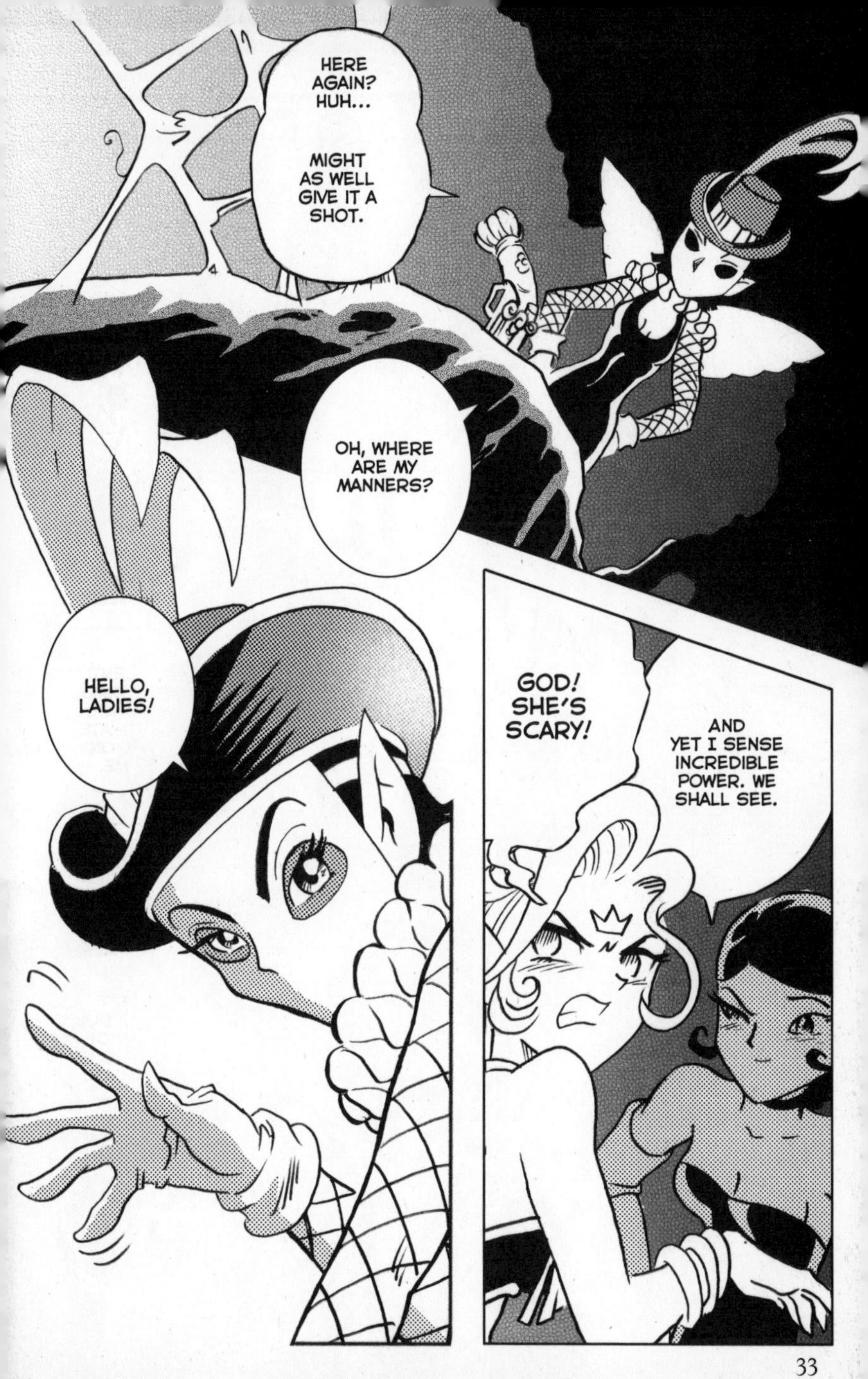
HERE AGAIN? HUH...
MIGHT AS WELL GIVE IT A SHOT.
OH, WHERE ARE MY MANNERS?
HELLO, LADIES!
GOD! SHE'S SCARY!
AND YET I SENSE INCREDIBLE POWER. WE SHALL SEE.

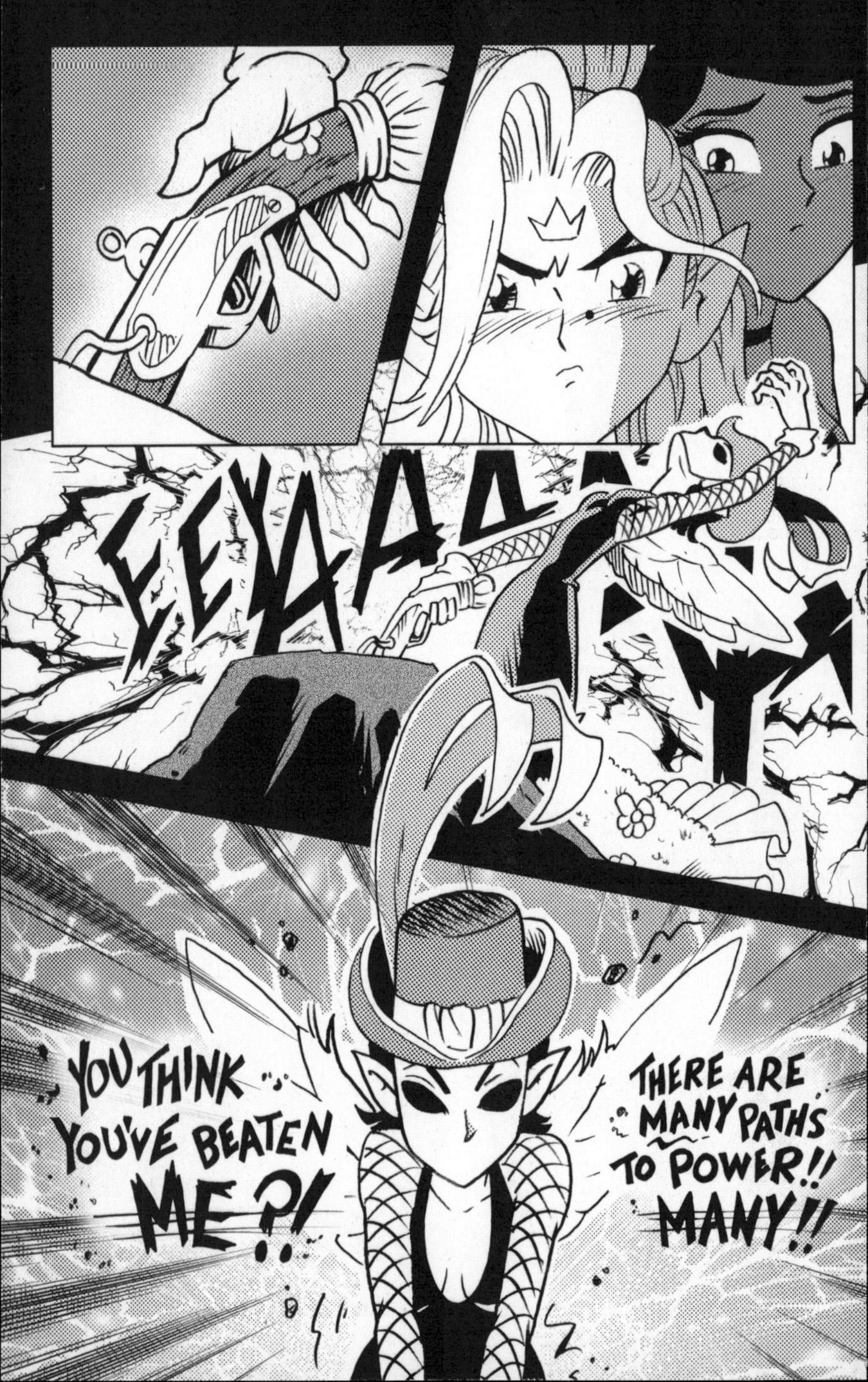
EEYAAA
YOU THINK YOU'VE BEATEN ME?!
THERE ARE MANY PATHS TO POWER!! MANY!!

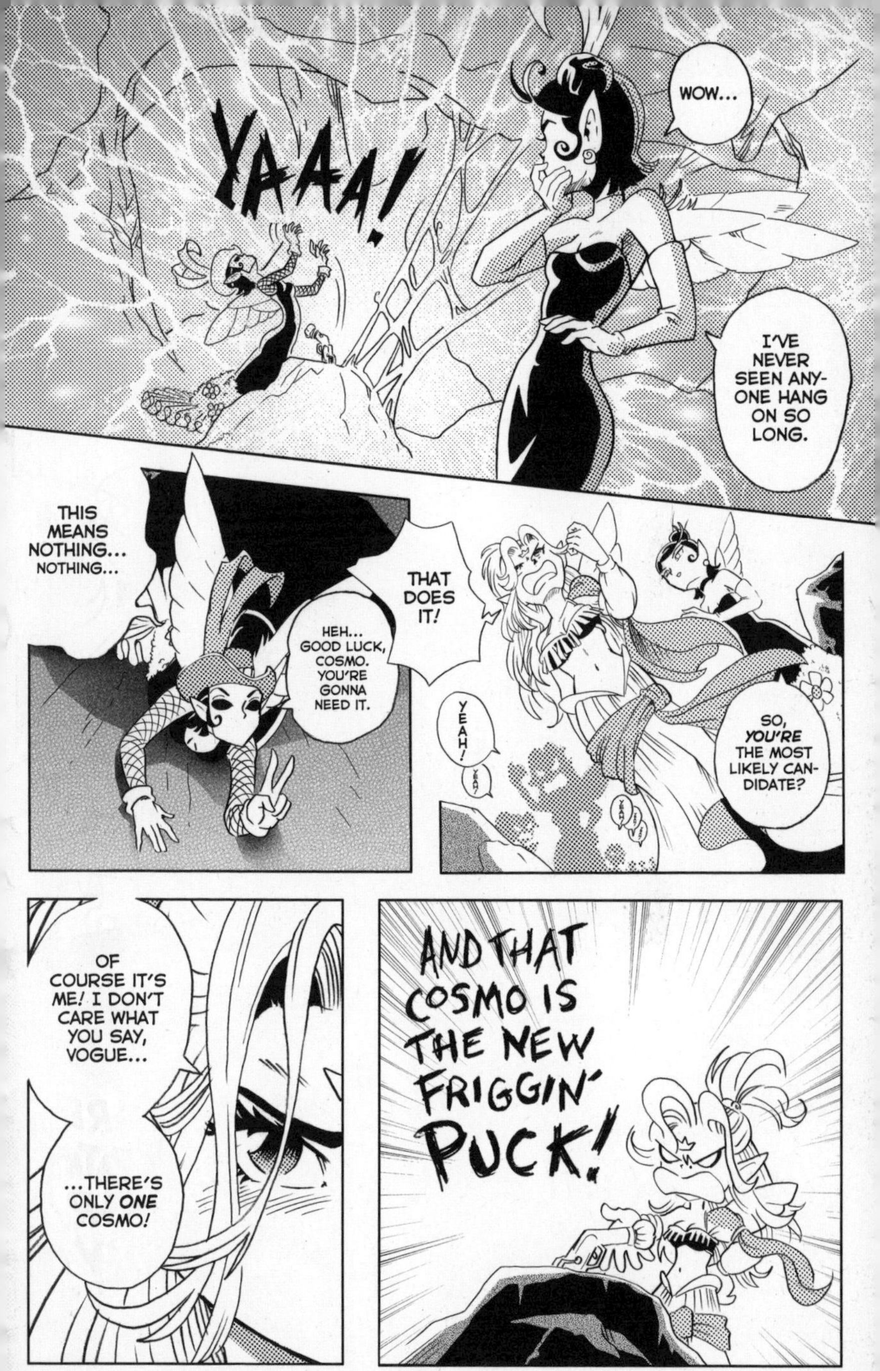

YAAA!
WOW...
I'VE NEVER SEEN ANYONE HANG ON SO LONG.
THIS MEANS NOTHING... NOTHING...
HEH... GOOD LUCK, COSMO. YOU'RE GONNA NEED IT.
THAT DOES IT!
YEAH!
SO, *YOU'RE* THE MOST LIKELY CANDIDATE?
OF COURSE IT'S ME! I DON'T CARE WHAT YOU SAY, VOGUE...
...THERE'S ONLY *ONE* COSMO!
AND THAT COSMO IS THE NEW FRIGGIN' PUCK!

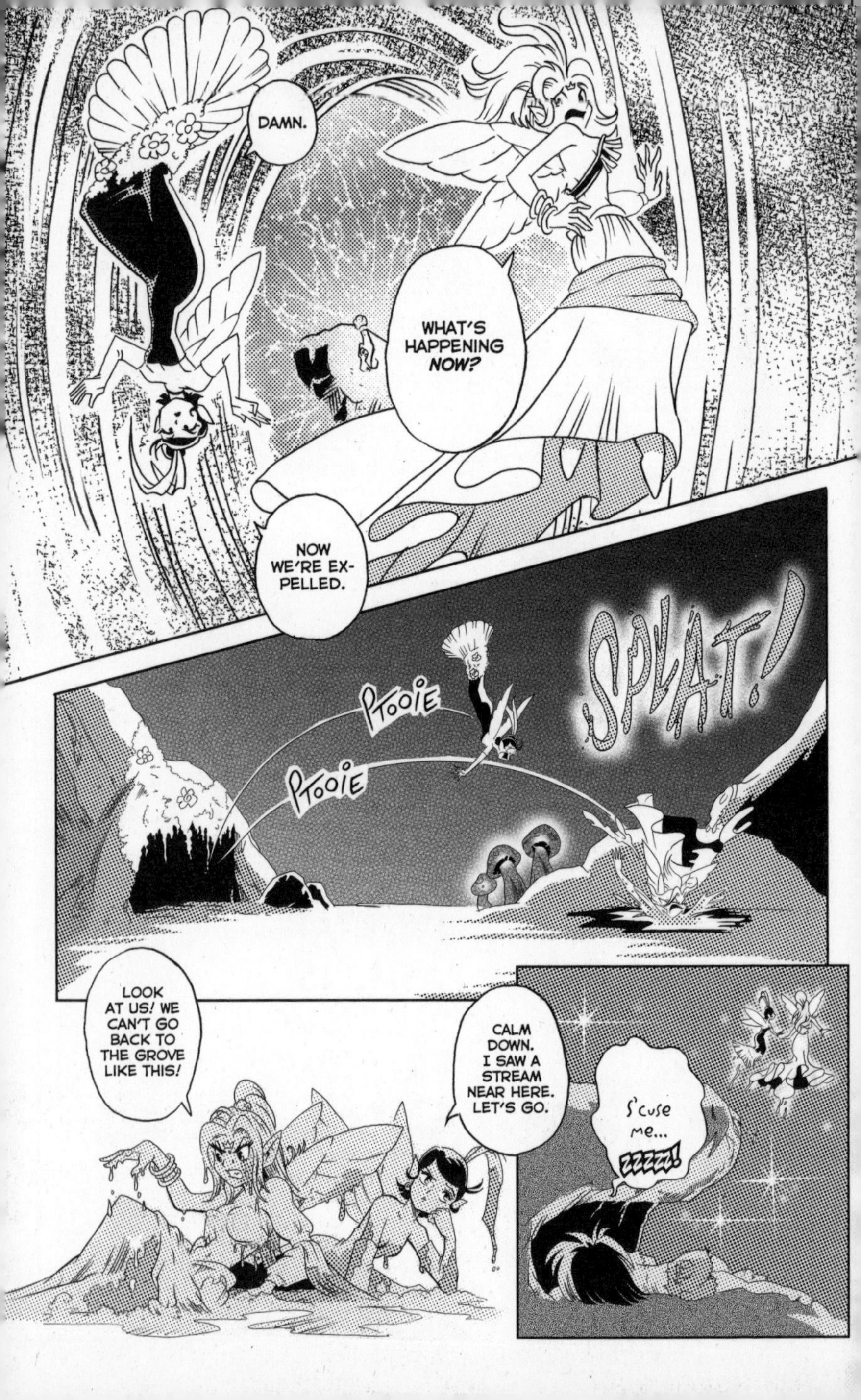
DAMN.
WHAT'S HAPPENING *NOW?*
NOW WE'RE EX-PELLED.
PTOOIE
PTOOIE
SPLAT!
LOOK AT US! WE CAN'T GO BACK TO THE GROVE LIKE THIS!
CALM DOWN. I SAW A STREAM NEAR HERE. LET'S GO.
S'cuse me...
ZZZZZ!

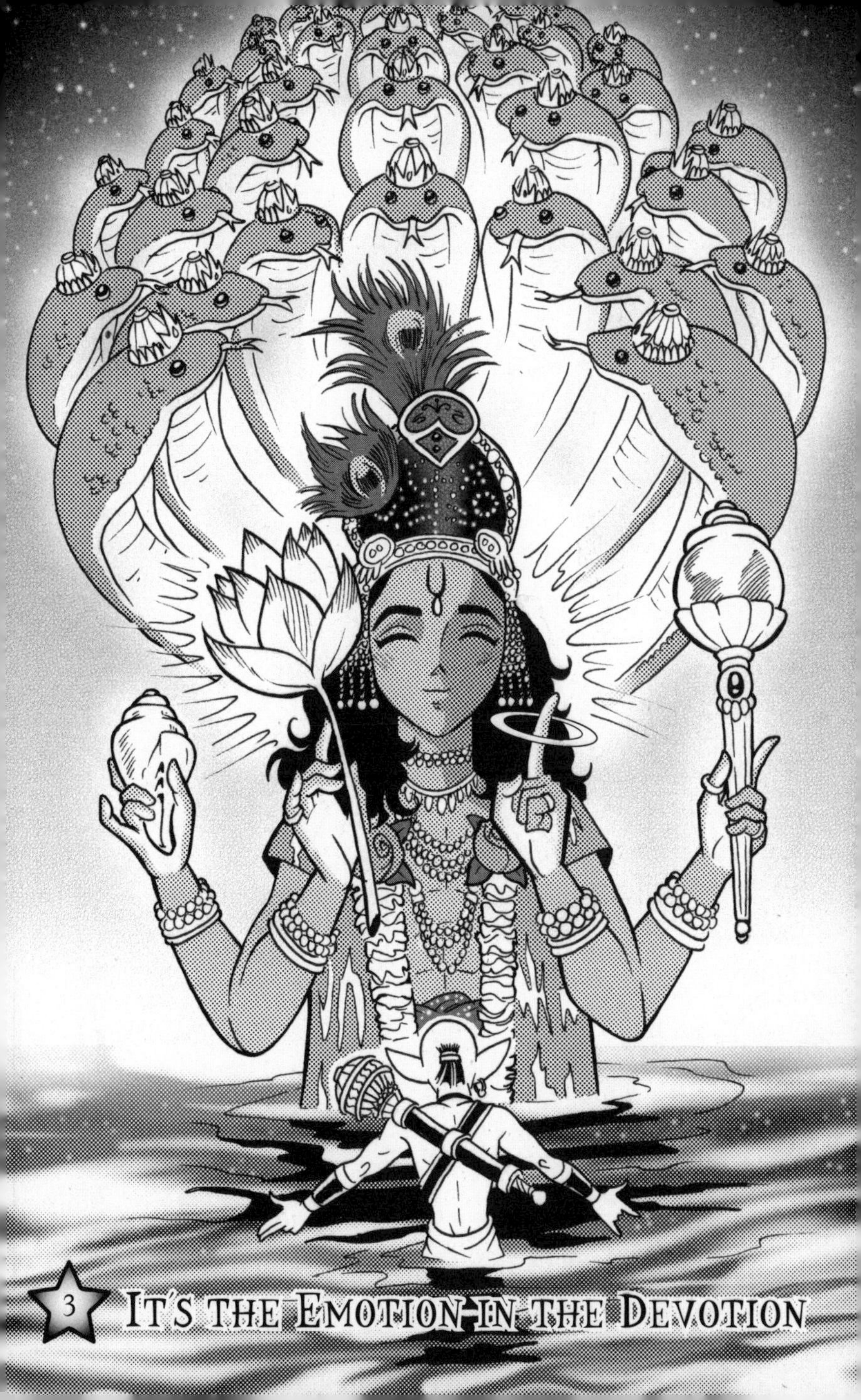

3 It's the Emotion in the Devotion

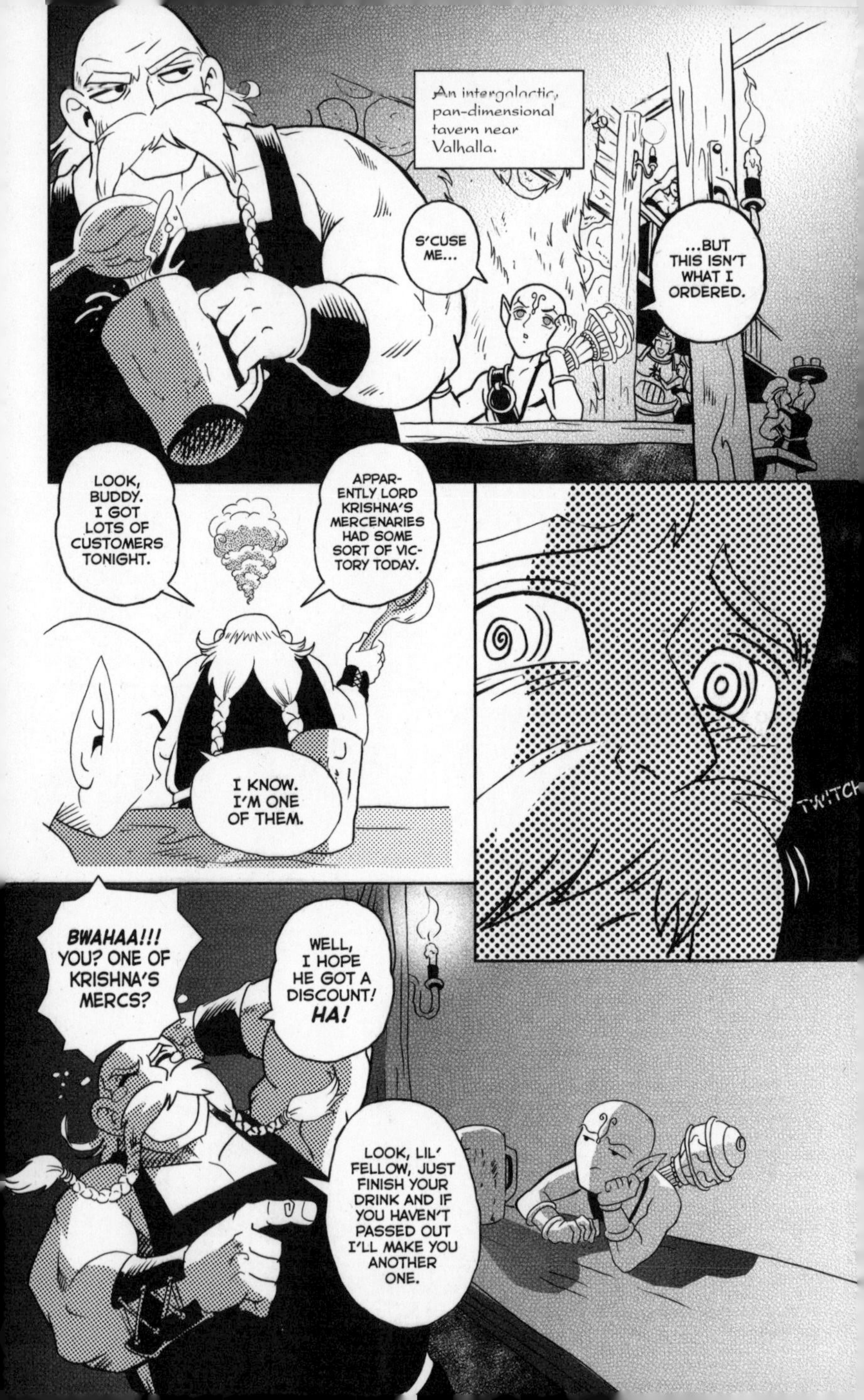
An intergalactic, pan-dimensional tavern near Valhalla.
S'CUSE ME...
...BUT THIS ISN'T WHAT I ORDERED.
LOOK, BUDDY. I GOT LOTS OF CUSTOMERS TONIGHT.
APPARENTLY LORD KRISHNA'S MERCENARIES HAD SOME SORT OF VICTORY TODAY.
I KNOW. I'M ONE OF THEM.
TWITCH
BWAHAA!!! YOU? ONE OF KRISHNA'S MERCS?
WELL, I HOPE HE GOT A DISCOUNT! HA!
LOOK, LIL' FELLOW, JUST FINISH YOUR DRINK AND IF YOU HAVEN'T PASSED OUT I'LL MAKE YOU ANOTHER ONE.

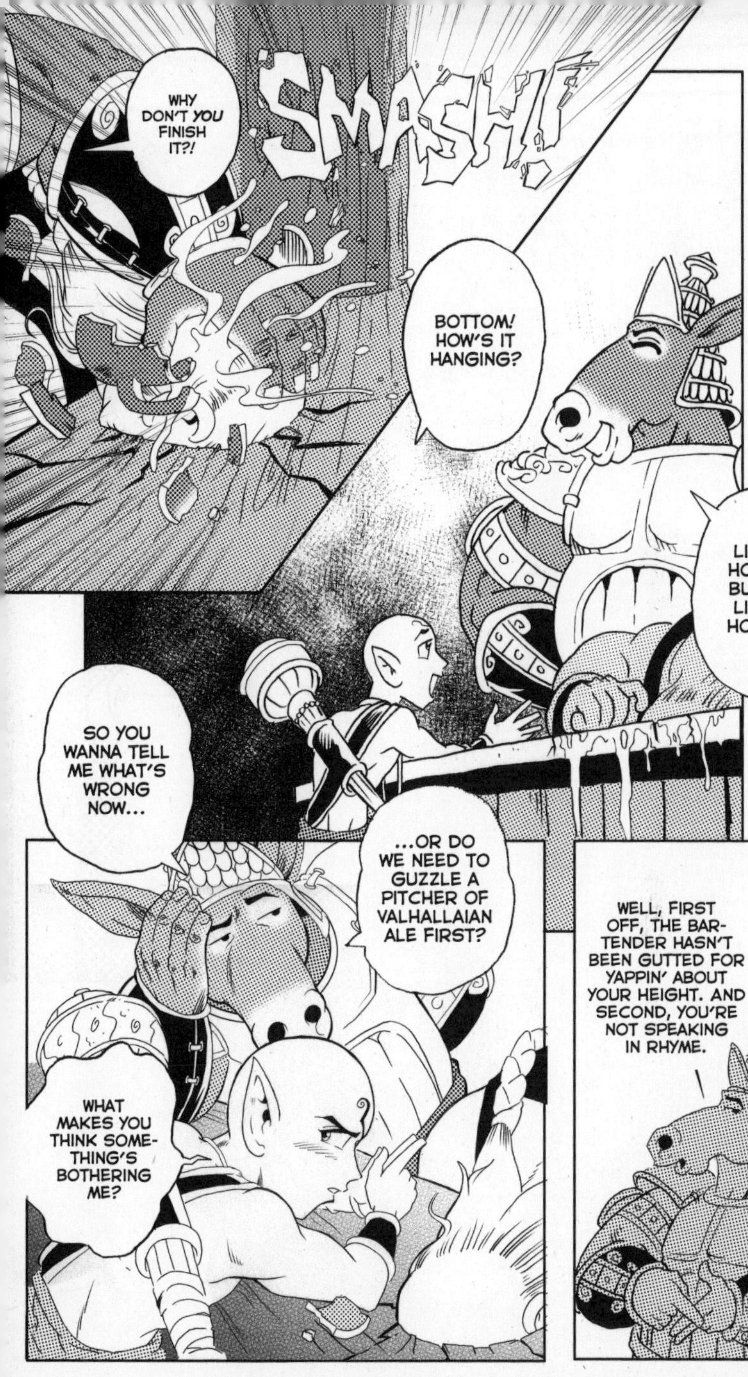
WHY DON'T *YOU* FINISH IT?!
SMASH!
BOTTOM! HOW'S IT HANGING?
LIKE A HORSE, BUDDY. LIKE A HORSE.
SO YOU WANNA TELL ME WHAT'S WRONG NOW...
...OR DO WE NEED TO GUZZLE A PITCHER OF VALHALLAIAN ALE FIRST?
WHAT MAKES YOU THINK SOME-THING'S BOTHERING ME?
WELL, FIRST OFF, THE BAR-TENDER HASN'T BEEN GUTTED FOR YAPPIN' ABOUT YOUR HEIGHT. AND SECOND, YOU'RE NOT SPEAKING IN RHYME.

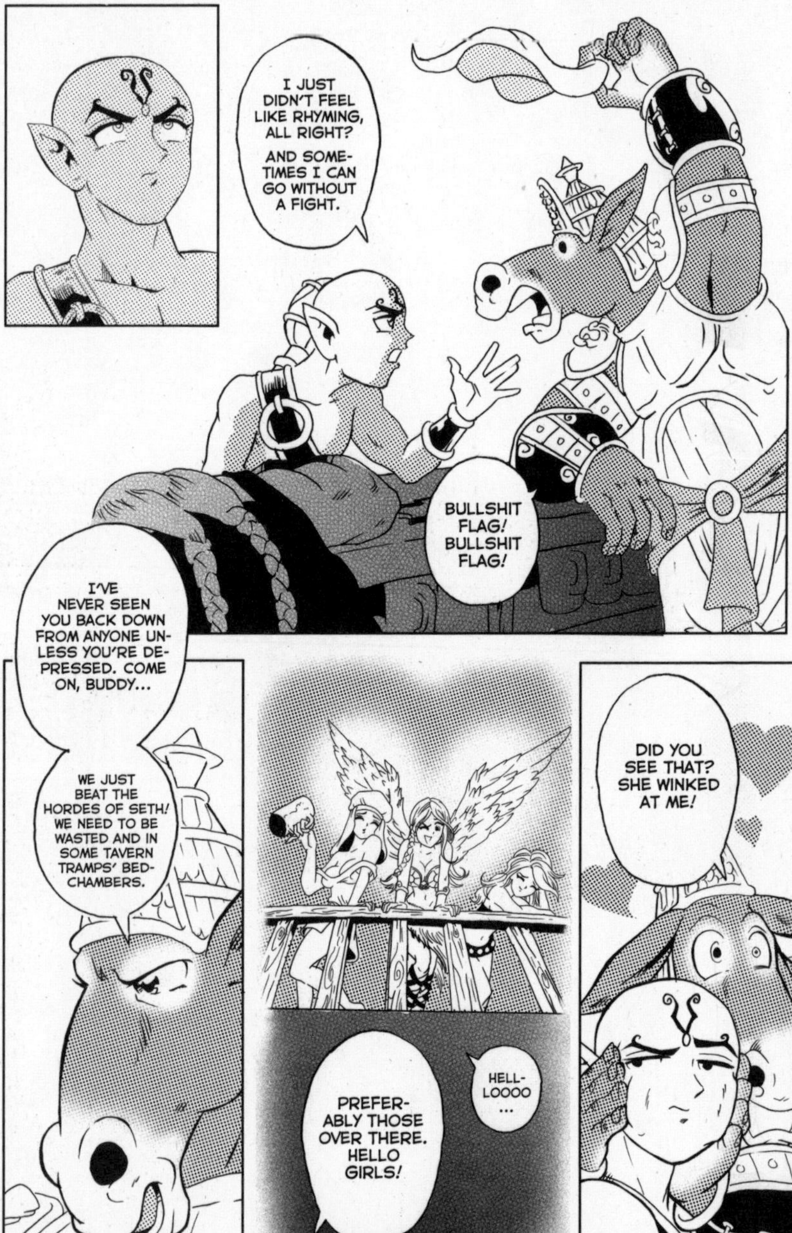
I JUST DIDN'T FEEL LIKE RHYMING, ALL RIGHT?
AND SOME-TIMES I CAN GO WITHOUT A FIGHT.
BULLSHIT FLAG! BULLSHIT FLAG!
I'VE NEVER SEEN YOU BACK DOWN FROM ANYONE UN-LESS YOU'RE DE-PRESSED. COME ON, BUDDY...
WE JUST BEAT THE HORDES OF SETH! WE NEED TO BE WASTED AND IN SOME TAVERN TRAMPS' BED-CHAMBERS.
PREFER-ABLY THOSE OVER THERE. HELLO GIRLS!
HELL-LOOOO ...
DID YOU SEE THAT? SHE WINKED AT ME!

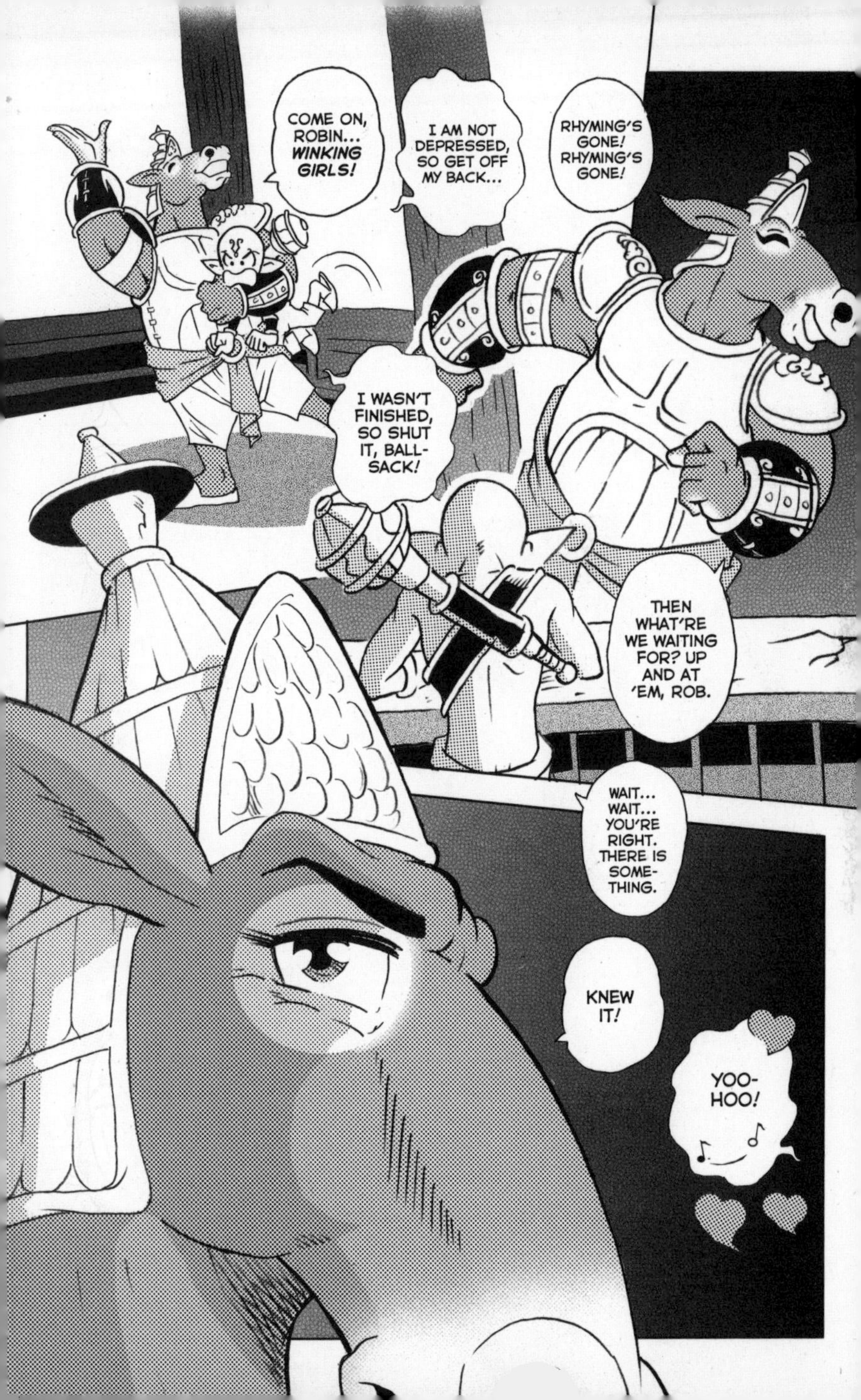
COME ON, ROBIN... ***WINKING GIRLS!***
I AM NOT DEPRESSED, SO GET OFF MY BACK...
RHYMING'S GONE! RHYMING'S GONE!
I WASN'T FINISHED, SO SHUT IT, BALL-SACK!
THEN WHAT'RE WE WAITING FOR? UP AND AT 'EM, ROB.
WAIT... WAIT... YOU'RE RIGHT. THERE IS SOME-THING.
KNEW IT!
YOO-HOO!

I'M...I'M NOT DE-PRESSED. I'M... *DONE.*

I DON'T FOLLOW YA.

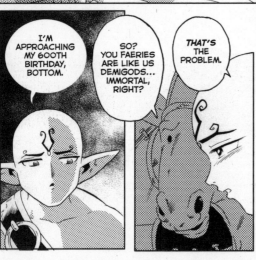

I'M APPROACHING MY 600TH BIRTHDAY, BOTTOM.

SO? YOU FAERIES ARE LIKE US DEMIGODS... IMMORTAL, RIGHT?

THAT'S THE PROBLEM.

I'M NOT A FULL FAERIE.

MY MOTHER WAS A HUMAN MILKMAID. AND MY FATHER WAS ONLY HALF FAERIE HIM-SELF.

THAT MAKES ME MORE HUMAN THAN ANY-THING.

HUMAN LIFE IS MEANT TO BE FLEETING. FOR THE LAST 100 YEARS I'VE FELT LIKE...

...LIKE MY SOUL WAS DYING. NOW... WELL, NOW THERE'S JUST NOTHING LEFT.

AW, COME ON, ROB. YOU'RE JUST IN A SLUMP, MAN. YOU'LL BOUNCE BACK.

4

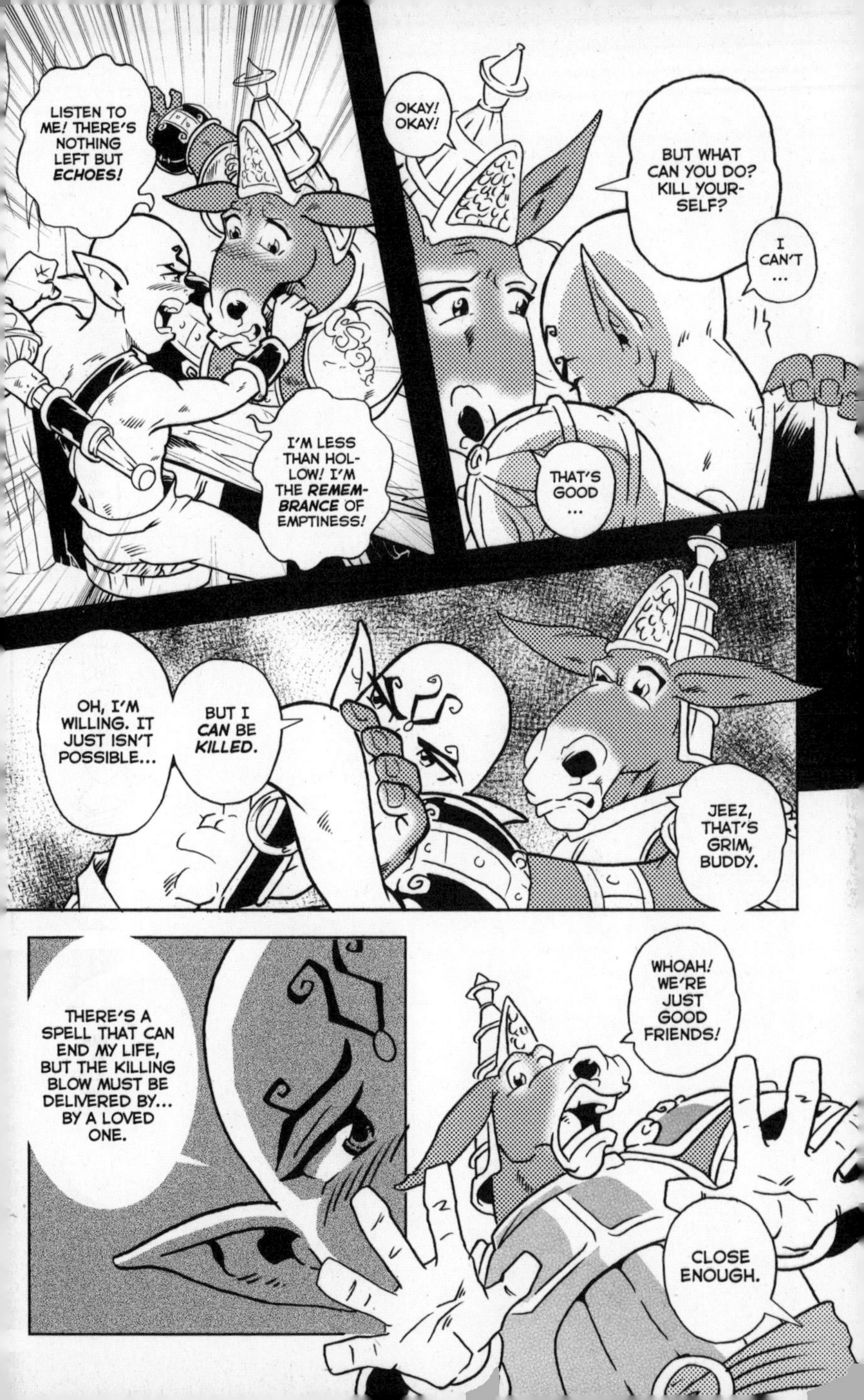
LISTEN TO ME! THERE'S NOTHING LEFT BUT ECHOES!
I'M LESS THAN HOL-LOW! I'M THE REMEMBRANCE OF EMPTINESS!
OKAY! OKAY!
BUT WHAT CAN YOU DO? KILL YOUR-SELF?
I CAN'T ...
THAT'S GOOD ...
OH, I'M WILLING. IT JUST ISN'T POSSIBLE...
BUT I CAN BE KILLED.
JEEZ, THAT'S GRIM, BUDDY.
THERE'S A SPELL THAT CAN END MY LIFE, BUT THE KILLING BLOW MUST BE DELIVERED BY... BY A LOVED ONE.
WHOAH! WE'RE JUST GOOD FRIENDS!
CLOSE ENOUGH.

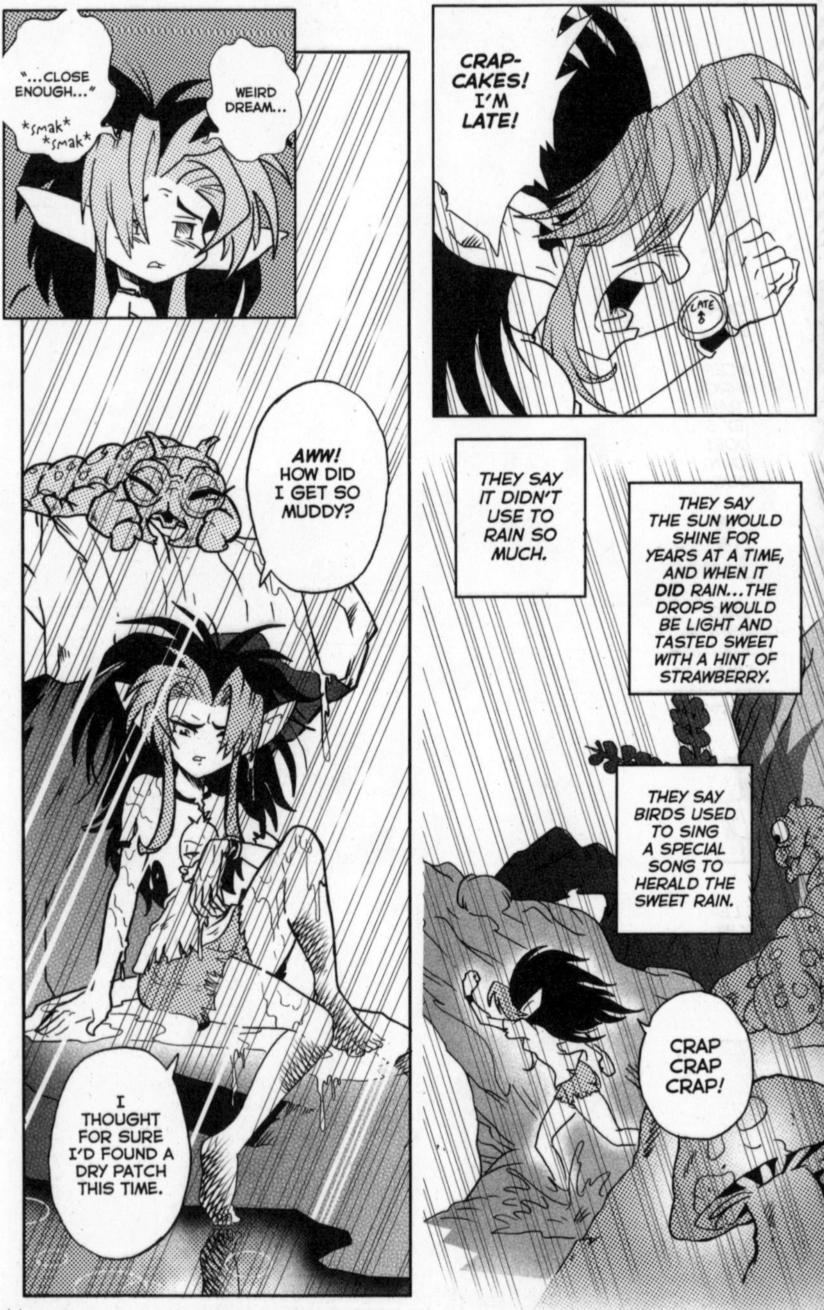
"...CLOSE ENOUGH..."
smak *smak*
WEIRD DREAM...
AWW! HOW DID I GET SO MUDDY?
I THOUGHT FOR SURE I'D FOUND A DRY PATCH THIS TIME.
CRAP-CAKES! I'M LATE!
LATE
THEY SAY IT DIDN'T USE TO RAIN SO MUCH.
THEY SAY THE SUN WOULD SHINE FOR YEARS AT A TIME, AND WHEN IT DID RAIN...THE DROPS WOULD BE LIGHT AND TASTED SWEET WITH A HINT OF STRAWBERRY.
THEY SAY BIRDS USED TO SING A SPECIAL SONG TO HERALD THE SWEET RAIN.
CRAP CRAP CRAP!

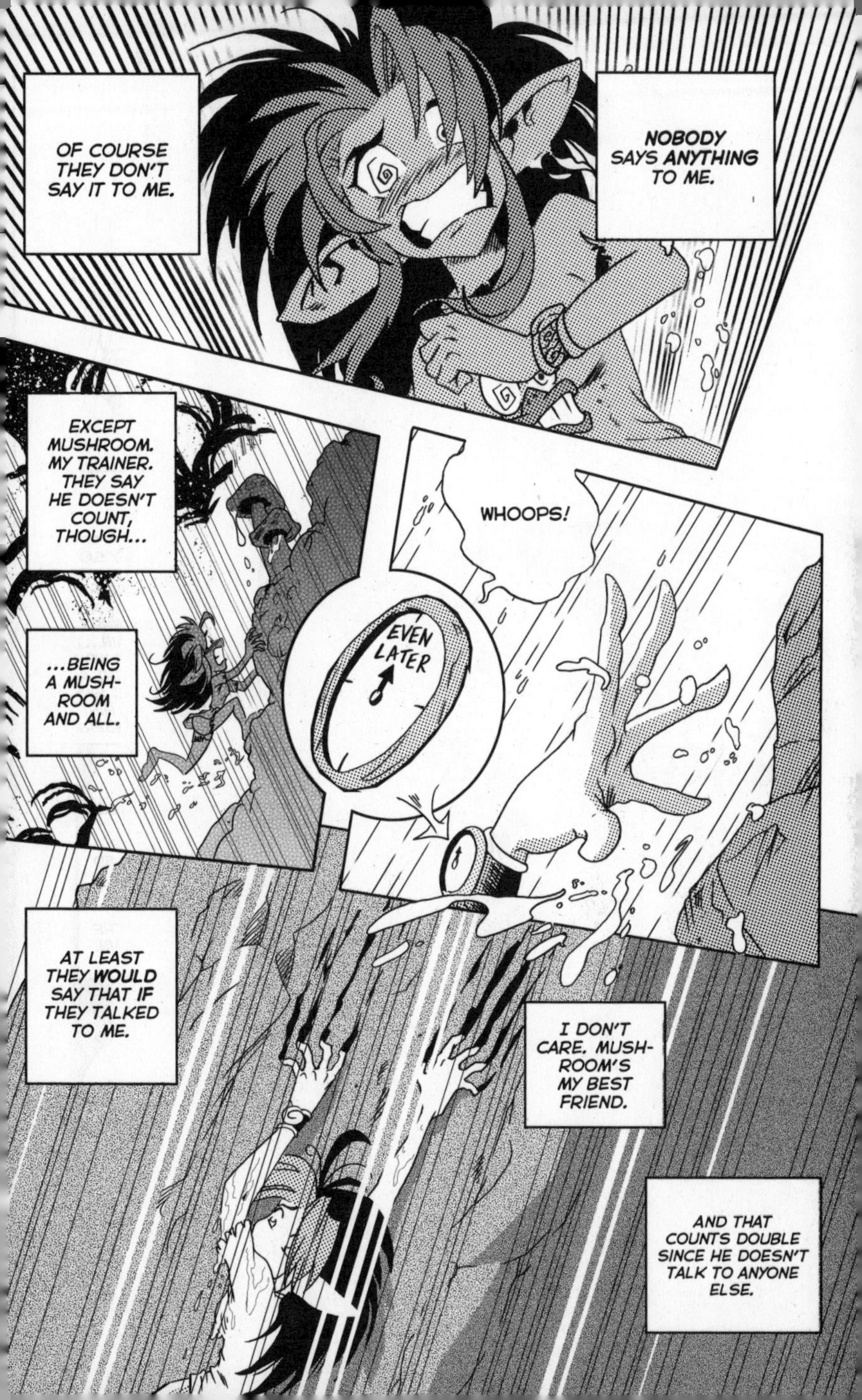
OF COURSE THEY DON'T SAY IT TO ME.
NOBODY SAYS ANYTHING TO ME.
EXCEPT MUSHROOM. MY TRAINER. THEY SAY HE DOESN'T COUNT, THOUGH...
...BEING A MUSH-ROOM AND ALL.
WHOOPS!
EVEN LATER
AT LEAST THEY WOULD SAY THAT IF THEY TALKED TO ME.
I DON'T CARE. MUSH-ROOM'S MY BEST FRIEND.
AND THAT COUNTS DOUBLE SINCE HE DOESN'T TALK TO ANYONE ELSE.

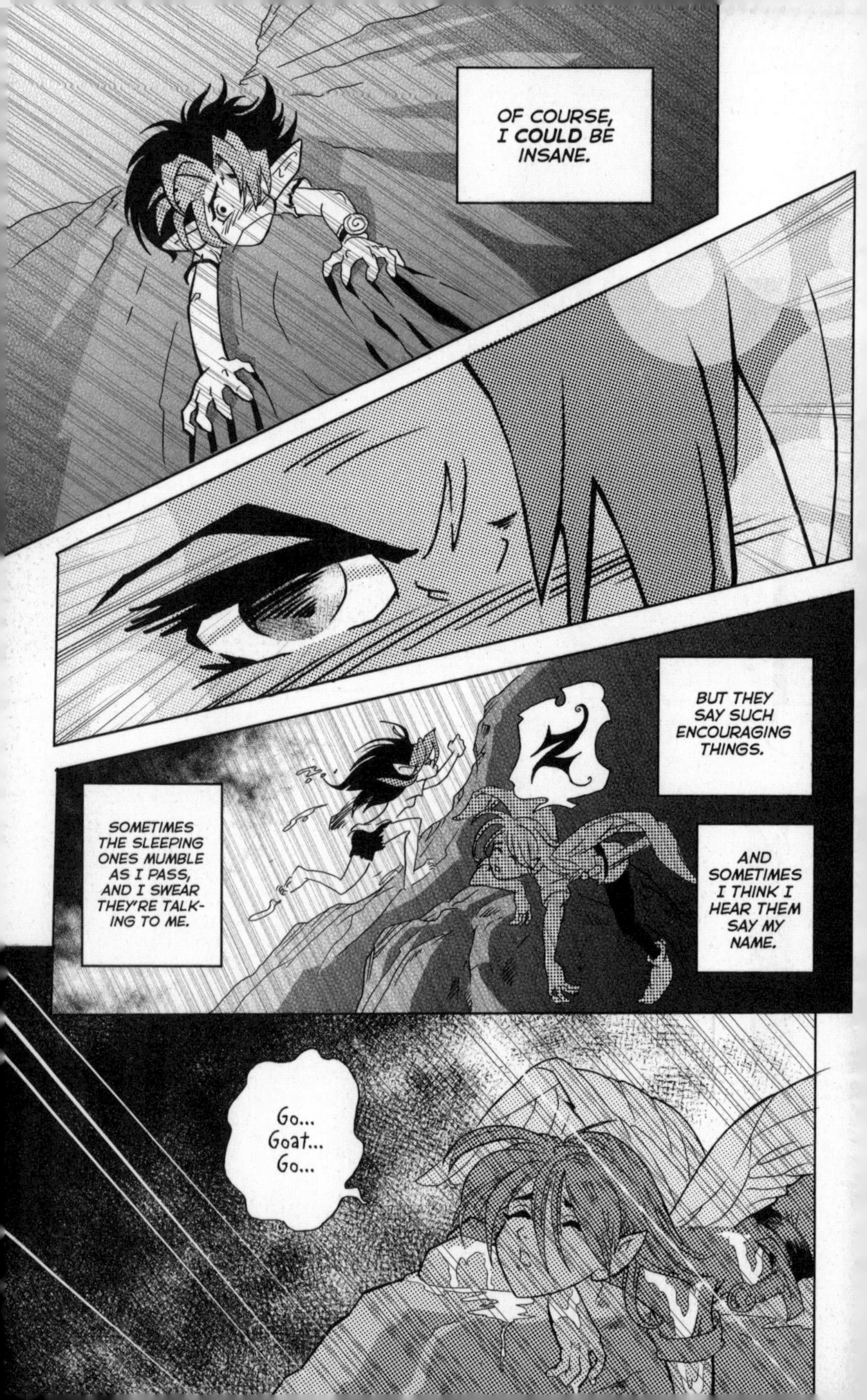
OF COURSE, I COULD BE INSANE.
SOMETIMES THE SLEEPING ONES MUMBLE AS I PASS, AND I SWEAR THEY'RE TALKING TO ME.
BUT THEY SAY SUCH ENCOURAGING THINGS.
AND SOMETIMES I THINK I HEAR THEM SAY MY NAME.
Go... Goat... Go...

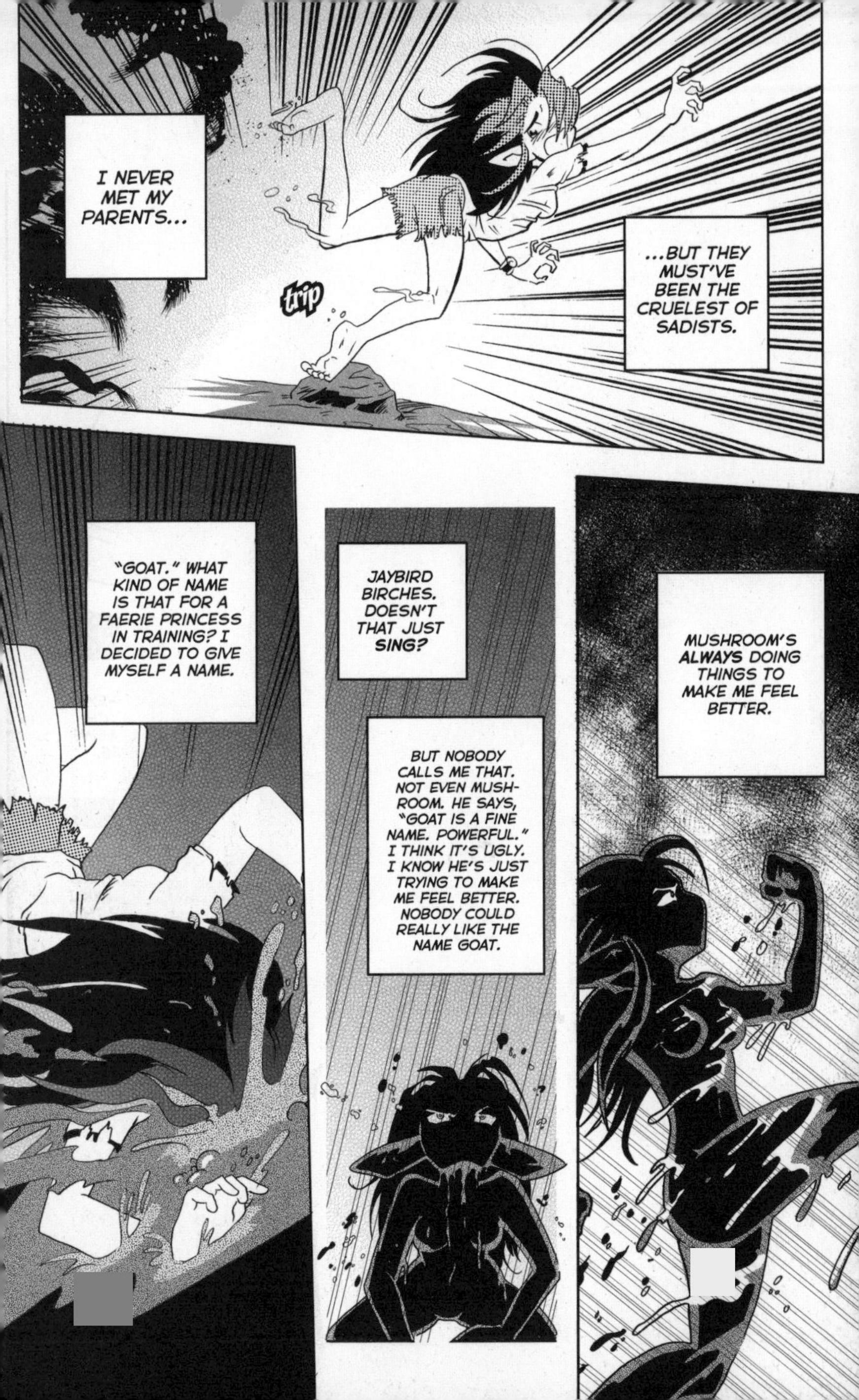
I NEVER MET MY PARENTS...
trip
...BUT THEY MUST'VE BEEN THE CRUELEST OF SADISTS.
"GOAT." WHAT KIND OF NAME IS THAT FOR A FAERIE PRINCESS IN TRAINING? I DECIDED TO GIVE MYSELF A NAME.
JAYBIRD BIRCHES. DOESN'T THAT JUST SING?
BUT NOBODY CALLS ME THAT. NOT EVEN MUSH-ROOM. HE SAYS, "GOAT IS A FINE NAME. POWERFUL." I THINK IT'S UGLY. I KNOW HE'S JUST TRYING TO MAKE ME FEEL BETTER. NOBODY COULD REALLY LIKE THE NAME GOAT.
MUSHROOM'S ALWAYS DOING THINGS TO MAKE ME FEEL BETTER.

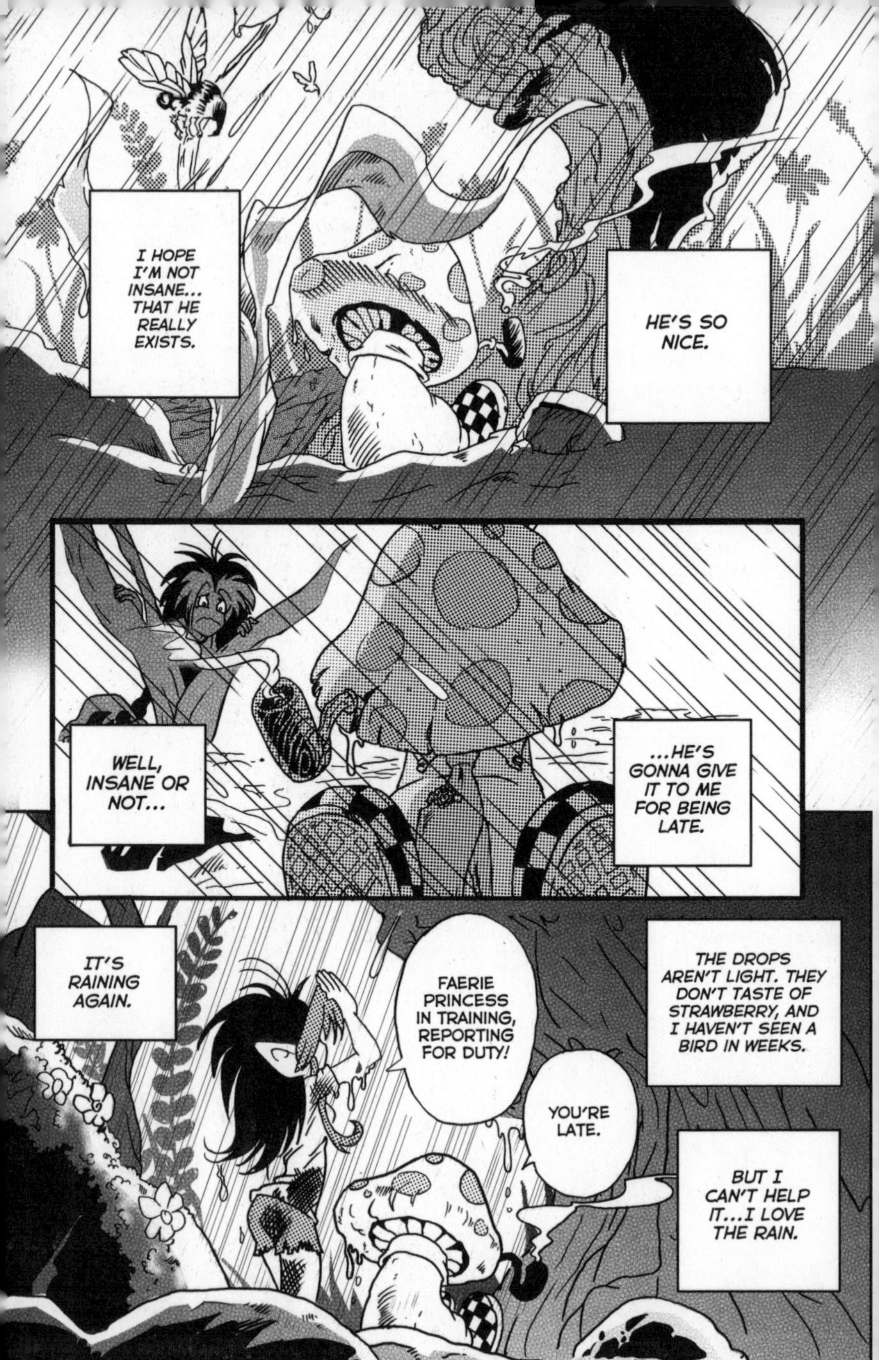
I HOPE I'M NOT INSANE... THAT HE REALLY EXISTS.
HE'S SO NICE.
WELL, INSANE OR NOT...
...HE'S GONNA GIVE IT TO ME FOR BEING LATE.
IT'S RAINING AGAIN.
FAERIE PRINCESS IN TRAINING, REPORTING FOR DUTY!
YOU'RE LATE.
THE DROPS AREN'T LIGHT. THEY DON'T TASTE OF STRAWBERRY, AND I HAVEN'T SEEN A BIRD IN WEEKS.
BUT I CAN'T HELP IT...I LOVE THE RAIN.

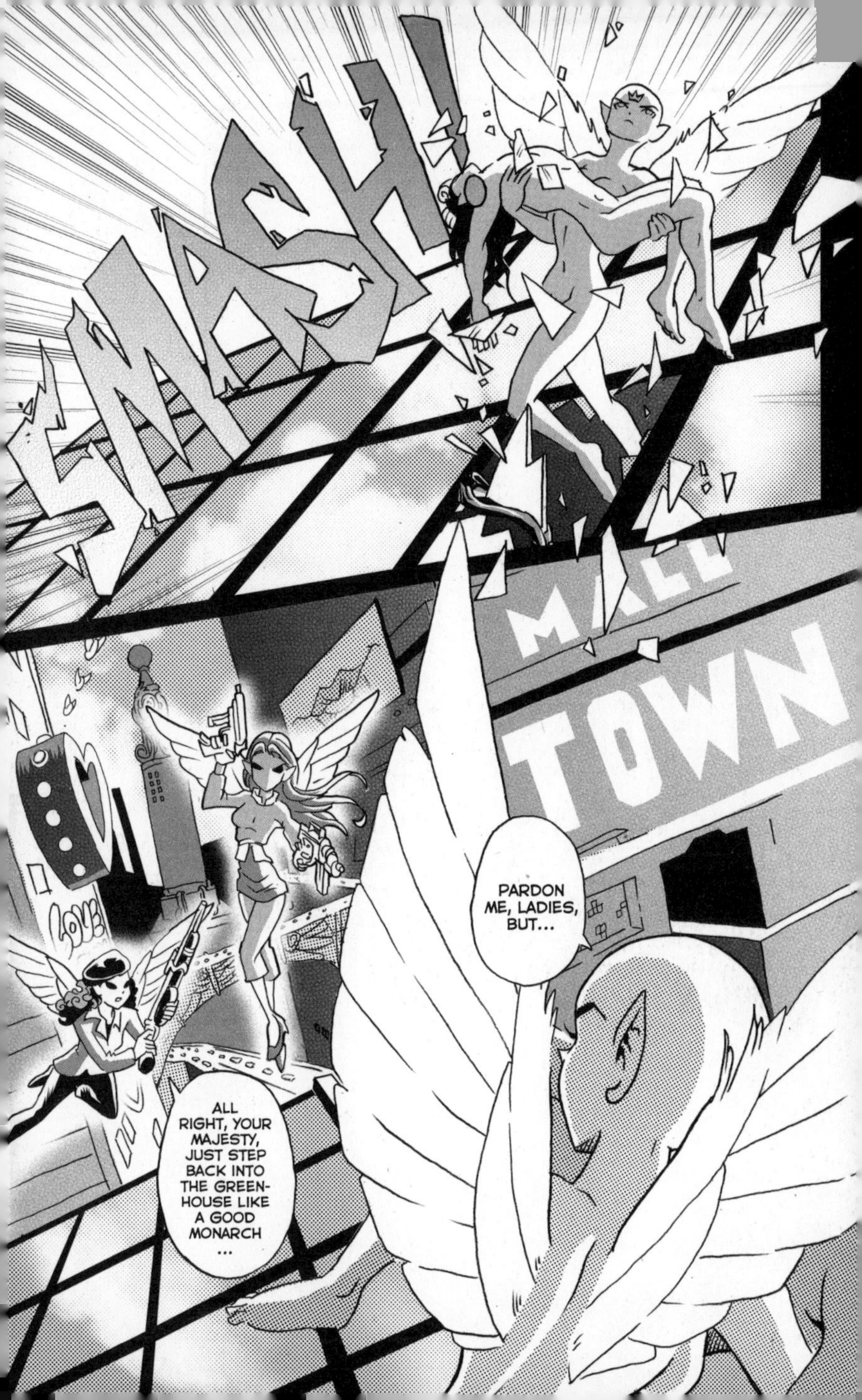
SMASH!
MALL TOWN
ALL RIGHT, YOUR MAJESTY, JUST STEP BACK INTO THE GREEN-HOUSE LIKE A GOOD MONARCH...
PARDON ME, LADIES, BUT...

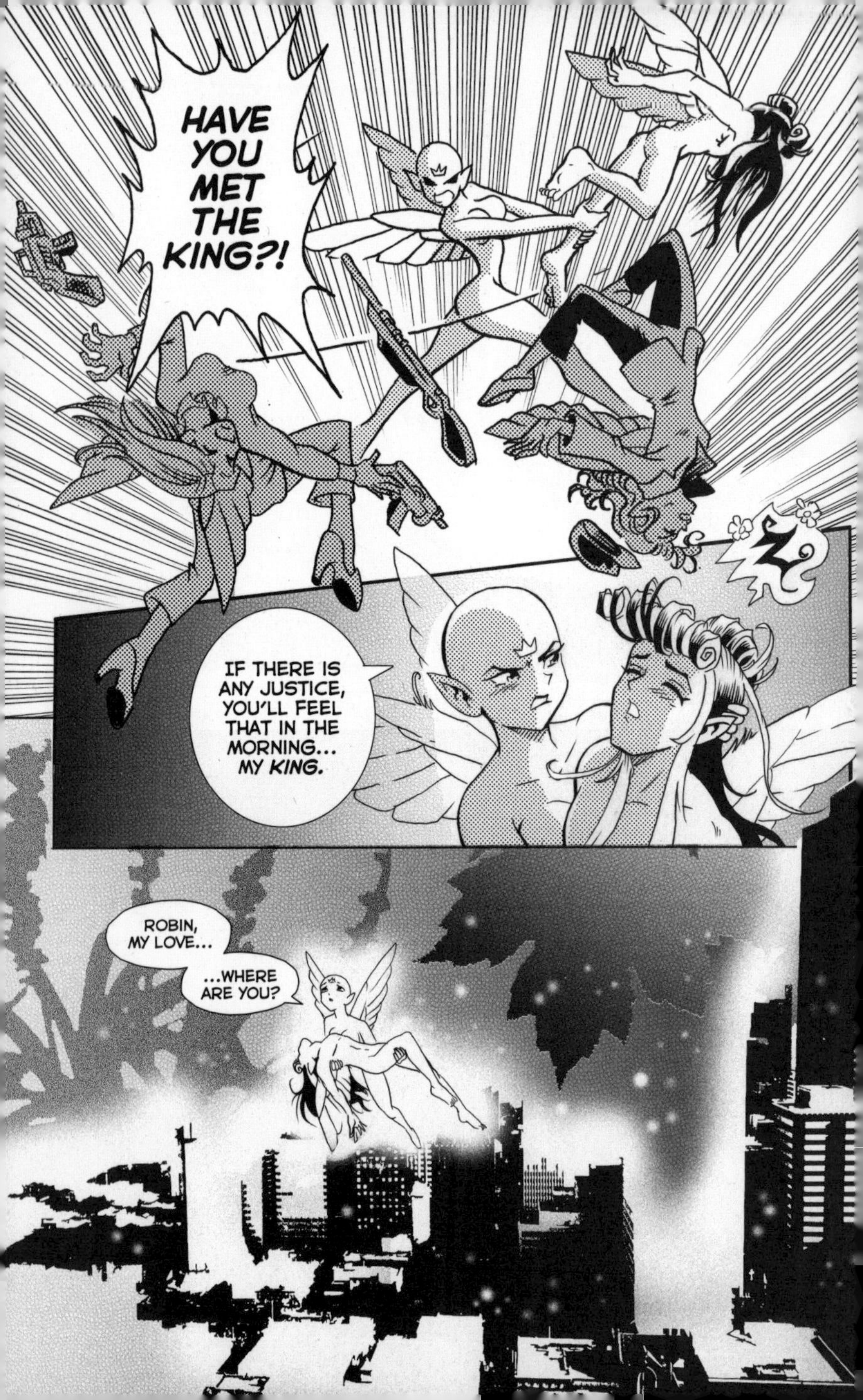
HAVE YOU MET THE KING?!
IF THERE IS ANY JUSTICE, YOU'LL FEEL THAT IN THE MORNING... MY KING.
ROBIN, MY LOVE...
...WHERE ARE YOU?

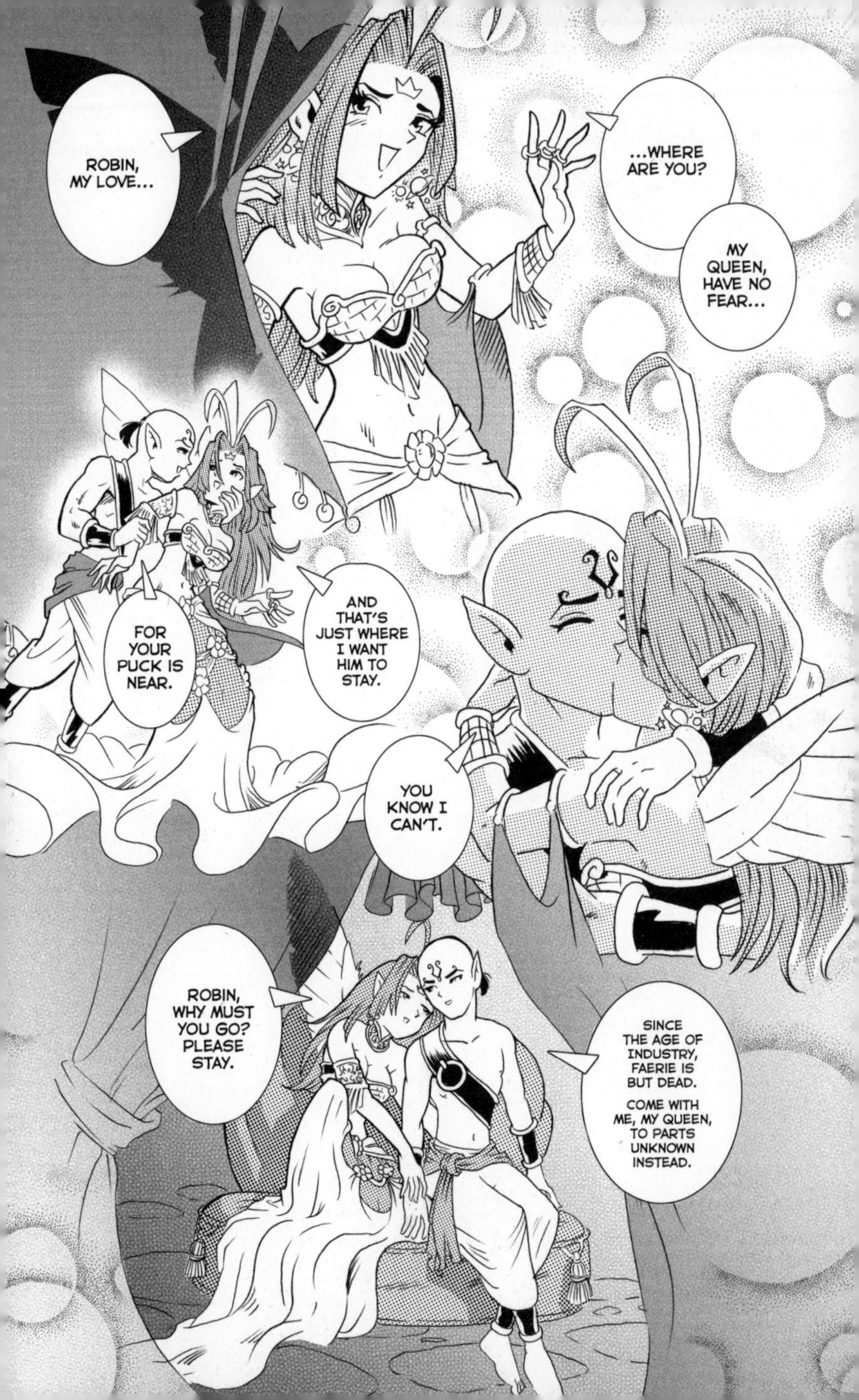
ROBIN, MY LOVE...
...WHERE ARE YOU?
MY QUEEN, HAVE NO FEAR...
FOR YOUR PUCK IS NEAR.
AND THAT'S JUST WHERE I WANT HIM TO STAY.
YOU KNOW I CAN'T.
ROBIN, WHY MUST YOU GO? PLEASE STAY.
SINCE THE AGE OF INDUSTRY, FAERIE IS BUT DEAD.
COME WITH ME, MY QUEEN, TO PARTS UNKNOWN INSTEAD.

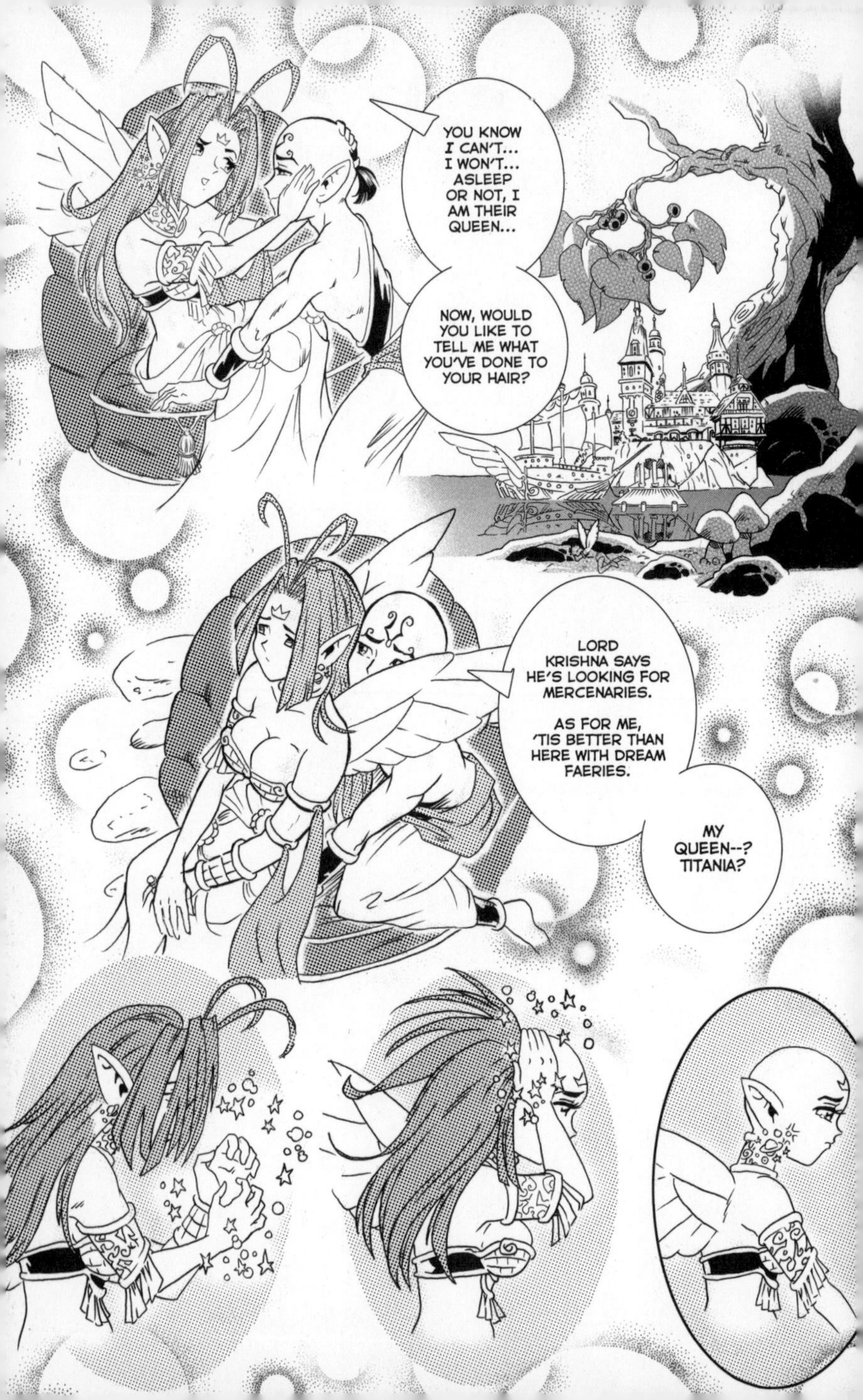
YOU KNOW *I* CAN'T... I WON'T... ASLEEP OR NOT, I AM THEIR QUEEN...
NOW, WOULD YOU LIKE TO TELL ME WHAT YOU'VE DONE TO YOUR HAIR?
LORD KRISHNA SAYS HE'S LOOKING FOR MERCENARIES.
AS FOR ME, 'TIS BETTER THAN HERE WITH DREAM FAERIES.
MY QUEEN--? TITANIA?

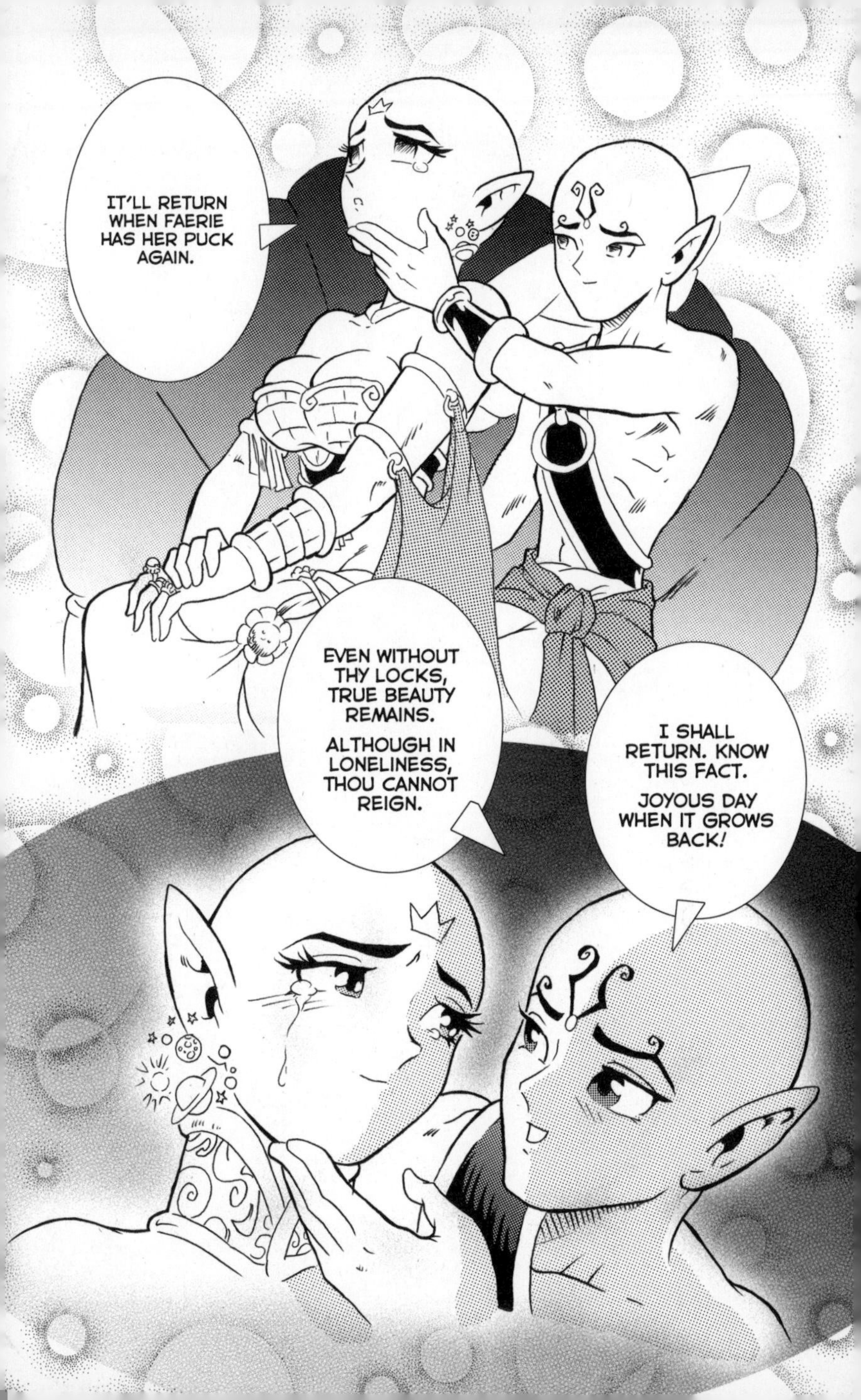
IT'LL RETURN WHEN FAERIE HAS HER PUCK AGAIN.
EVEN WITHOUT THY LOCKS, TRUE BEAUTY REMAINS.
ALTHOUGH IN LONELINESS, THOU CANNOT REIGN.
I SHALL RETURN. KNOW THIS FACT.
JOYOUS DAY WHEN IT GROWS BACK!

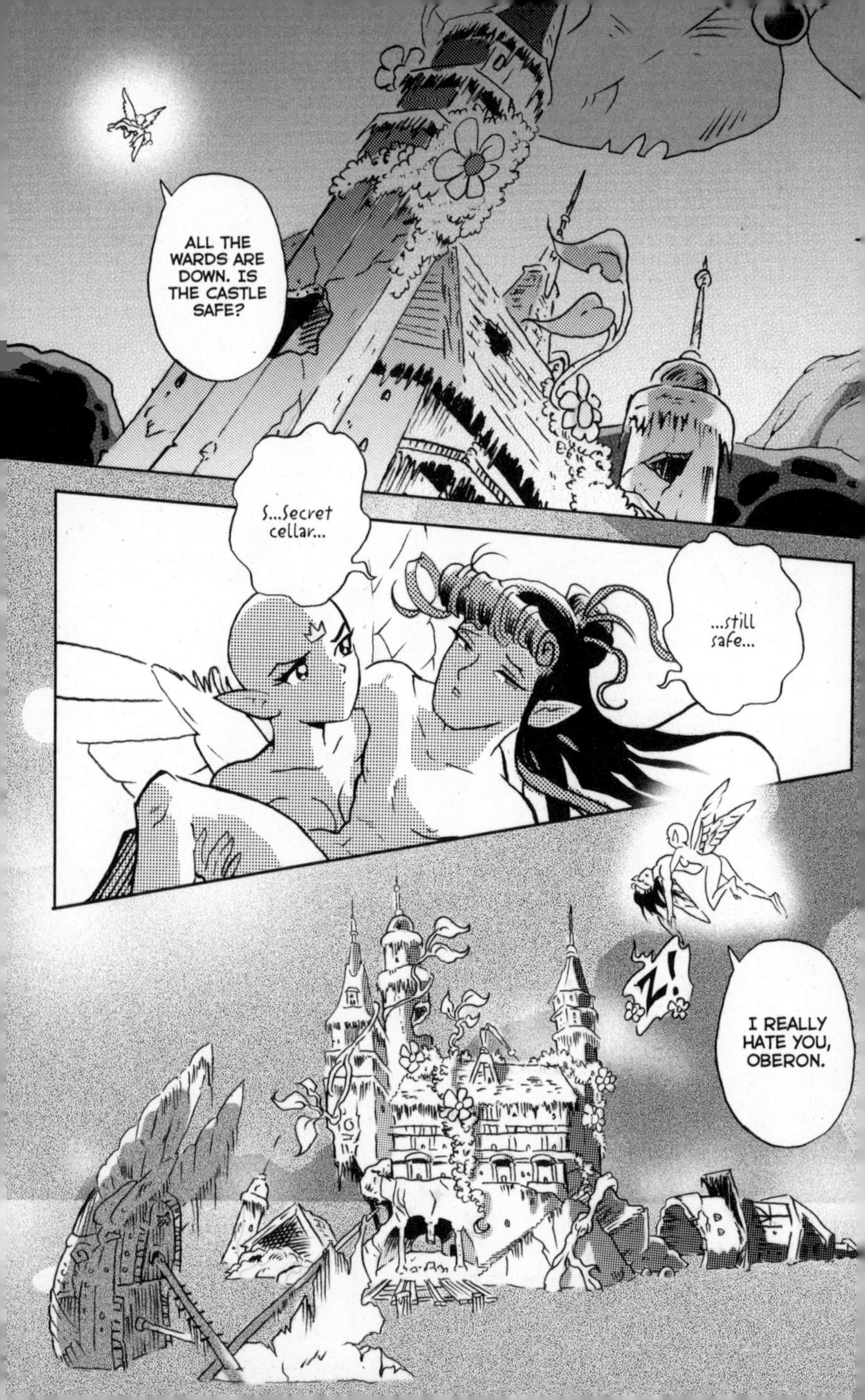

ALL THE WARDS ARE DOWN. IS THE CASTLE SAFE?
S...Secret cellar...
...still safe...
Z!
I REALLY HATE YOU, OBERON.

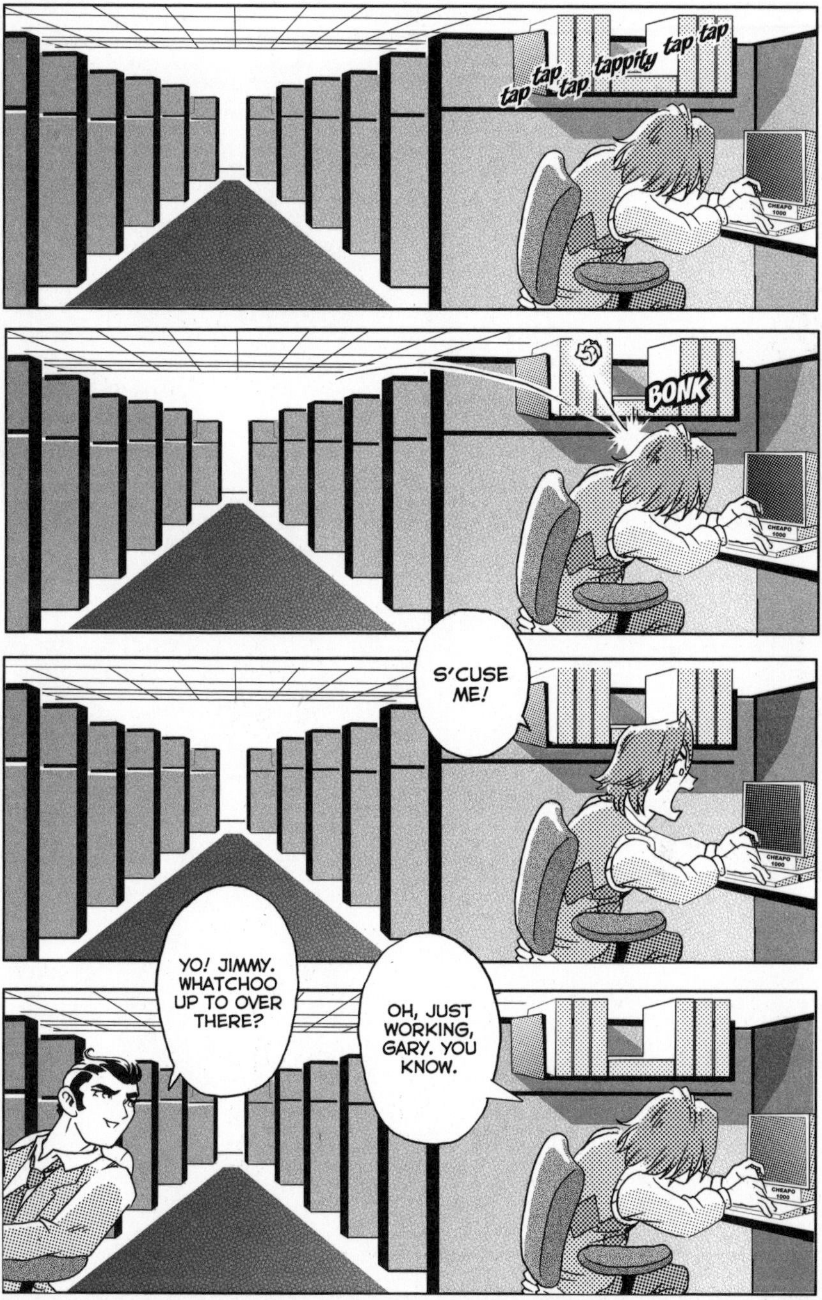
tap tap tap tap tappity tap tap
CHEAPO 1000
BONK
S'CUSE ME!
YO! JIMMY. WHATCHOO UP TO OVER THERE?
OH, JUST WORKING, GARY. YOU KNOW.

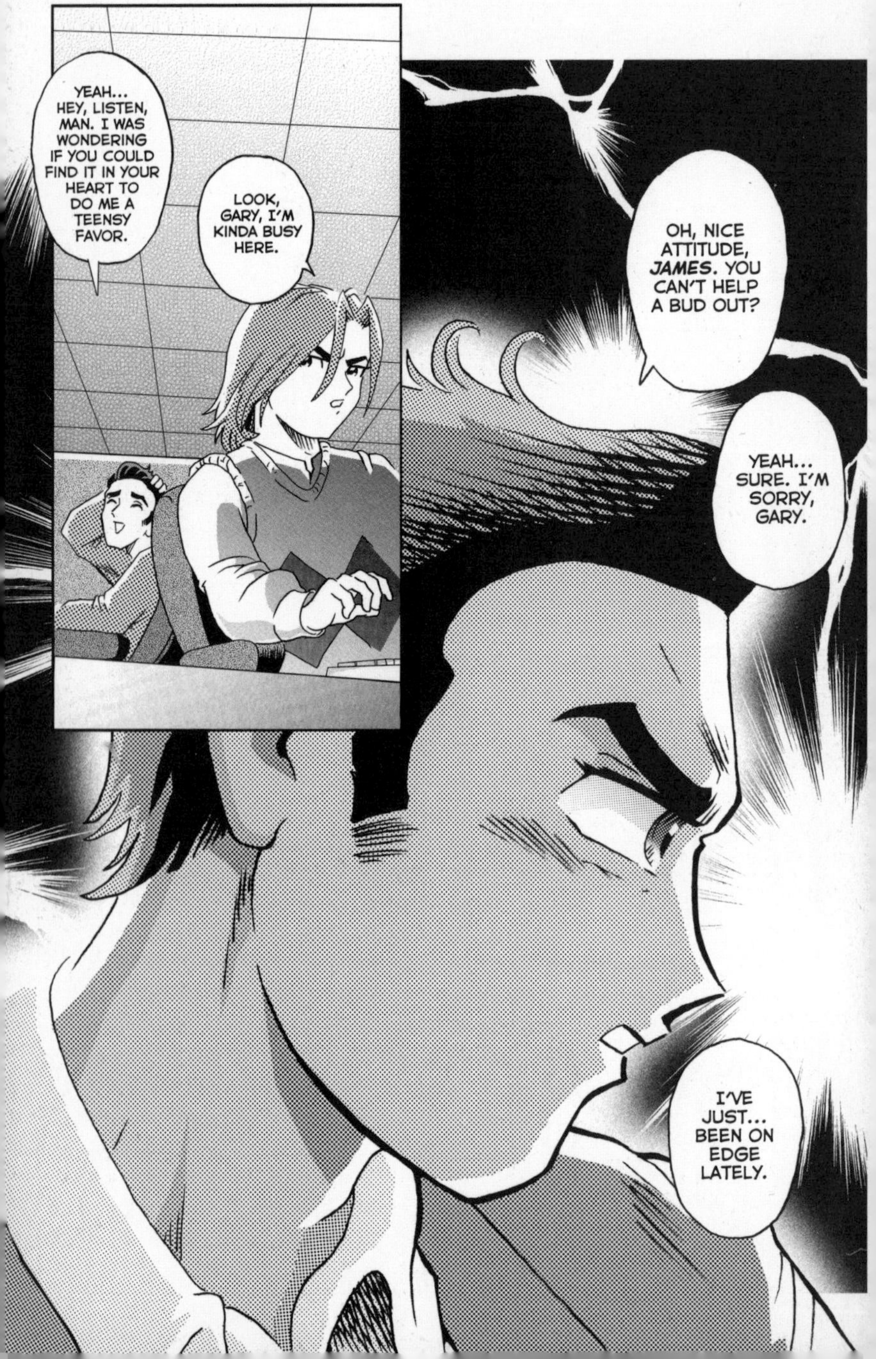
YEAH... HEY, LISTEN, MAN. I WAS WONDERING IF YOU COULD FIND IT IN YOUR HEART TO DO ME A TEENSY FAVOR.
LOOK, GARY, I'M KINDA BUSY HERE.
OH, NICE ATTITUDE, ***JAMES***. YOU CAN'T HELP A BUD OUT?
YEAH... SURE. I'M SORRY, GARY.
I'VE JUST... BEEN ON EDGE LATELY.

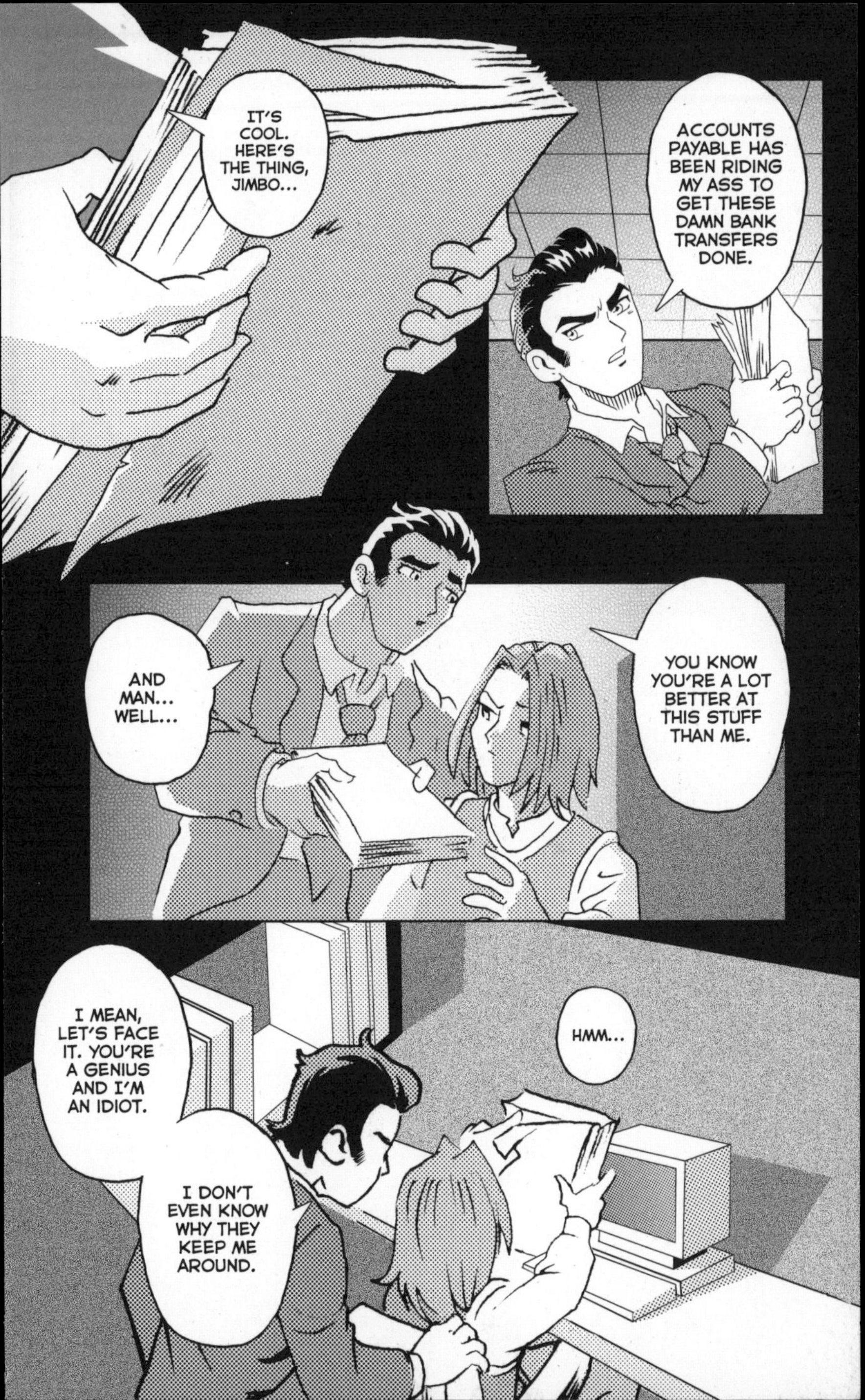
IT'S COOL. HERE'S THE THING, JIMBO...
ACCOUNTS PAYABLE HAS BEEN RIDING MY ASS TO GET THESE DAMN BANK TRANSFERS DONE.
AND MAN... WELL...
YOU KNOW YOU'RE A LOT BETTER AT THIS STUFF THAN ME.
I MEAN, LET'S FACE IT. YOU'RE A GENIUS AND I'M AN IDIOT.
I DON'T EVEN KNOW WHY THEY KEEP ME AROUND.
HMM...

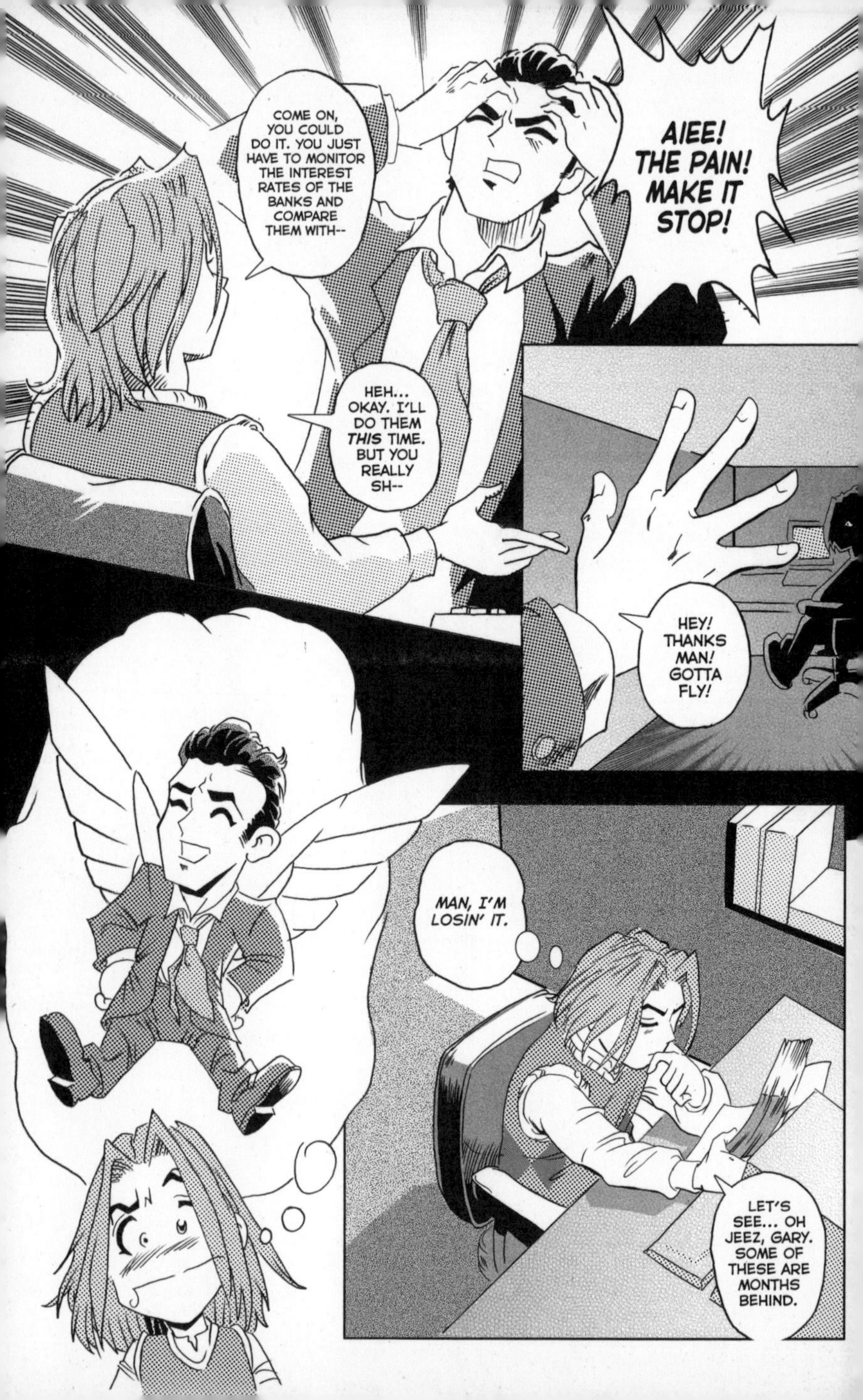
COME ON, YOU COULD DO IT. YOU JUST HAVE TO MONITOR THE INTEREST RATES OF THE BANKS AND COMPARE THEM WITH--
AIEE! THE PAIN! MAKE IT STOP!
HEH... OKAY. I'LL DO THEM *THIS* TIME. BUT YOU REALLY SH--
HEY! THANKS MAN! GOTTA FLY!
MAN, I'M LOSIN' IT.
LET'S SEE... OH JEEZ, GARY. SOME OF THESE ARE MONTHS BEHIND.

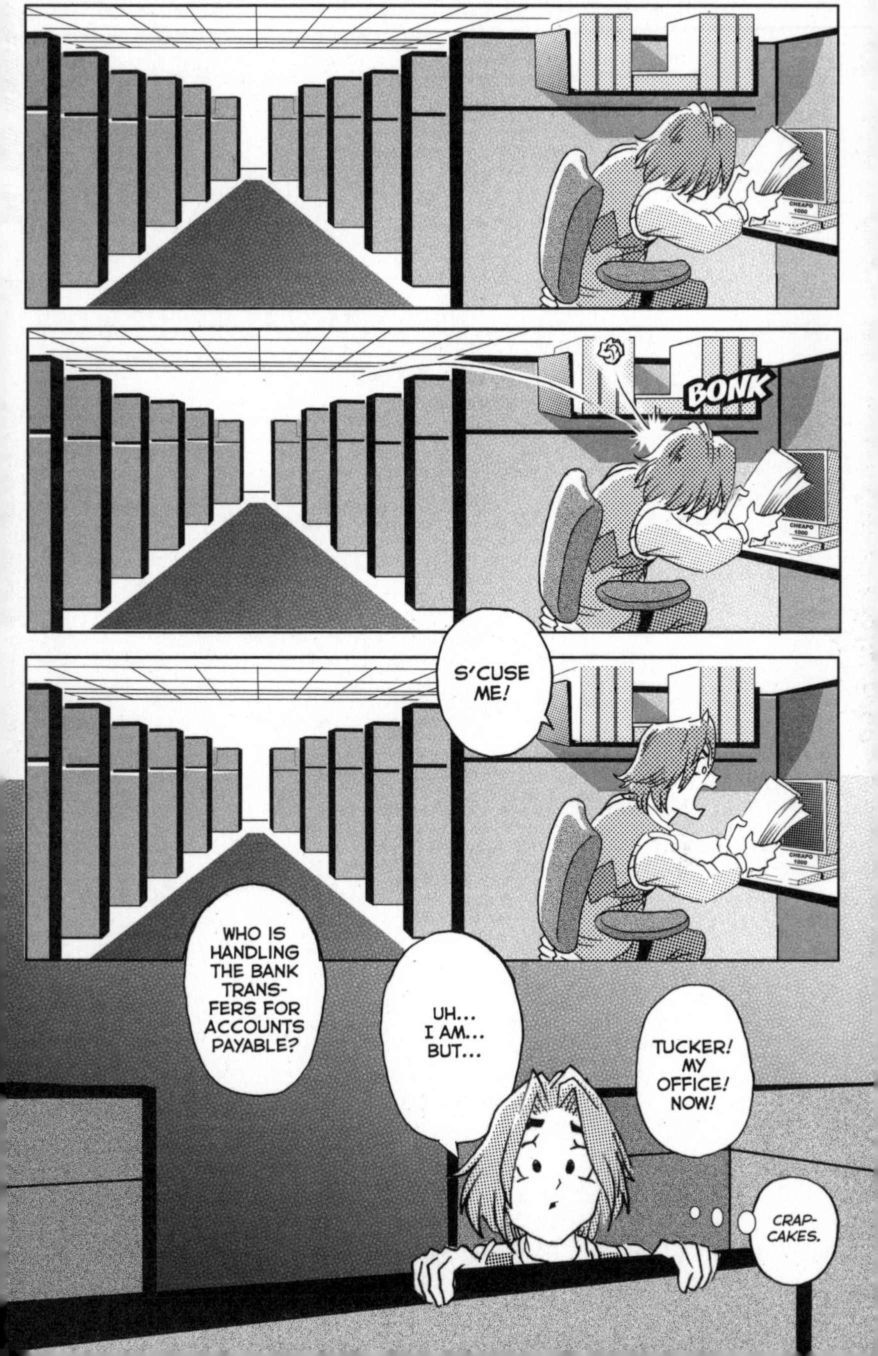
CHEAPO 1000
CHEAPO 1000
BONK
S'CUSE ME!
CHEAPO 1000
WHO IS HANDLING THE BANK TRANS-FERS FOR ACCOUNTS PAYABLE?
UH... I AM... BUT...
TUCKER! MY OFFICE! NOW!
CRAP-CAKES.

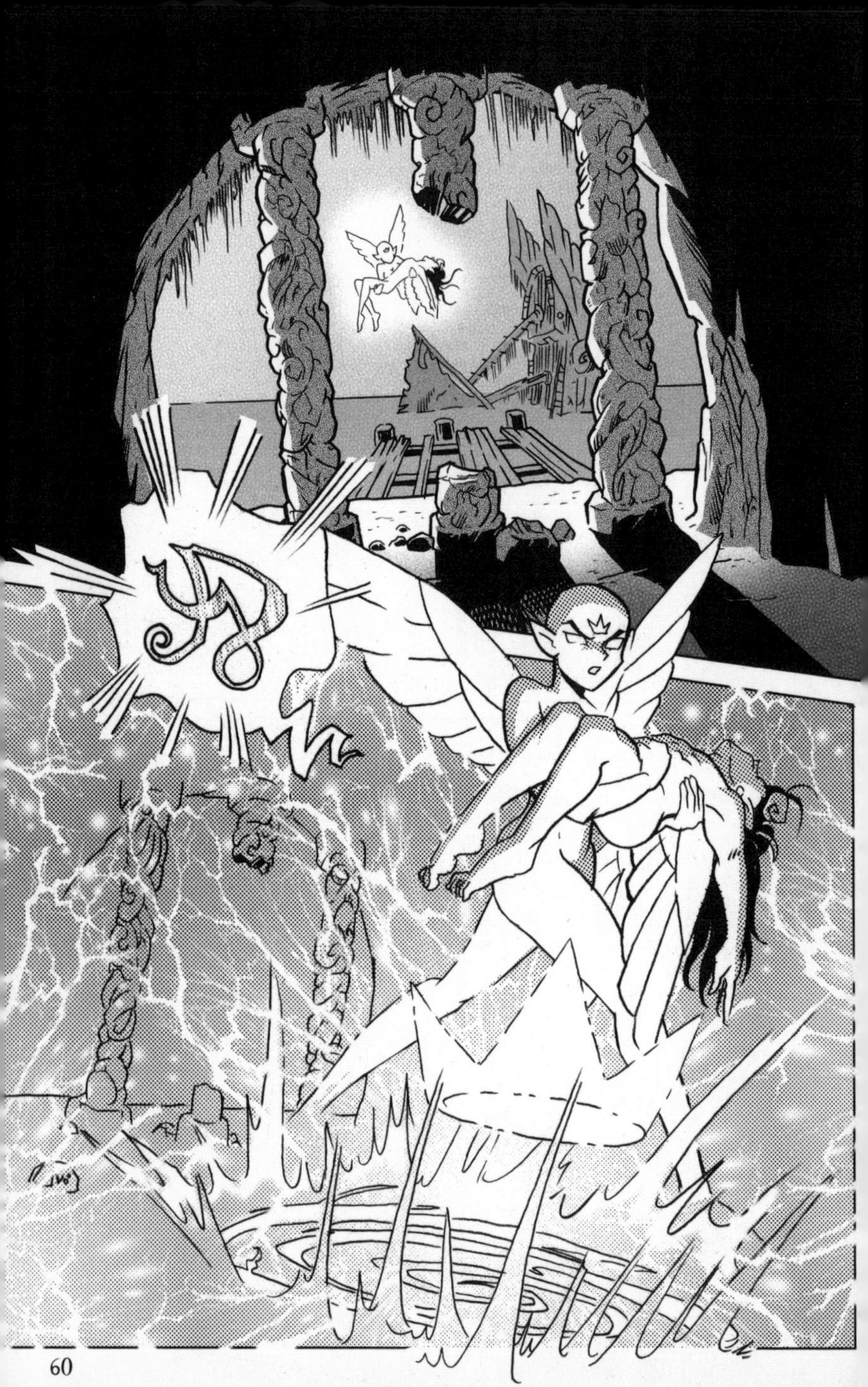

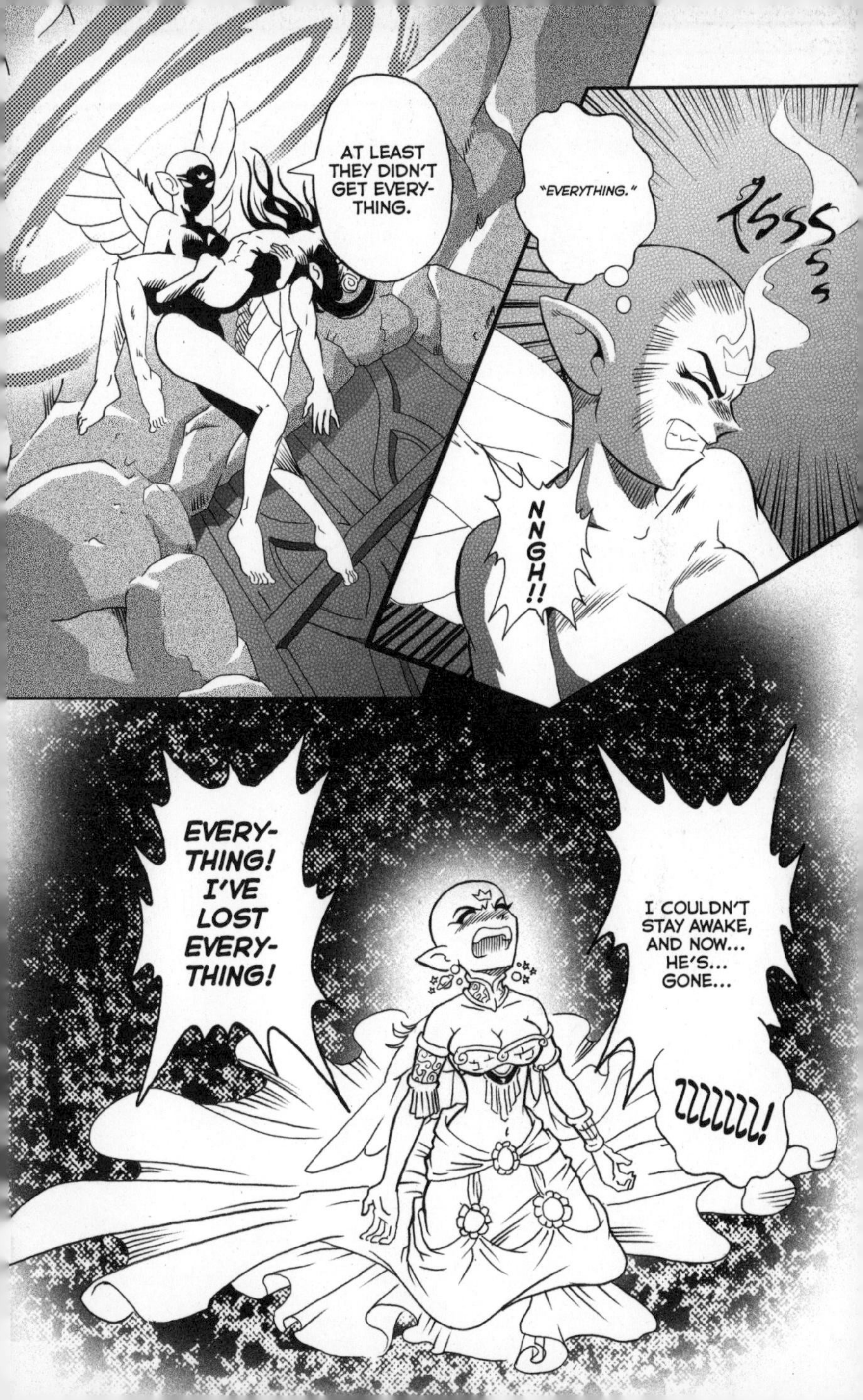

AT LEAST THEY DIDN'T GET EVERY-THING.
"EVERYTHING."
NNGH!!
EVERY-THING! I'VE LOST EVERY-THING!
I COULDN'T STAY AWAKE, AND NOW... HE'S... GONE...
ZZZZZZZ!

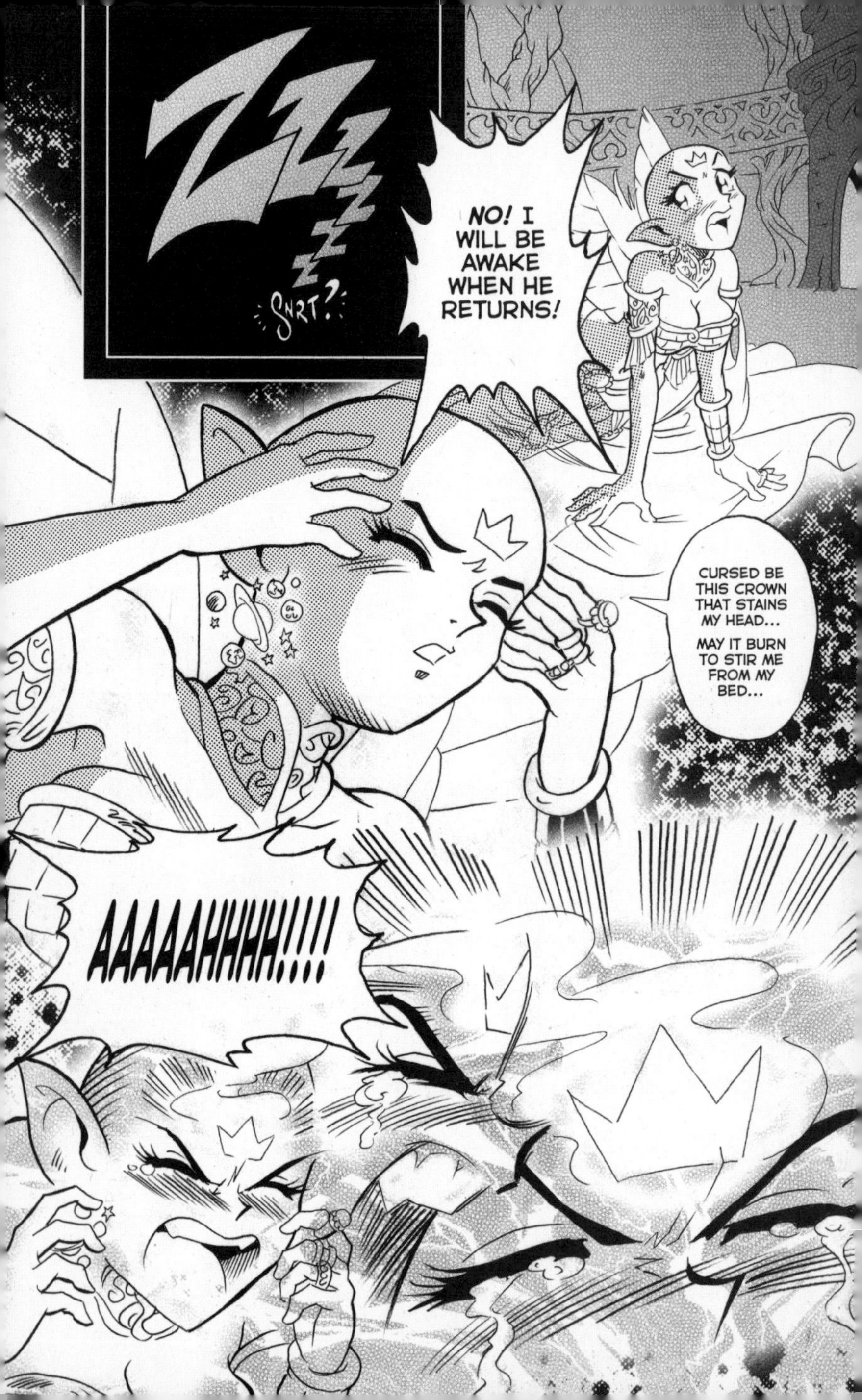
ZZZZZZ
SNRT?
NO! I WILL BE AWAKE WHEN HE RETURNS!
CURSED BE THIS CROWN THAT STAINS MY HEAD...
MAY IT BURN TO STIR ME FROM MY BED...
AAAAAHHHH!!!!!

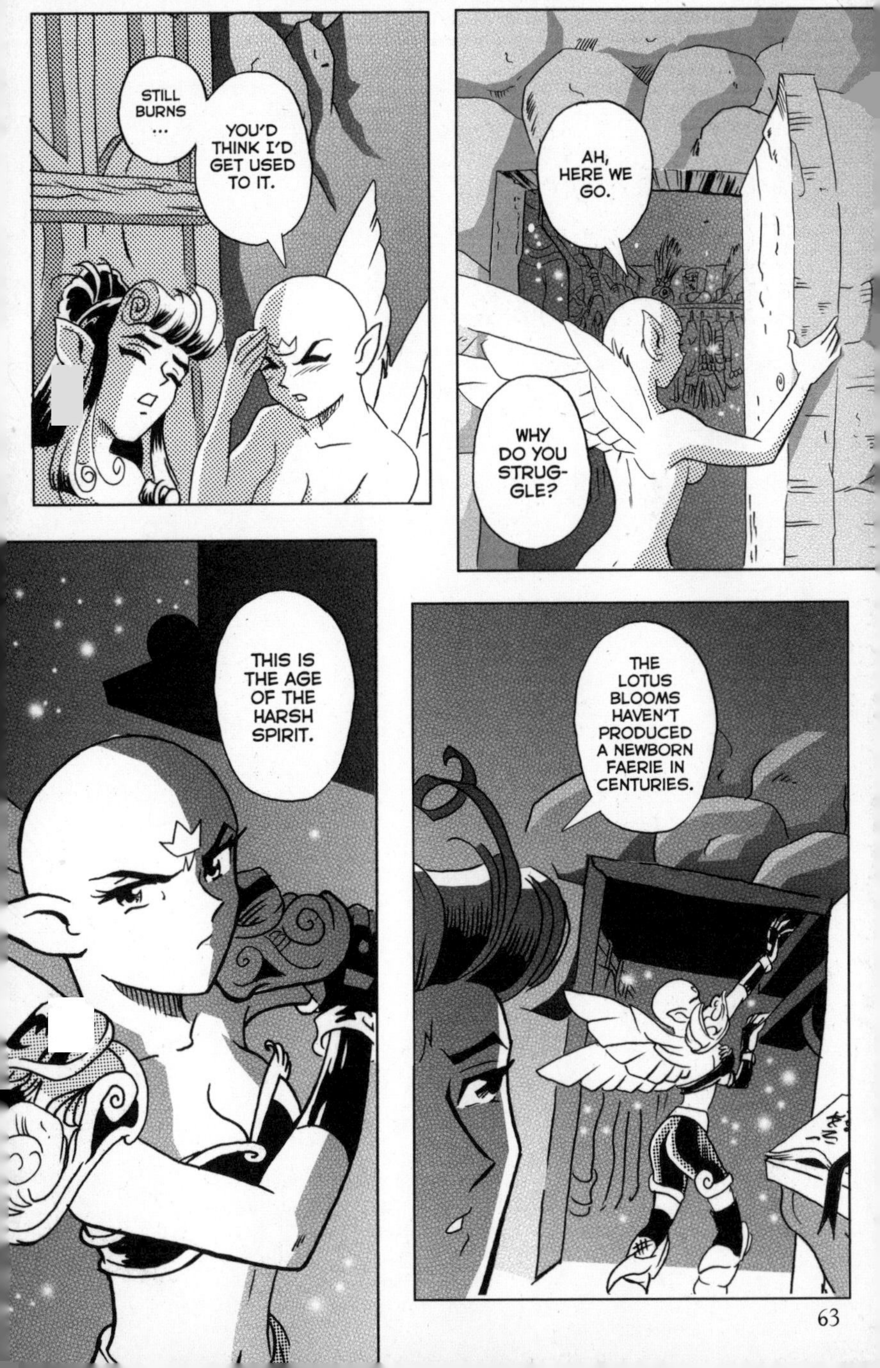
STILL BURNS ...
YOU'D THINK I'D GET USED TO IT.
AH, HERE WE GO.
WHY DO YOU STRUG-GLE?
THIS IS THE AGE OF THE HARSH SPIRIT.
THE LOTUS BLOOMS HAVEN'T PRODUCED A NEWBORN FAERIE IN CENTURIES.

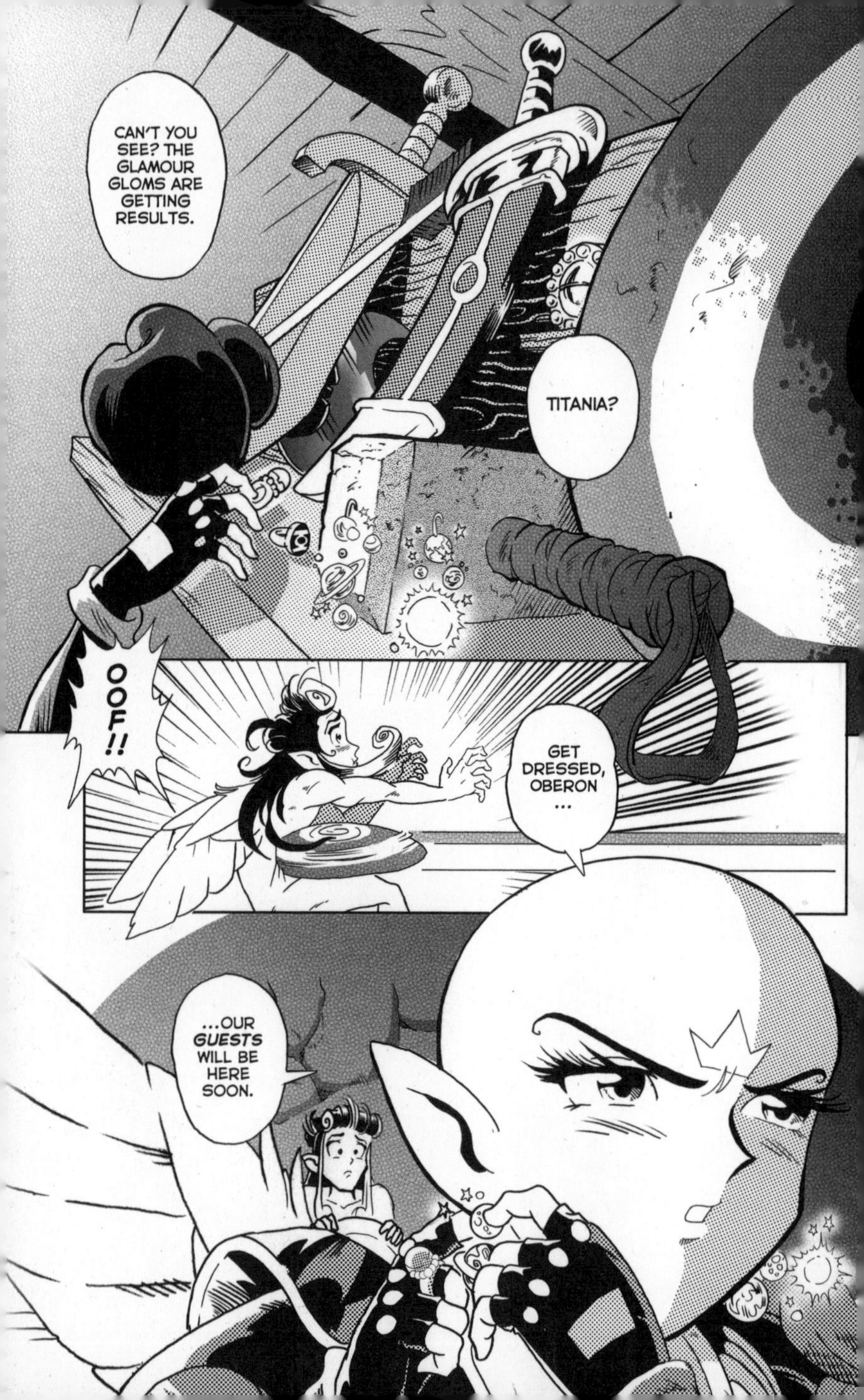
CAN'T YOU SEE? THE GLAMOUR GLOMS ARE GETTING RESULTS.
TITANIA?
OOF!!
GET DRESSED, OBERON ...
...OUR GUESTS WILL BE HERE SOON.

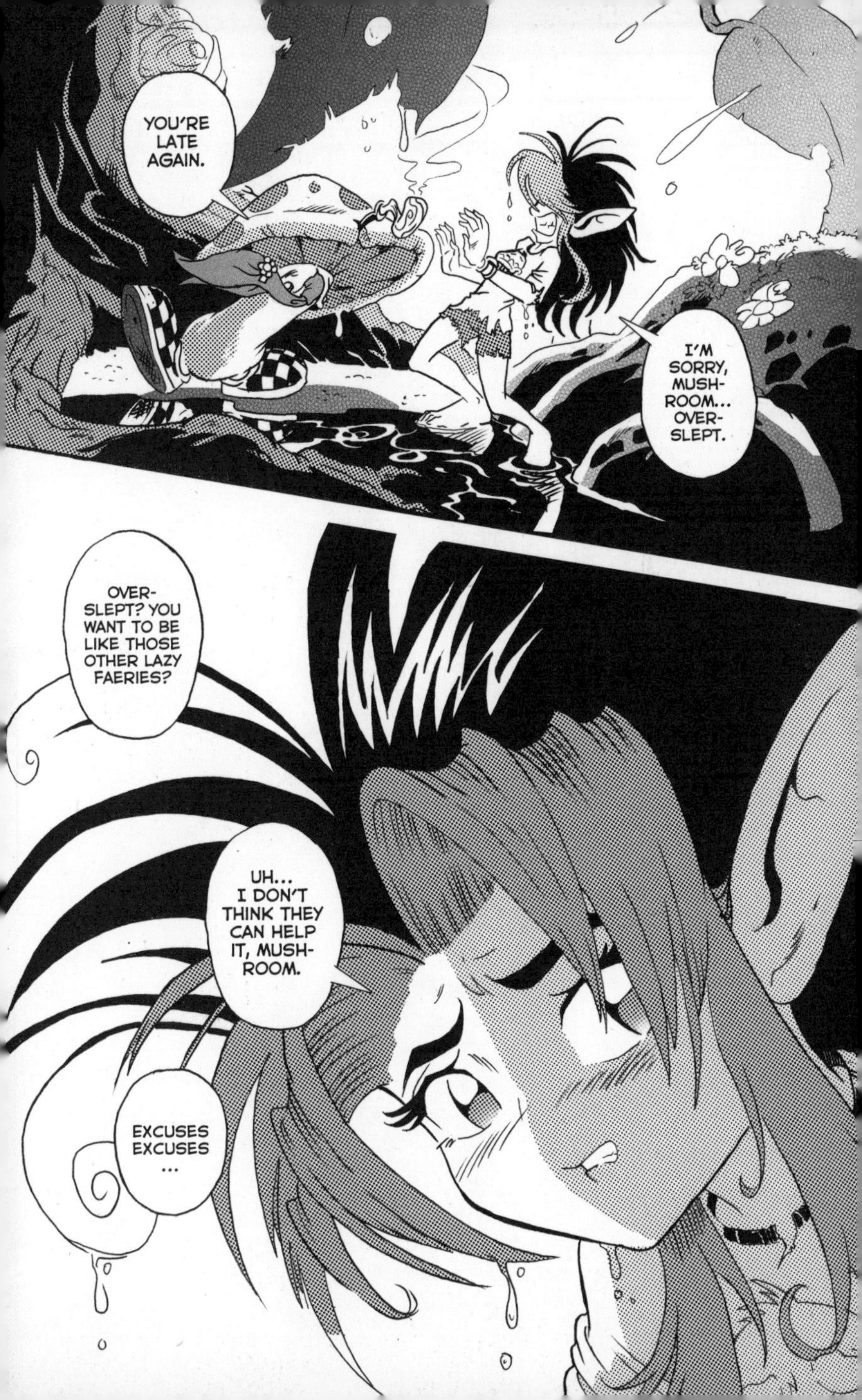
YOU'RE LATE AGAIN.
I'M SORRY, MUSH-ROOM... OVER-SLEPT.
OVER-SLEPT? YOU WANT TO BE LIKE THOSE OTHER LAZY FAERIES?
UH... I DON'T THINK THEY CAN HELP IT, MUSH-ROOM.
EXCUSES EXCUSES ...

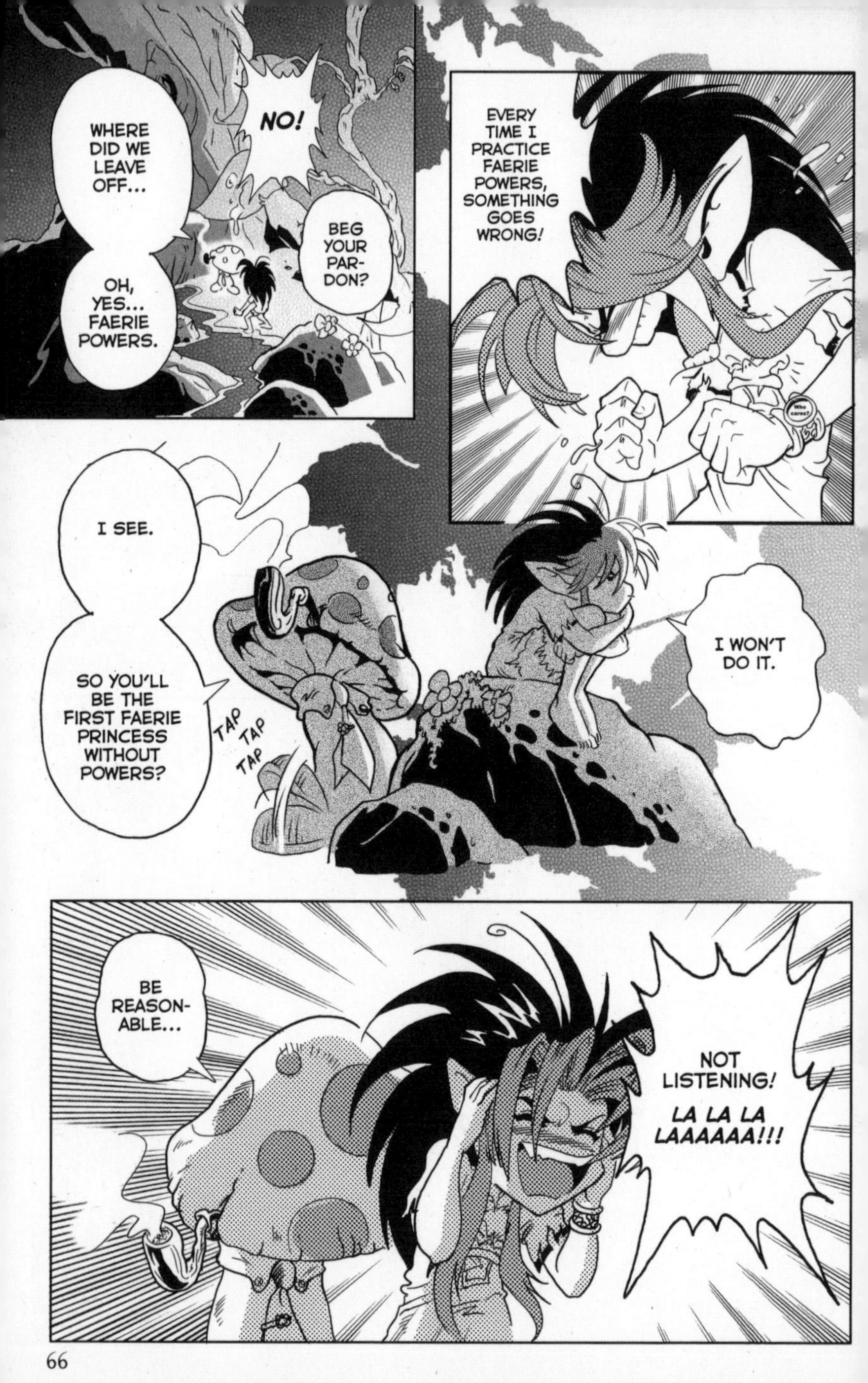

WHERE DID WE LEAVE OFF...
OH, YES... FAERIE POWERS.
NO!
BEG YOUR PAR- DON?
EVERY TIME I PRACTICE FAERIE POWERS, SOMETHING GOES WRONG!
I SEE.
SO YOU'LL BE THE FIRST FAERIE PRINCESS WITHOUT POWERS?
TAP TAP TAP
I WON'T DO IT.
BE REASON- ABLE...
NOT LISTENING!
LA LA LA LAAAAAA!!!

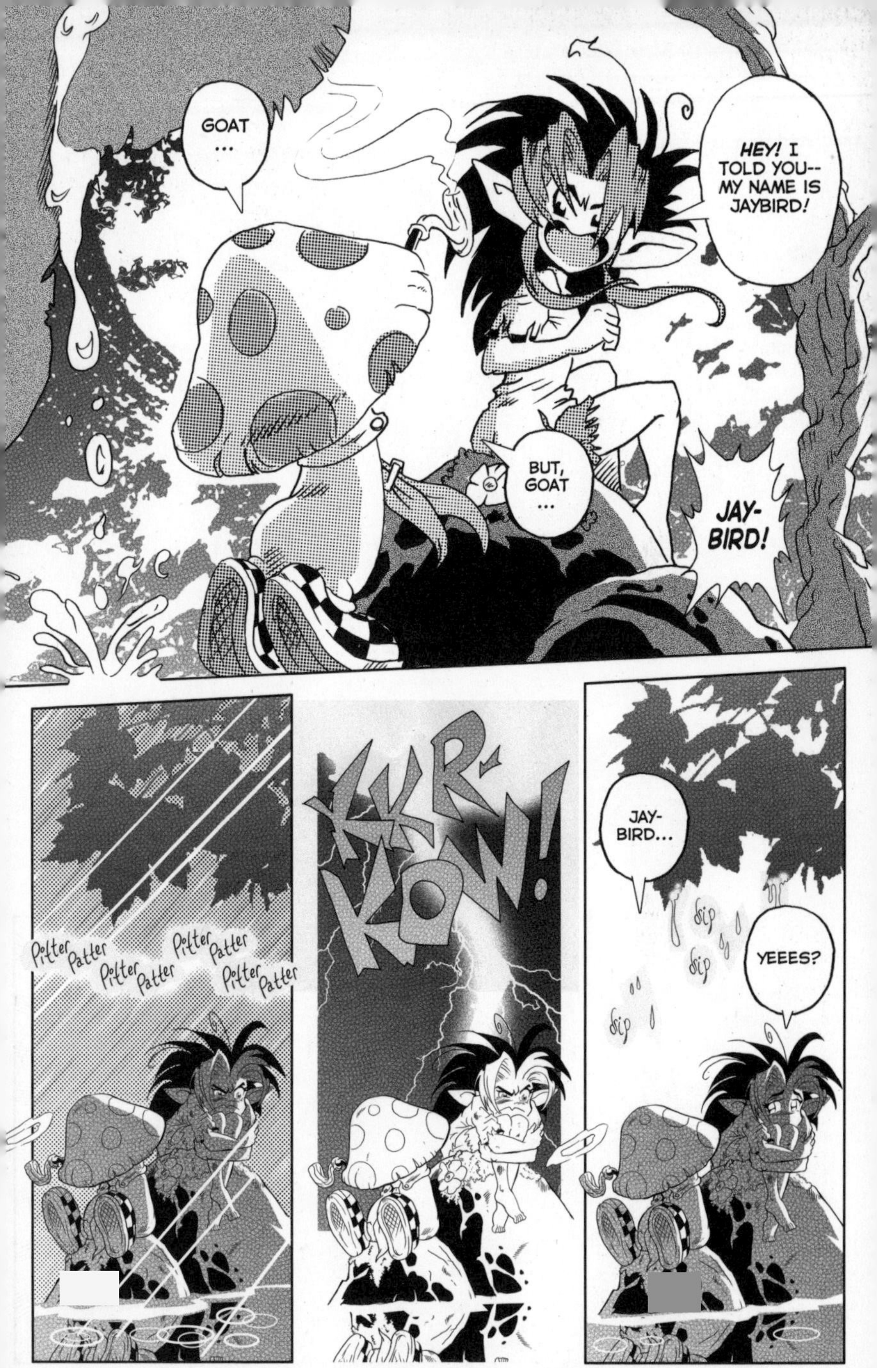
GOAT ...
HEY! I TOLD YOU-- MY NAME IS JAYBIRD!
BUT, GOAT ...
JAY-BIRD!
Pitter Patter Pitter Patter Pitter Patter Pitter Patter
KKR-KOW!
JAY-BIRD...
drip drip drip
YEEES?

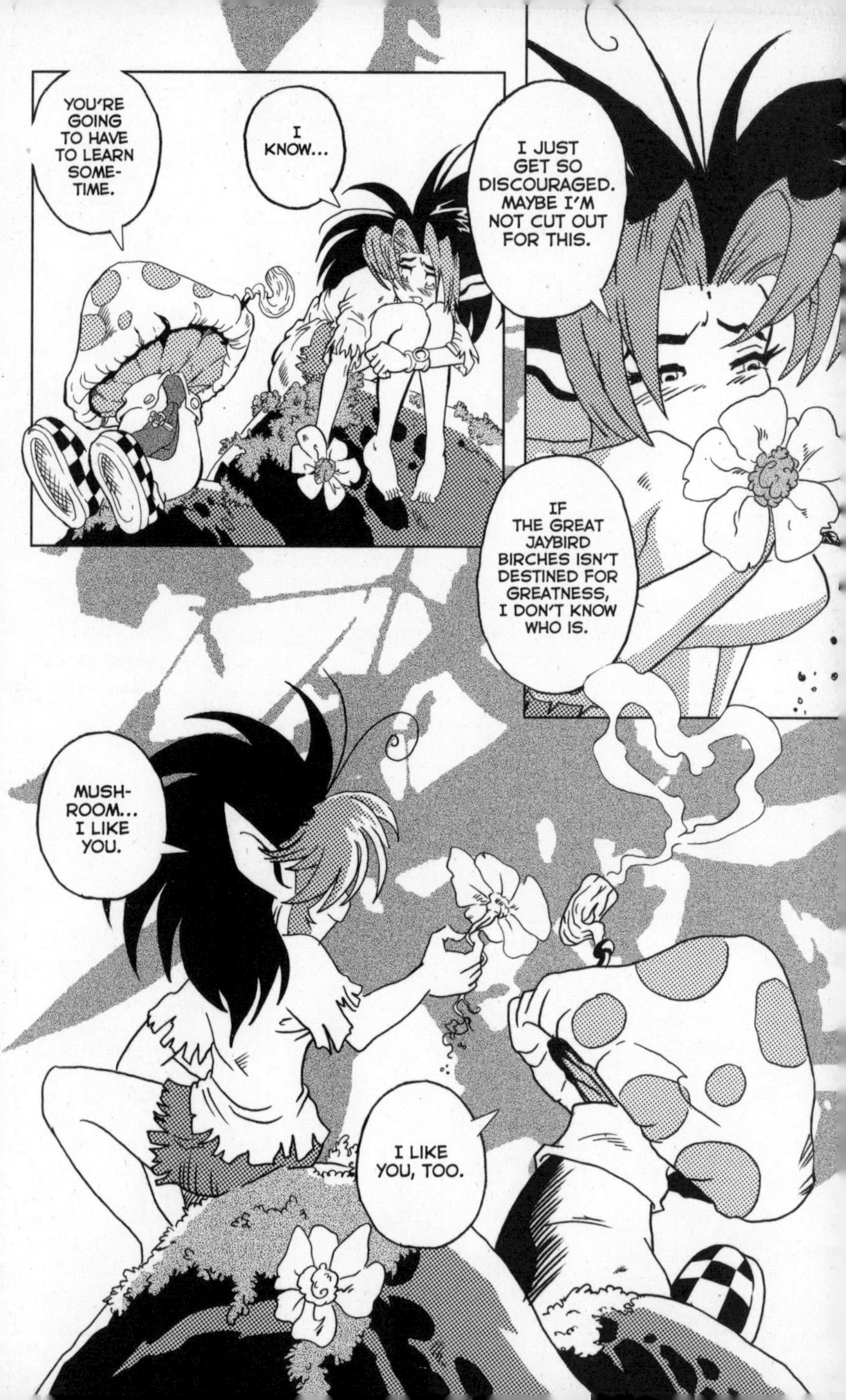
YOU'RE GOING TO HAVE TO LEARN SOME-TIME.
I KNOW...
I JUST GET SO DISCOURAGED. MAYBE I'M NOT CUT OUT FOR THIS.
IF THE GREAT JAYBIRD BIRCHES ISN'T DESTINED FOR GREATNESS, I DON'T KNOW WHO IS.
MUSH-ROOM... I LIKE YOU.
I LIKE YOU, TOO.

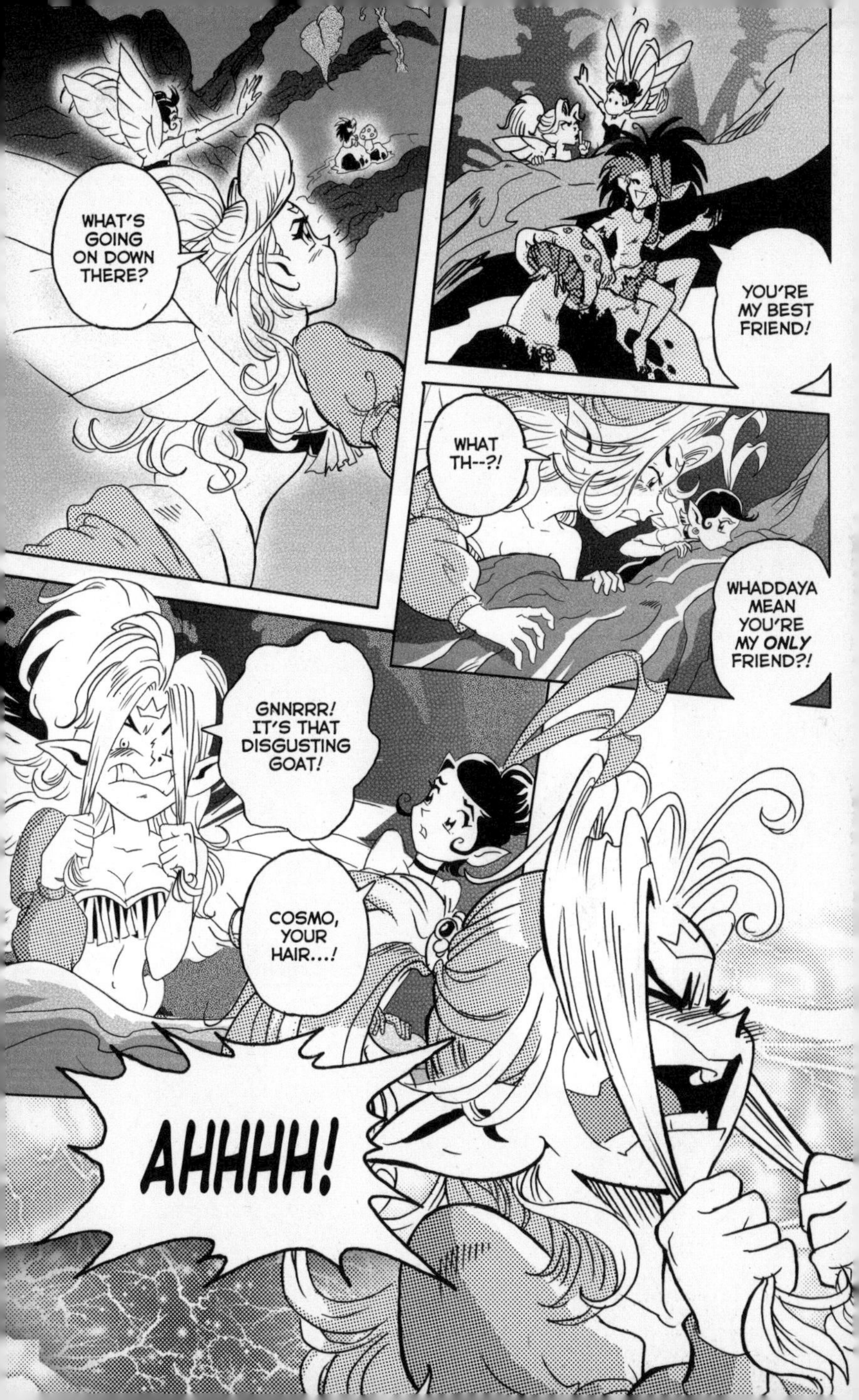
WHAT'S GOING ON DOWN THERE?
YOU'RE MY BEST FRIEND!
WHAT TH--?!
WHADDAYA MEAN YOU'RE MY *ONLY* FRIEND?!
GNNRRR! IT'S THAT DISGUSTING GOAT!
COSMO, YOUR HAIR...!
AHHHH!

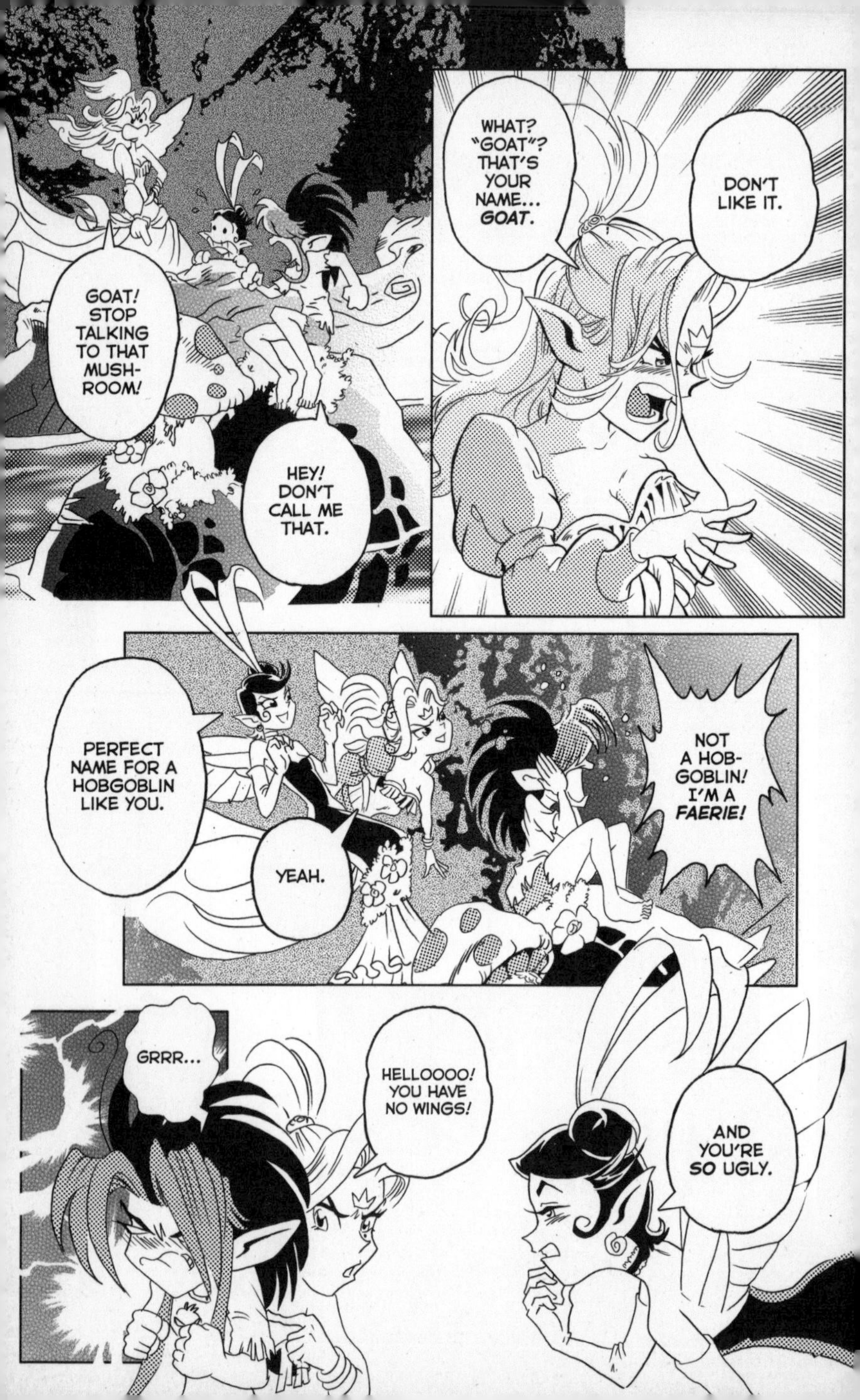
GOAT! STOP TALKING TO THAT MUSH-ROOM!
HEY! DON'T CALL ME THAT.
WHAT? "GOAT"? THAT'S YOUR NAME... GOAT.
DON'T LIKE IT.
PERFECT NAME FOR A HOBGOBLIN LIKE YOU.
YEAH.
NOT A HOB-GOBLIN! I'M A FAERIE!
GRRR...
HELLOOOO! YOU HAVE NO WINGS!
AND YOU'RE SO UGLY.

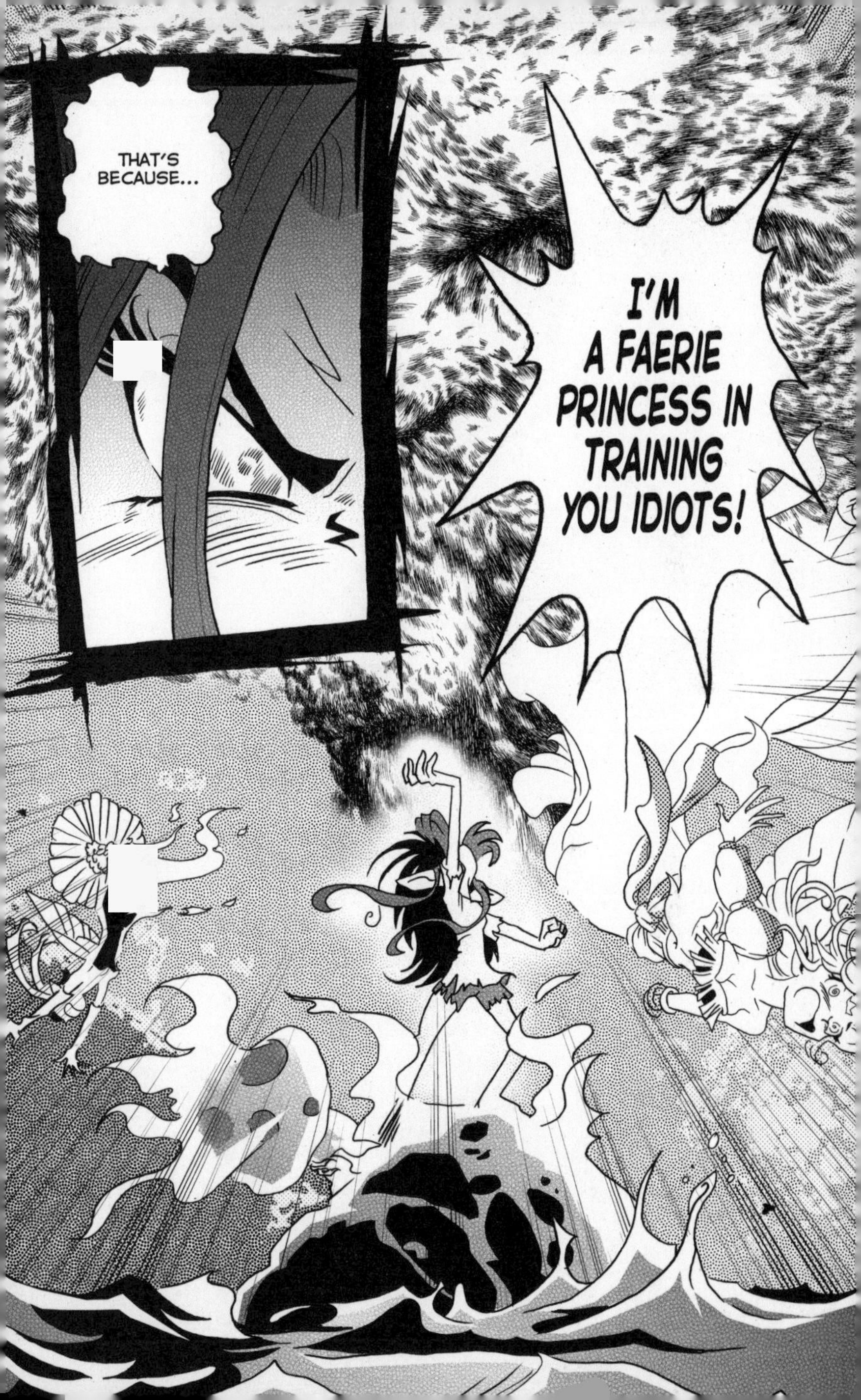
THAT'S BECAUSE...
I'M A FAERIE PRINCESS IN TRAINING YOU IDIOTS!

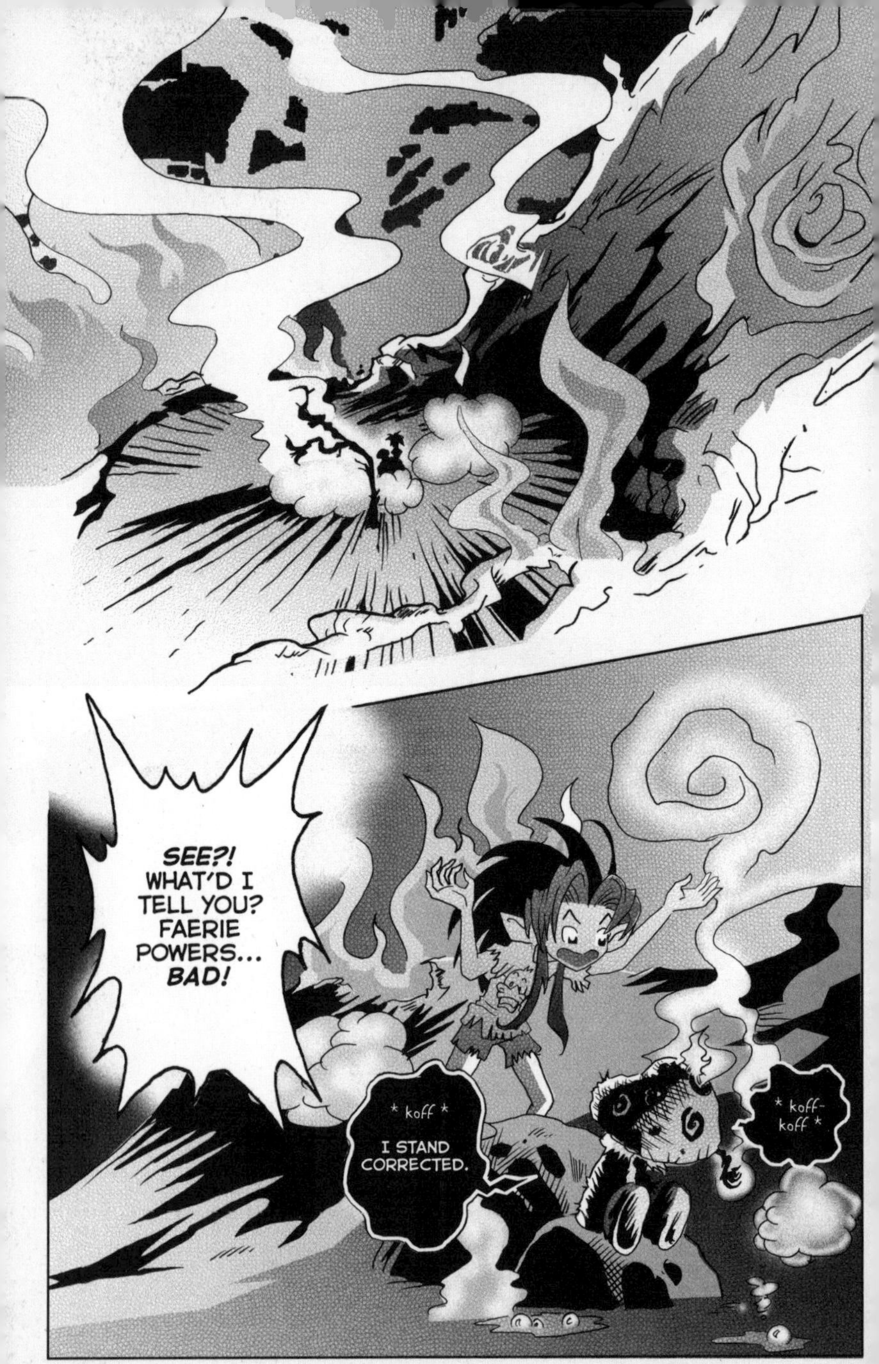
SEE?! WHAT'D I TELL YOU? FAERIE POWERS... BAD!
* koff * I STAND CORRECTED.
* koff-koff *

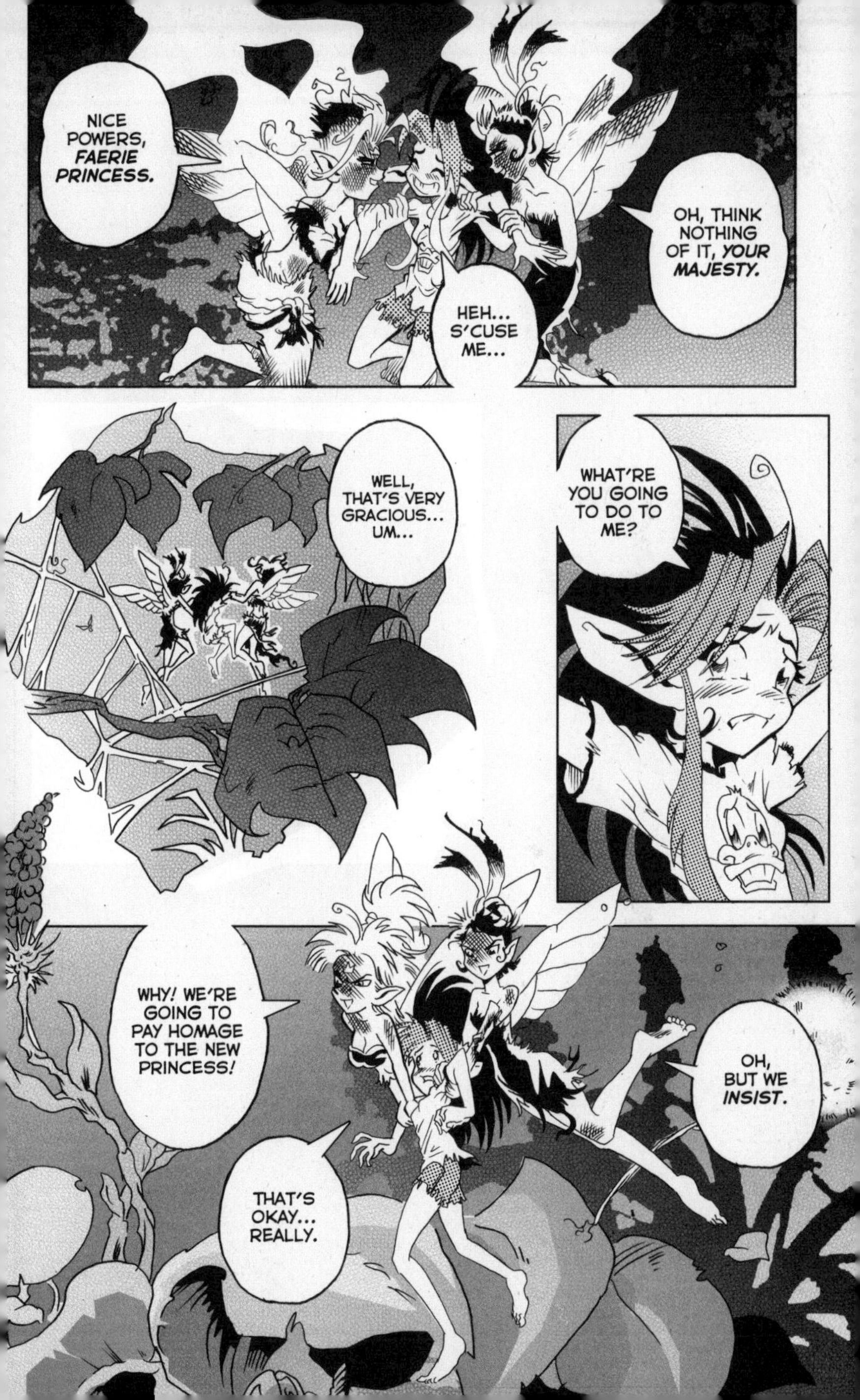
NICE POWERS, *FAERIE PRINCESS.*
HEH... S'CUSE ME...
OH, THINK NOTHING OF IT, *YOUR MAJESTY.*
WELL, THAT'S VERY GRACIOUS... UM...
WHAT'RE YOU GOING TO DO TO ME?
WHY! WE'RE GOING TO PAY HOMAGE TO THE NEW PRINCESS!
THAT'S OKAY... REALLY.
OH, BUT WE *INSIST.*

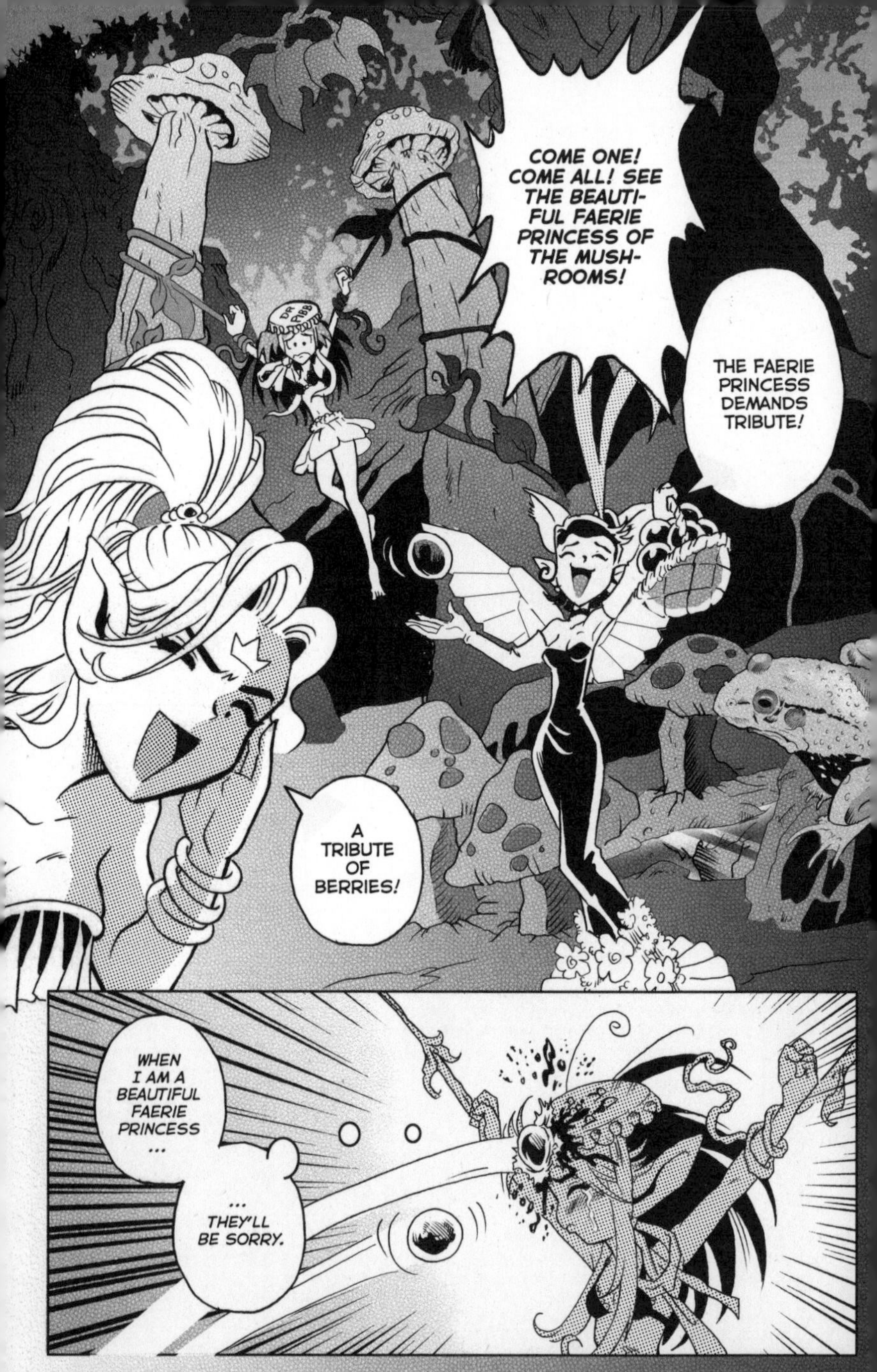
COME ONE! COME ALL! SEE THE BEAUTI-FUL FAERIE PRINCESS OF THE MUSH-ROOMS!
THE FAERIE PRINCESS DEMANDS TRIBUTE!
A TRIBUTE OF BERRIES!
WHEN I AM A BEAUTIFUL FAERIE PRINCESS ...
... THEY'LL BE SORRY.

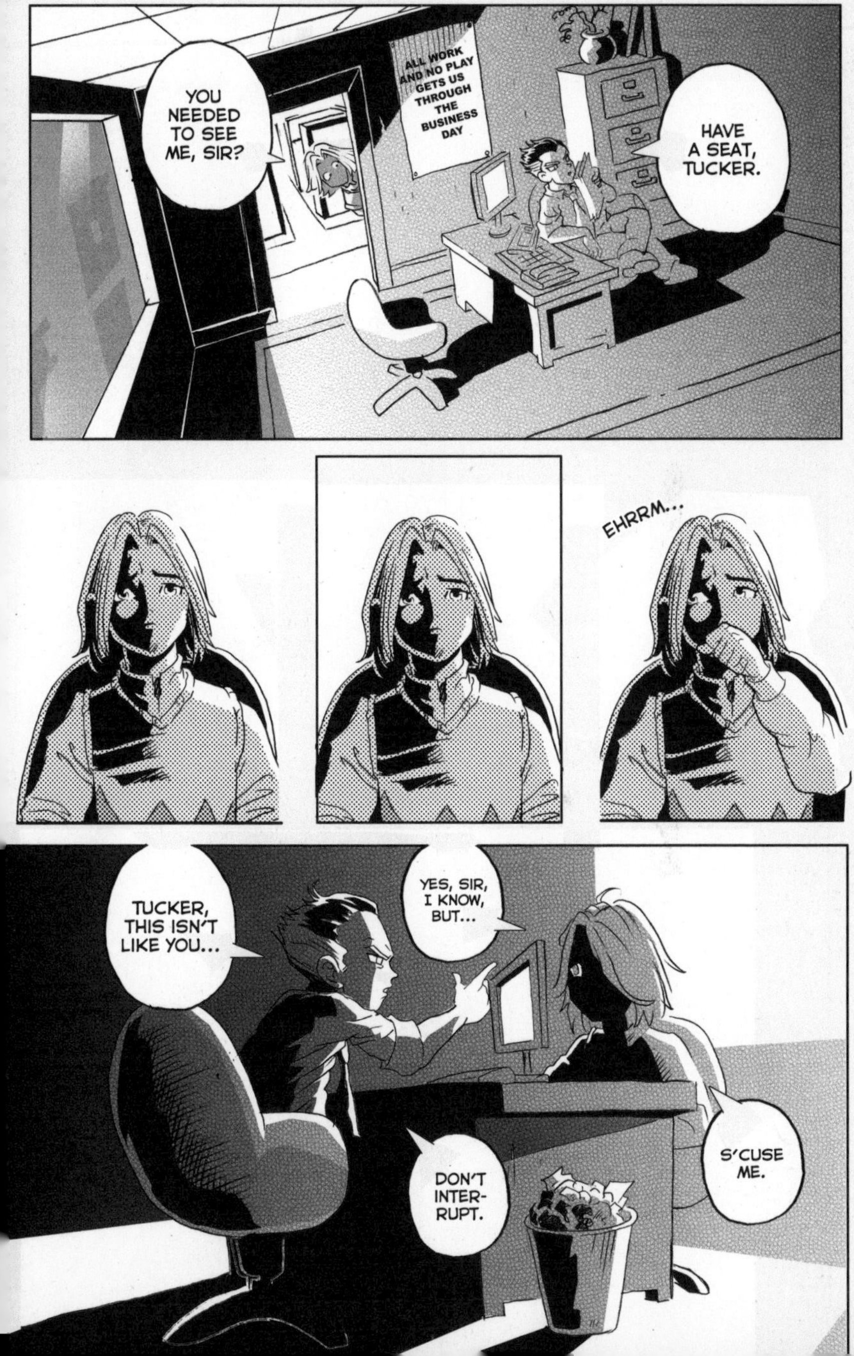
YOU NEEDED TO SEE ME, SIR?
ALL WORK AND NO PLAY GETS US THROUGH THE BUSINESS DAY
HAVE A SEAT, TUCKER.
EHRRM...
TUCKER, THIS ISN'T LIKE YOU...
YES, SIR, I KNOW, BUT...
DON'T INTER-RUPT.
S'CUSE ME.

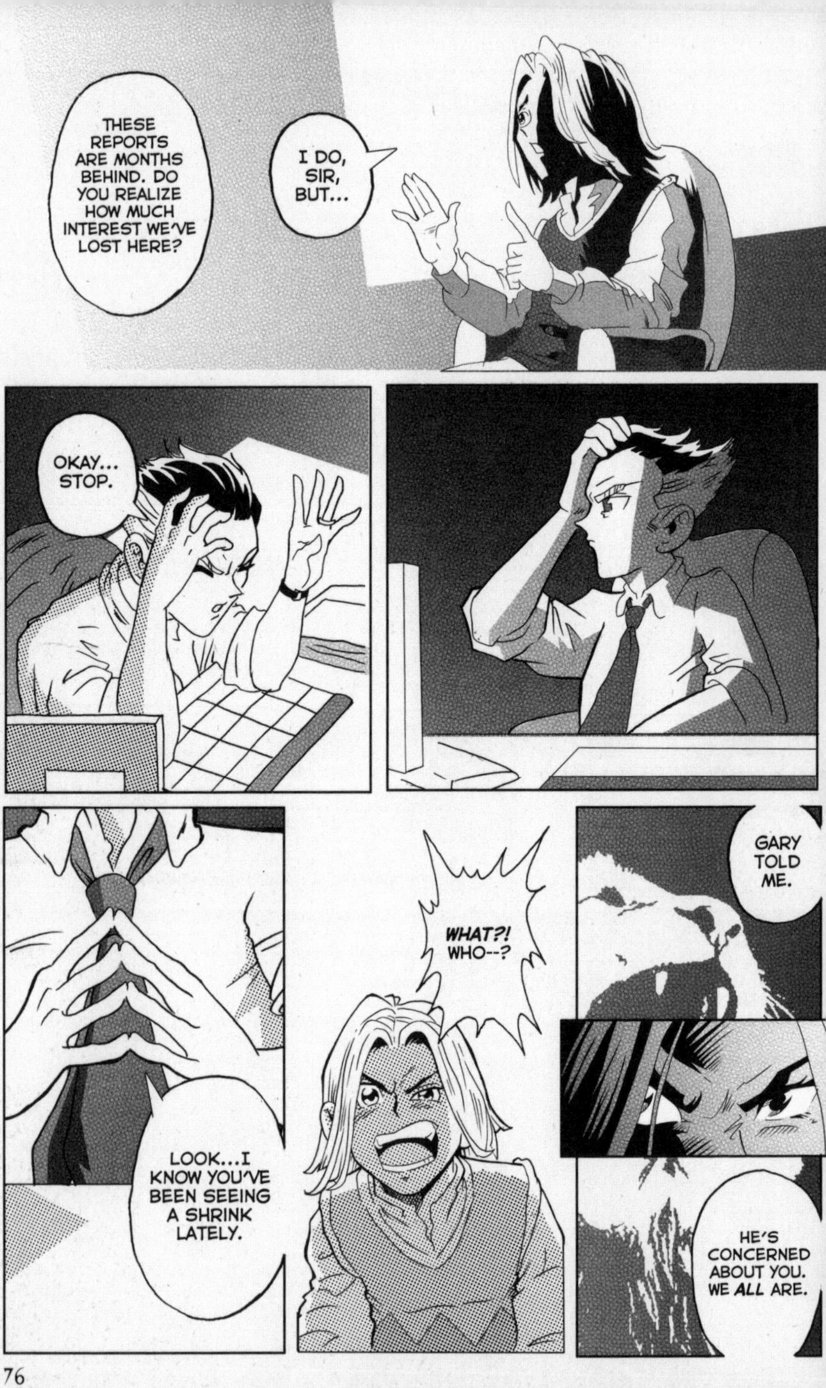
THESE REPORTS ARE MONTHS BEHIND. DO YOU REALIZE HOW MUCH INTEREST WE'VE LOST HERE?
I DO, SIR, BUT...
OKAY... STOP.
LOOK...I KNOW YOU'VE BEEN SEEING A SHRINK LATELY.
WHAT?! WHO--?
GARY TOLD ME.
HE'S CONCERNED ABOUT YOU. WE *ALL* ARE.

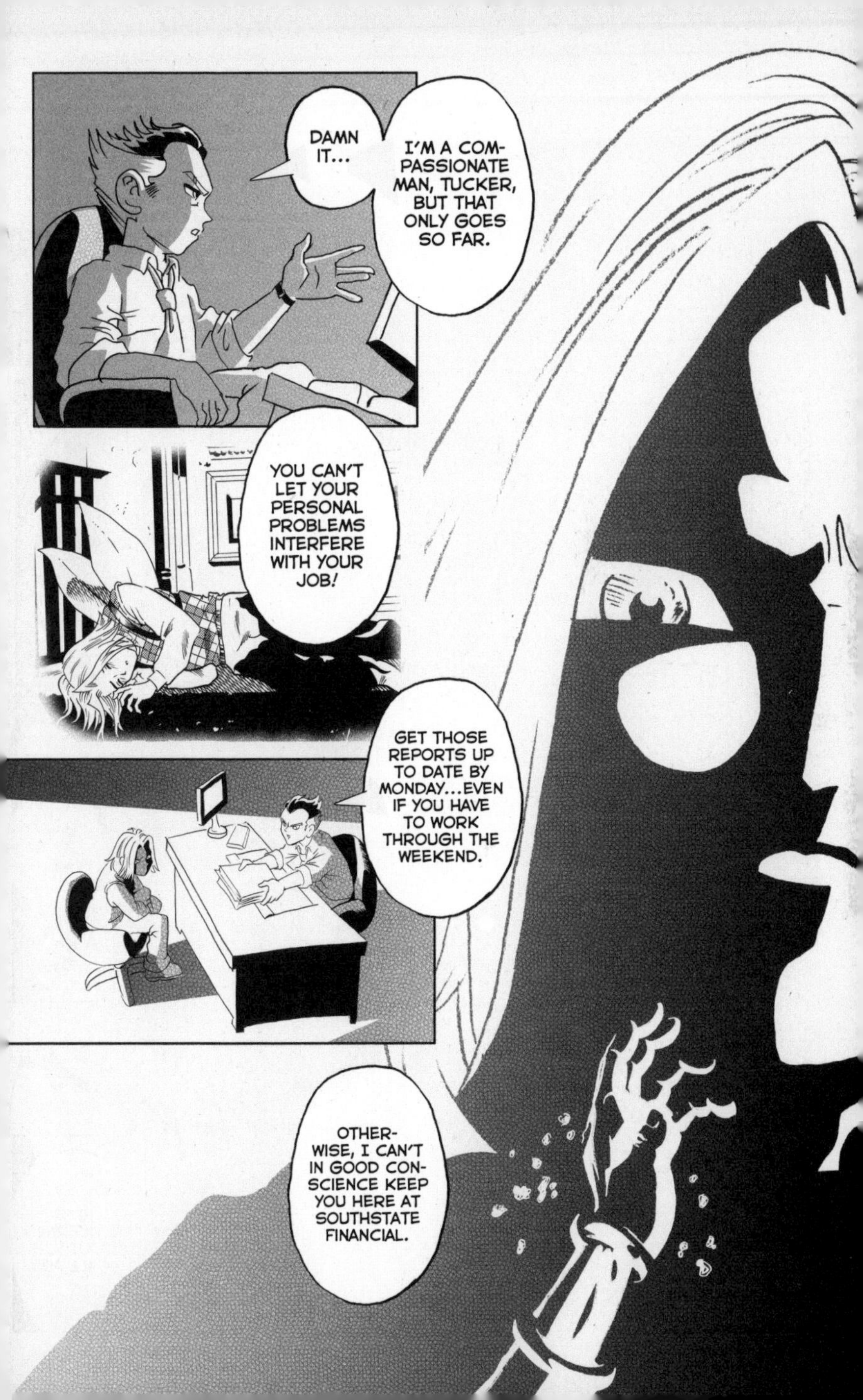
DAMN IT...
I'M A COMPASSIONATE MAN, TUCKER, BUT THAT ONLY GOES SO FAR.
YOU CAN'T LET YOUR PERSONAL PROBLEMS INTERFERE WITH YOUR JOB!
GET THOSE REPORTS UP TO DATE BY MONDAY...EVEN IF YOU HAVE TO WORK THROUGH THE WEEKEND.
OTHERWISE, I CAN'T IN GOOD CONSCIENCE KEEP YOU HERE AT SOUTHSTATE FINANCIAL.

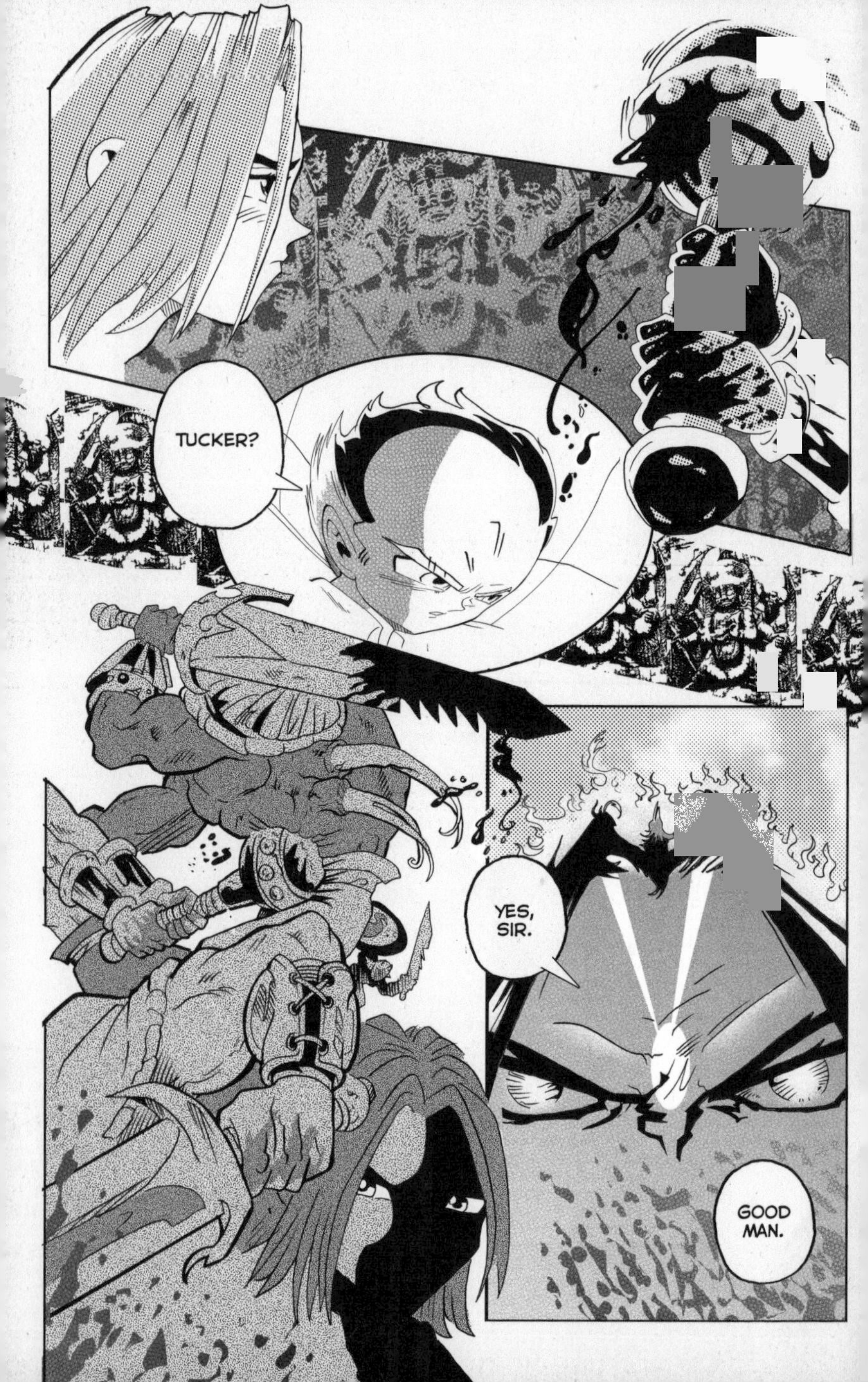
TUCKER?
YES, SIR.
GOOD MAN.

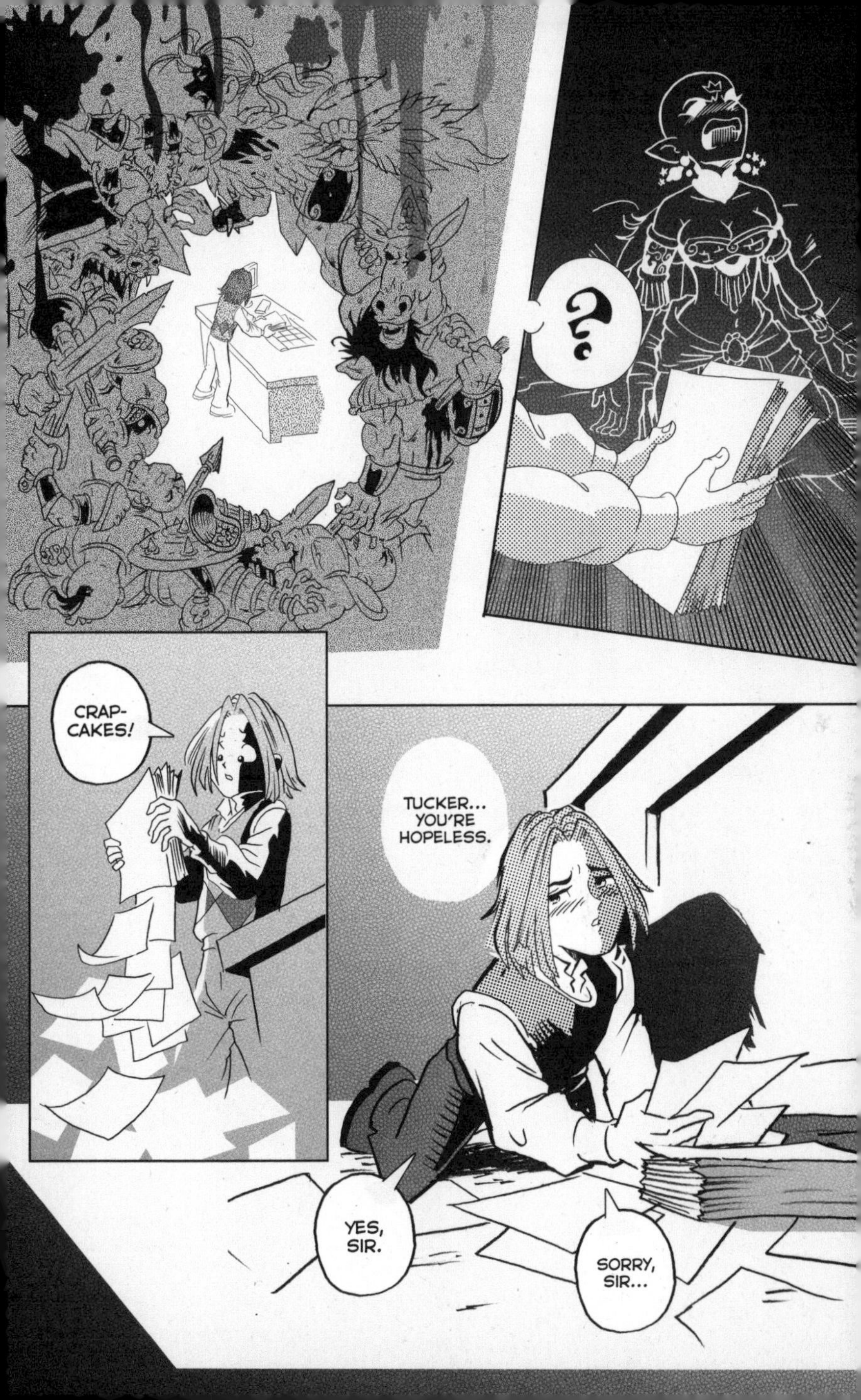
?
CRAP-CAKES!
TUCKER... YOU'RE HOPELESS.
YES, SIR.
SORRY, SIR...

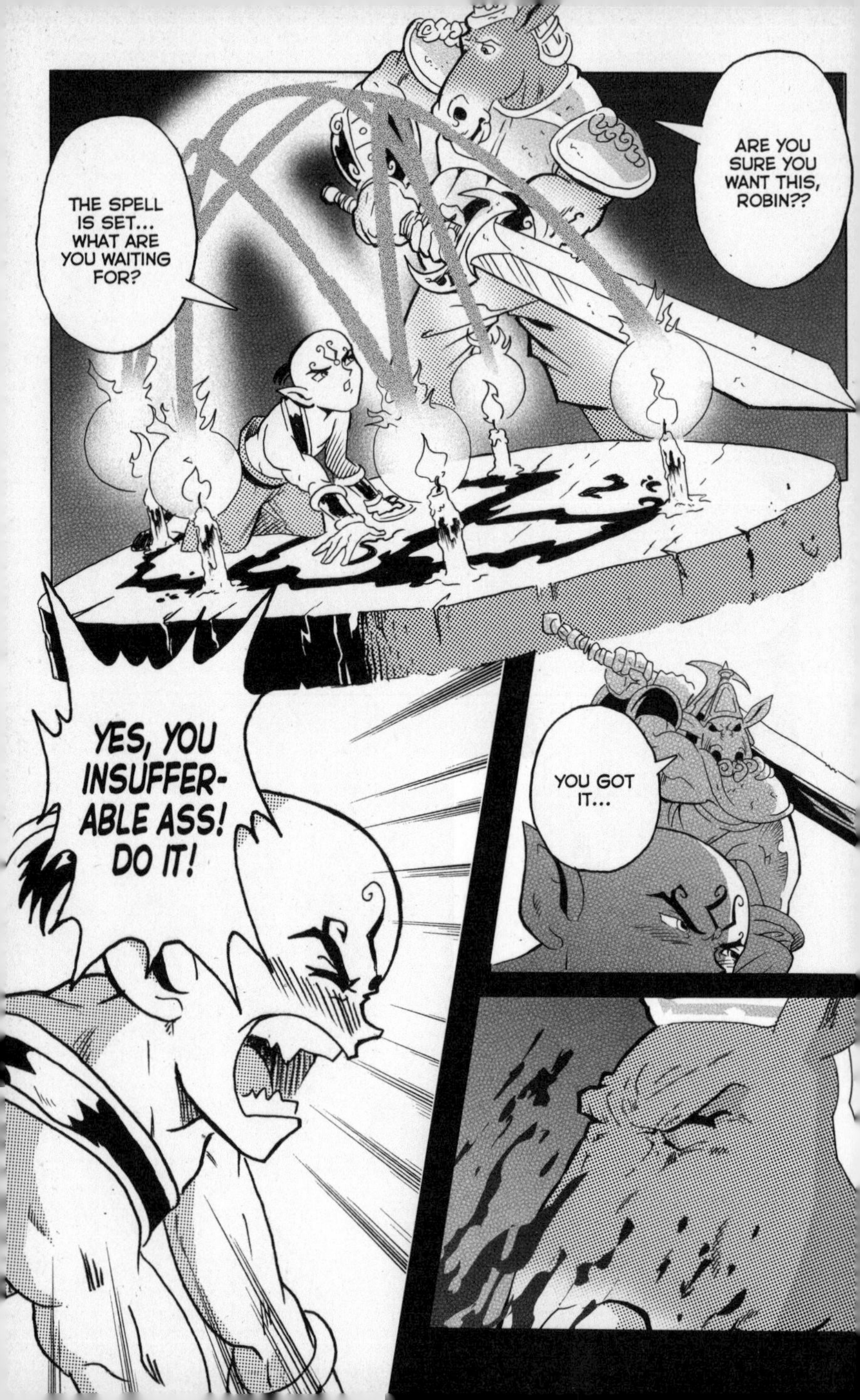
THE SPELL IS SET... WHAT ARE YOU WAITING FOR?
ARE YOU SURE YOU WANT THIS, ROBIN??
YES, YOU INSUFFER-ABLE ASS! DO IT!
YOU GOT IT...

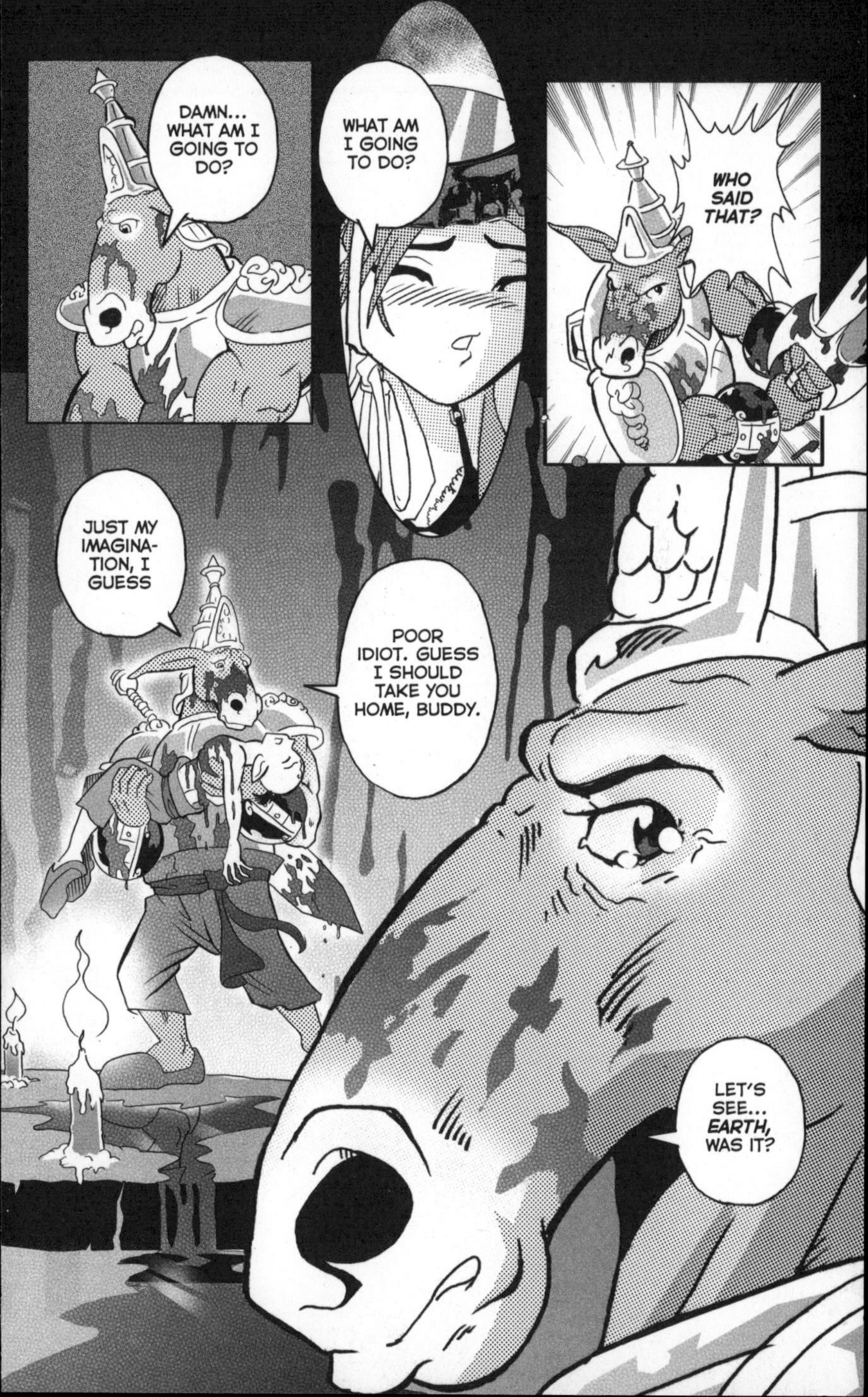

DAMN... WHAT AM I GOING TO DO?
WHAT AM I GOING TO DO?
WHO SAID THAT?
JUST MY IMAGINA-TION, I GUESS
POOR IDIOT. GUESS I SHOULD TAKE YOU HOME, BUDDY.
LET'S SEE... *EARTH*, WAS IT?

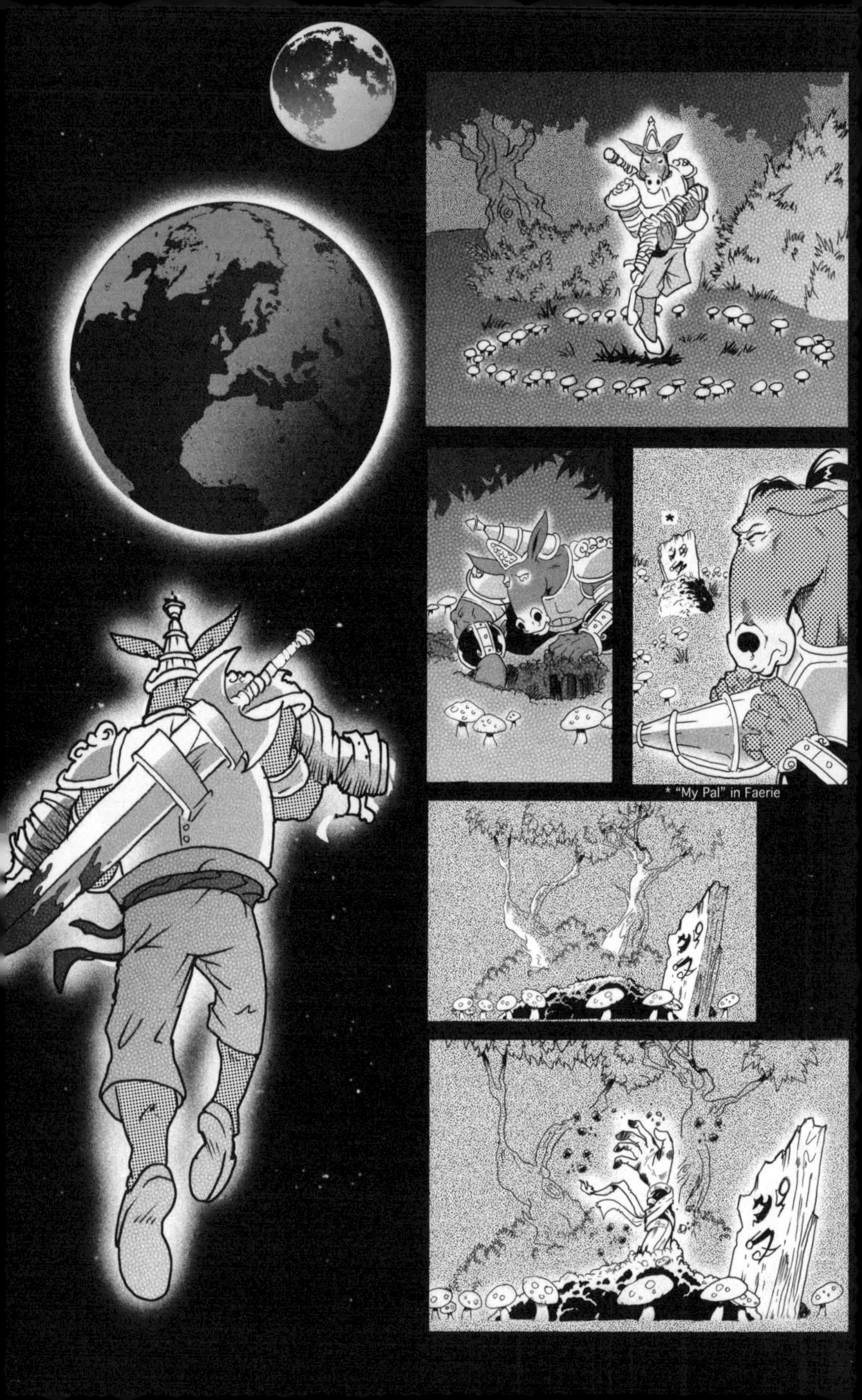
*
* “My Pal” in Faerie

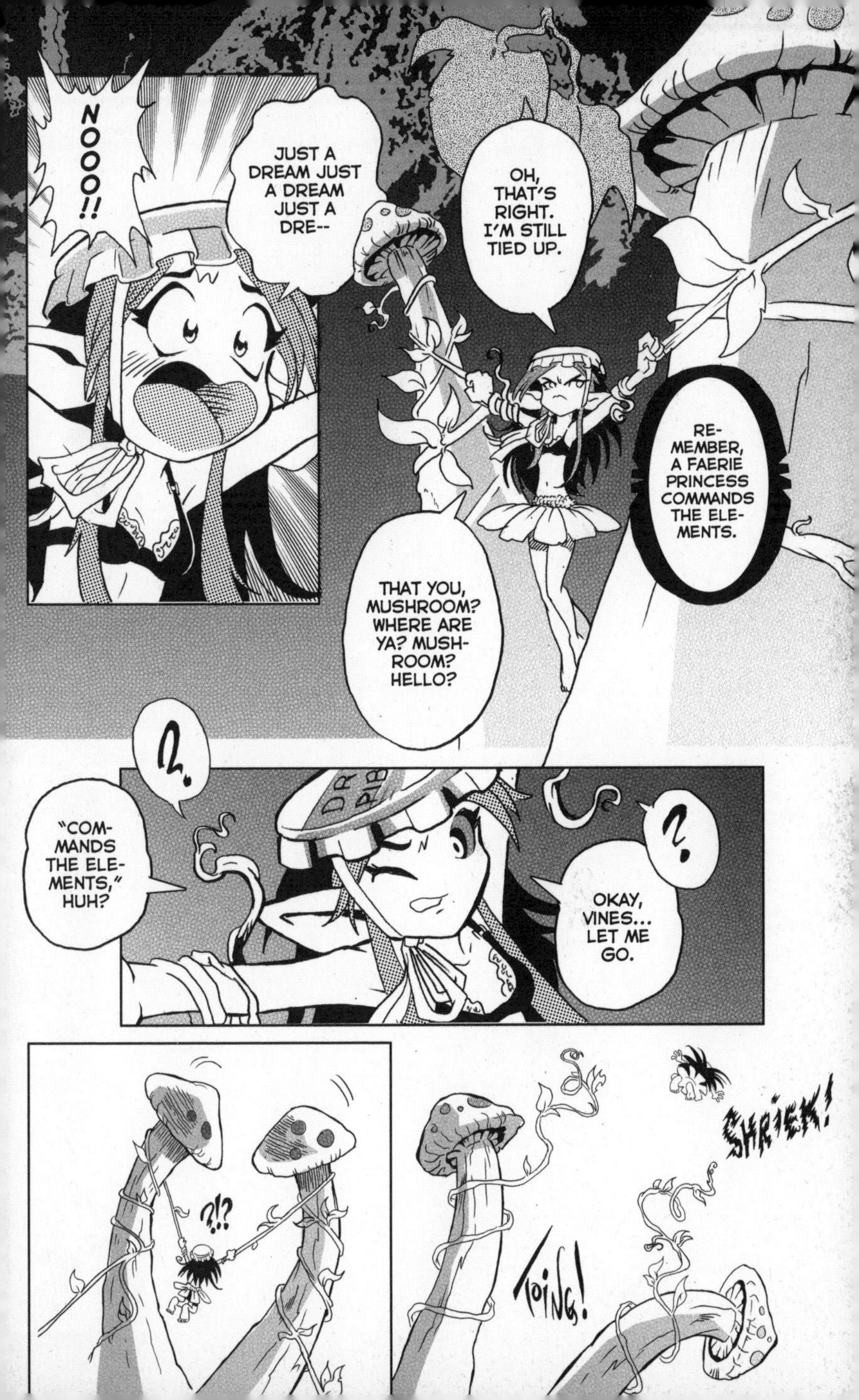
NOOOO!!
JUST A DREAM JUST A DREAM JUST A DRE--
OH, THAT'S RIGHT. I'M STILL TIED UP.
RE-MEMBER, A FAERIE PRINCESS COMMANDS THE ELE-MENTS.
THAT YOU, MUSHROOM? WHERE ARE YA? MUSH-ROOM? HELLO?
?
"COM-MANDS THE ELE-MENTS," HUH?
?
OKAY, VINES... LET ME GO.
?!?
TOING!
SHRIEK!

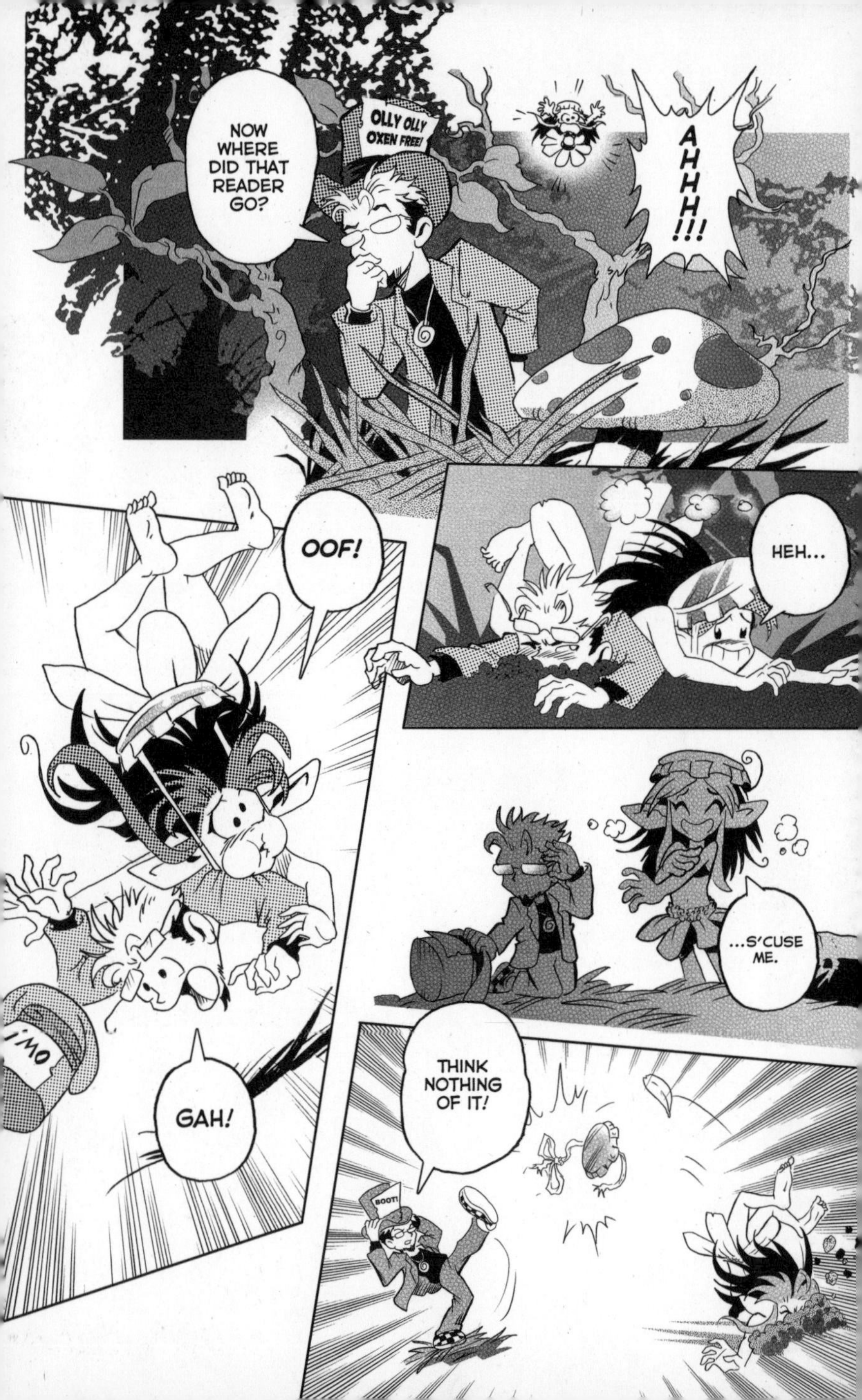
NOW WHERE DID THAT READER GO?
OLLY OLLY OXEN FREE!
AHHH!!!
OOF!
OW!
GAH!
HEH...
...S'CUSE ME.
THINK NOTHING OF IT!
BOOT!

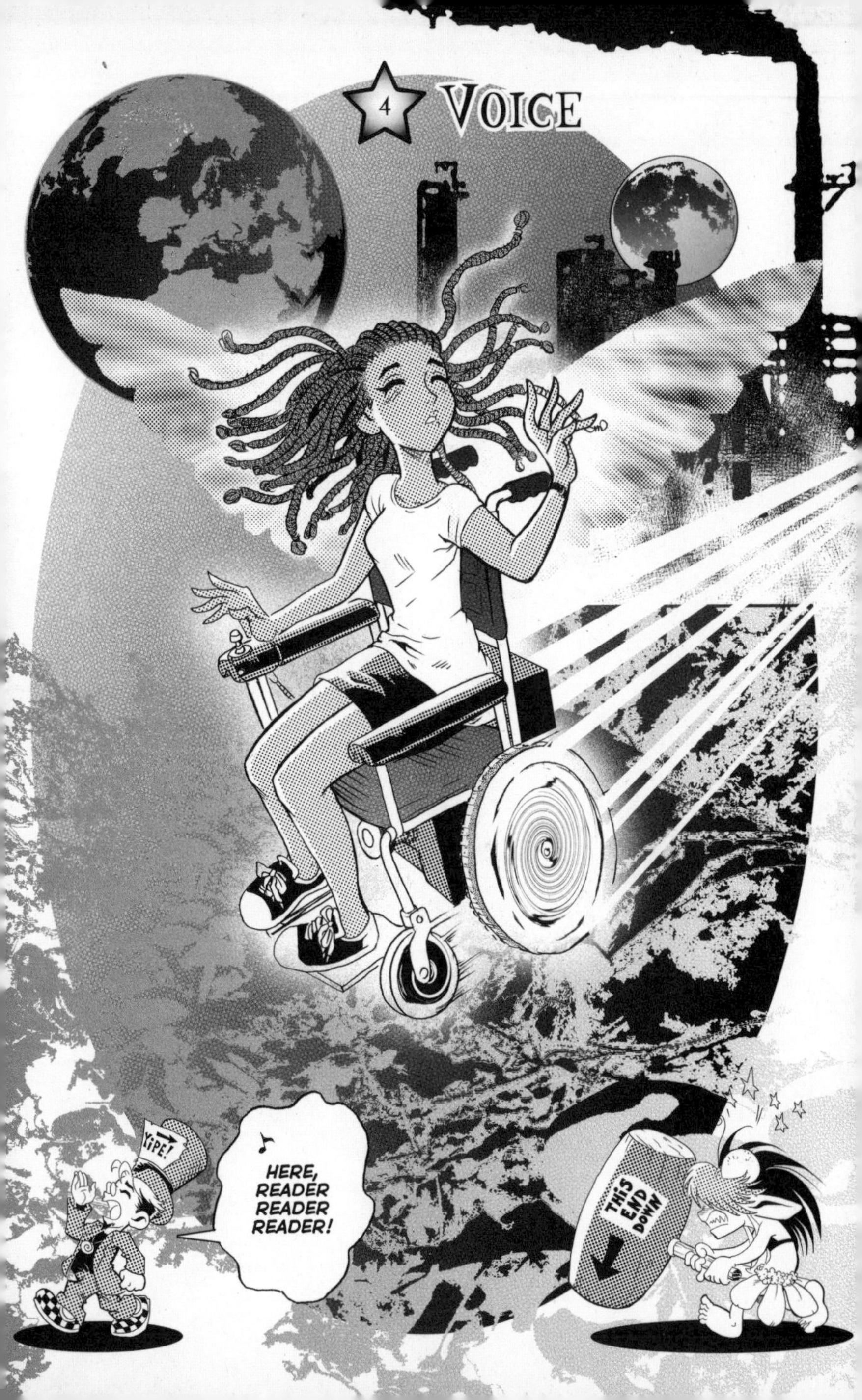
4 VOICE
YIPE!
HERE, READER READER READER!
THIS END DOWN

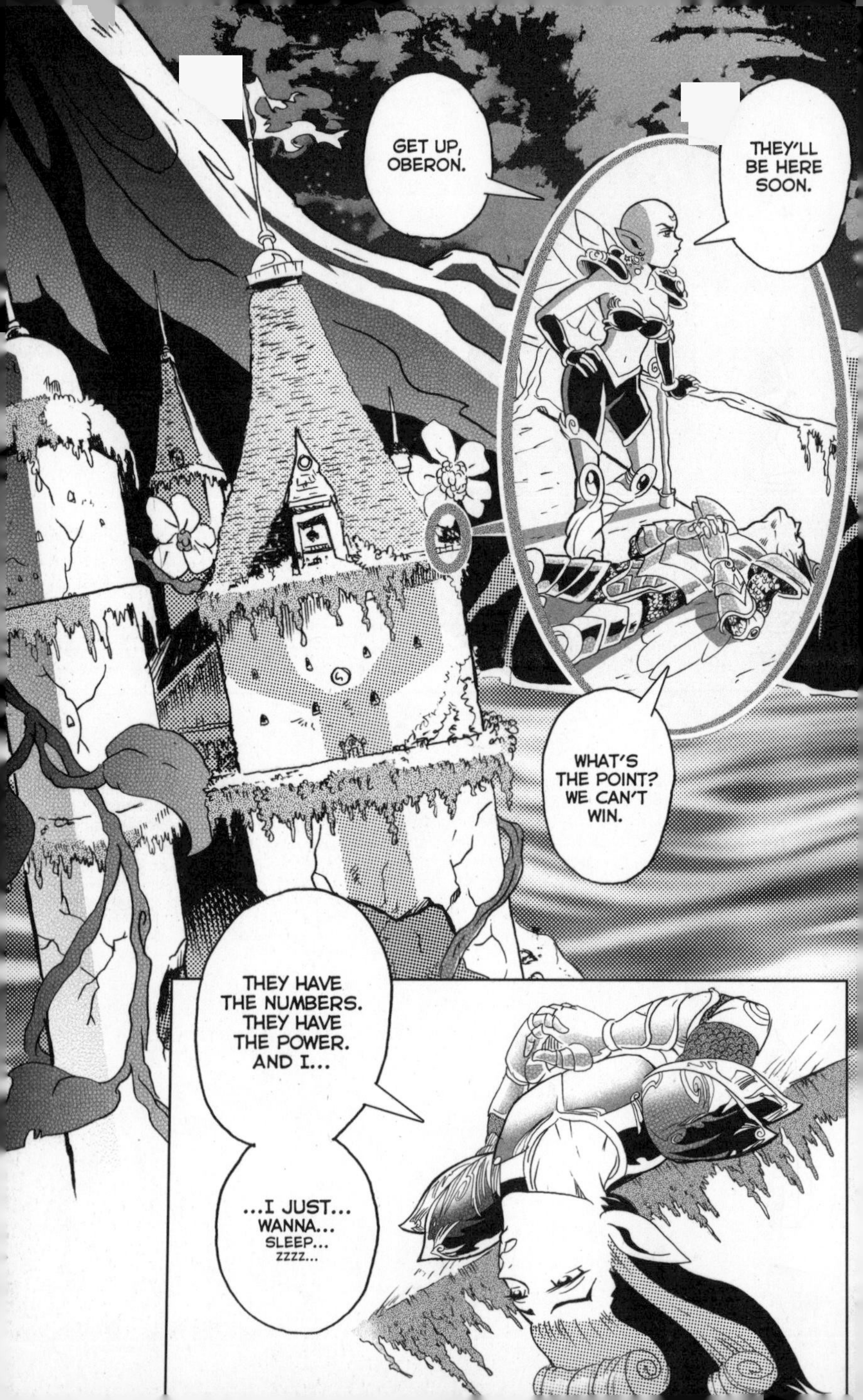
GET UP, OBERON.
THEY'LL BE HERE SOON.
WHAT'S THE POINT? WE CAN'T WIN.
THEY HAVE THE NUMBERS. THEY HAVE THE POWER. AND I...
...I JUST... WANNA... SLEEP... ZZZZ...

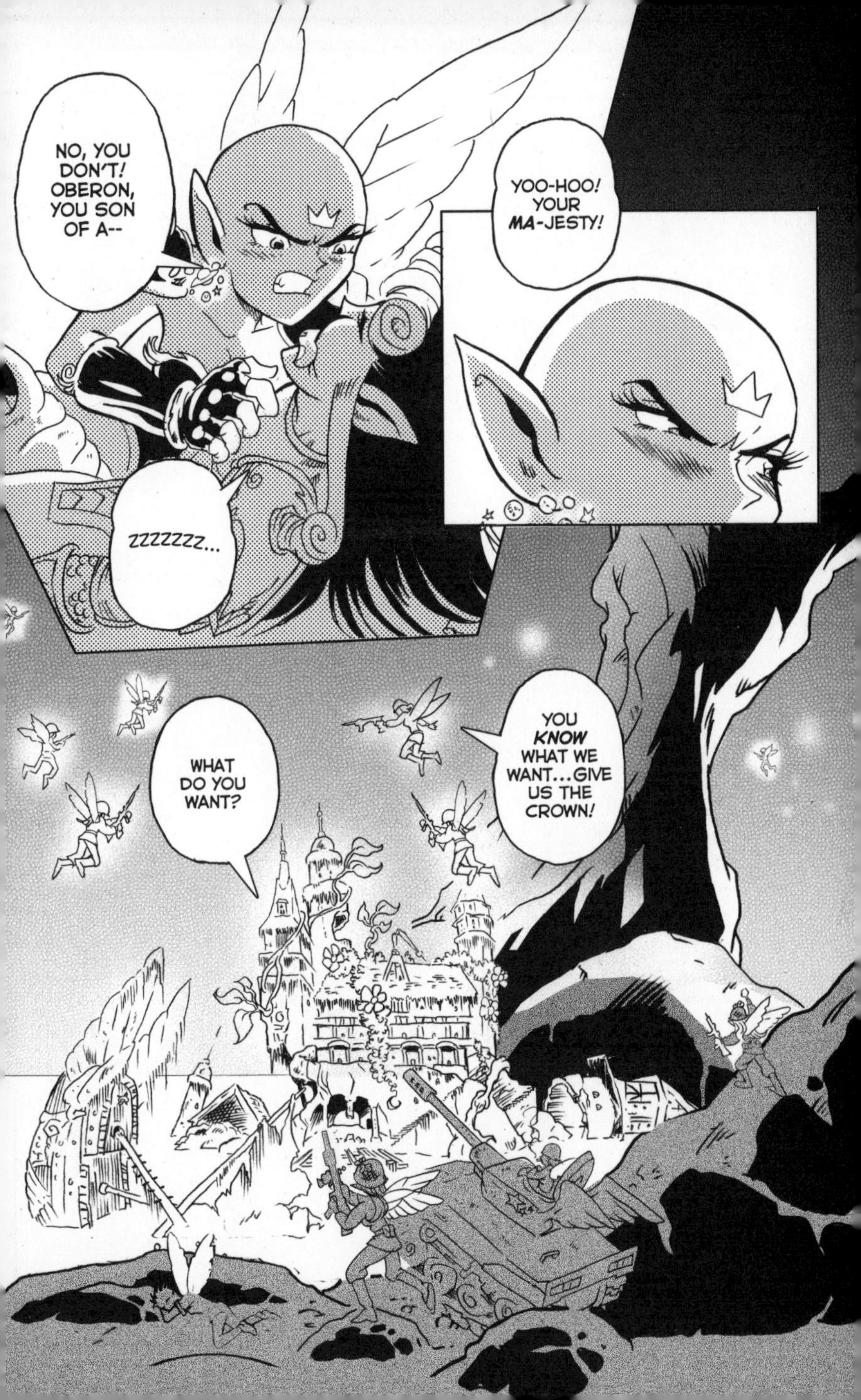
NO, YOU DON'T! OBERON, YOU SON OF A--
ZZZZZZZ...
YOO-HOO! YOUR *MA*-JESTY!
WHAT DO YOU WANT?
YOU *KNOW* WHAT WE WANT...GIVE US THE CROWN!

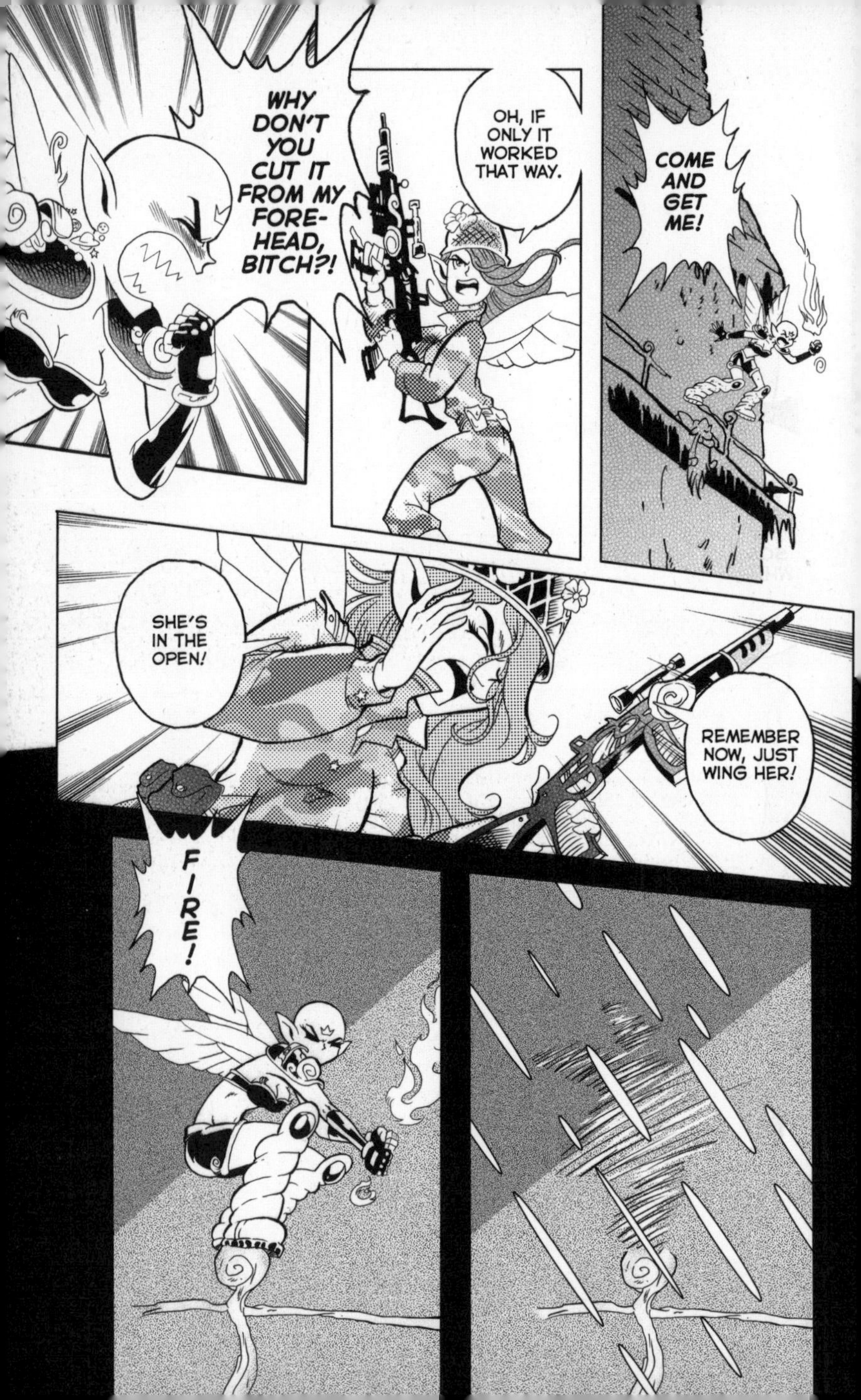
WHY DON'T YOU CUT IT FROM MY FORE-HEAD, BITCH?!
OH, IF ONLY IT WORKED THAT WAY.
COME AND GET ME!
SHE'S IN THE OPEN!
REMEMBER NOW, JUST WING HER!
FIRE!

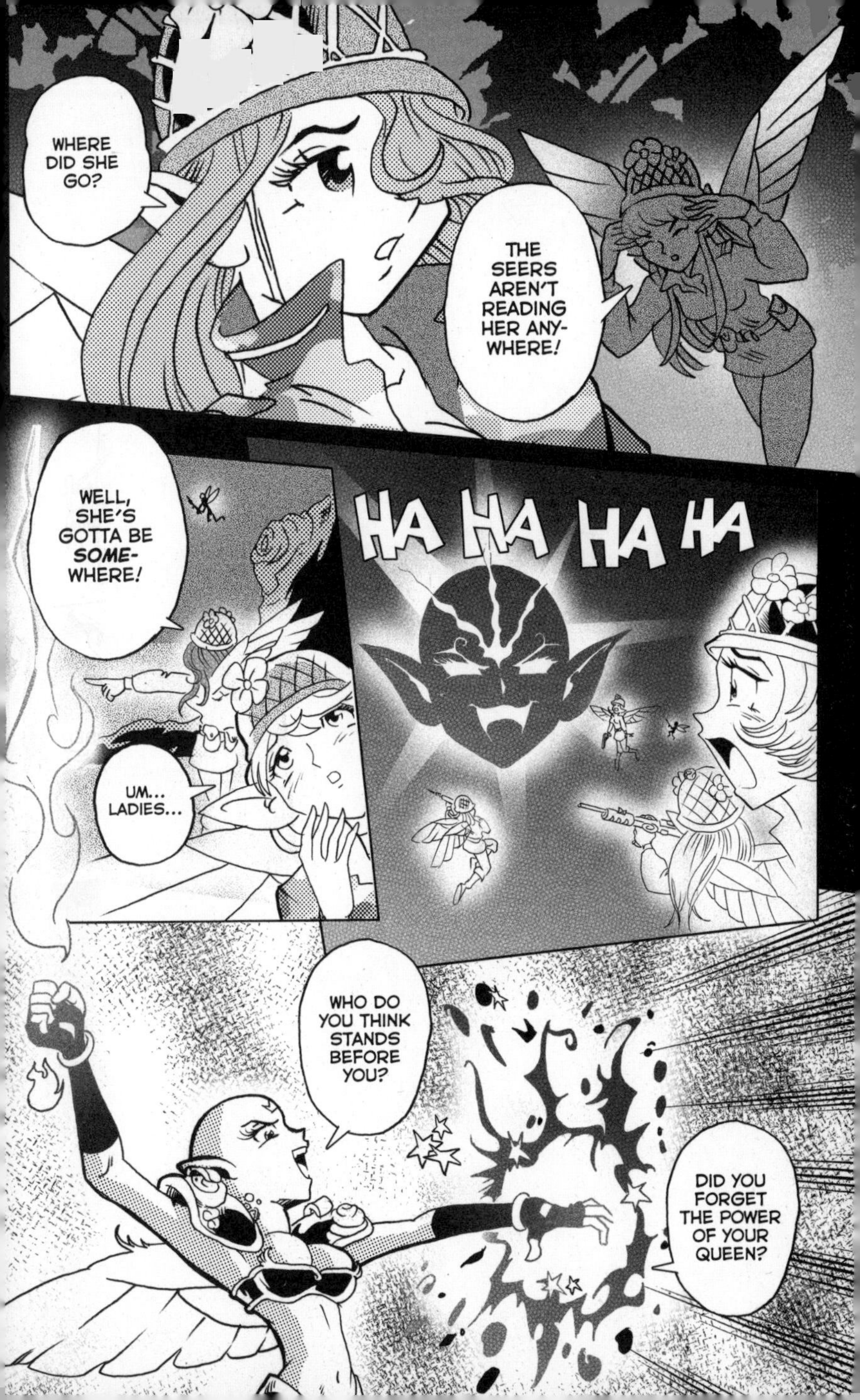
WHERE DID SHE GO?
THE SEERS AREN'T READING HER ANY-WHERE!
WELL, SHE'S GOTTA BE SOME-WHERE!
UM... LADIES...
HA HA HA HA
WHO DO YOU THINK STANDS BEFORE YOU?
DID YOU FORGET THE POWER OF YOUR QUEEN?

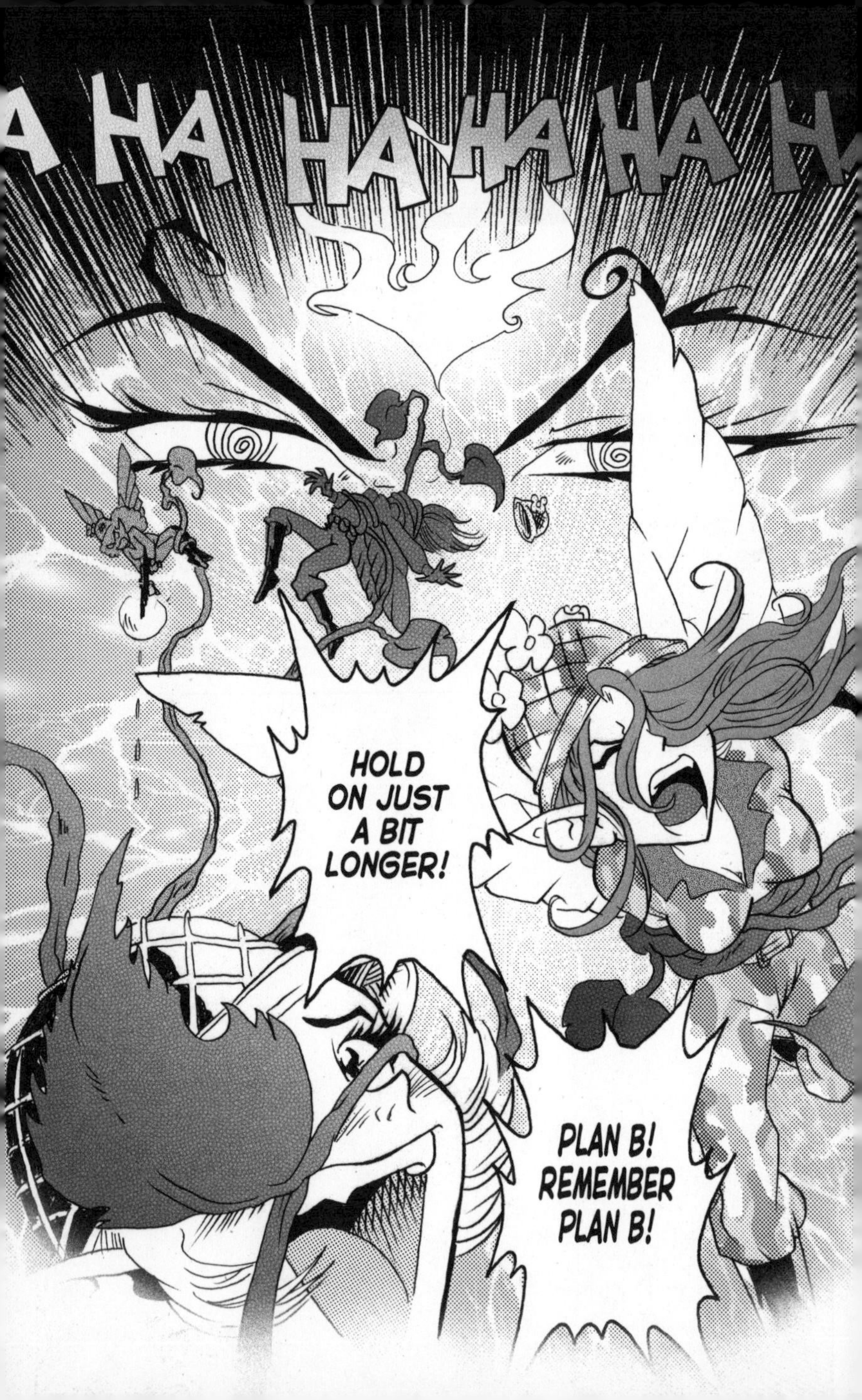
HA HA HA HA HA HA HA
HOLD ON JUST A BIT LONGER!
PLAN B! REMEMBER PLAN B!

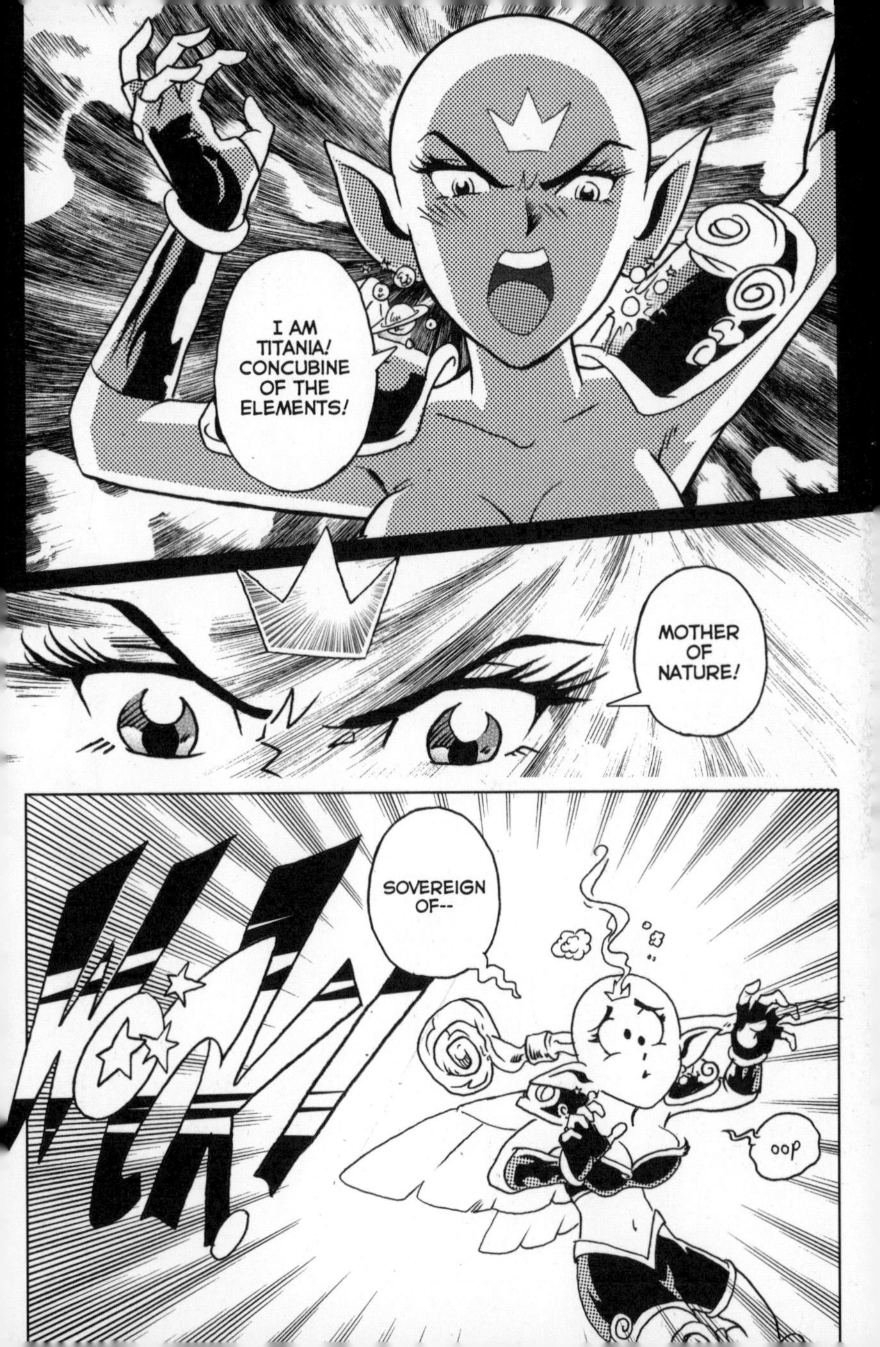
I AM TITANIA! CONCUBINE OF THE ELEMENTS!
MOTHER OF NATURE!
SOVEREIGN OF--
oop

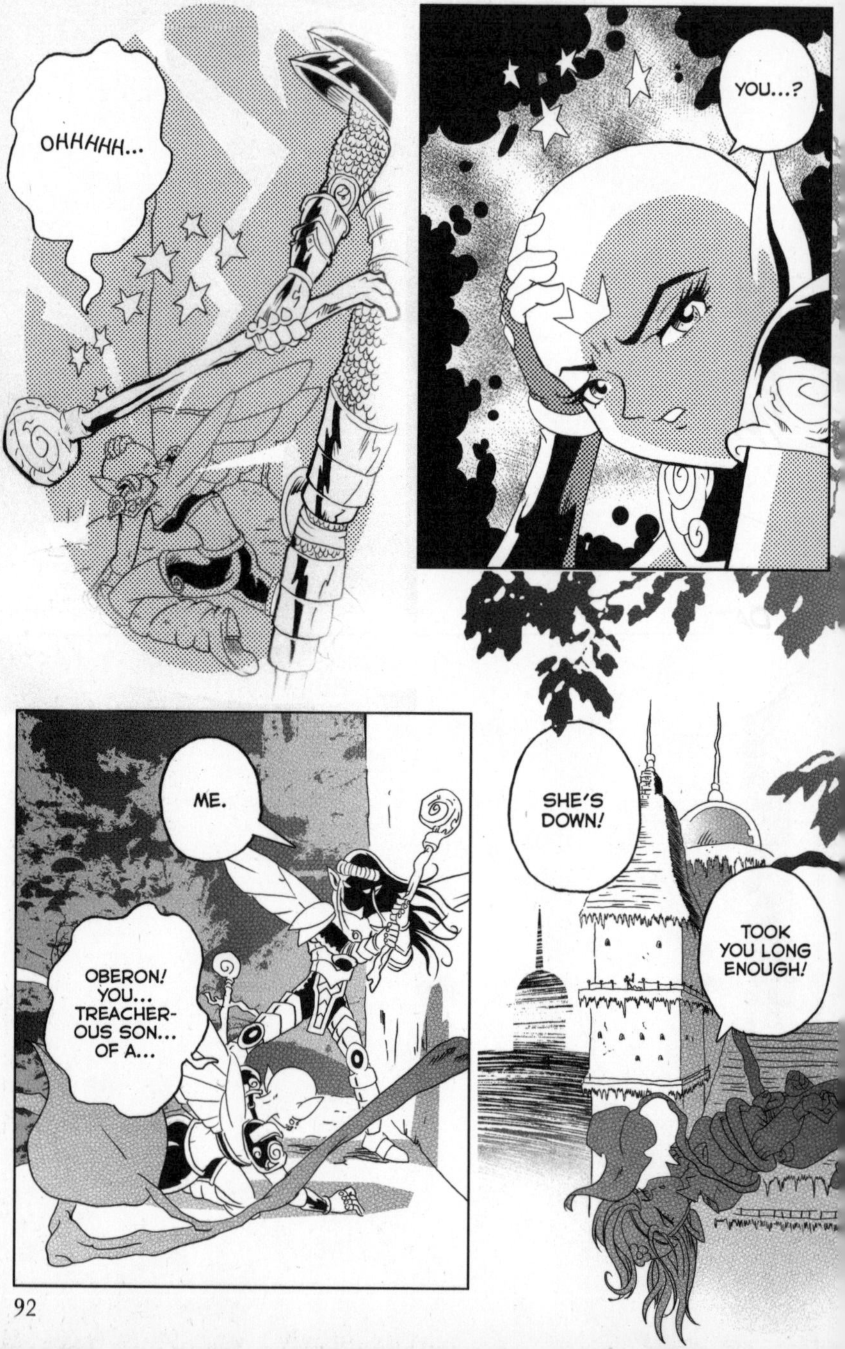
OHHHHH...
YOU...?
ME.
OBERON! YOU... TREACHER-OUS SON... OF A...
SHE'S DOWN!
TOOK YOU LONG ENOUGH!

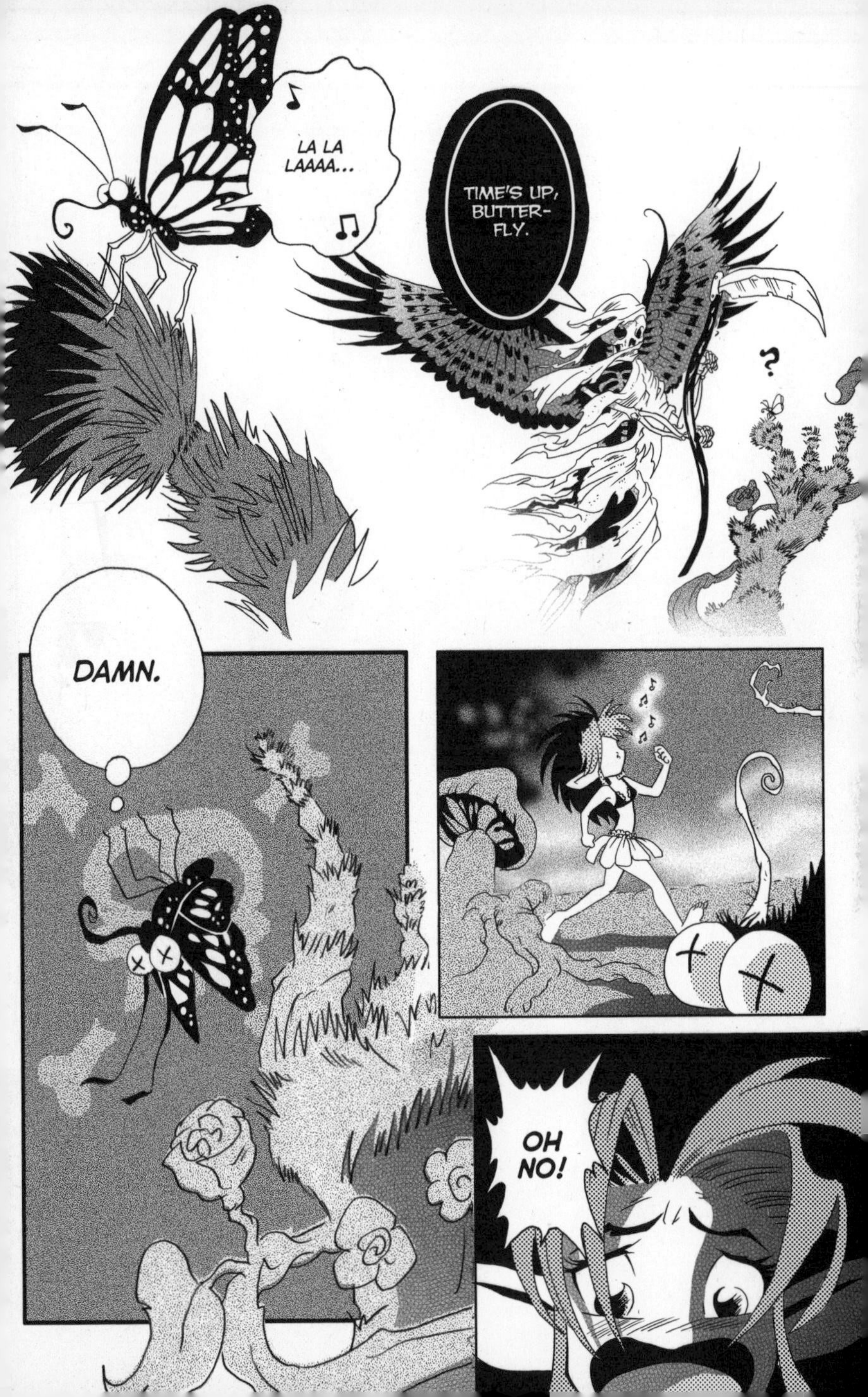
LA LA LAAAA...
TIME'S UP, BUTTER-FLY.
?
DAMN.
OH NO!

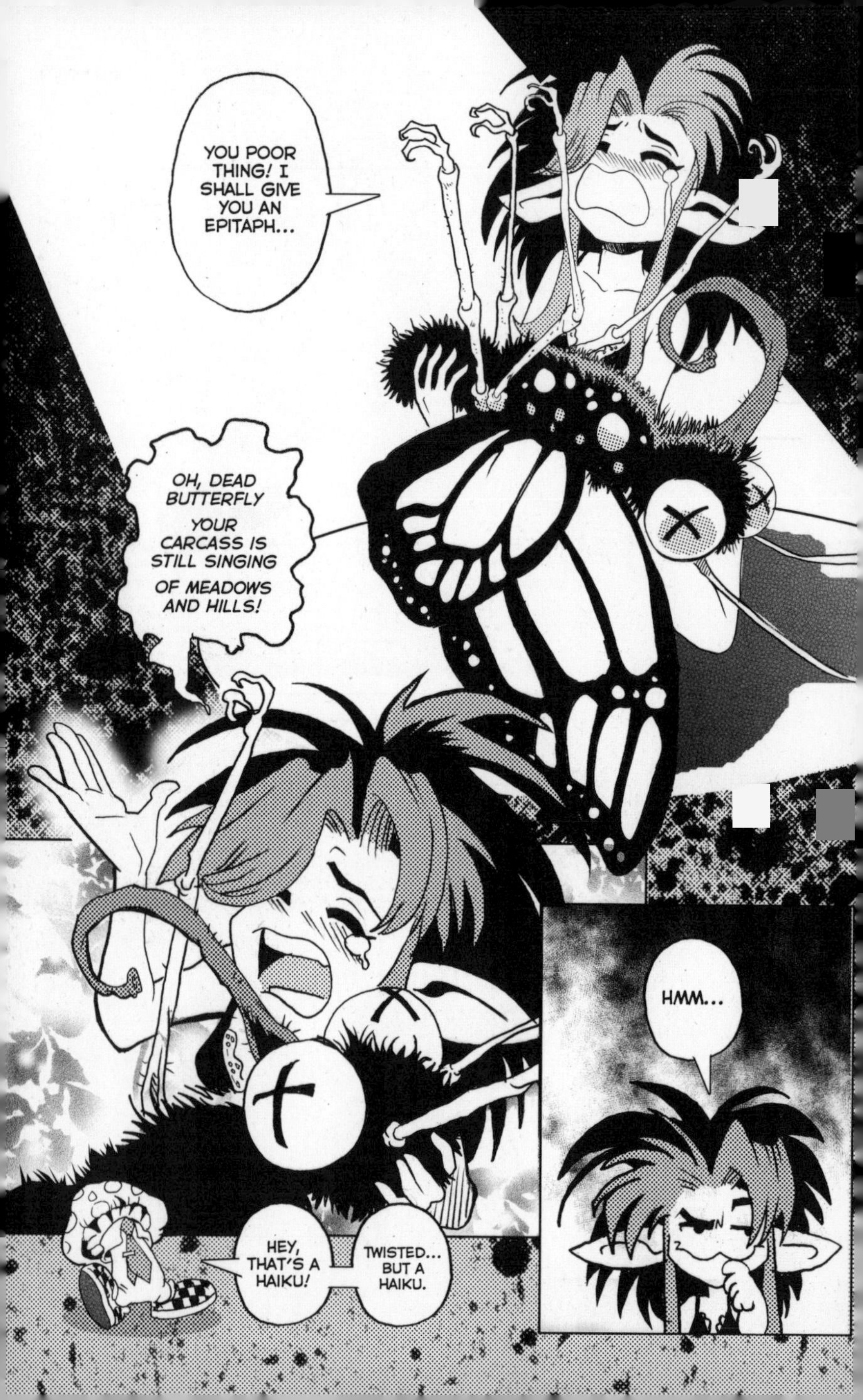
YOU POOR THING! I SHALL GIVE YOU AN EPITAPH...
OH, DEAD BUTTERFLY
YOUR CARCASS IS STILL SINGING
OF MEADOWS AND HILLS!
HEY, THAT'S A HAIKU!
TWISTED... BUT A HAIKU.
HMM...

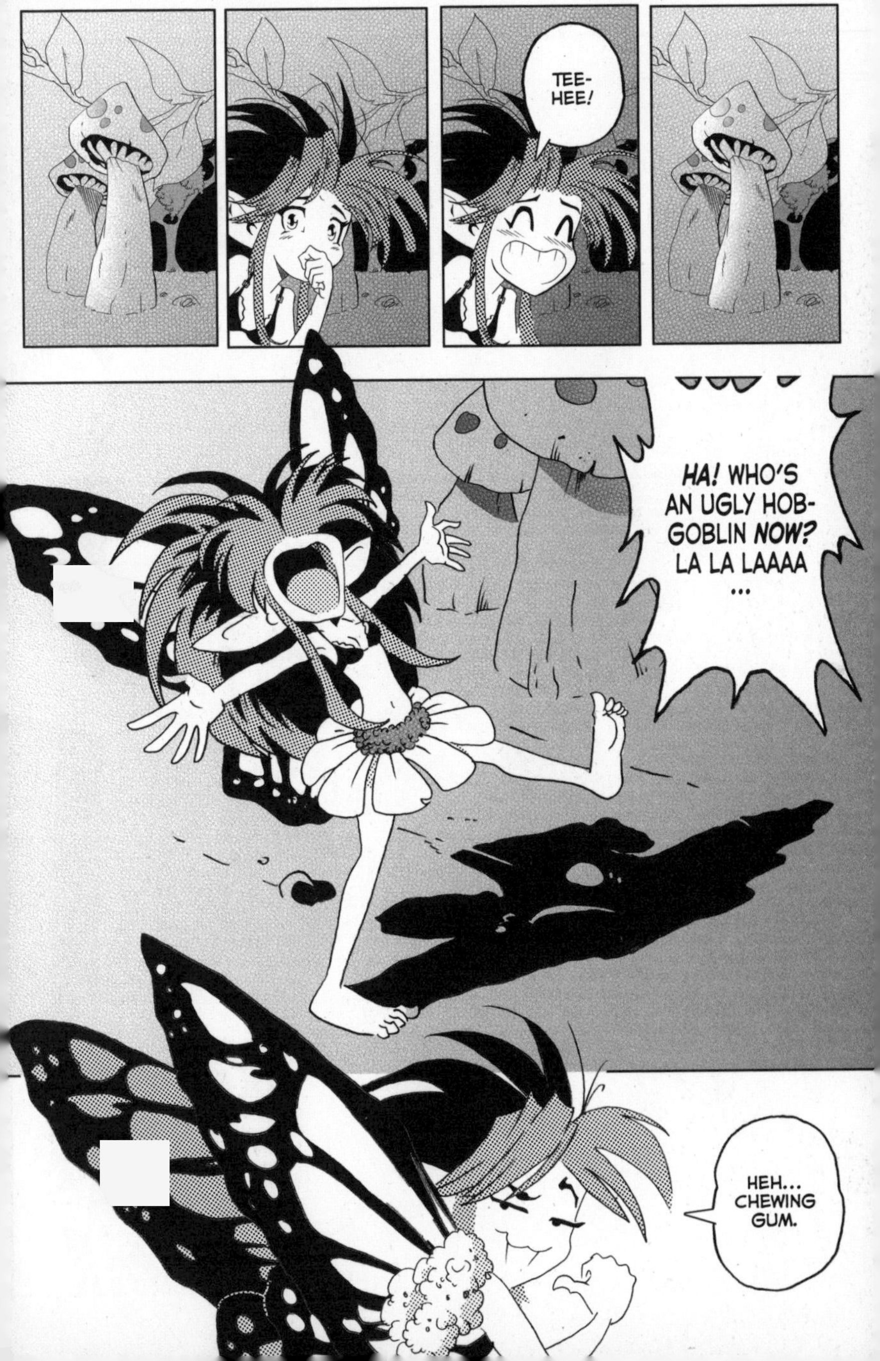
TEE-HEE!
HA! WHO'S AN UGLY HOB-GOBLIN NOW? LA LA LAAAA ...
HEH... CHEWING GUM.

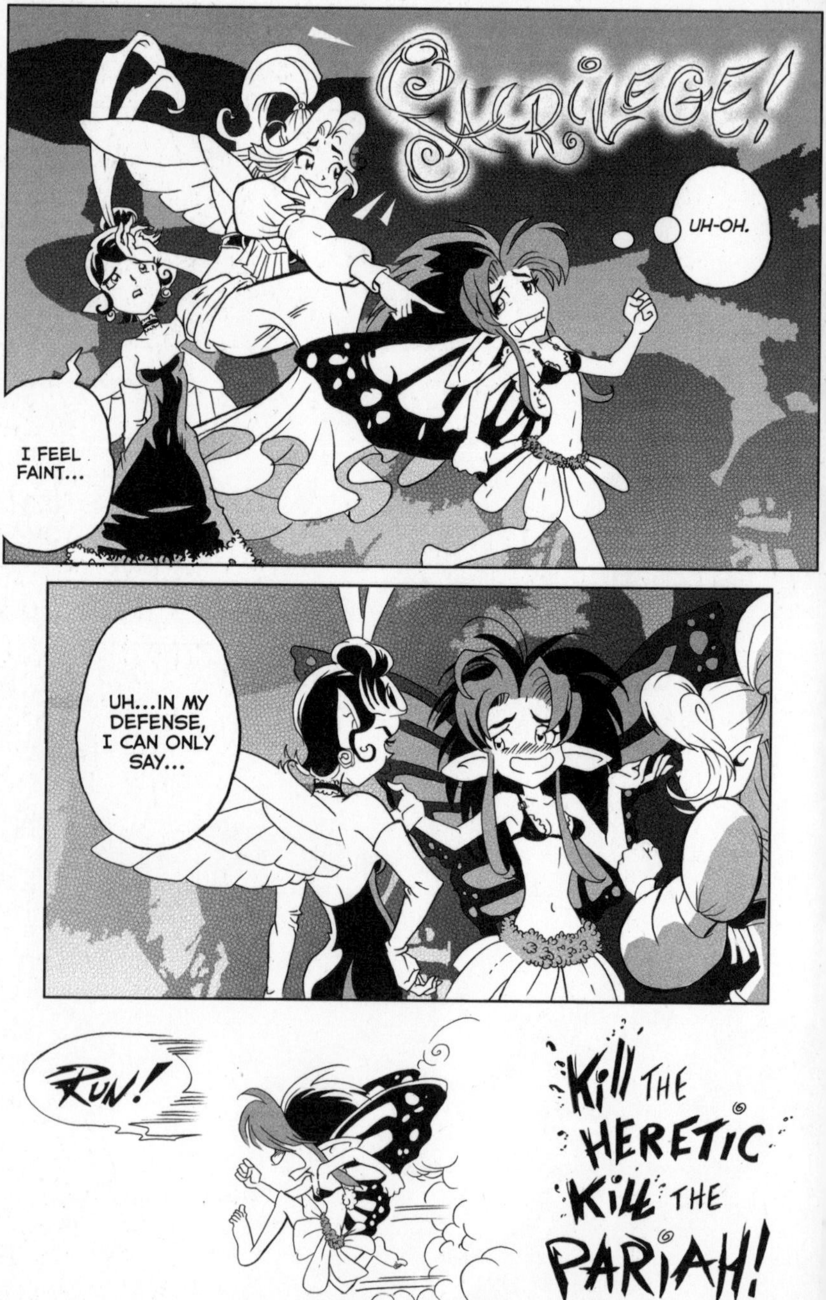
SACRILEGE!
UH-OH.
I FEEL FAINT...
UH...IN MY DEFENSE, I CAN ONLY SAY...
RUN!
KILL THE HERETIC KILL THE PARIAH!

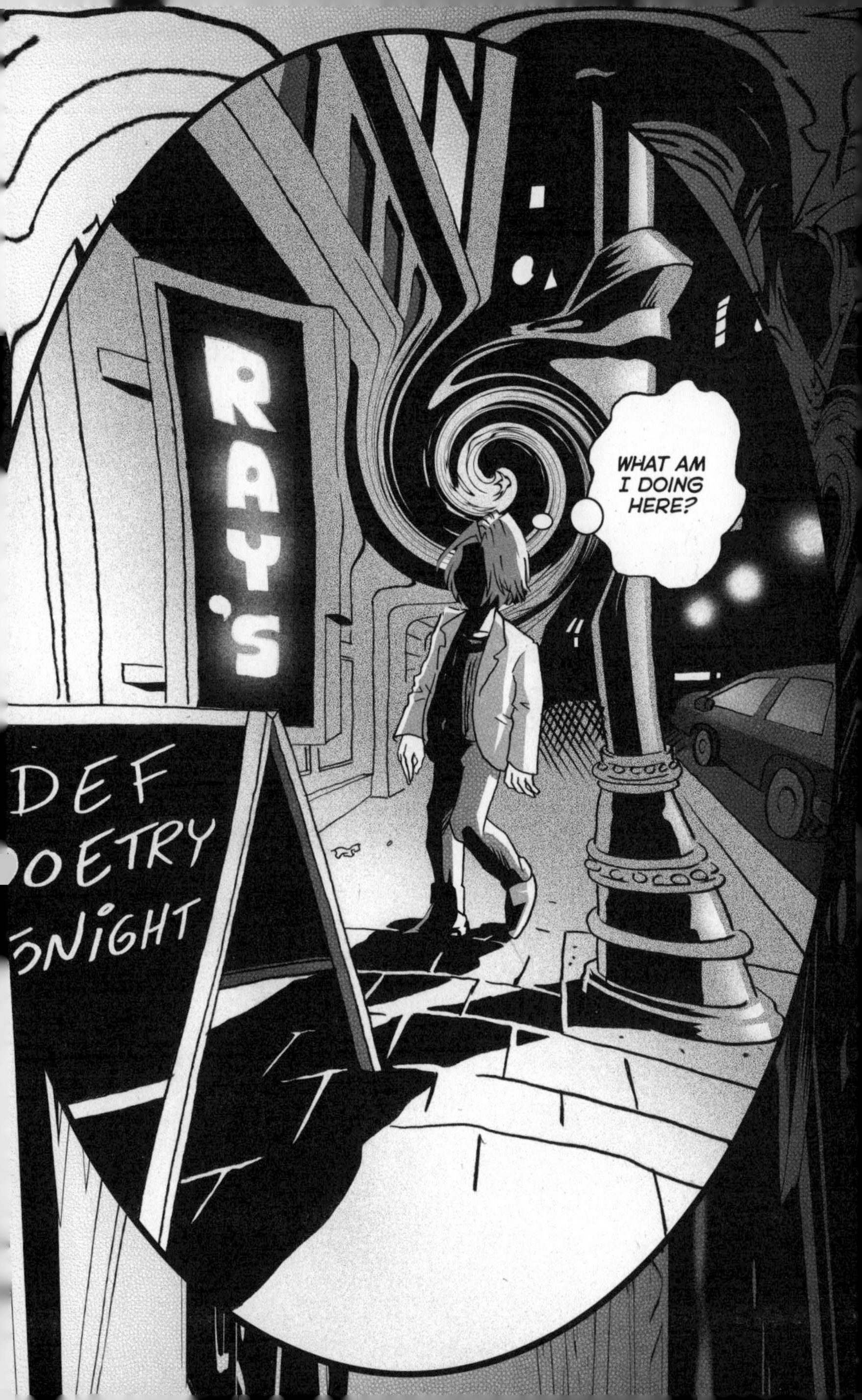
RAY'S
DEF
POETRY
TONIGHT
WHAT AM I DOING HERE?

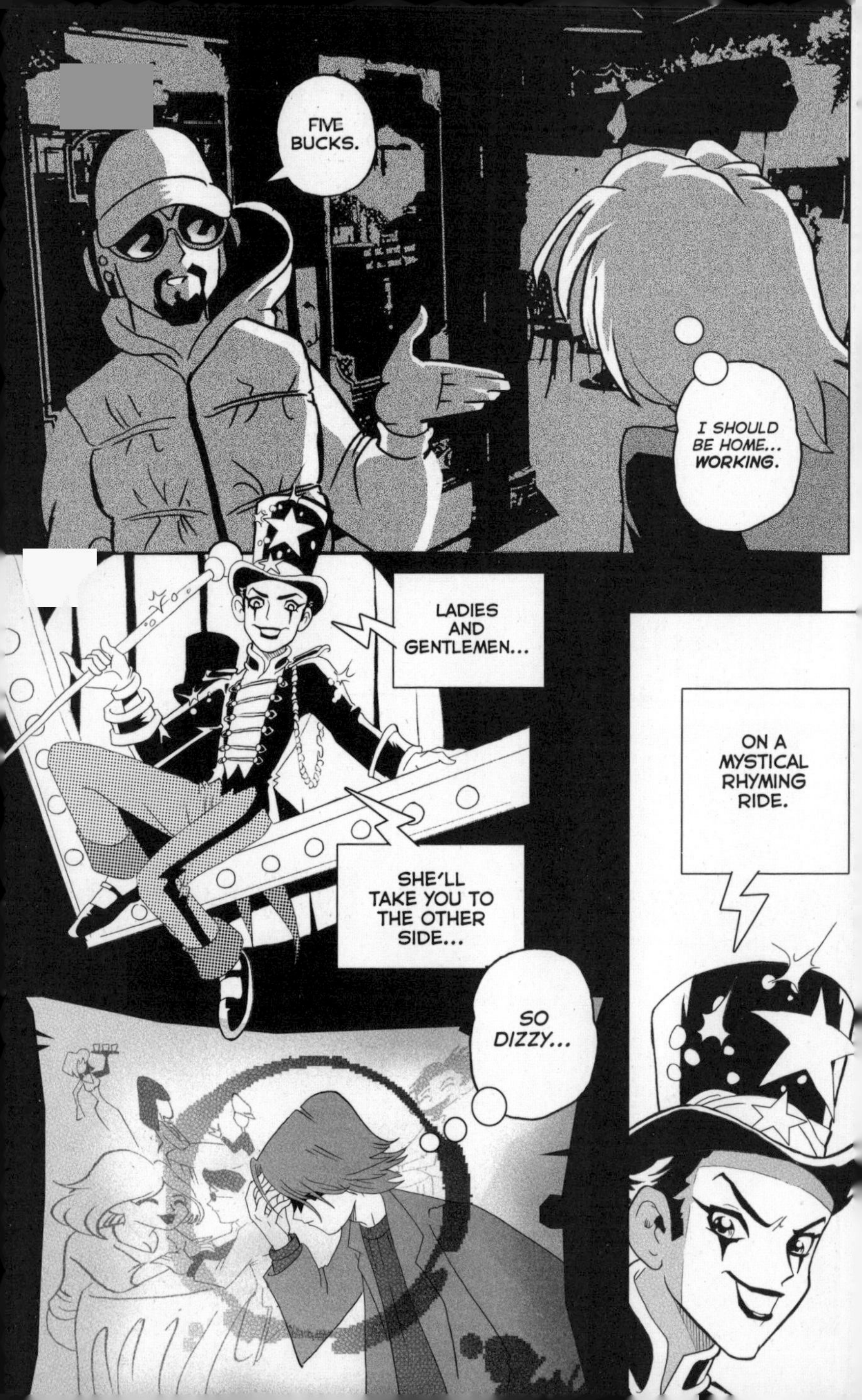
FIVE BUCKS.
I SHOULD BE HOME... WORKING.
LADIES AND GENTLEMEN...
SHE'LL TAKE YOU TO THE OTHER SIDE...
SO DIZZY...
ON A MYSTICAL RHYMING RIDE.

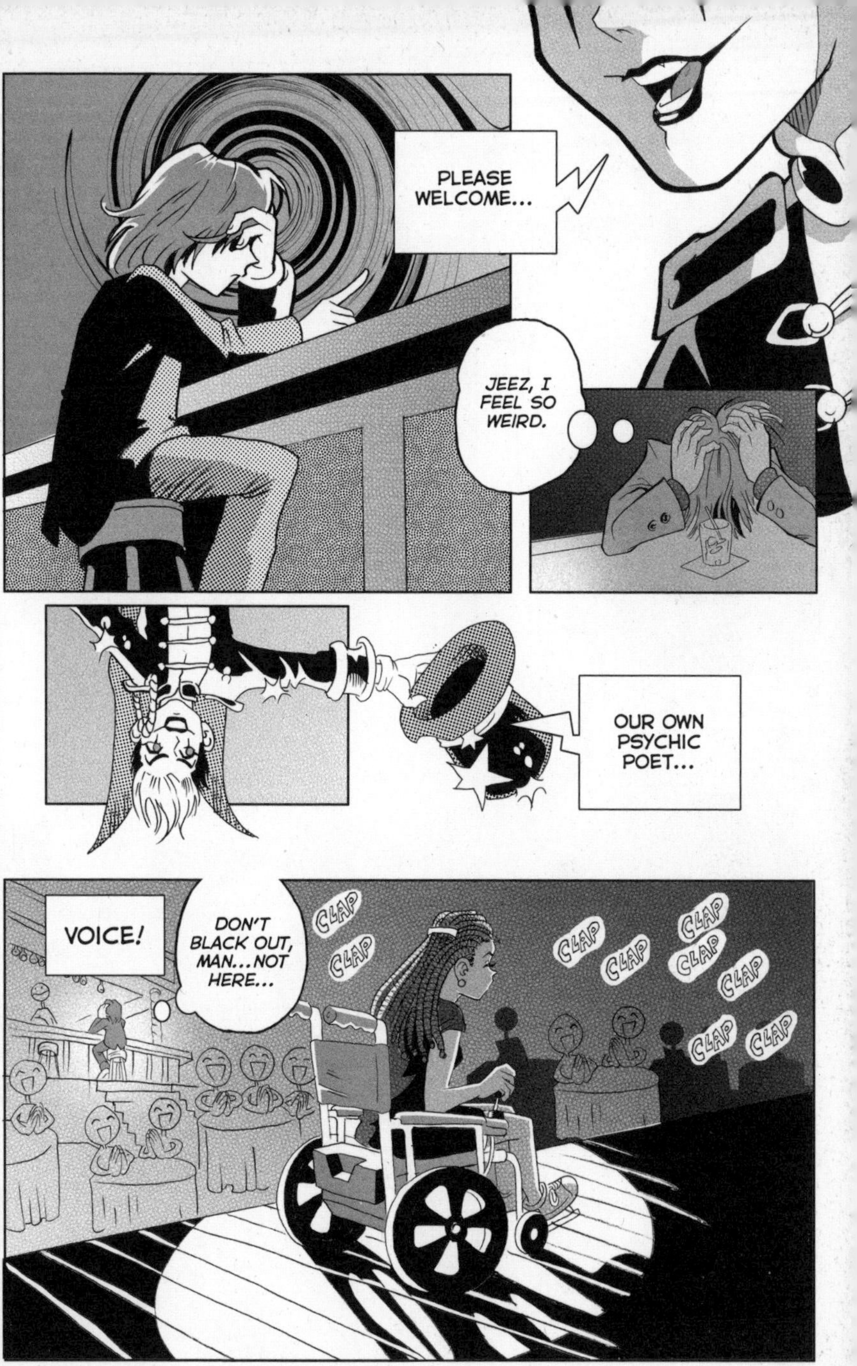
PLEASE WELCOME...
JEEZ, I FEEL SO WEIRD.
OUR OWN PSYCHIC POET...
VOICE!
DON'T BLACK OUT, MAN...NOT HERE...
CLAP
CLAP
CLAP
CLAP
CLAP
CLAP
CLAP
CLAP
CLAP
CLAP

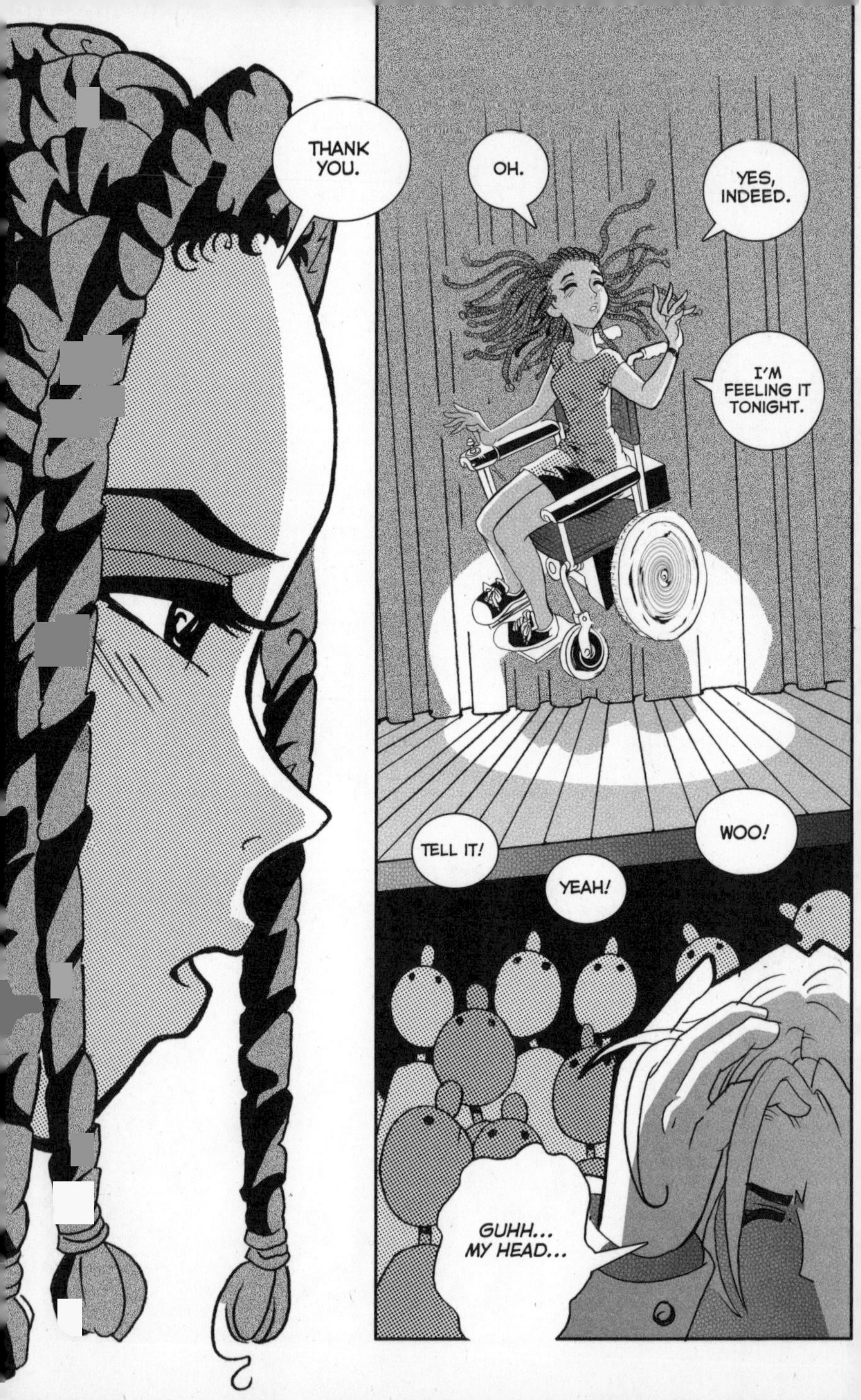
THANK YOU.
OH.
YES, INDEED.
I'M FEELING IT TONIGHT.
TELL IT!
WOO!
YEAH!
GUHH... MY HEAD...

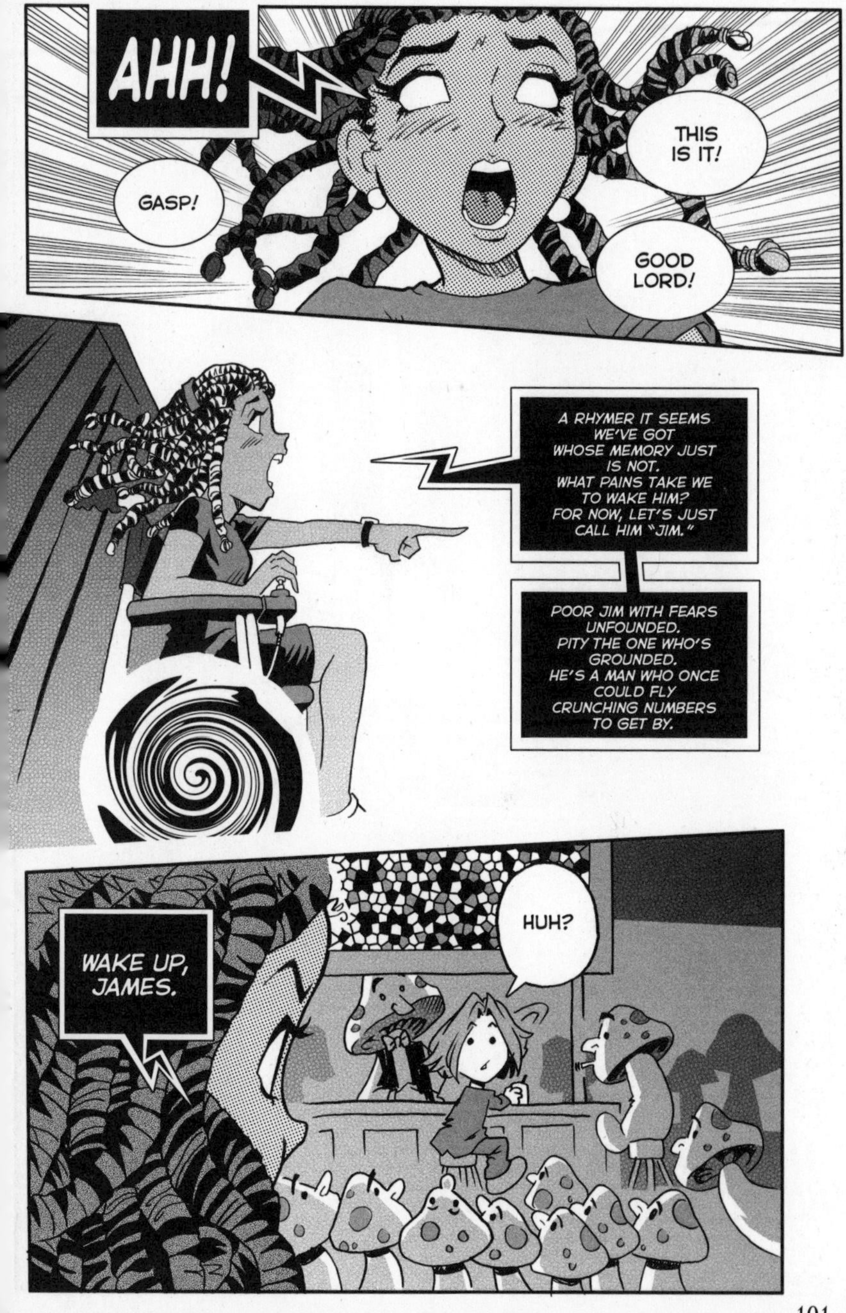

AHH!
GASP!
THIS IS IT!
GOOD LORD!
A RHYMER IT SEEMS WE'VE GOT WHOSE MEMORY JUST IS NOT. WHAT PAINS TAKE WE TO WAKE HIM? FOR NOW, LET'S JUST CALL HIM "JIM."
POOR JIM WITH FEARS UNFOUNDED. PITY THE ONE WHO'S GROUNDED. HE'S A MAN WHO ONCE COULD FLY CRUNCHING NUMBERS TO GET BY.
WAKE UP, JAMES.
HUH?

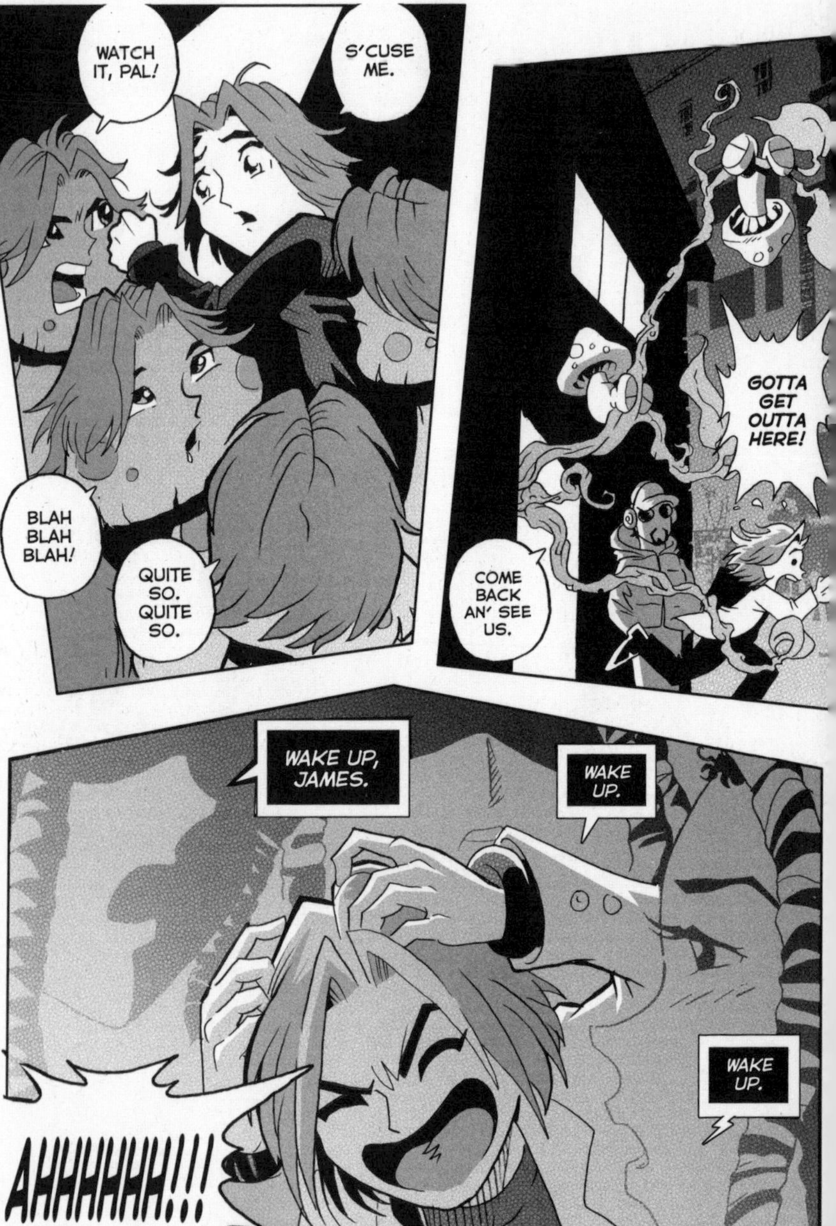
WATCH IT, PAL!
S'CUSE ME.
BLAH BLAH BLAH!
QUITE SO. QUITE SO.
GOTTA GET OUTTA HERE!
COME BACK AN' SEE US.
WAKE UP, JAMES.
WAKE UP.
AHHHHHH!!!
WAKE UP.

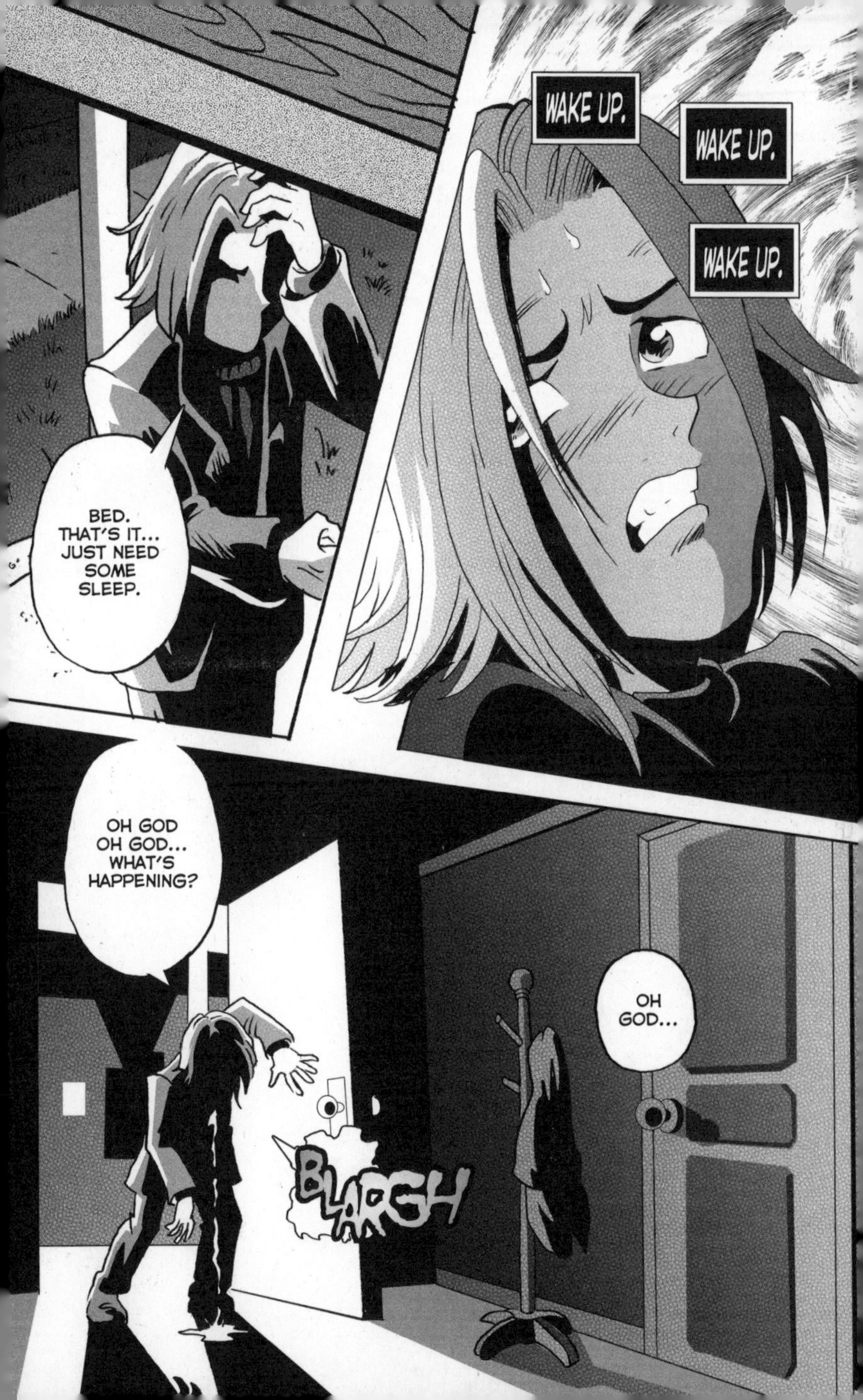
BED. THAT'S IT... JUST NEED SOME SLEEP.
WAKE UP.
WAKE UP.
WAKE UP.
OH GOD OH GOD... WHAT'S HAPPENING?
BLARGH
OH GOD...

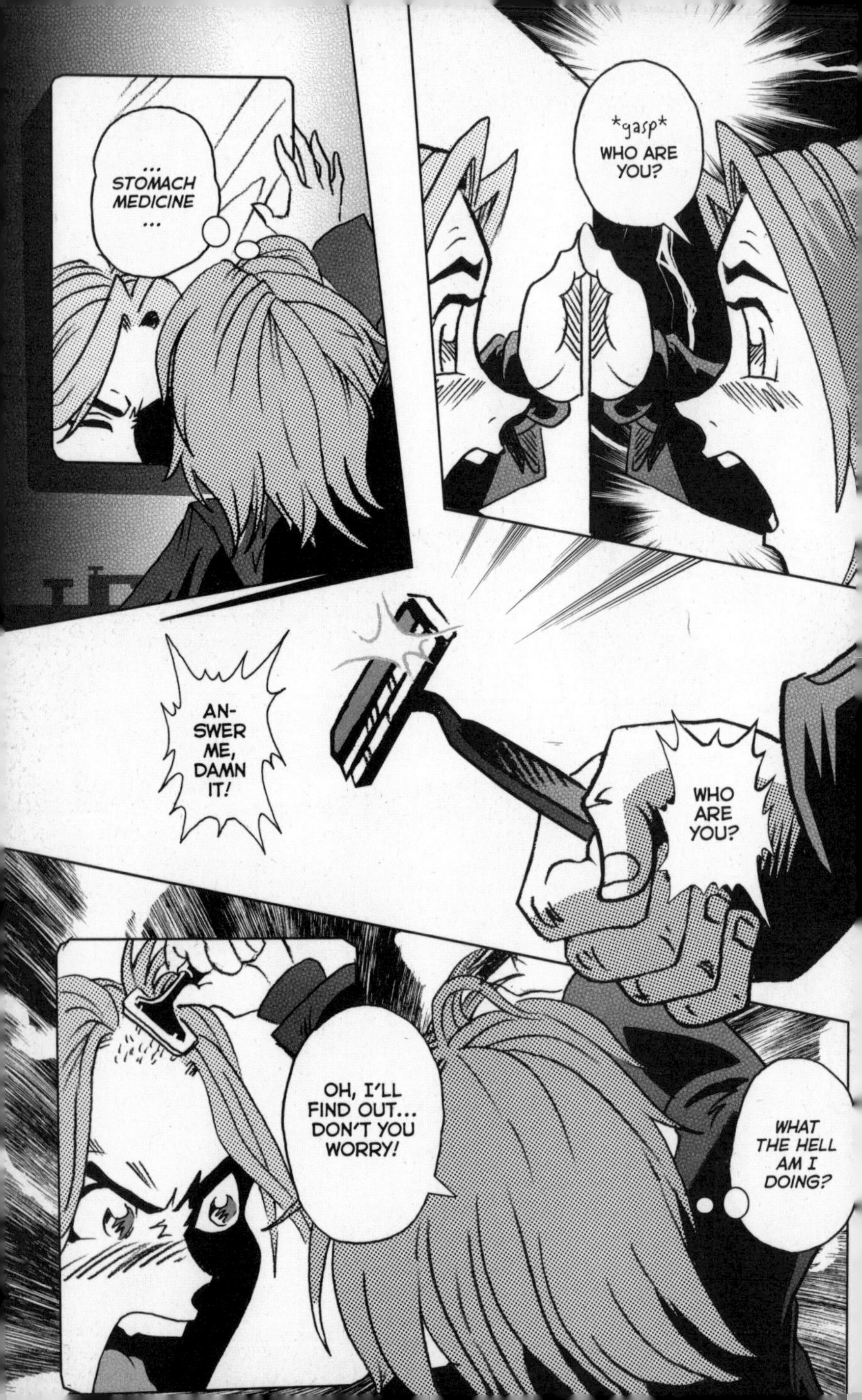

... STOMACH MEDICINE ...
gasp WHO ARE YOU?
AN-SWER ME, DAMN IT!
WHO ARE YOU?
OH, I'LL FIND OUT... DON'T YOU WORRY!
WHAT THE HELL AM I DOING?

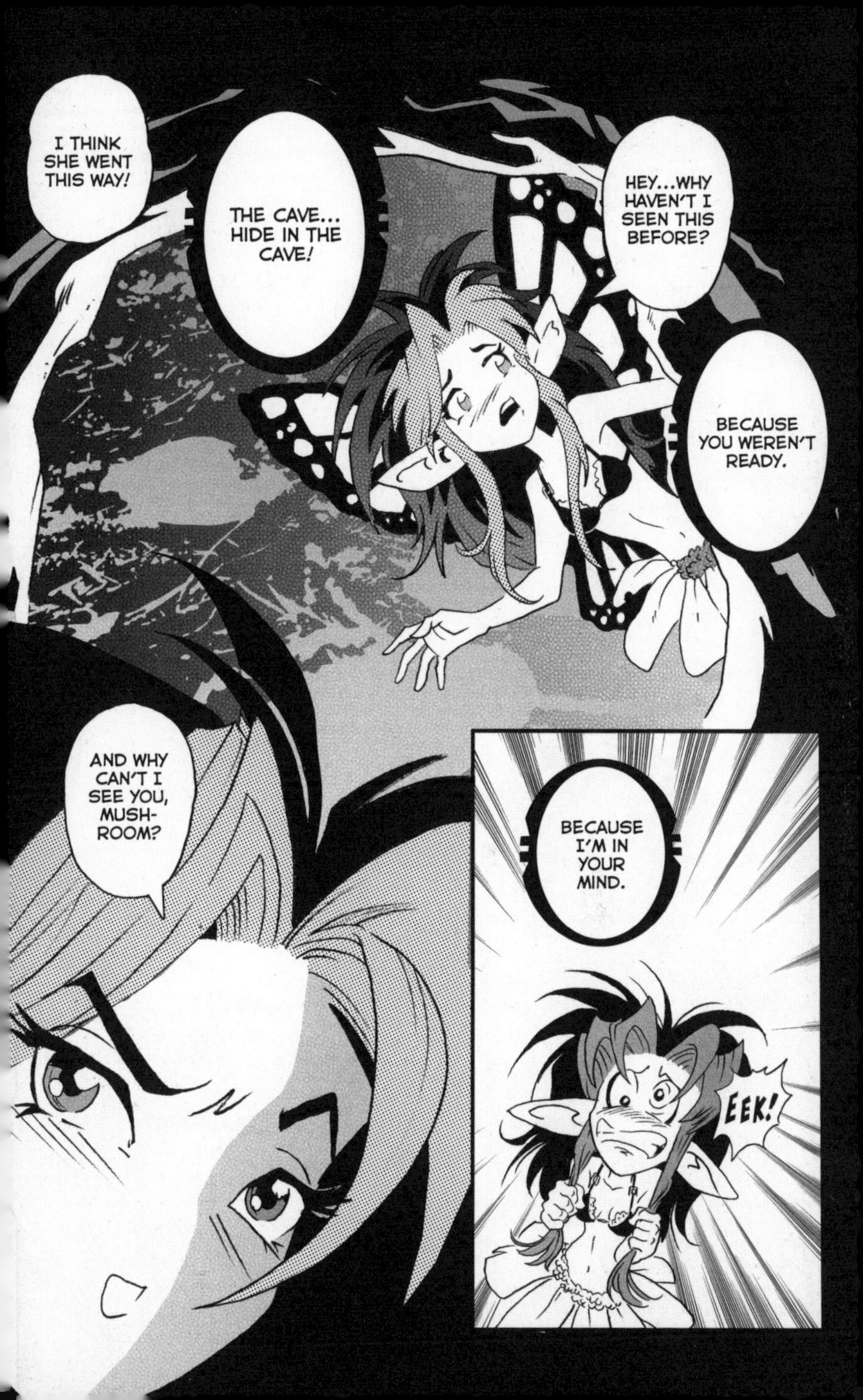
I THINK SHE WENT THIS WAY!
THE CAVE... HIDE IN THE CAVE!
HEY...WHY HAVEN'T I SEEN THIS BEFORE?
BECAUSE YOU WEREN'T READY.
AND WHY CAN'T I SEE YOU, MUSH-ROOM?
BECAUSE I'M IN YOUR MIND.
EEK!

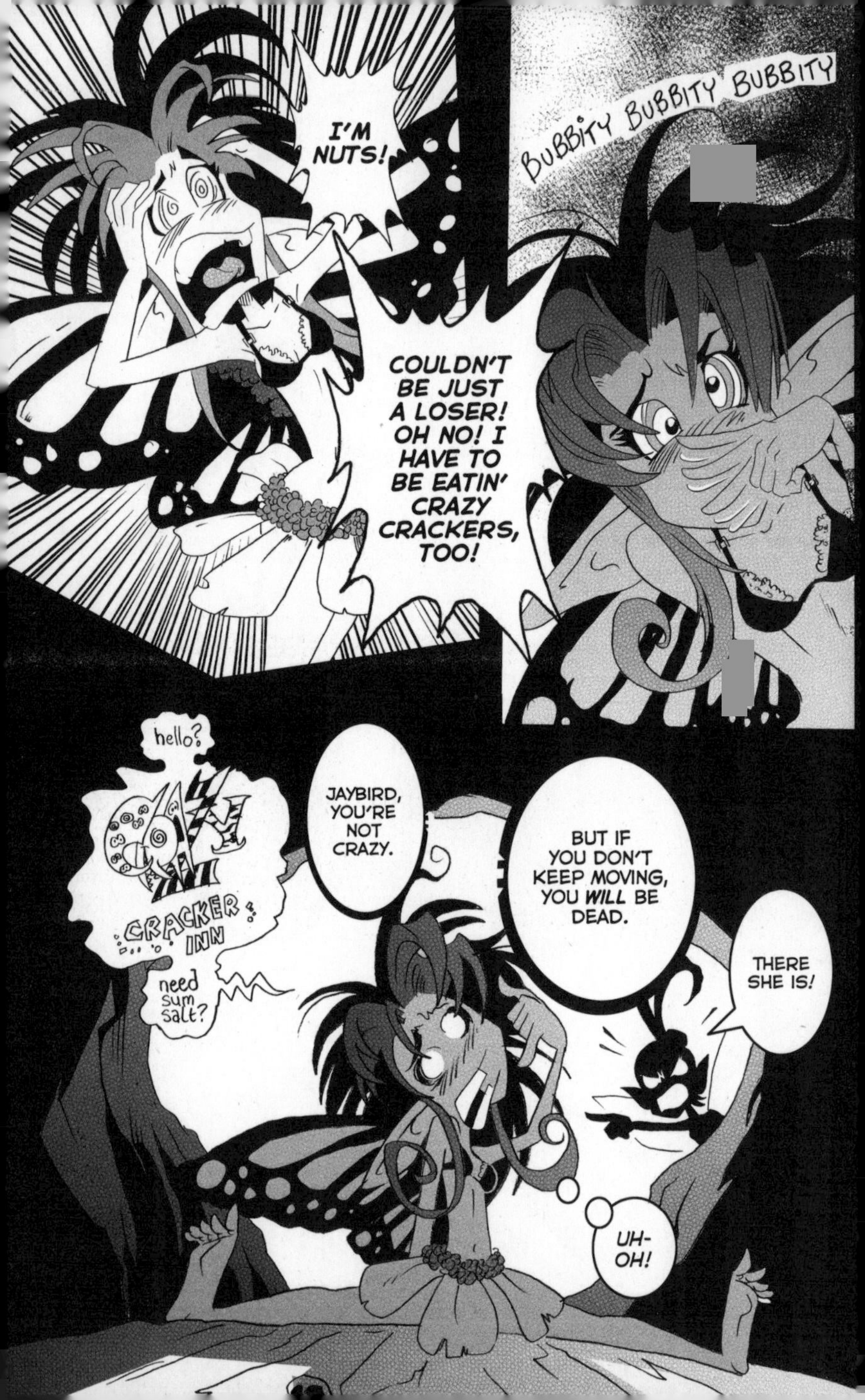
I'M NUTS!
COULDN'T BE JUST A LOSER! OH NO! I HAVE TO BE EATIN' CRAZY CRACKERS, TOO!
BUBBITY BUBBITY BUBBITY
hello?
CRACKER INN
need sum salt?
JAYBIRD, YOU'RE NOT CRAZY.
BUT IF YOU DON'T KEEP MOVING, YOU *WILL* BE DEAD.
THERE SHE IS!
UH-OH!

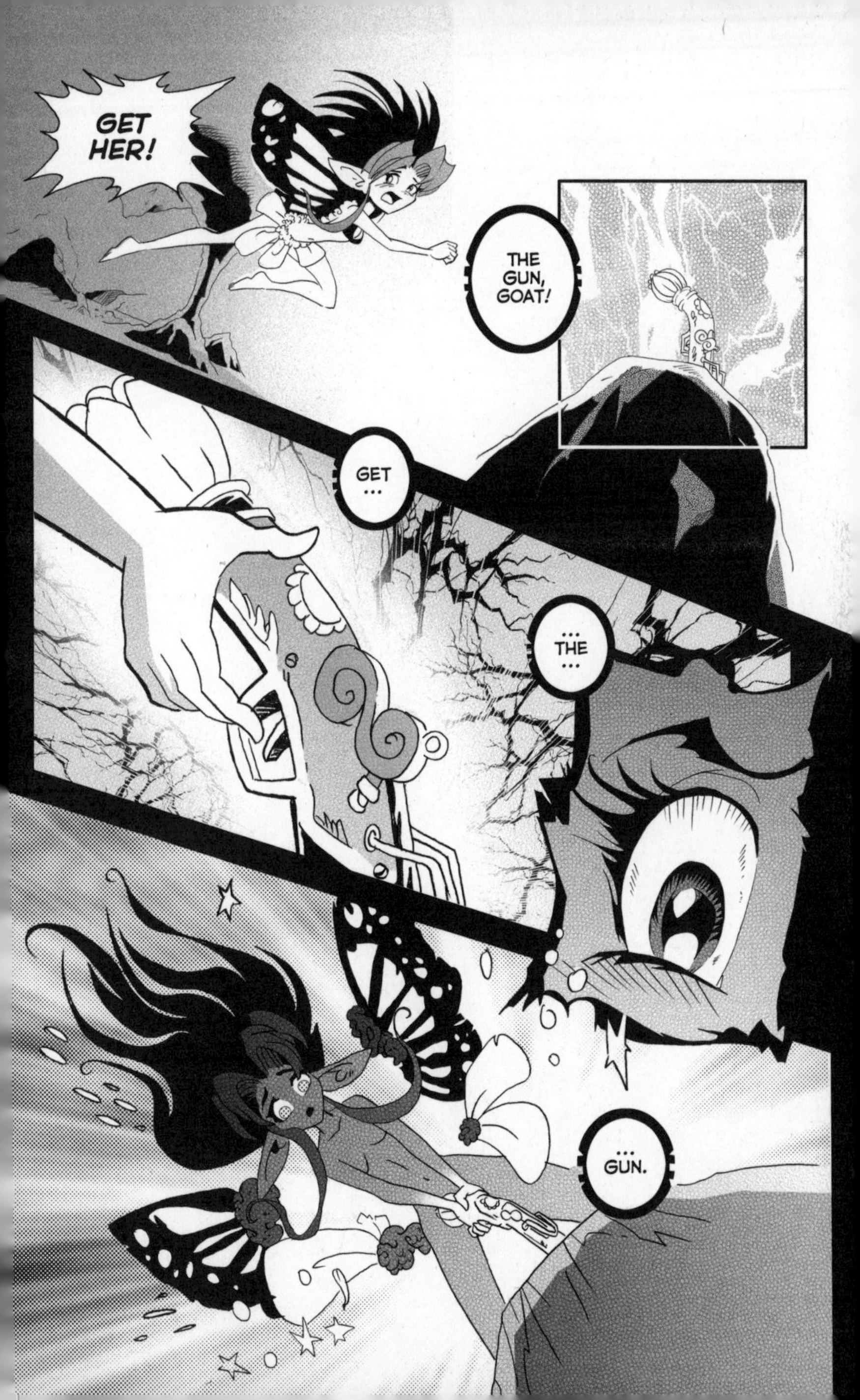
GET HER!
THE GUN, GOAT!
GET ...
... THE ...
... GUN.

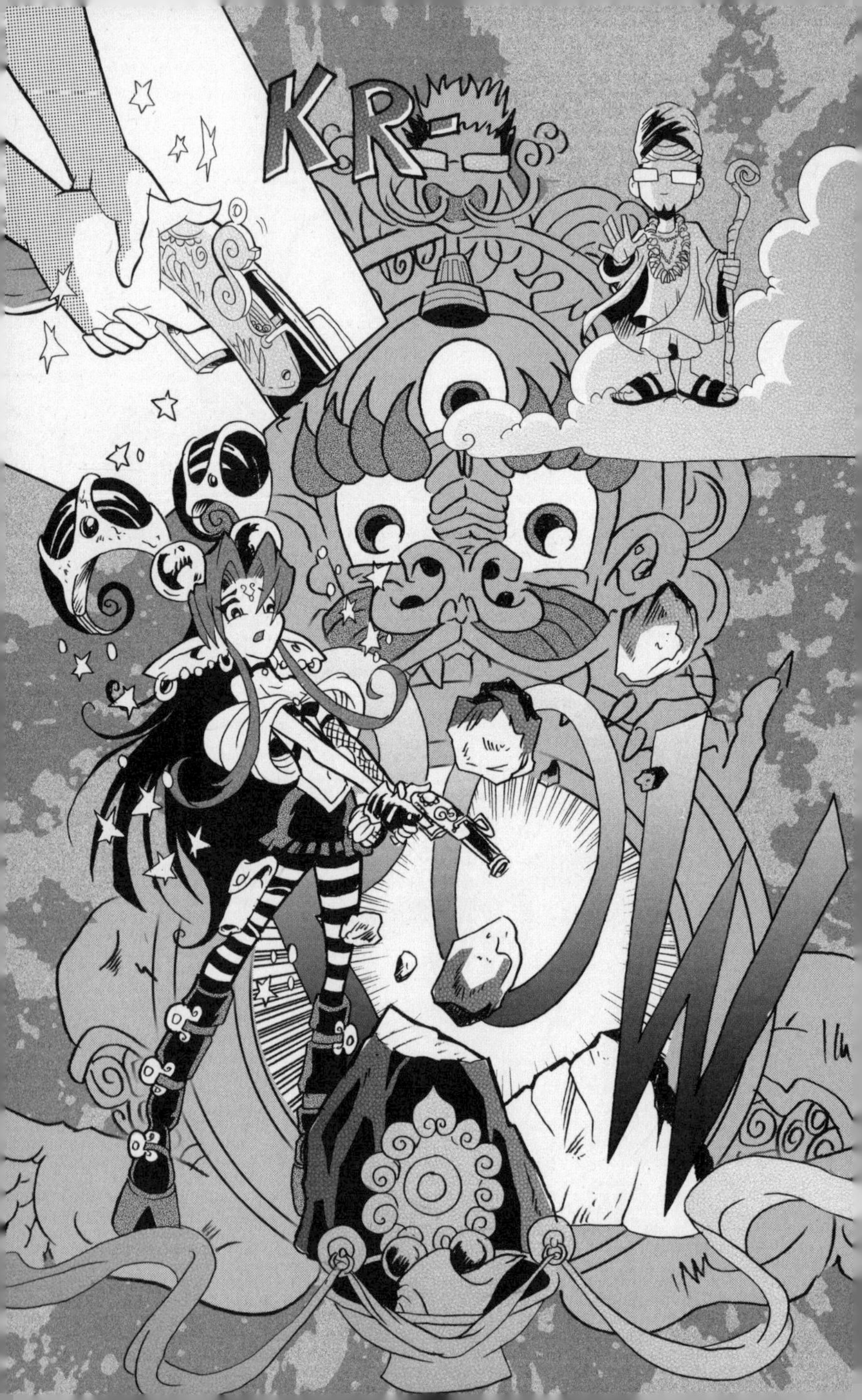
KR--
OW

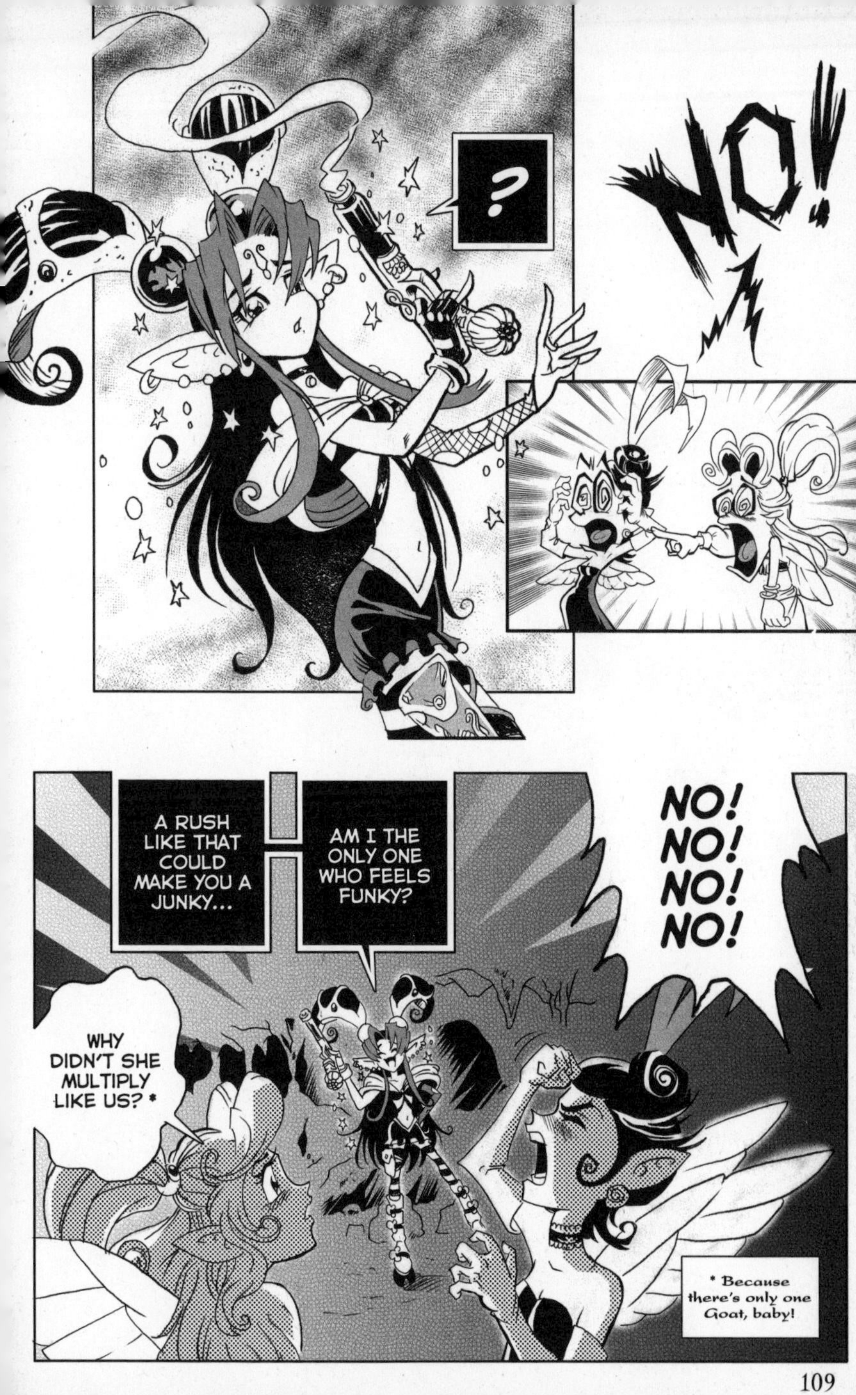
?
NO!!
A RUSH LIKE THAT COULD MAKE YOU A JUNKY...
AM I THE ONLY ONE WHO FEELS FUNKY?
NO! NO! NO! NO!
WHY DIDN'T SHE MULTIPLY LIKE US? *
* Because there's only one Goat, baby!

5 Long Live the Puck

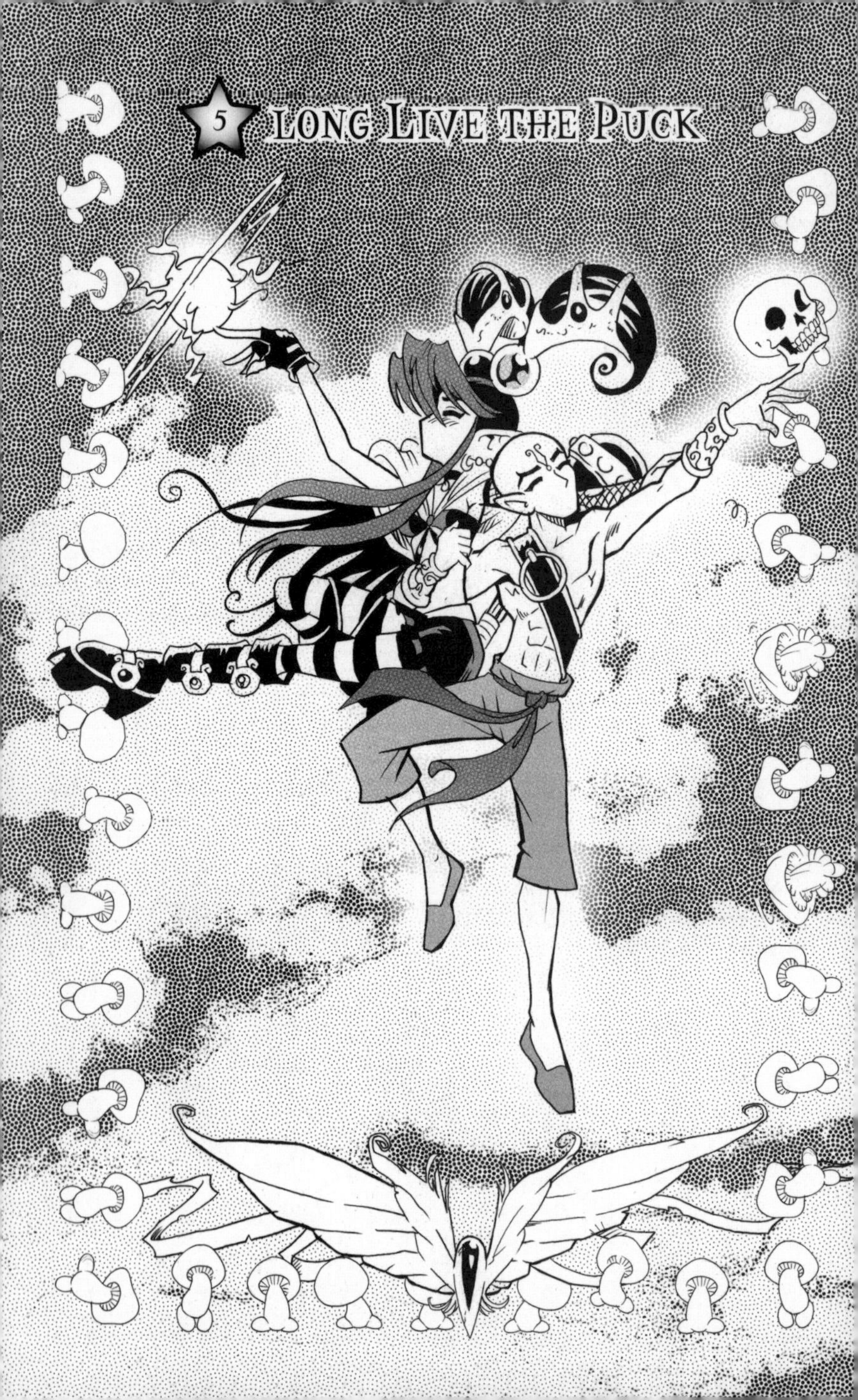

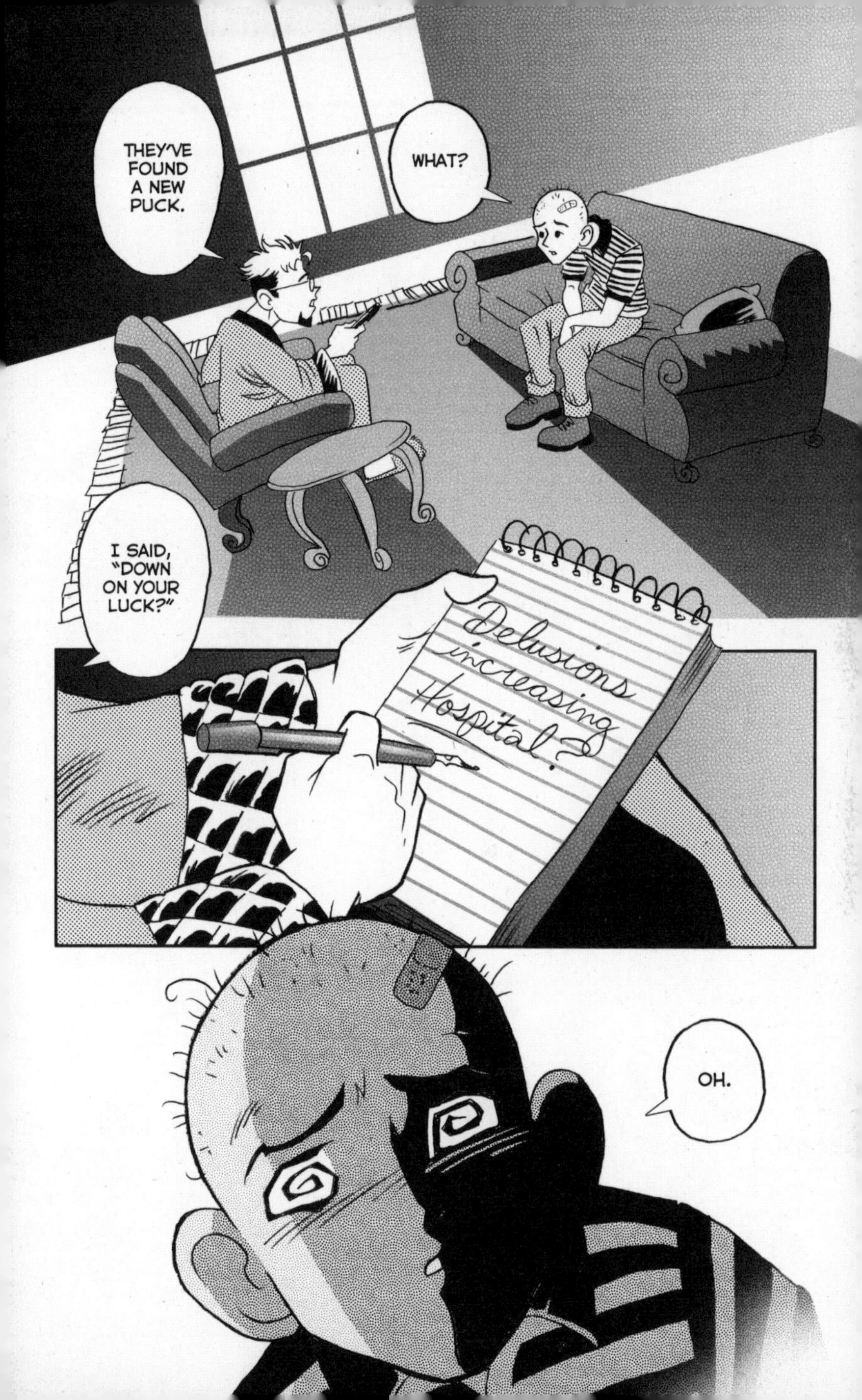
THEY'VE FOUND A NEW PUCK.
WHAT?
I SAID, "DOWN ON YOUR LUCK?"
Delusions increasing Hospital?
OH.

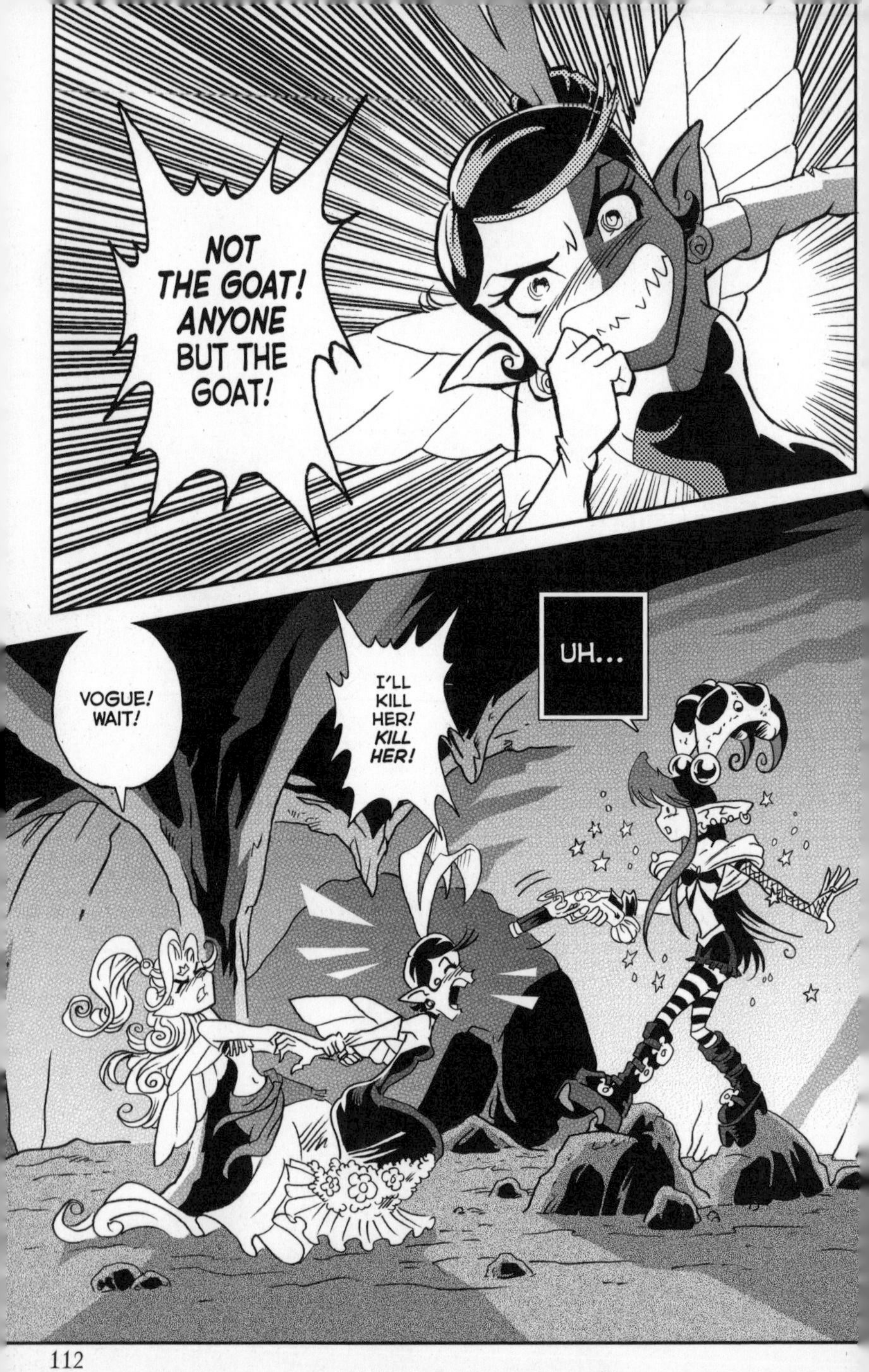
NOT THE GOAT! ANYONE BUT THE GOAT!
VOGUE! WAIT!
I'LL KILL HER! KILL HER!
UH...

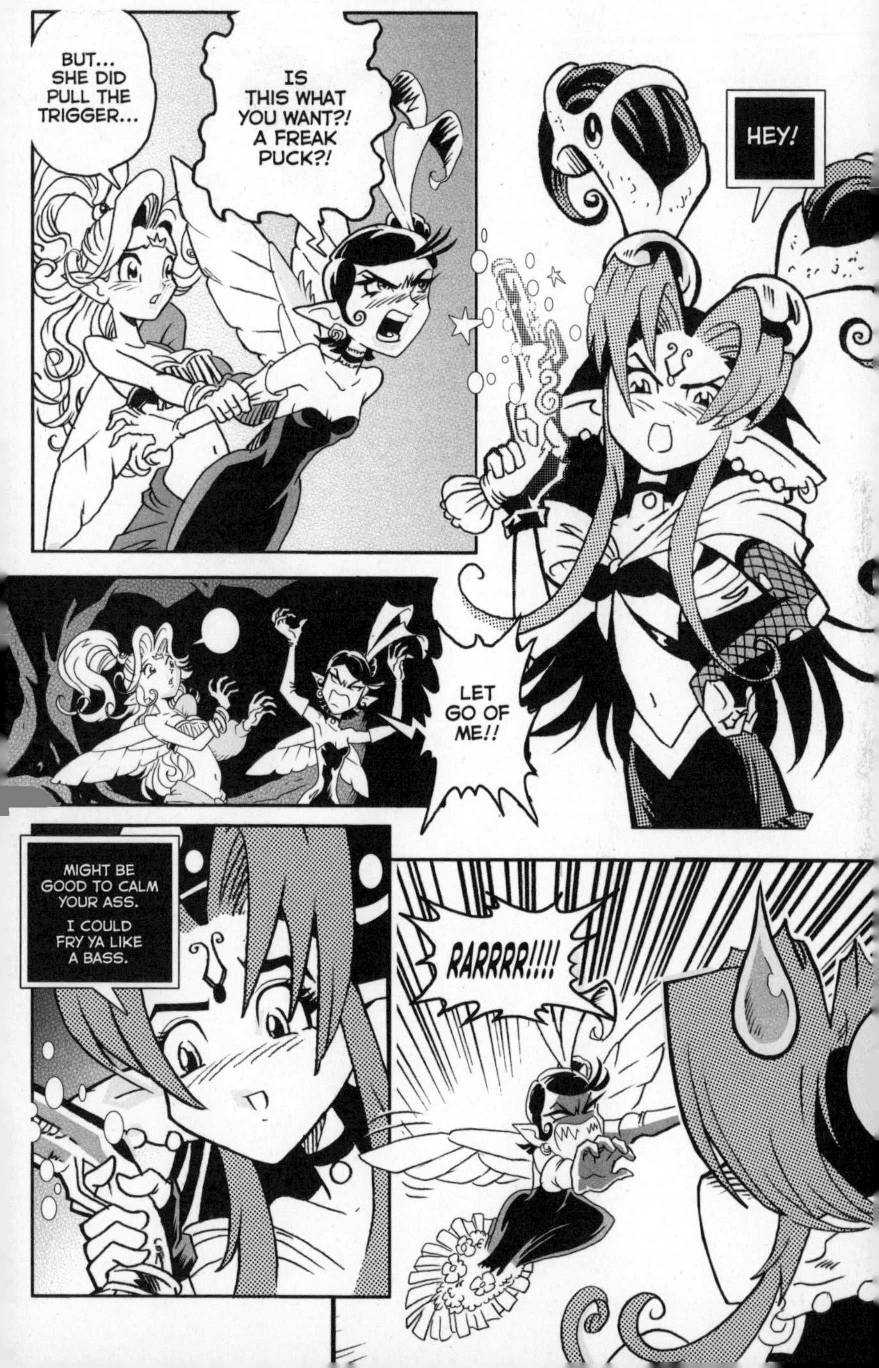
BUT... SHE DID PULL THE TRIGGER...
IS THIS WHAT YOU WANT?! A FREAK PUCK?!
HEY!
LET GO OF ME!!
MIGHT BE GOOD TO CALM YOUR ASS.
I COULD FRY YA LIKE A BASS.
RARRRR!!!!

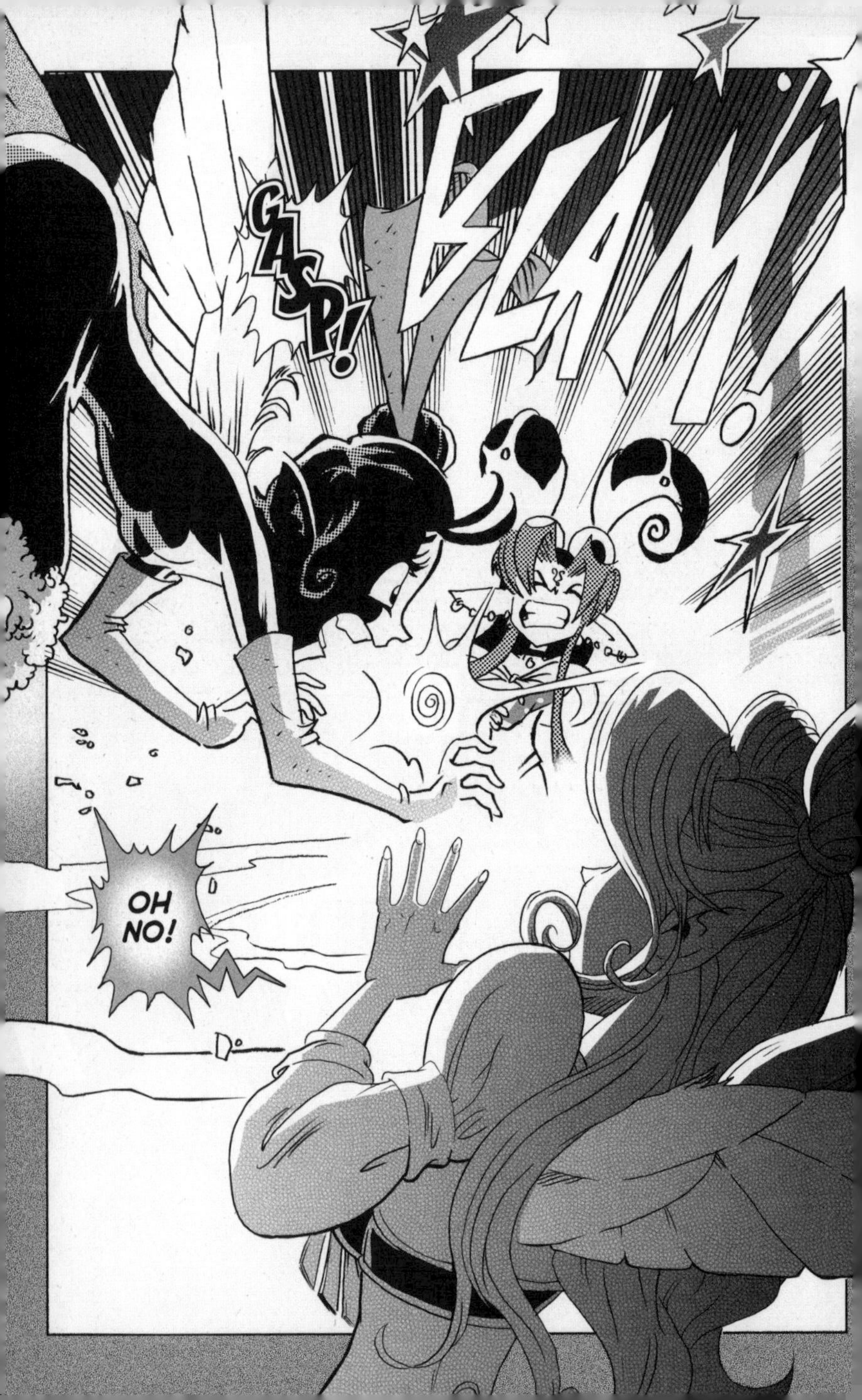
GASP!
BLAM!
OH NO!

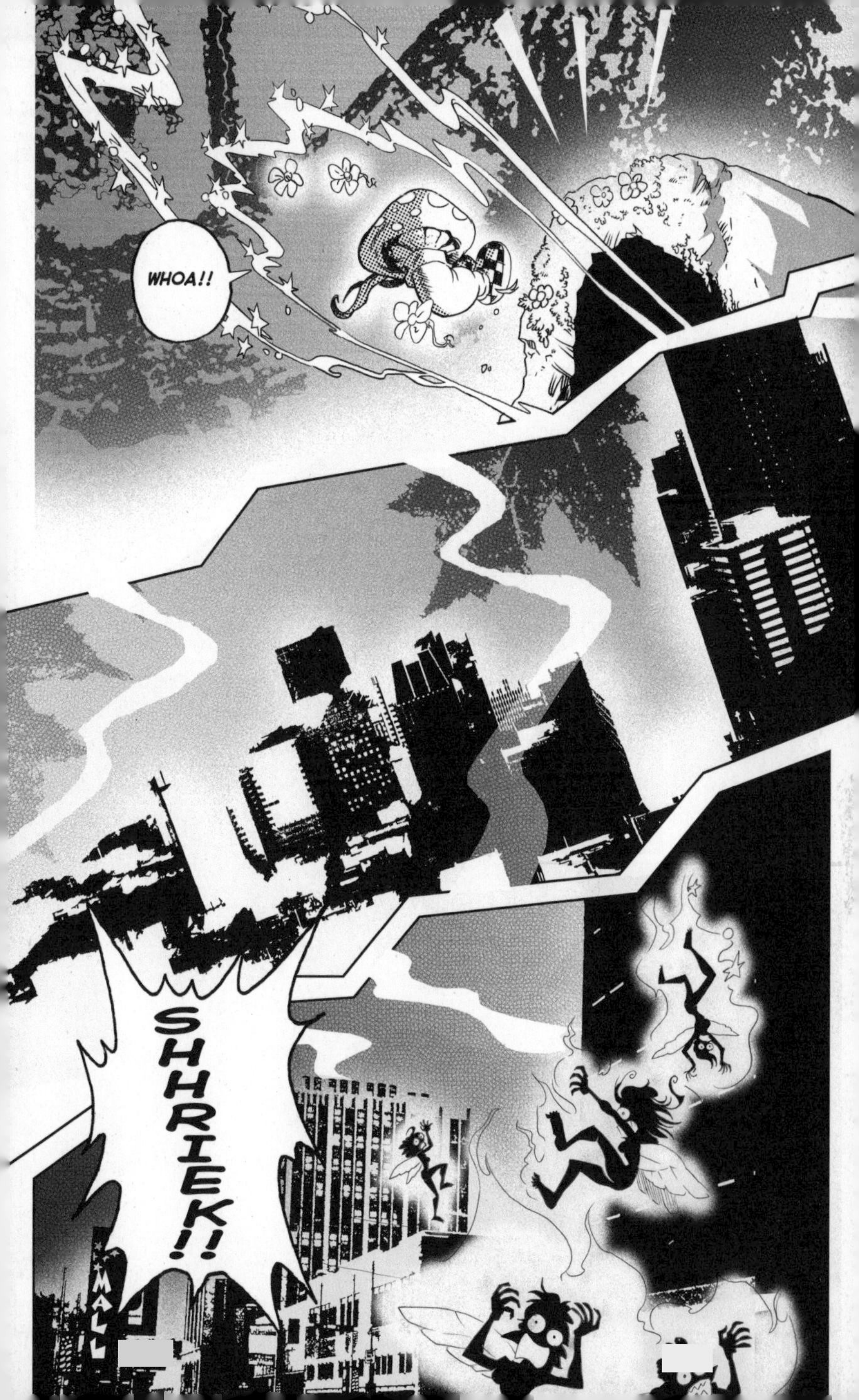
WHOA!!
SHRIEK!!
MALL

SNORT?
AHHH!
AT LEAST IT STOPPED HER MOUTH A FLAPPIN'.
SOMEONE TELL ME, WHAT THE HELL HAPPENED?
AAAHHH!!!
I BELIEVE I CAN ANSWER THAT.

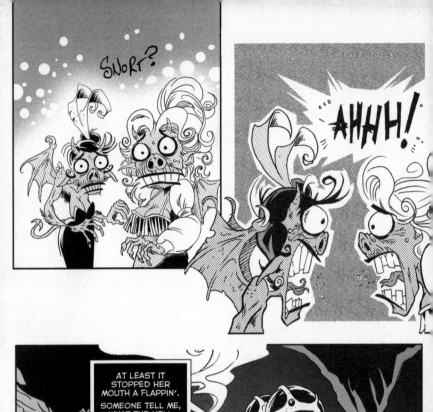

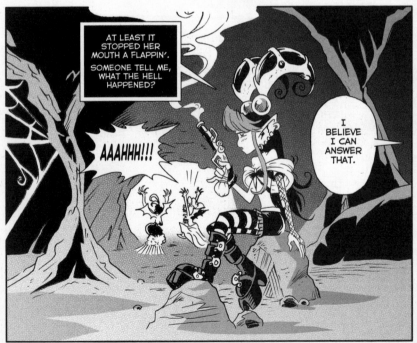

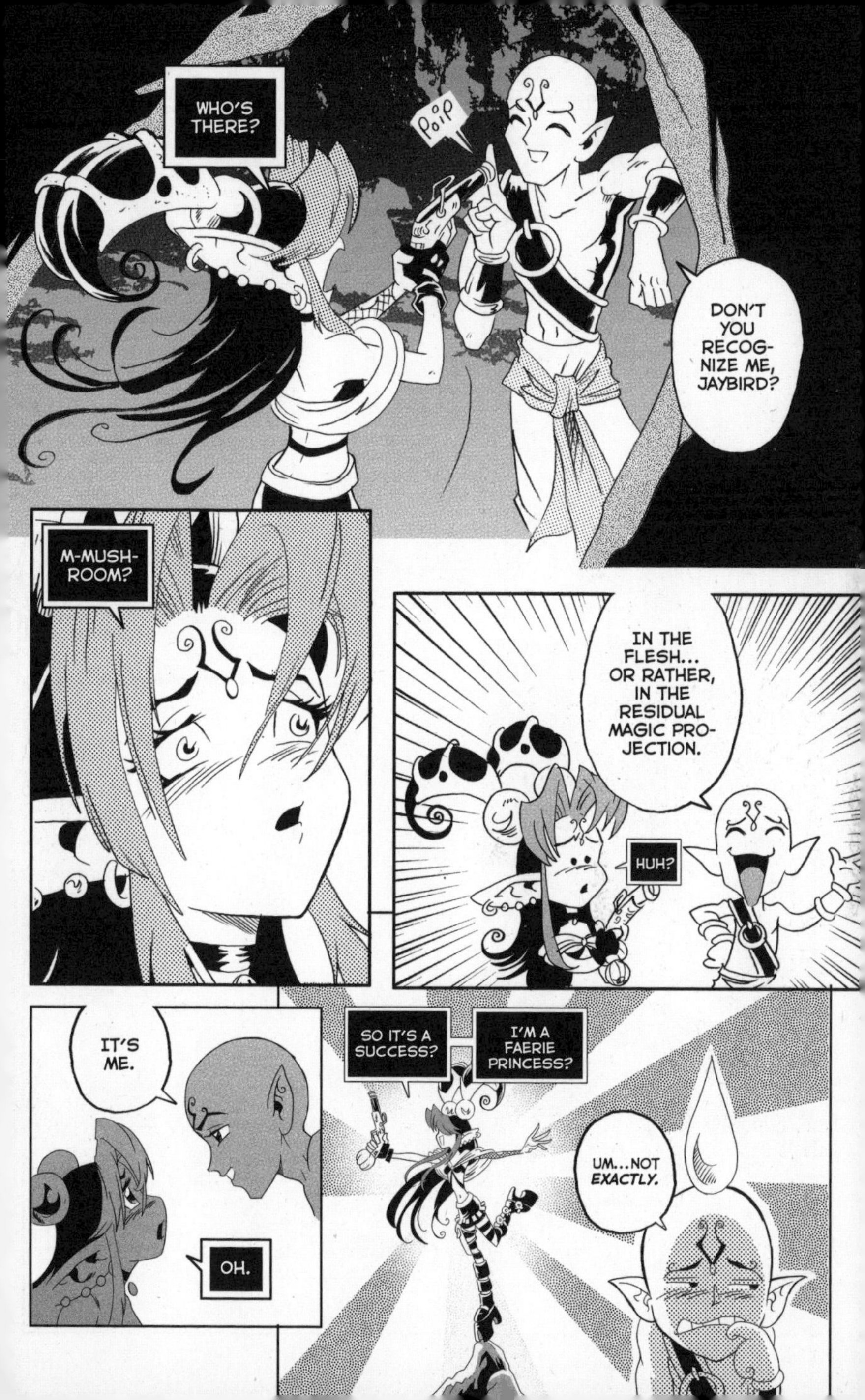
WHO'S THERE?
POIP
DON'T YOU RECOG- NIZE ME, JAYBIRD?
M-MUSH- ROOM?
IN THE FLESH... OR RATHER, IN THE RESIDUAL MAGIC PRO- JECTION.
HUH?
IT'S ME.
OH.
SO IT'S A SUCCESS?
I'M A FAERIE PRINCESS?
UM...NOT *EXACTLY.*

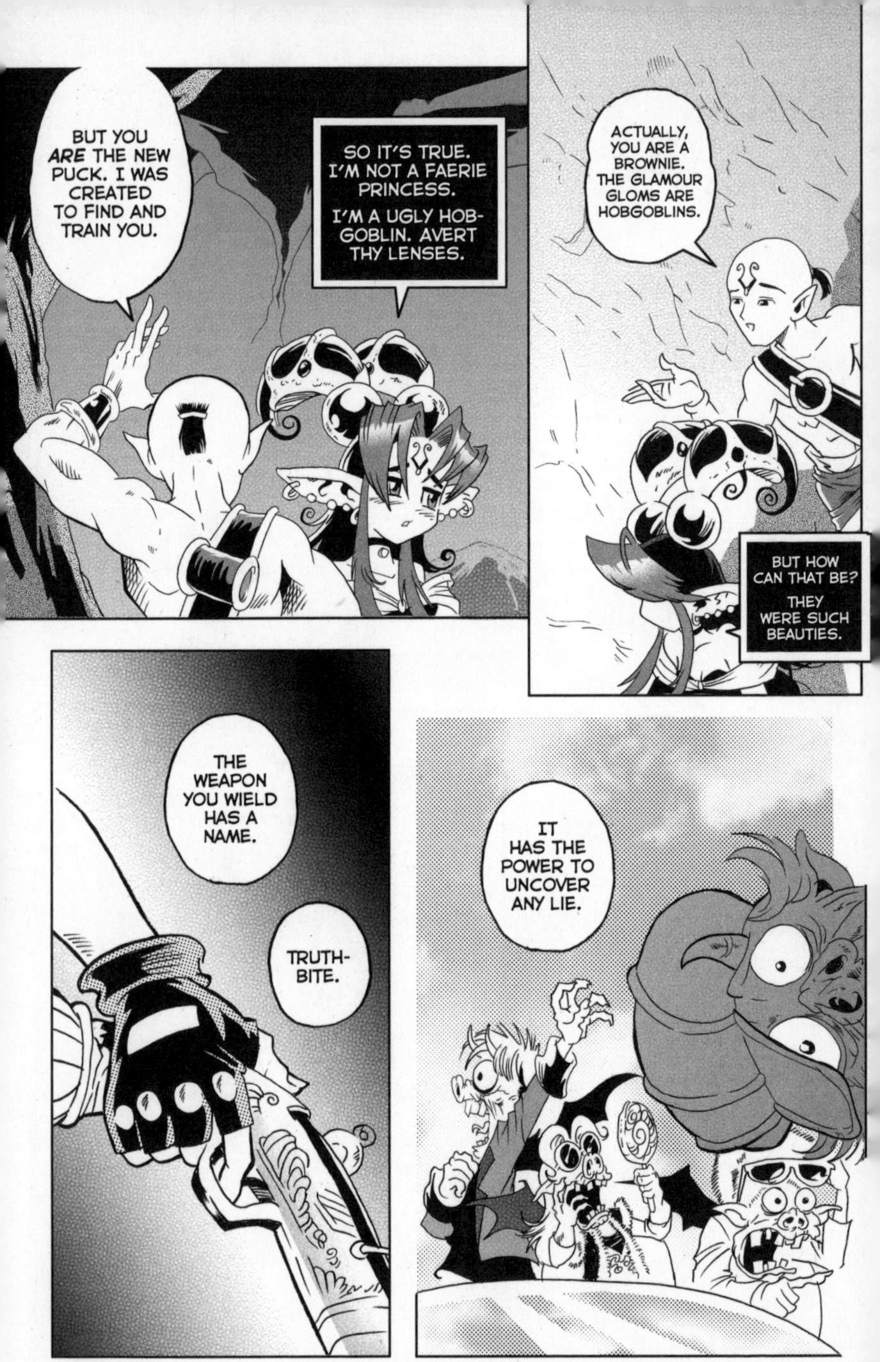
BUT YOU *ARE* THE NEW PUCK. I WAS CREATED TO FIND AND TRAIN YOU.
SO IT'S TRUE. I'M NOT A FAERIE PRINCESS.
I'M A UGLY HOB-GOBLIN. AVERT THY LENSES.
ACTUALLY, YOU ARE A BROWNIE. THE GLAMOUR GLOMS ARE HOBGOBLINS.
BUT HOW CAN THAT BE?
THEY WERE SUCH BEAUTIES.
THE WEAPON YOU WIELD HAS A NAME.
TRUTH-BITE.
IT HAS THE POWER TO UNCOVER ANY LIE.

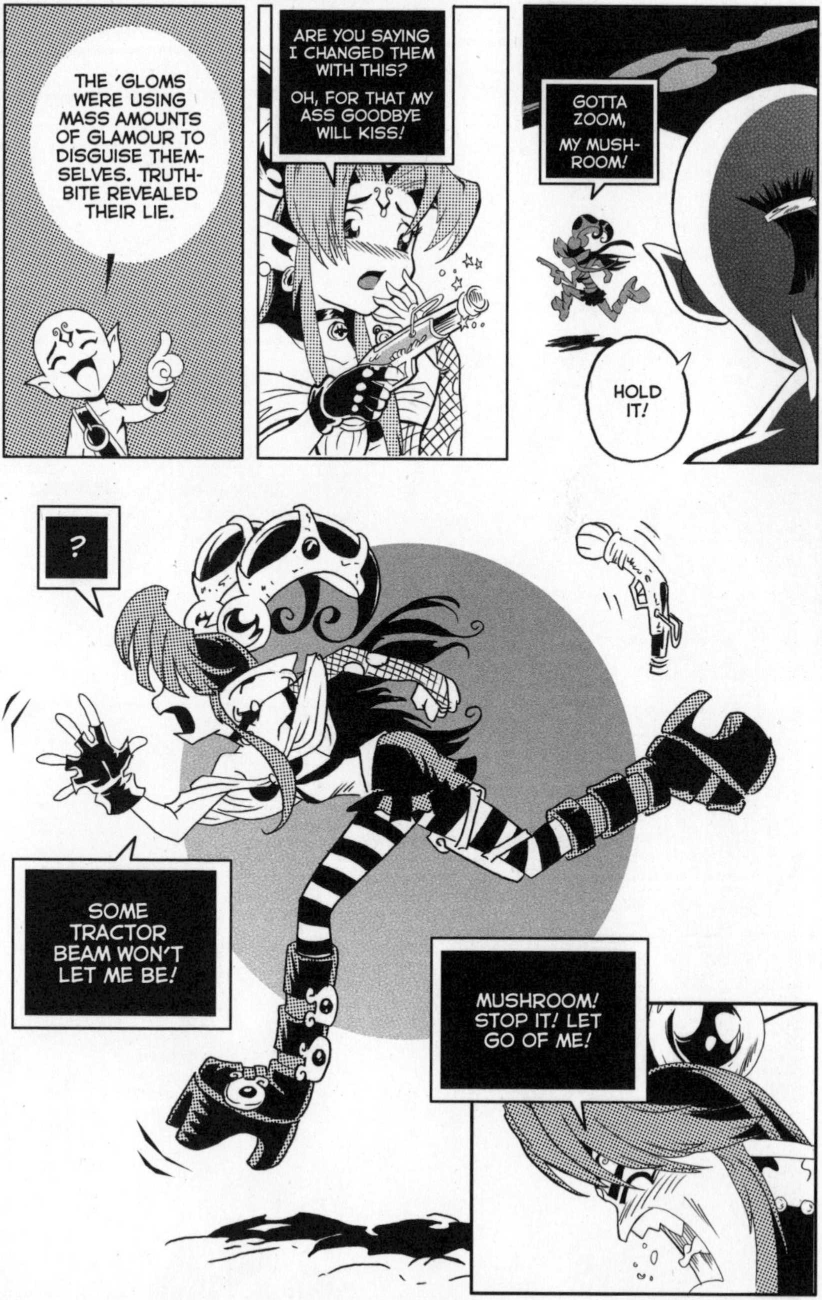
THE 'GLOMS WERE USING MASS AMOUNTS OF GLAMOUR TO DISGUISE THEMSELVES. TRUTHBITE REVEALED THEIR LIE.
ARE YOU SAYING I CHANGED THEM WITH THIS?
OH, FOR THAT MY ASS GOODBYE WILL KISS!
GOTTA ZOOM, MY MUSHROOM!
HOLD IT!
?
SOME TRACTOR BEAM WON'T LET ME BE!
MUSHROOM! STOP IT! LET GO OF ME!

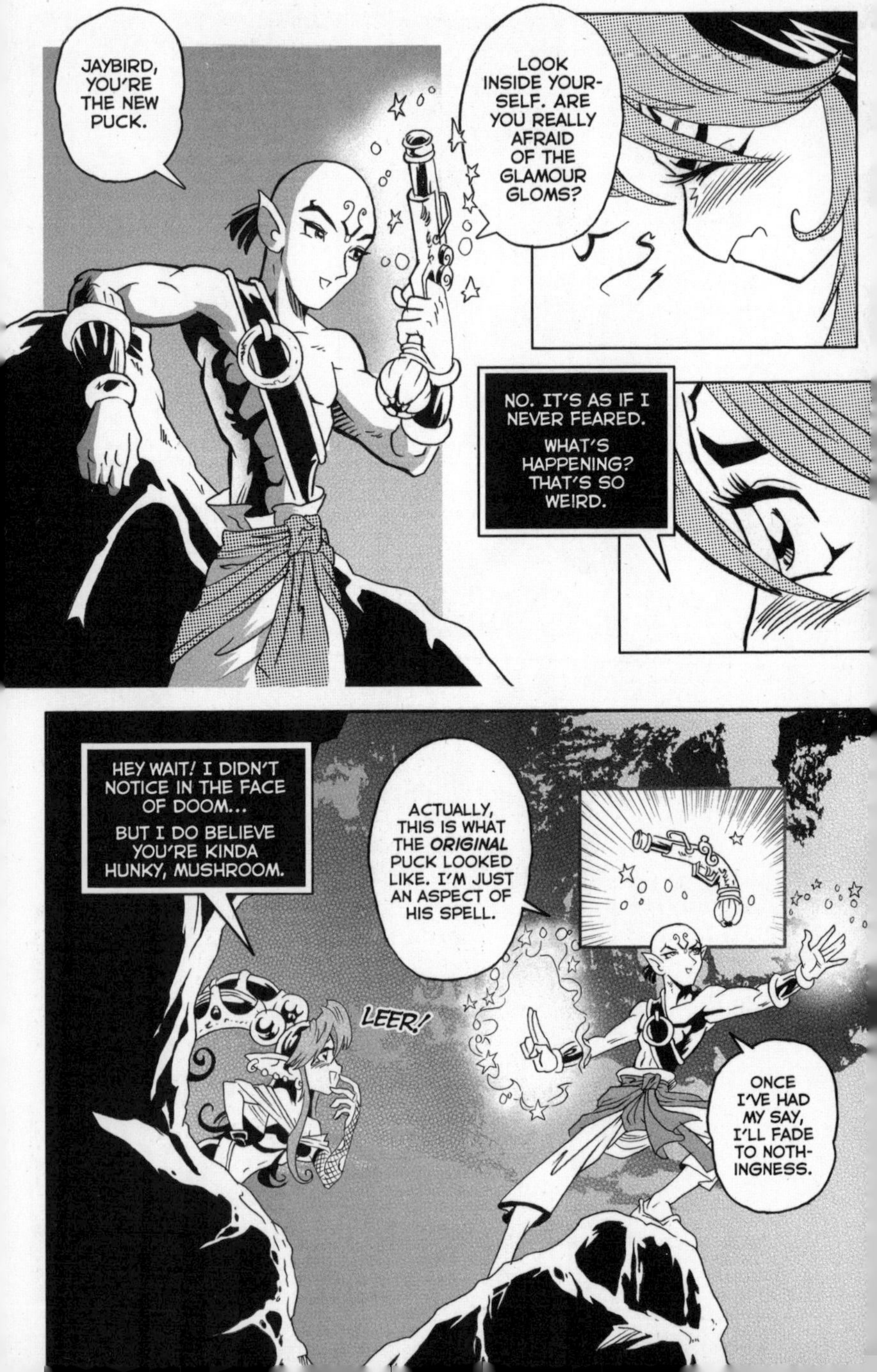
JAYBIRD, YOU'RE THE NEW PUCK.
LOOK INSIDE YOURSELF. ARE YOU REALLY AFRAID OF THE GLAMOUR GLOMS?
NO. IT'S AS IF I NEVER FEARED.
WHAT'S HAPPENING? THAT'S SO WEIRD.
HEY WAIT! I DIDN'T NOTICE IN THE FACE OF DOOM...
BUT I DO BELIEVE YOU'RE KINDA HUNKY, MUSHROOM.
ACTUALLY, THIS IS WHAT THE *ORIGINAL* PUCK LOOKED LIKE. I'M JUST AN ASPECT OF HIS SPELL.
LEER!
ONCE I'VE HAD *MY* SAY, I'LL FADE TO NOTHINGNESS.

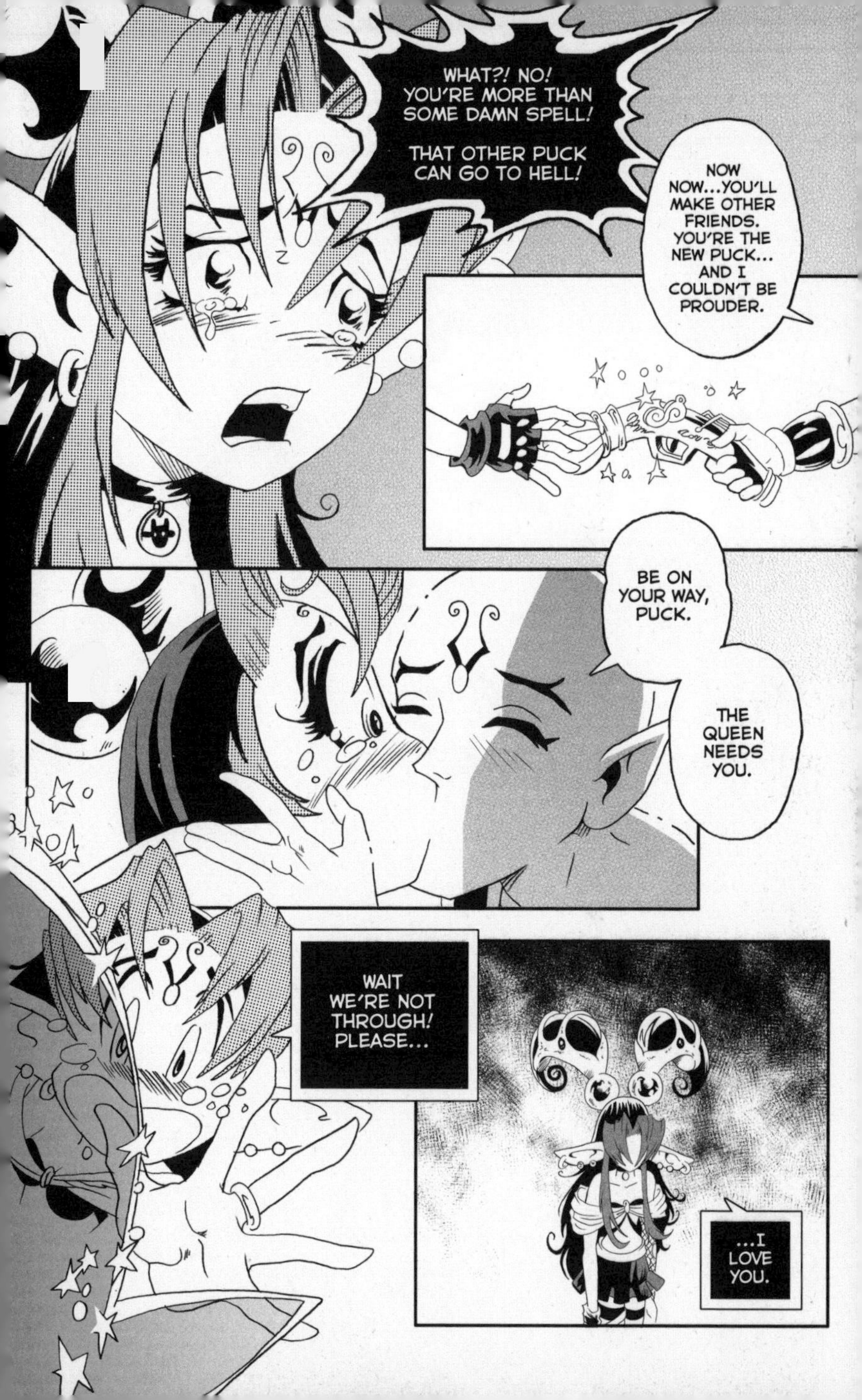
WHAT?! NO! YOU'RE MORE THAN SOME DAMN SPELL!
THAT OTHER PUCK CAN GO TO HELL!
NOW NOW...YOU'LL MAKE OTHER FRIENDS. YOU'RE THE NEW PUCK... AND I COULDN'T BE PROUDER.
BE ON YOUR WAY, PUCK.
THE QUEEN NEEDS YOU.
WAIT WE'RE NOT THROUGH! PLEASE...
...I LOVE YOU.

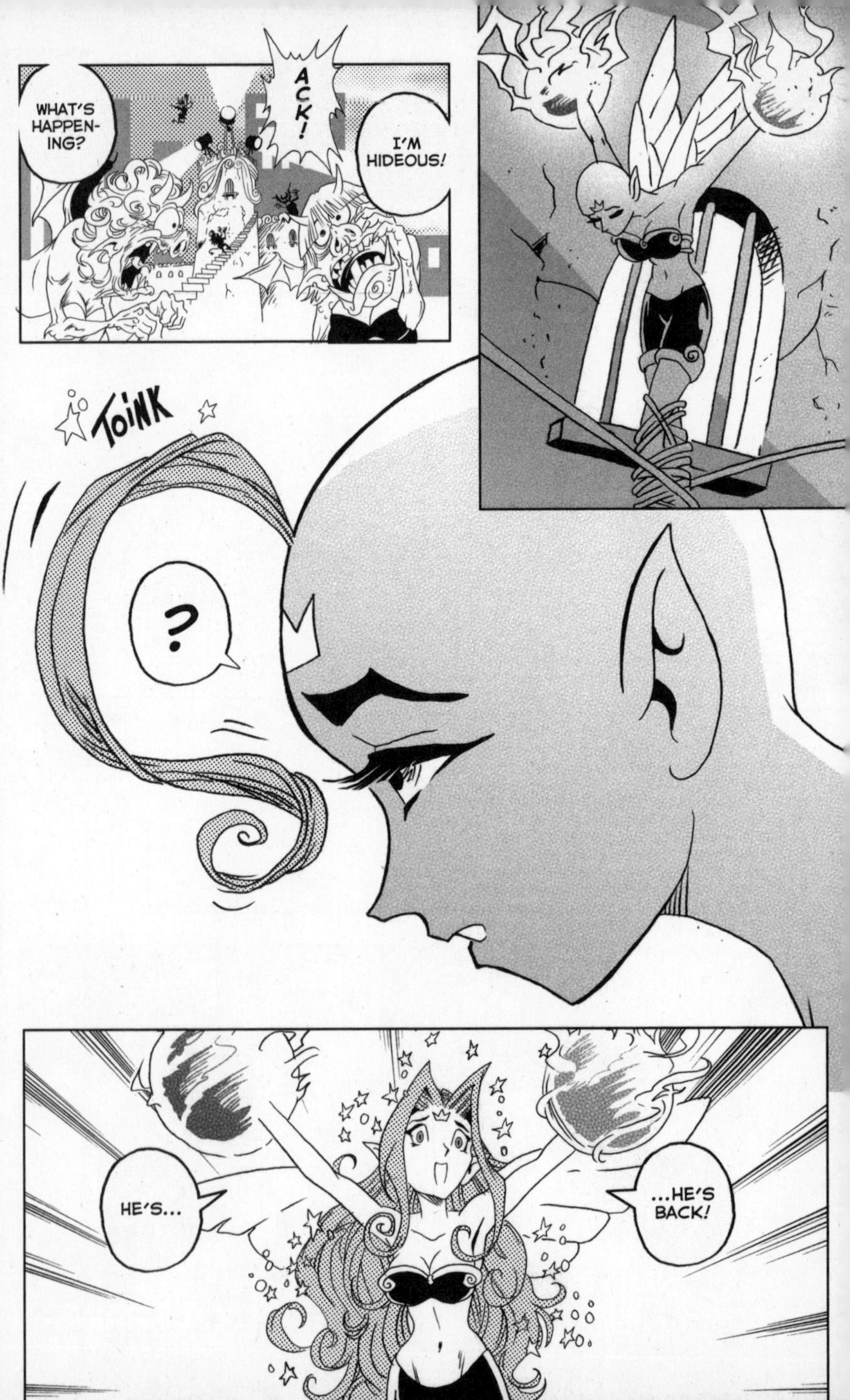
WHAT'S HAPPEN-ING?
ACK!
I'M HIDEOUS!
TOINK
?
HE'S...
...HE'S BACK!

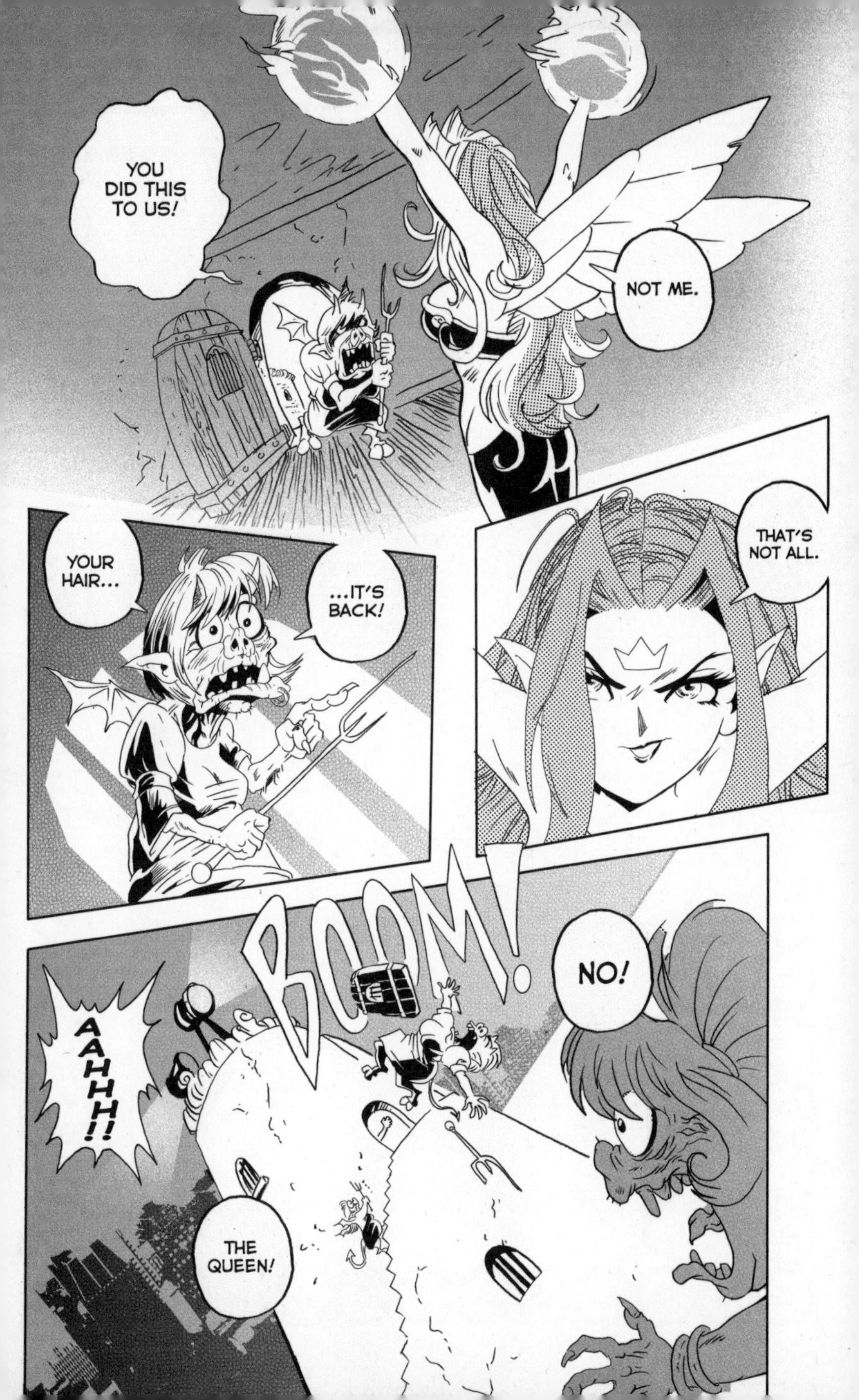
YOU DID THIS TO US!
NOT ME.
YOUR HAIR...
...IT'S BACK!
THAT'S NOT ALL.
BOOM!
NO!
AAHHH!!
THE QUEEN!

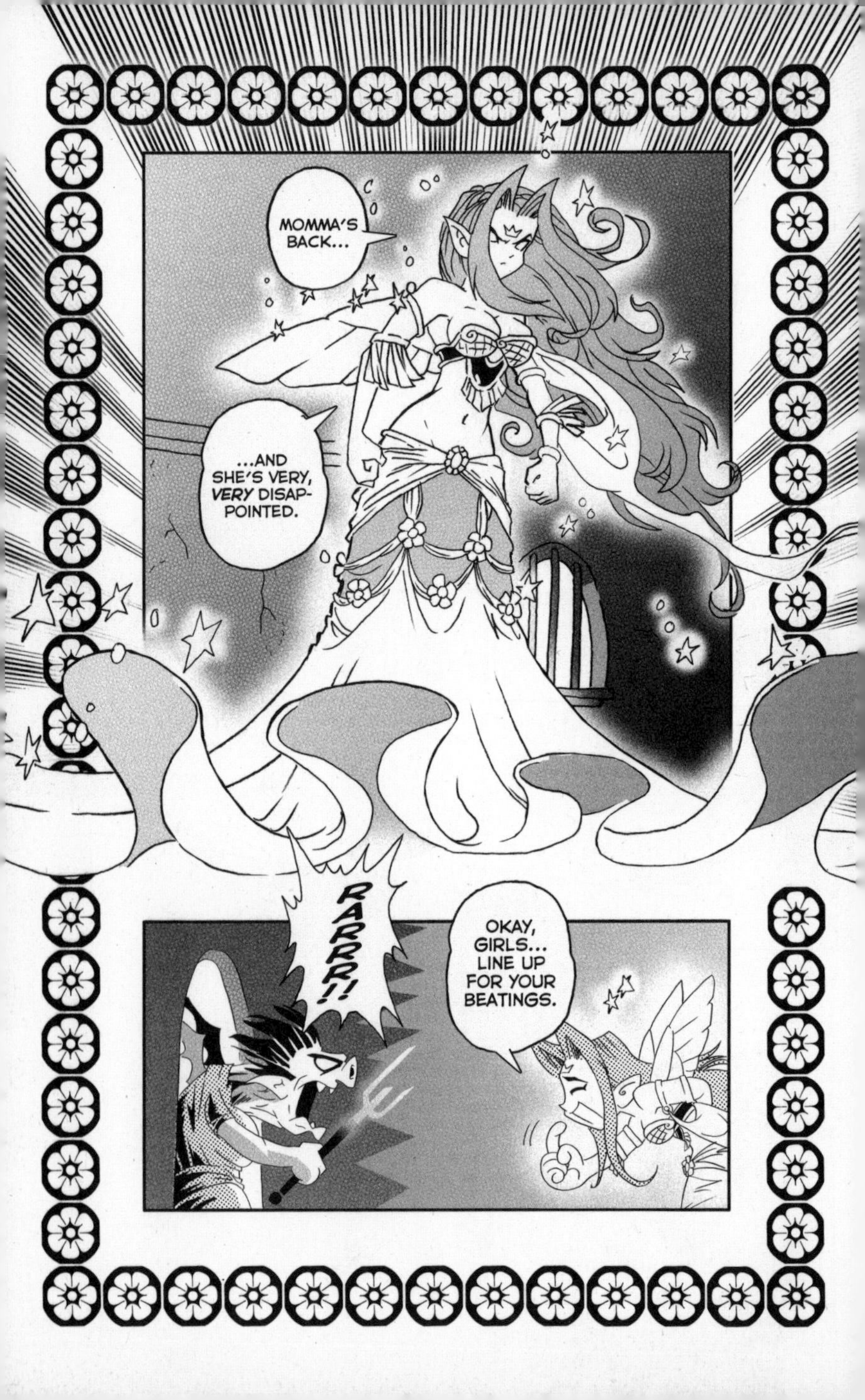
MOMMA'S BACK...
...AND SHE'S VERY, *VERY* DISAPPOINTED.
RARRR!!
OKAY, GIRLS... LINE UP FOR YOUR BEATINGS.

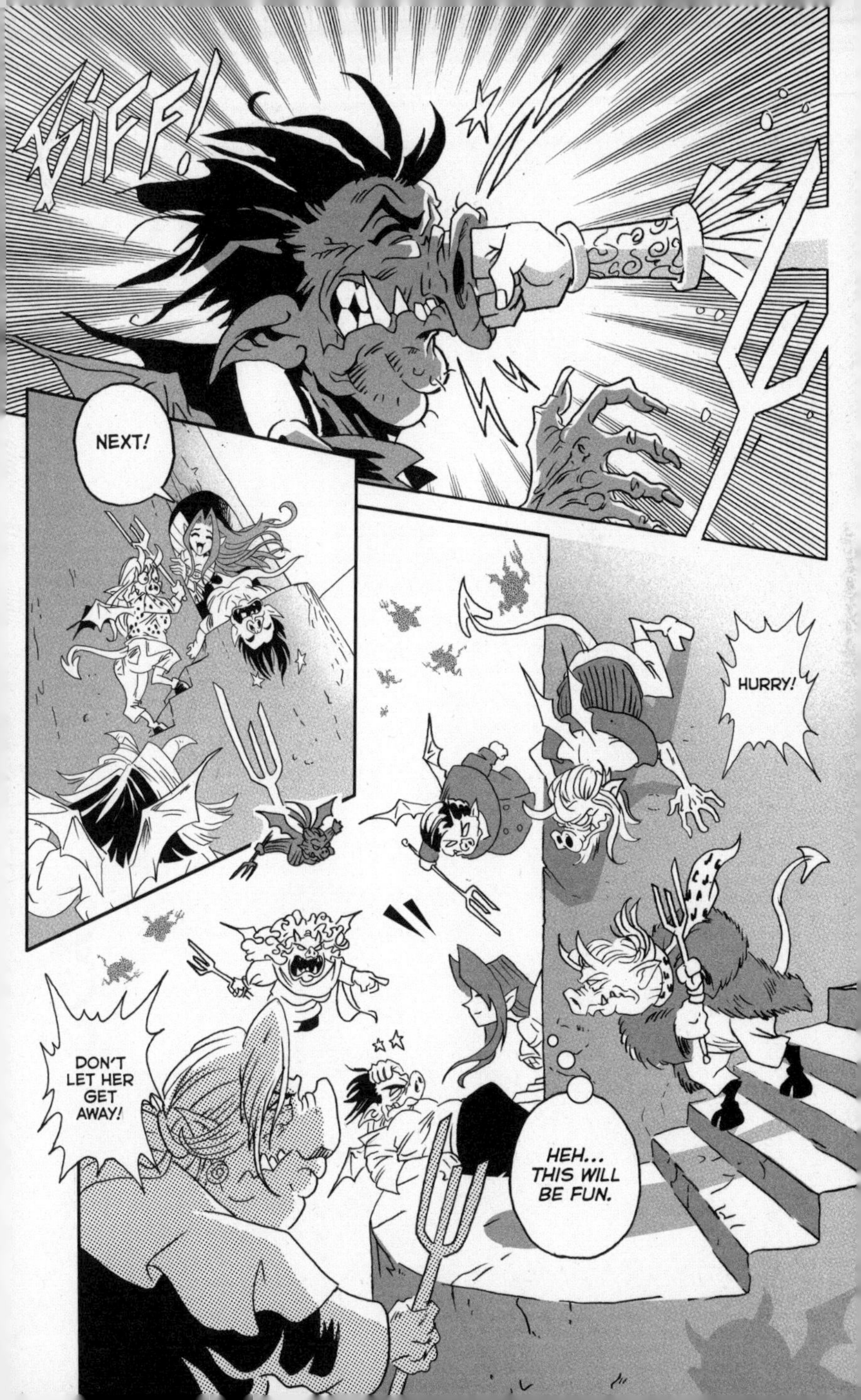
BIFF!
NEXT!
HURRY!
DON'T LET HER GET AWAY!
HEH... THIS WILL BE FUN.

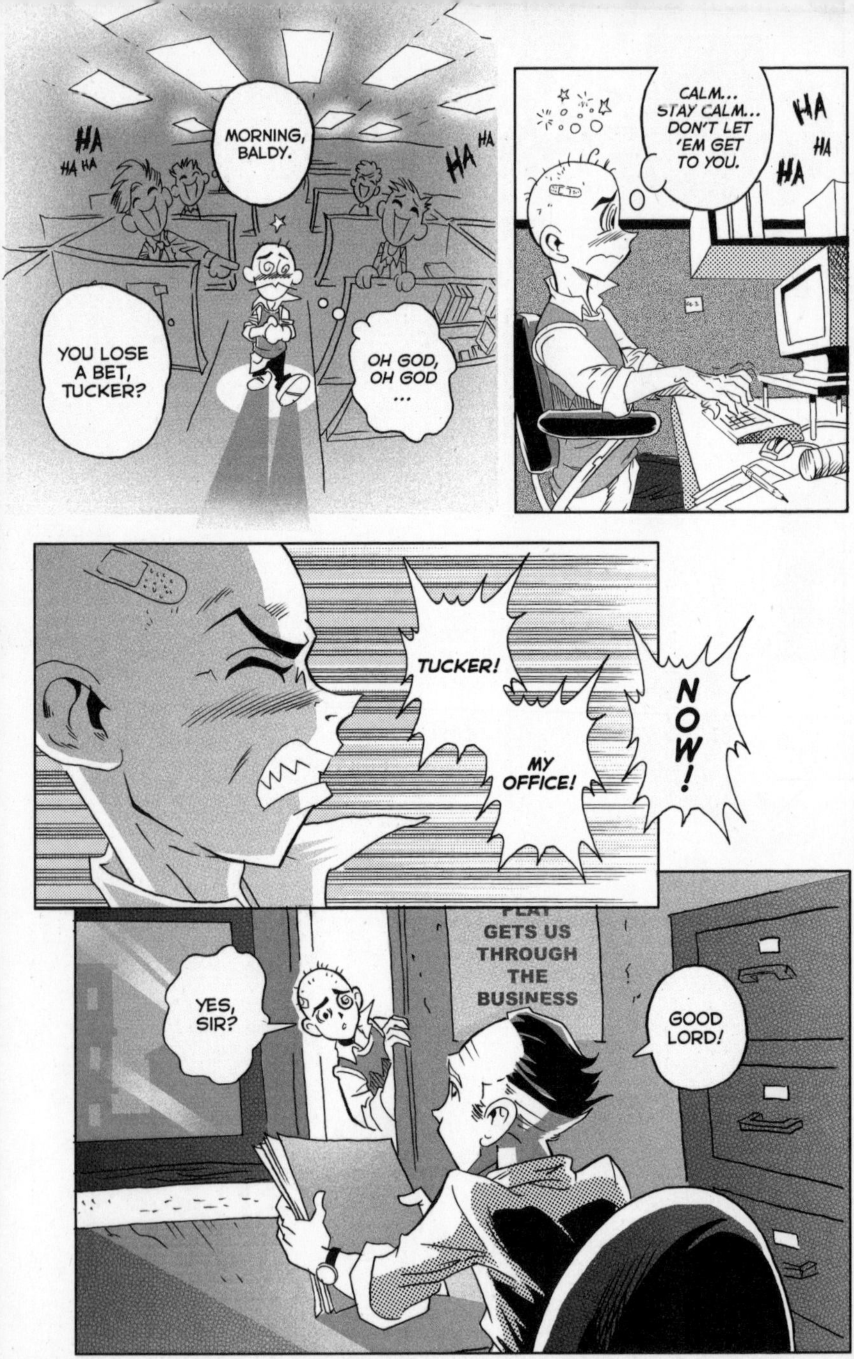
HA HA HA
MORNING, BALDY.
HA HA
YOU LOSE A BET, TUCKER?
OH GOD, OH GOD ...
CALM... STAY CALM... DON'T LET 'EM GET TO YOU.
HA HA HA
TUCKER!
MY OFFICE!
NOW!
GETS US THROUGH THE BUSINESS
YES, SIR?
GOOD LORD!

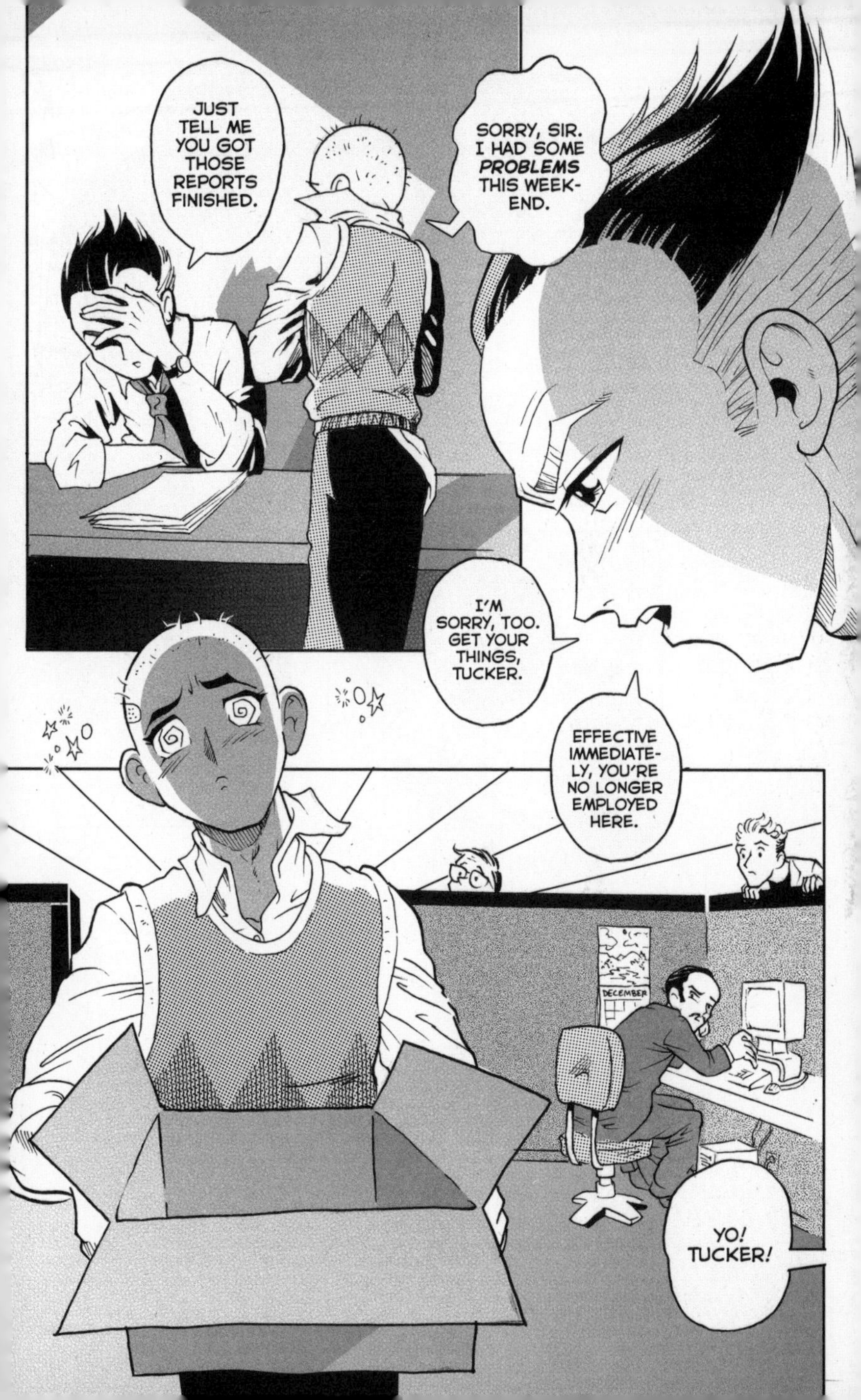
JUST TELL ME YOU GOT THOSE REPORTS FINISHED.
SORRY, SIR. I HAD SOME *PROBLEMS* THIS WEEK-END.
I'M SORRY, TOO. GET YOUR THINGS, TUCKER.
EFFECTIVE IMMEDIATE-LY, YOU'RE NO LONGER EMPLOYED HERE.
DECEMBER
YO! TUCKER!

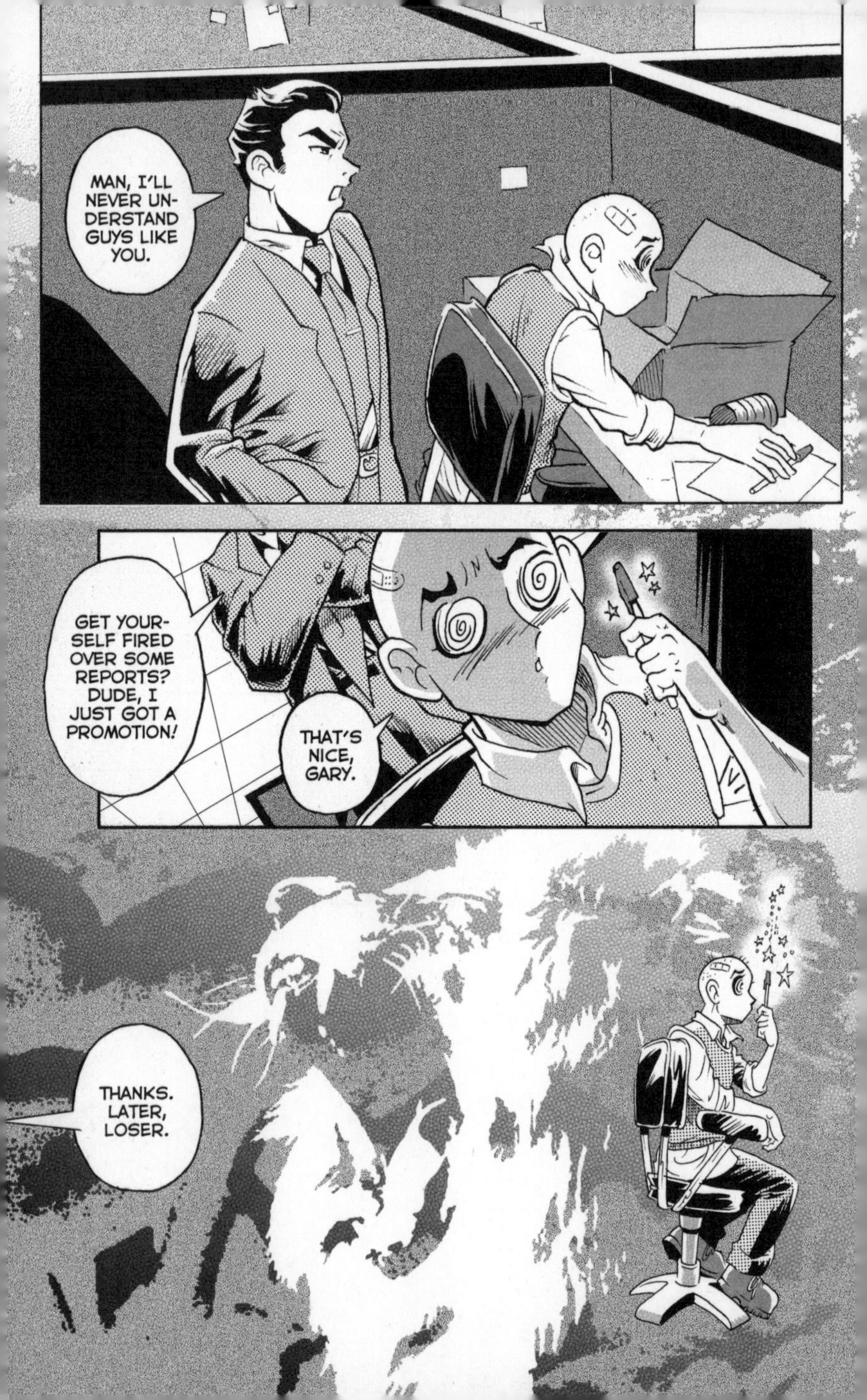
MAN, I'LL NEVER UNDERSTAND GUYS LIKE YOU.
GET YOURSELF FIRED OVER SOME REPORTS? DUDE, I JUST GOT A PROMOTION!
THAT'S NICE, GARY.
THANKS. LATER, LOSER.

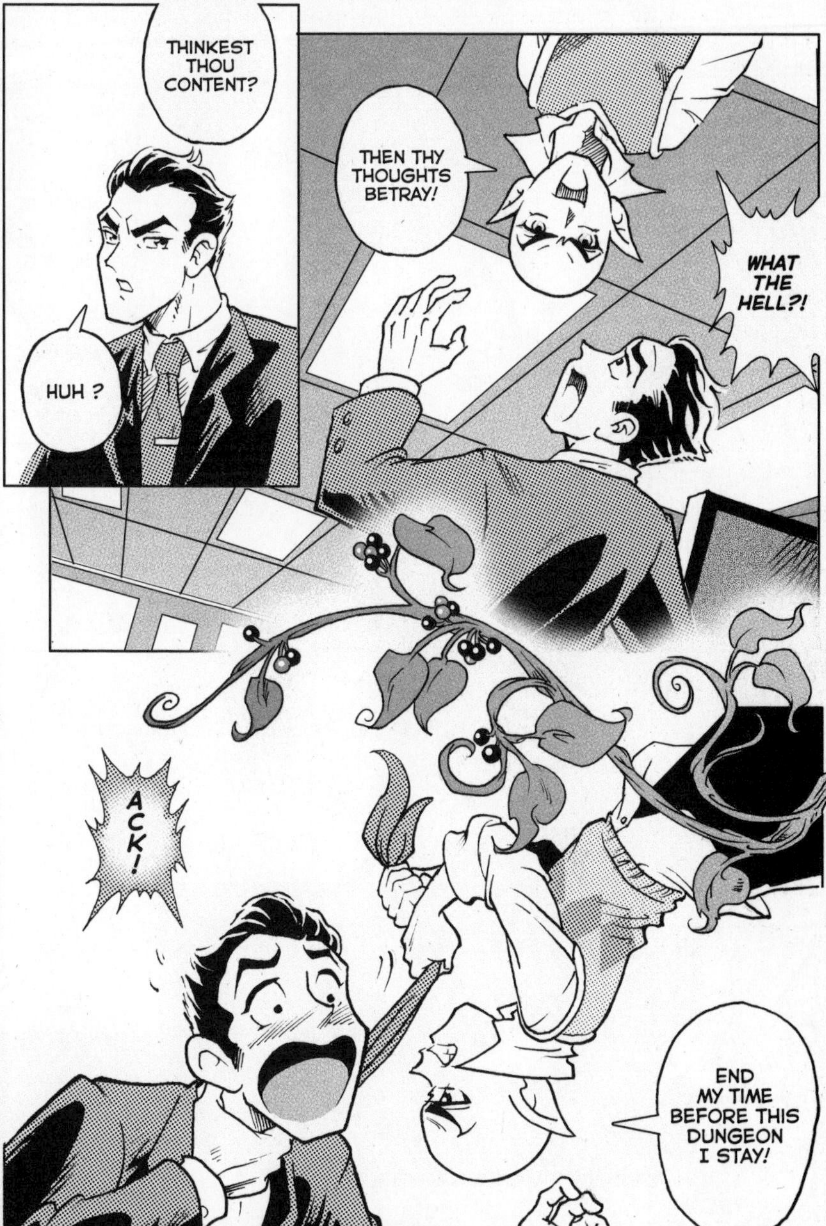
THINKEST THOU CONTENT?
HUH ?
THEN THY THOUGHTS BETRAY!
WHAT THE HELL?!
ACK!
END MY TIME BEFORE THIS DUNGEON I STAY!

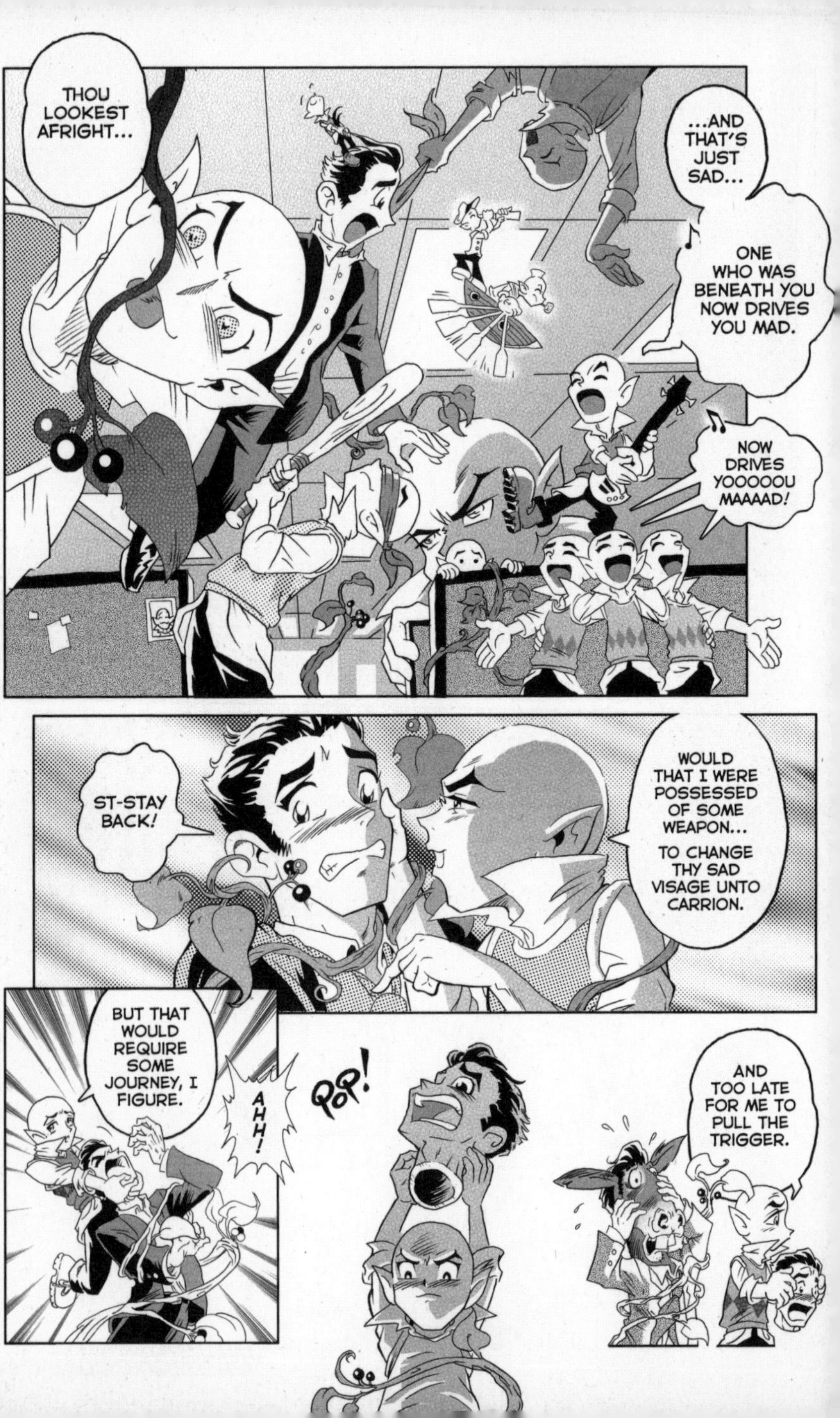
THOU LOOKEST AFRIGHT...
...AND THAT'S JUST SAD...
ONE WHO WAS BENEATH YOU NOW DRIVES YOU MAD.
NOW DRIVES YOOOOOU MAAAAD!
ST-STAY BACK!
WOULD THAT I WERE POSSESSED OF SOME WEAPON...
TO CHANGE THY SAD VISAGE UNTO CARRION.
BUT THAT WOULD REQUIRE SOME JOURNEY, I FIGURE.
AHH!
POP!
AND TOO LATE FOR ME TO PULL THE TRIGGER.

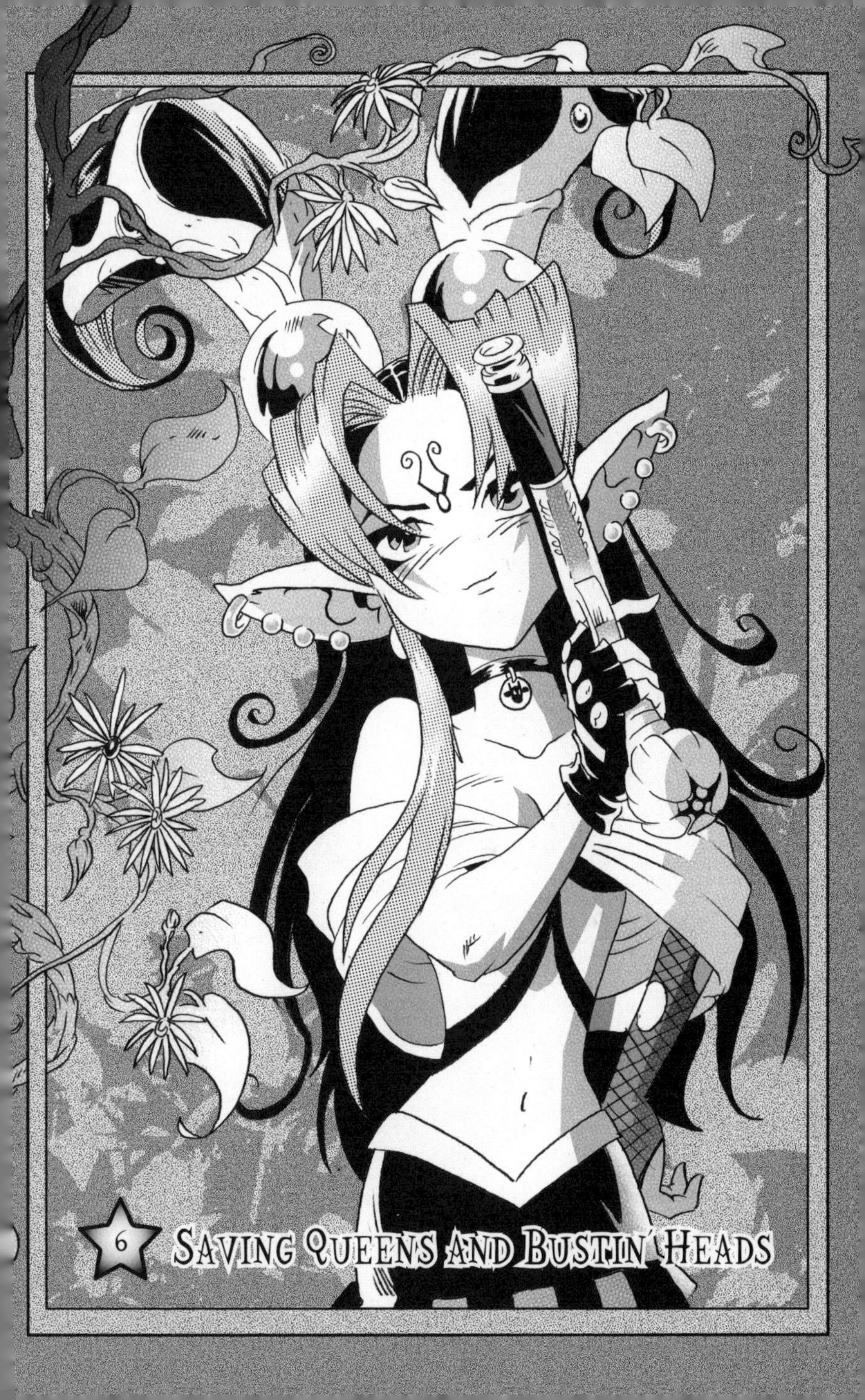

6 Saving Queens and Bustin' Heads

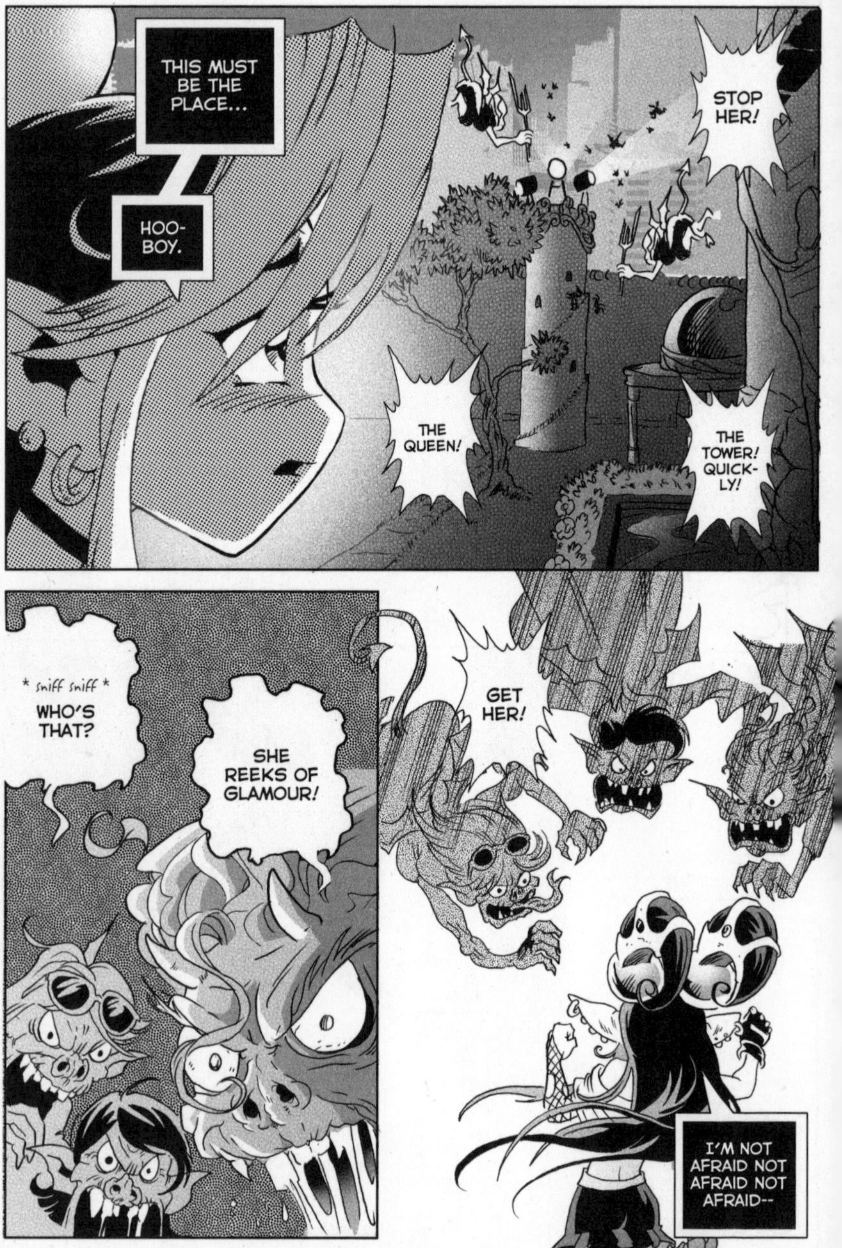
THIS MUST BE THE PLACE...
HOO-BOY.
STOP HER!
THE QUEEN!
THE TOWER! QUICKLY!
* sniff sniff * WHO'S THAT?
SHE REEKS OF GLAMOUR!
GET HER!
I'M NOT AFRAID NOT AFRAID NOT AFRAID--

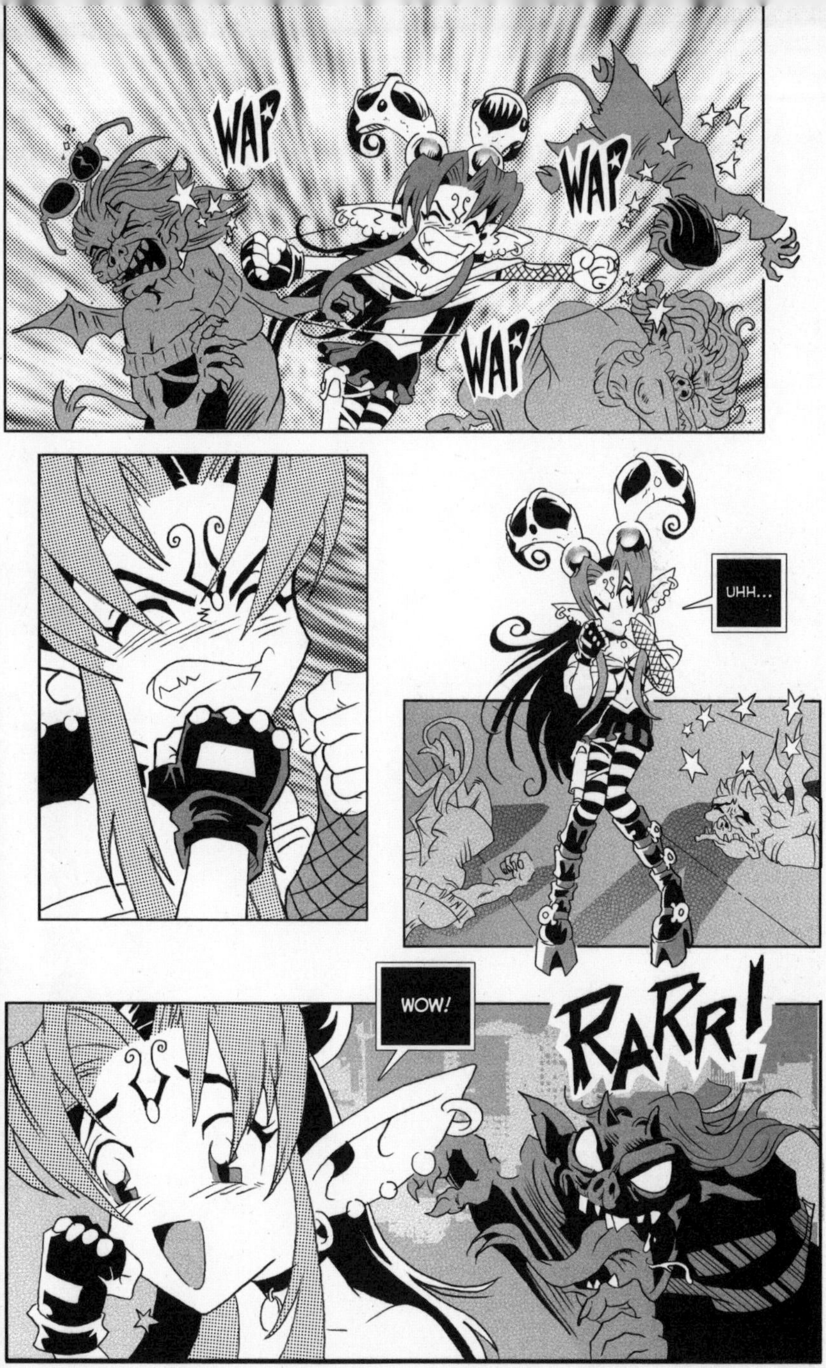
WAP
WAP
WAP
UHH...
WOW!
RARR!

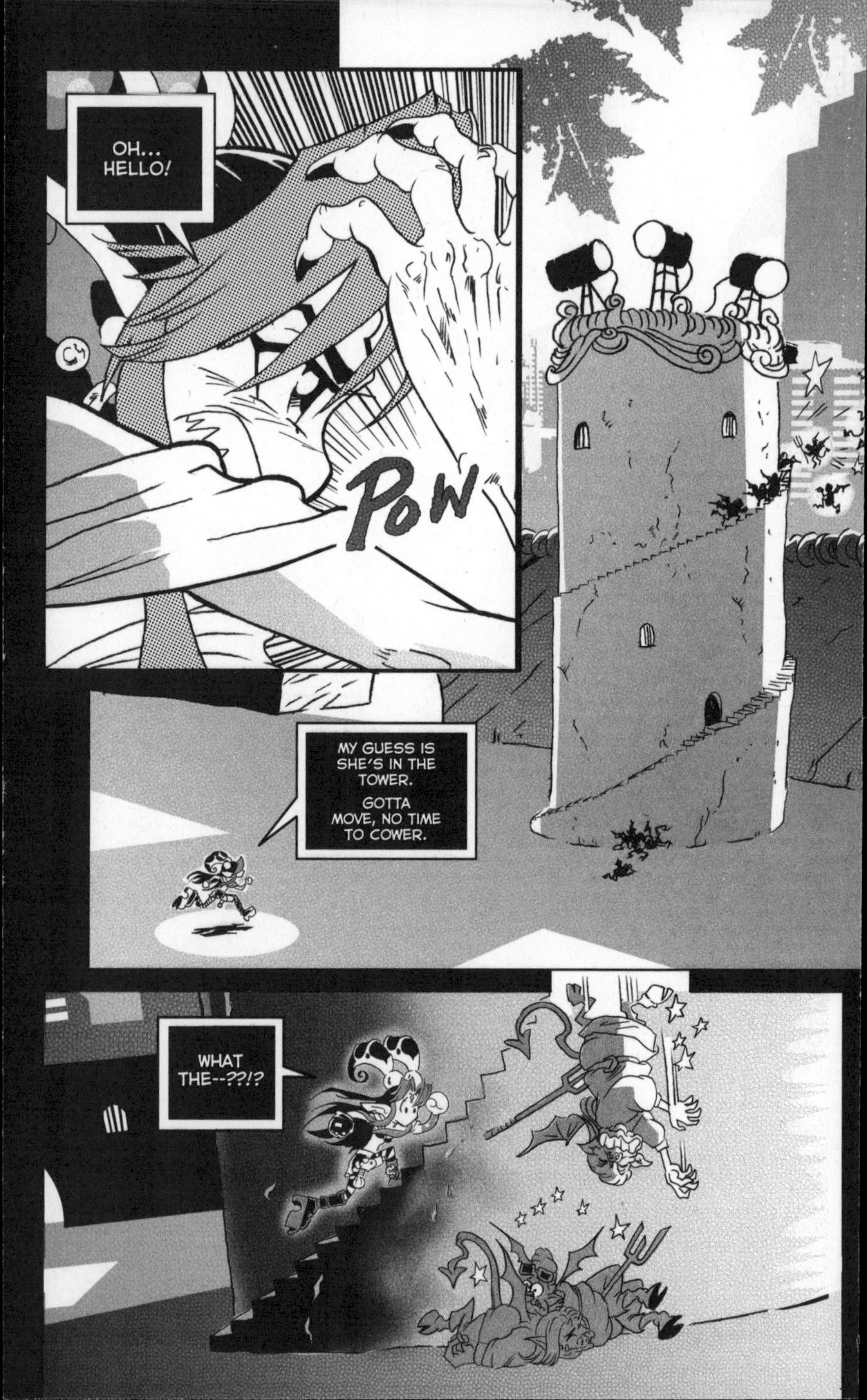
OH... HELLO!
POW
MY GUESS IS SHE'S IN THE TOWER.
GOTTA MOVE, NO TIME TO COWER.
WHAT THE--??!?

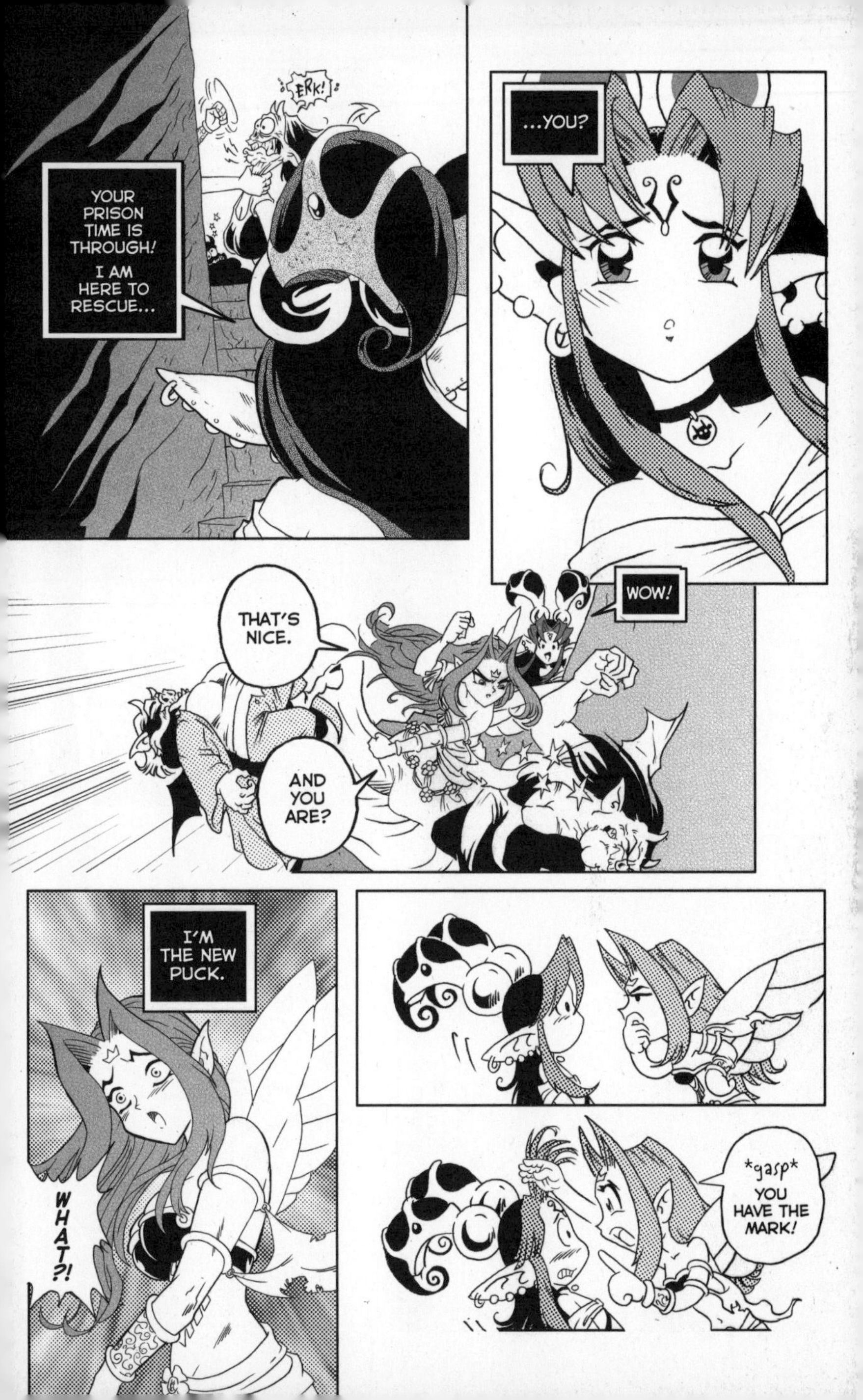
ERK!
YOUR PRISON TIME IS THROUGH! I AM HERE TO RESCUE...
...YOU?
THAT'S NICE.
WOW!
AND YOU ARE?
I'M THE NEW PUCK.
WHAT?!
gasp YOU HAVE THE MARK!

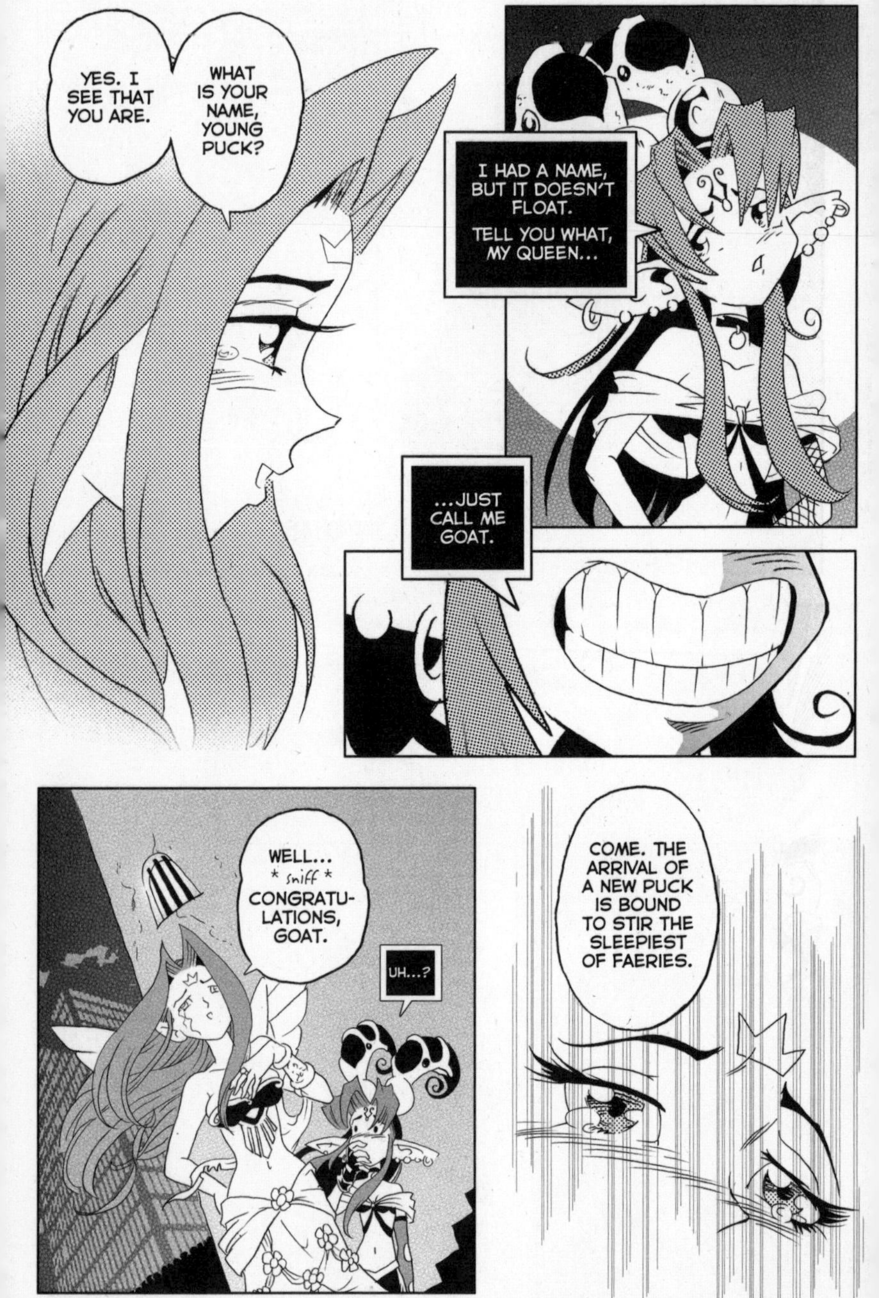
YES. I SEE THAT YOU ARE.
WHAT IS YOUR NAME, YOUNG PUCK?
I HAD A NAME, BUT IT DOESN'T FLOAT.
TELL YOU WHAT, MY QUEEN...
...JUST CALL ME GOAT.
WELL... * sniff * CONGRATU-LATIONS, GOAT.
UH...?
COME. THE ARRIVAL OF A NEW PUCK IS BOUND TO STIR THE SLEEPIEST OF FAERIES.

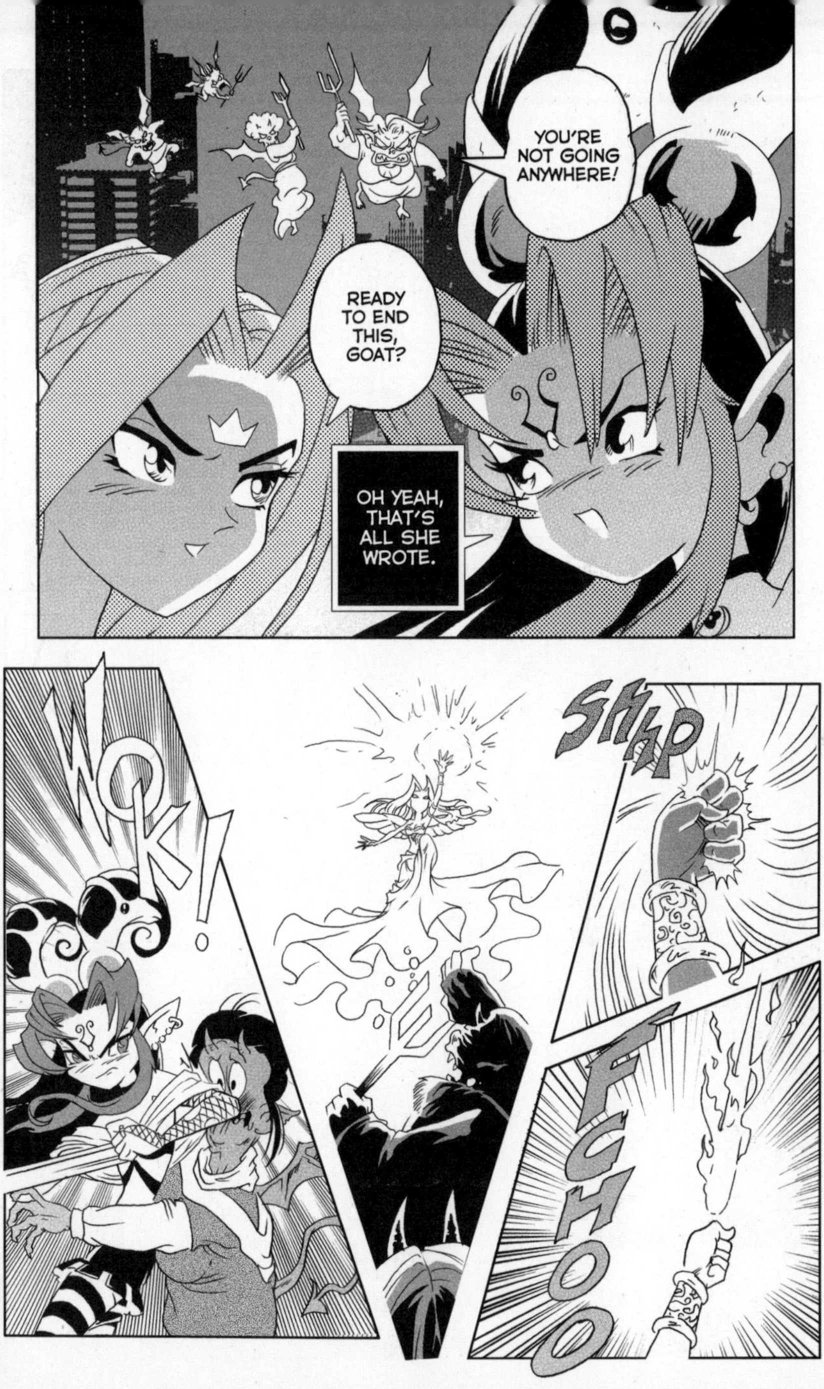
YOU'RE NOT GOING ANYWHERE!
READY TO END THIS, GOAT?
OH YEAH, THAT'S ALL SHE WROTE.
WOK!
SHHP
FCHOOO

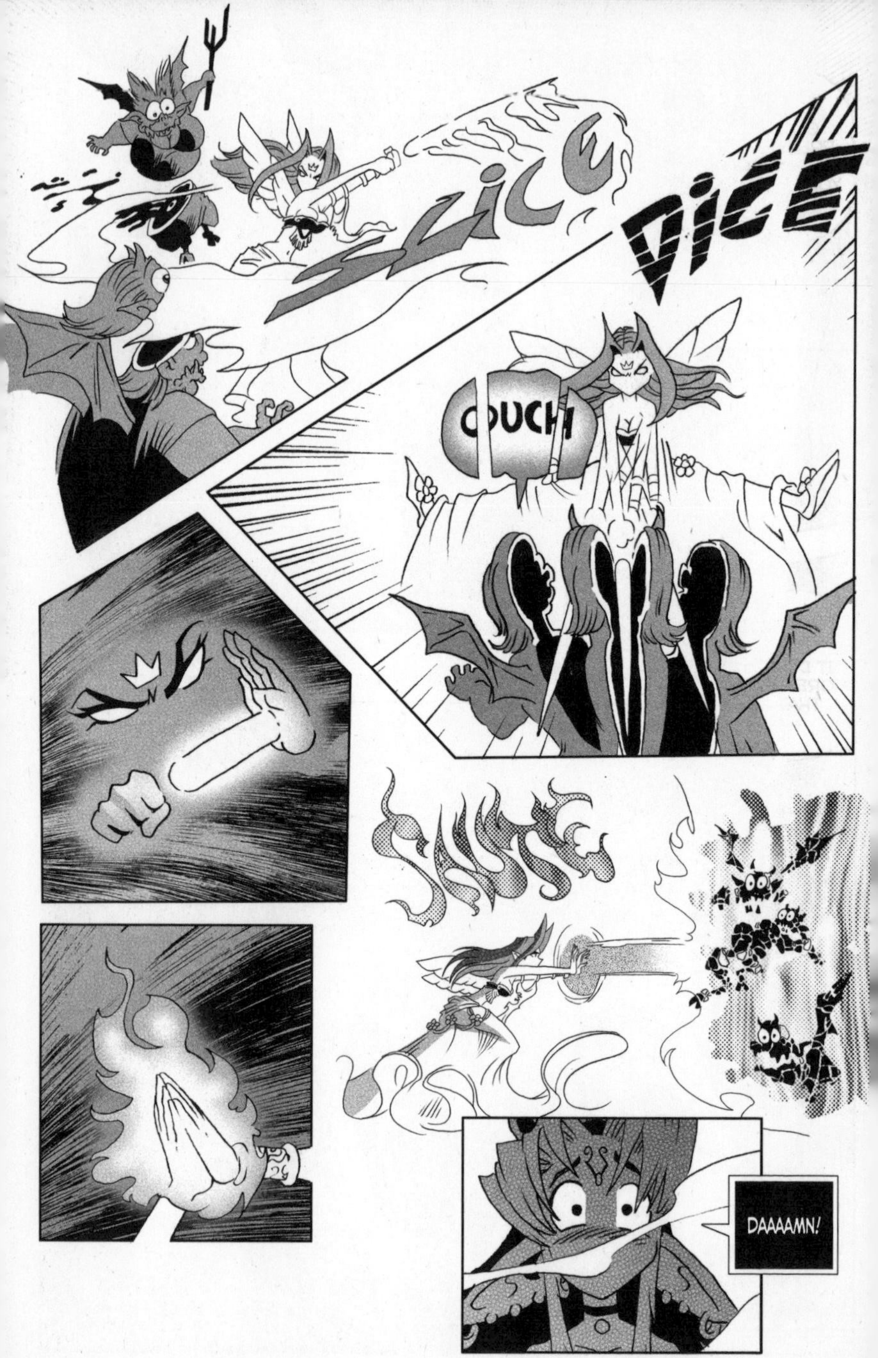
SLICE
DICE
OUCH
DAAAAMN!

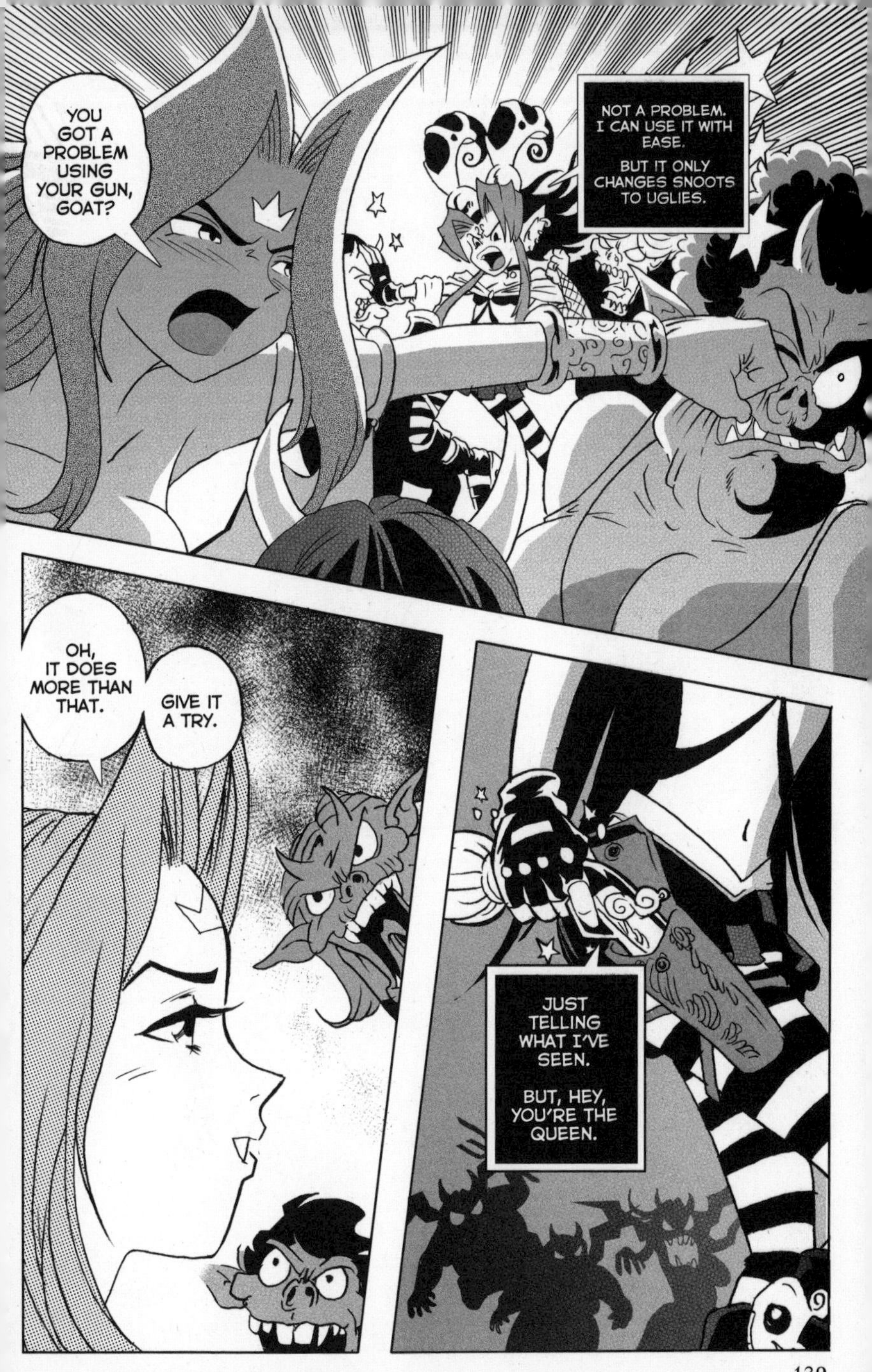
YOU GOT A PROBLEM USING YOUR GUN, GOAT?
NOT A PROBLEM. I CAN USE IT WITH EASE.
BUT IT ONLY CHANGES SNOOTS TO UGLIES.
OH, IT DOES MORE THAN THAT.
GIVE IT A TRY.
JUST TELLING WHAT I'VE SEEN.
BUT, HEY, YOU'RE THE QUEEN.

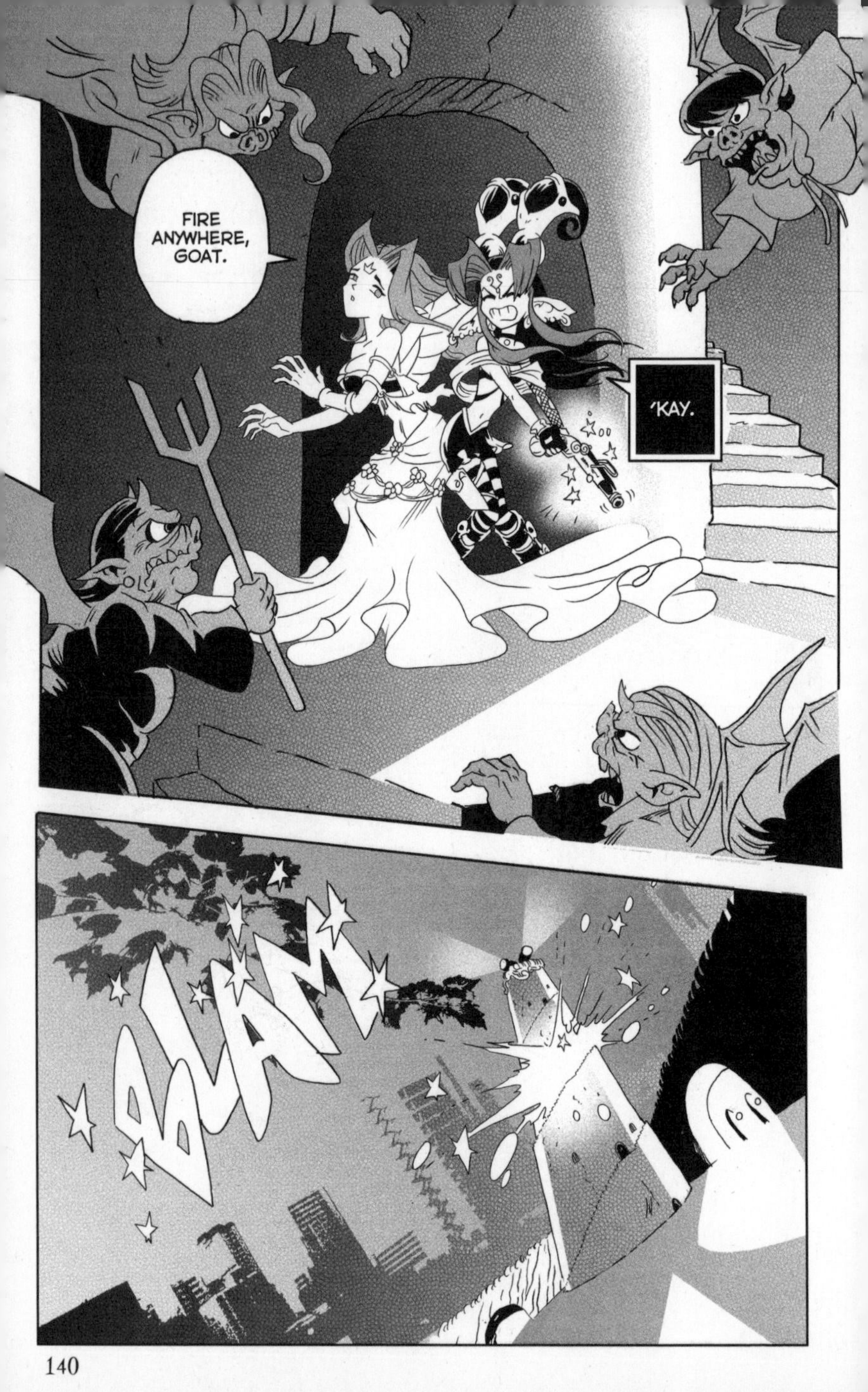
FIRE ANYWHERE, GOAT.
'KAY.
BLAM

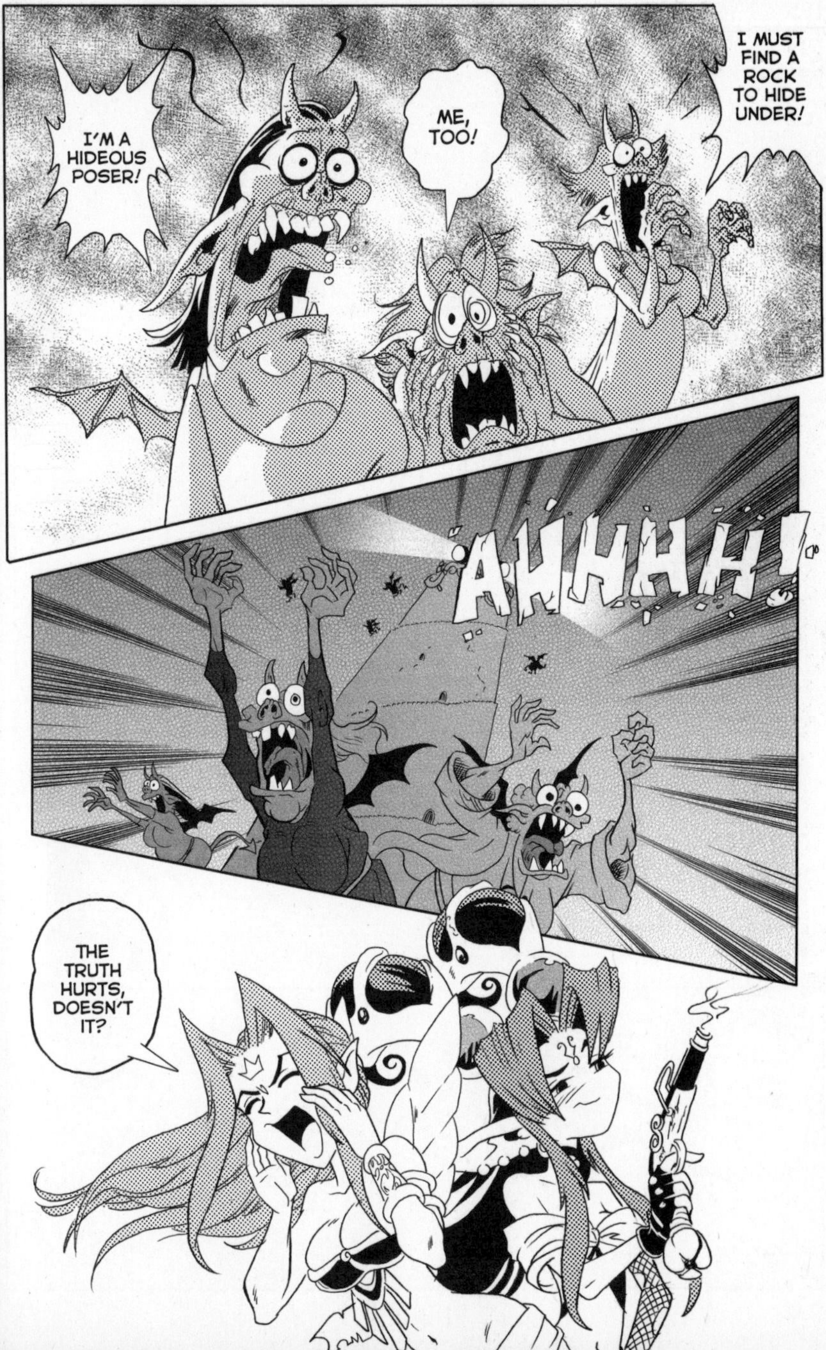
I'M A HIDEOUS POSER!
ME, TOO!
I MUST FIND A ROCK TO HIDE UNDER!
AHHHH!
THE TRUTH HURTS, DOESN'T IT?

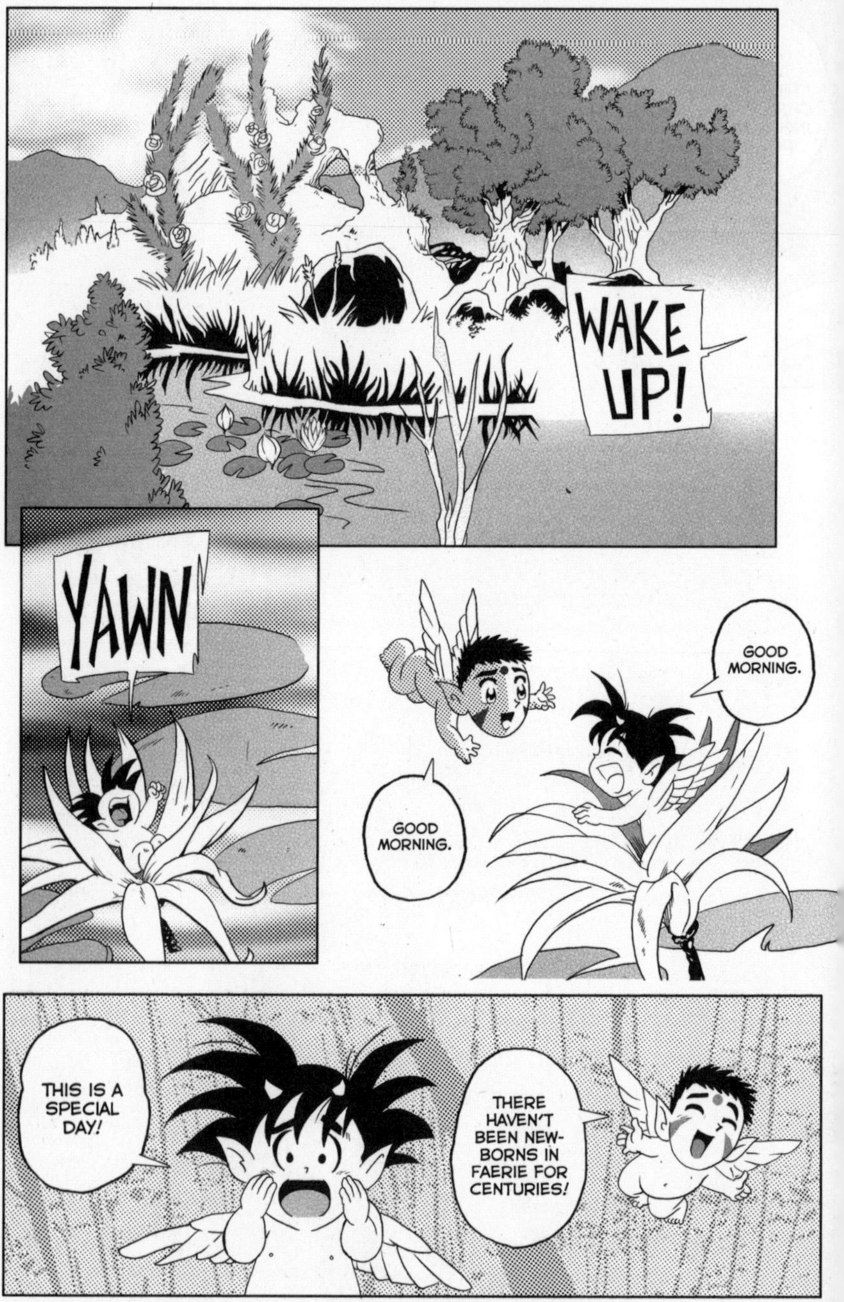
WAKE UP!
YAWN
GOOD MORNING.
GOOD MORNING.
THIS IS A SPECIAL DAY!
THERE HAVEN'T BEEN NEW-BORNS IN FAERIE FOR CENTURIES!

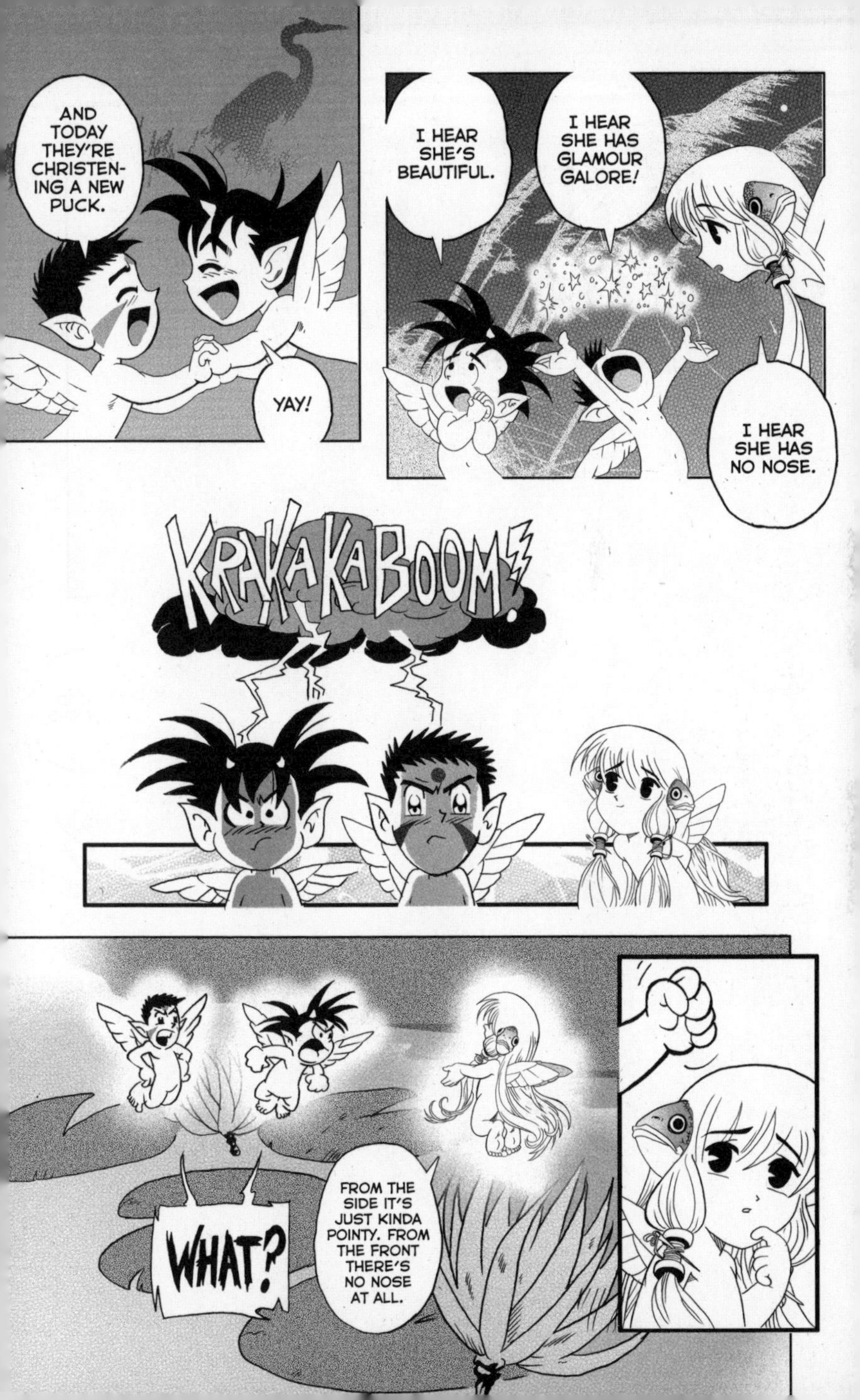
AND TODAY THEY'RE CHRISTEN-ING A NEW PUCK.
YAY!
I HEAR SHE'S BEAUTIFUL.
I HEAR SHE HAS GLAMOUR GALORE!
I HEAR SHE HAS NO NOSE.
KRAKAKABOOM!
WHAT?
FROM THE SIDE IT'S JUST KINDA POINTY. FROM THE FRONT THERE'S NO NOSE AT ALL.

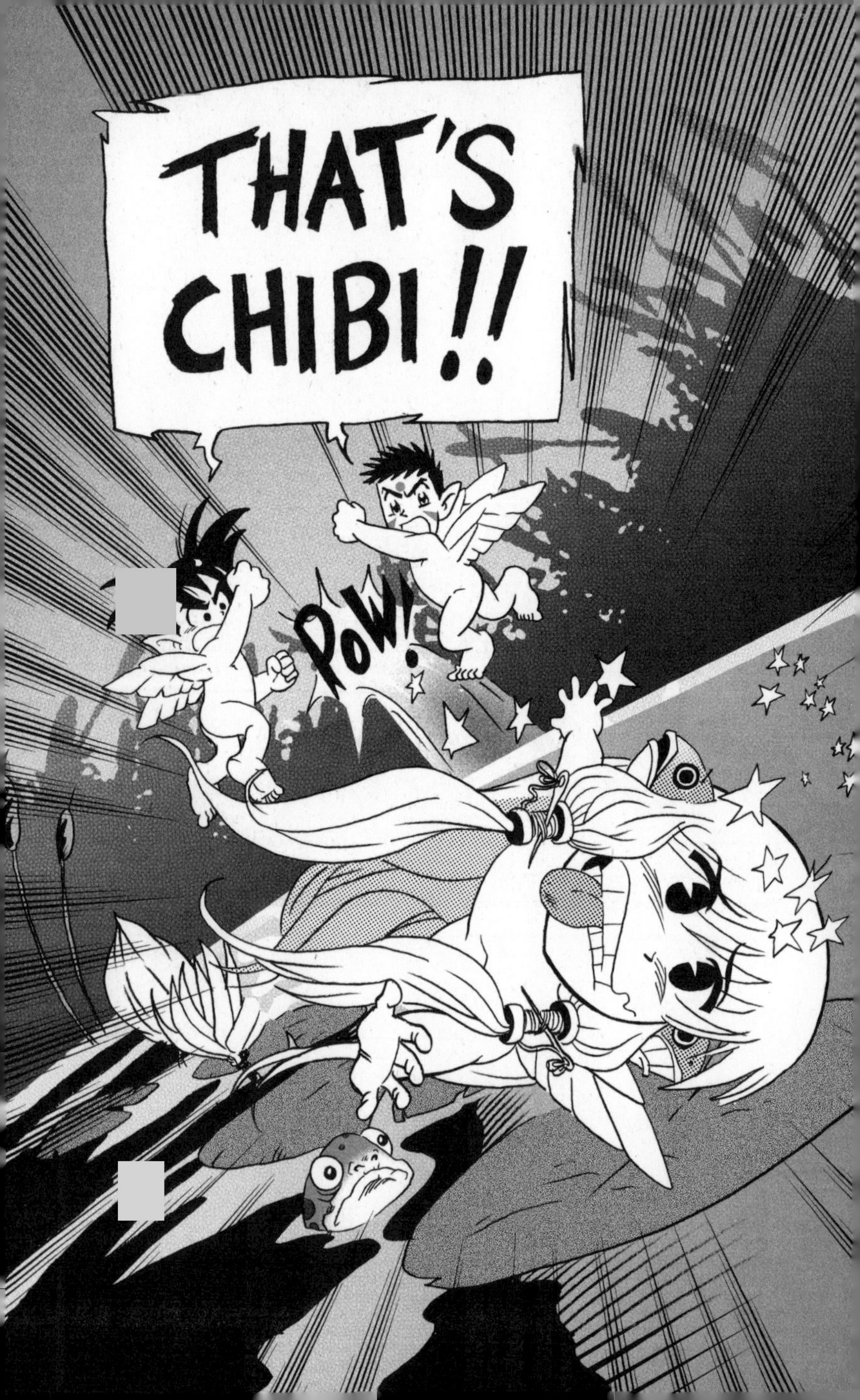
THAT'S CHIBI!!
POW!

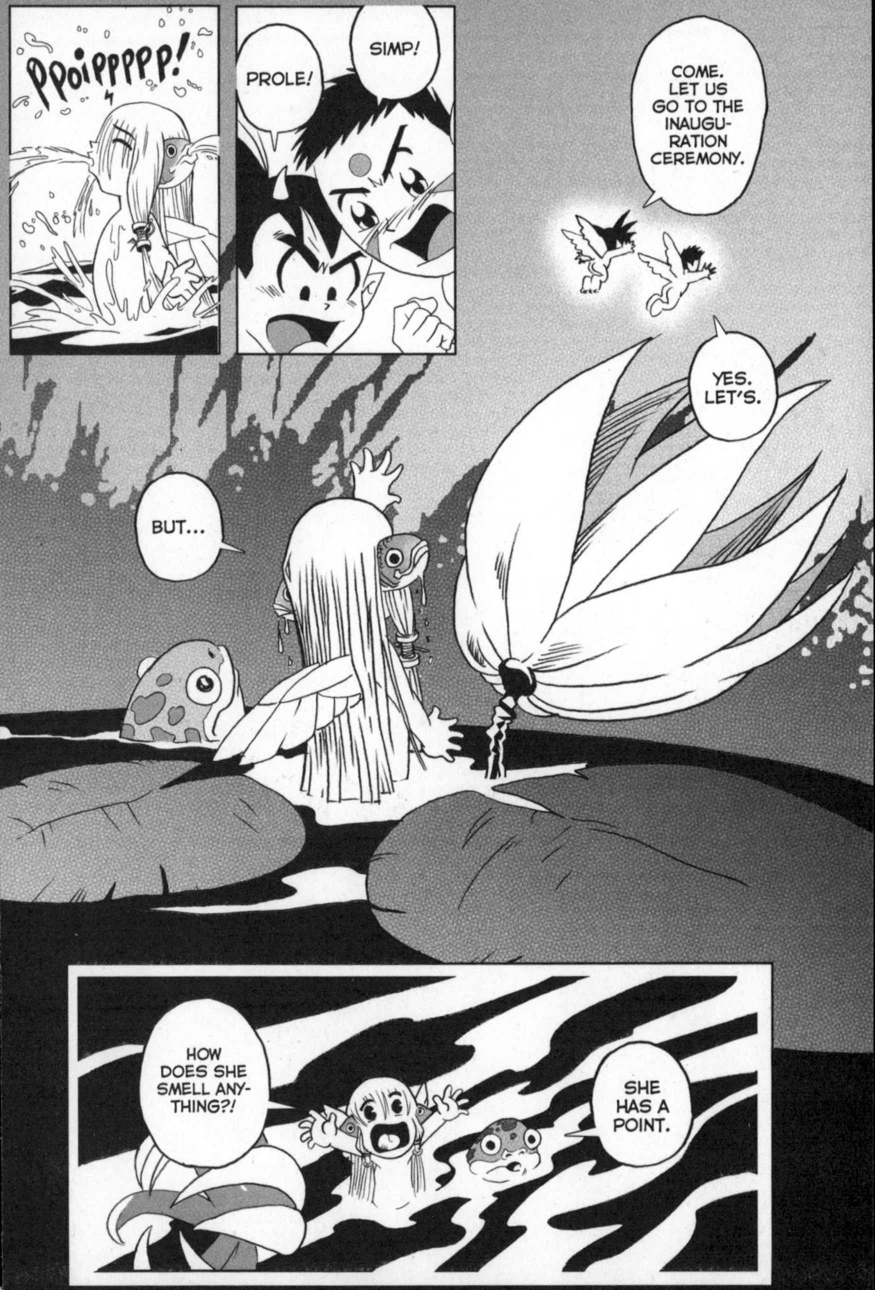
PPOIPPPPP!
PROLE!
SIMP!
COME. LET US GO TO THE INAUGU-RATION CEREMONY.
YES. LET'S.
BUT...
HOW DOES SHE SMELL ANY-THING?!
SHE HAS A POINT.

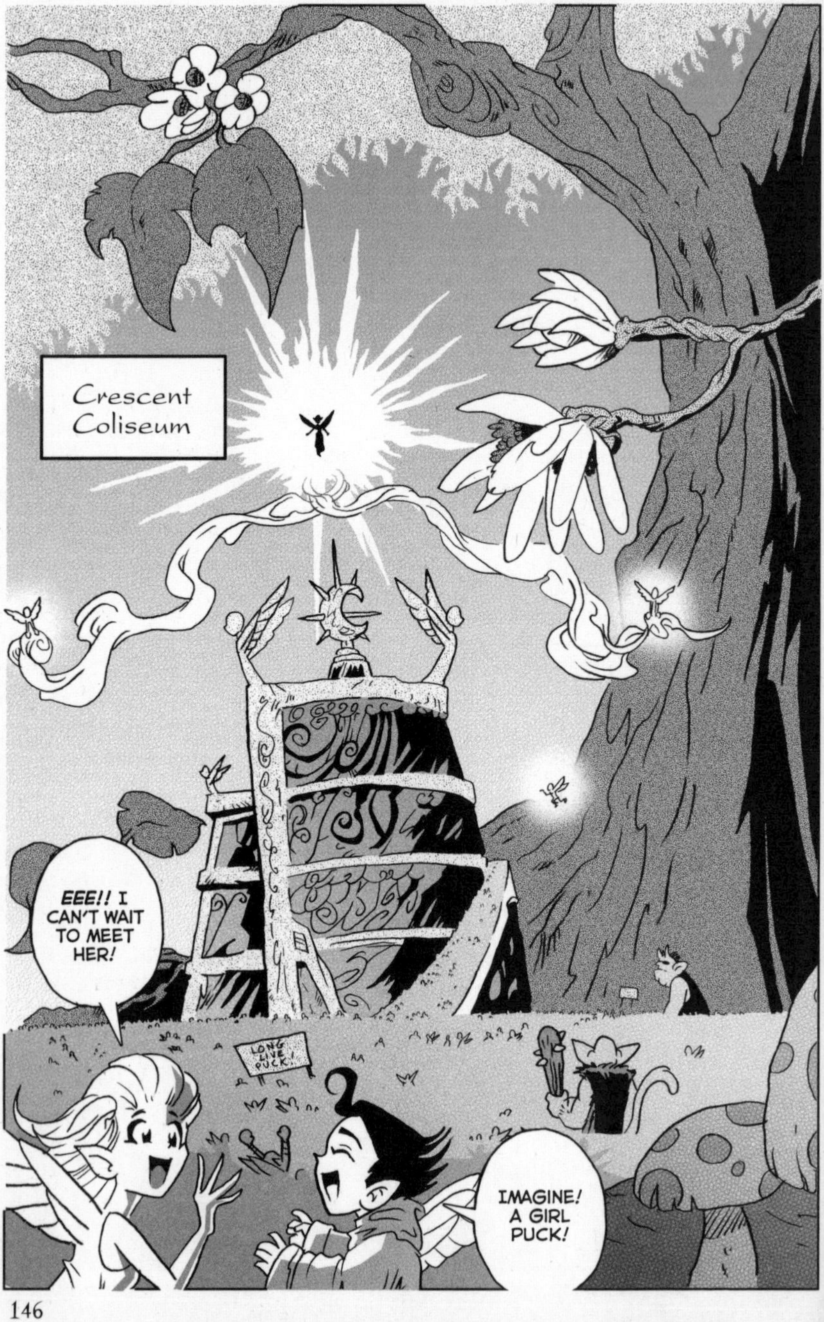
Crescent Coliseum
EEE!! I CAN'T WAIT TO MEET HER!
LONG LIVE PUCK!
IMAGINE! A GIRL PUCK!

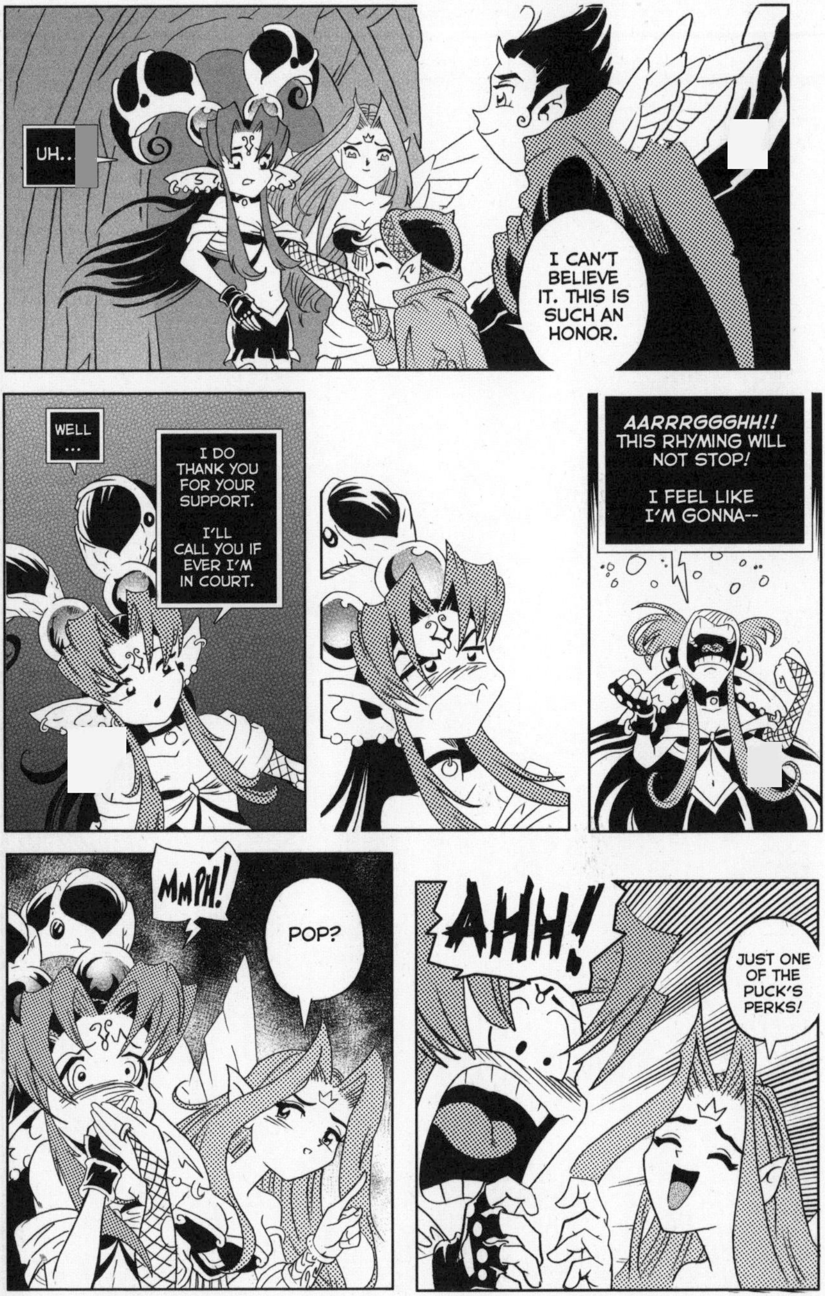
UH..
I CAN'T BELIEVE IT. THIS IS SUCH AN HONOR.
WELL ...
I DO THANK YOU FOR YOUR SUPPORT.
I'LL CALL YOU IF EVER I'M IN COURT.
AARRRGGGHH!! THIS RHYMING WILL NOT STOP!
I FEEL LIKE I'M GONNA--
MMPH!
POP?
AHH!
JUST ONE OF THE PUCK'S PERKS!

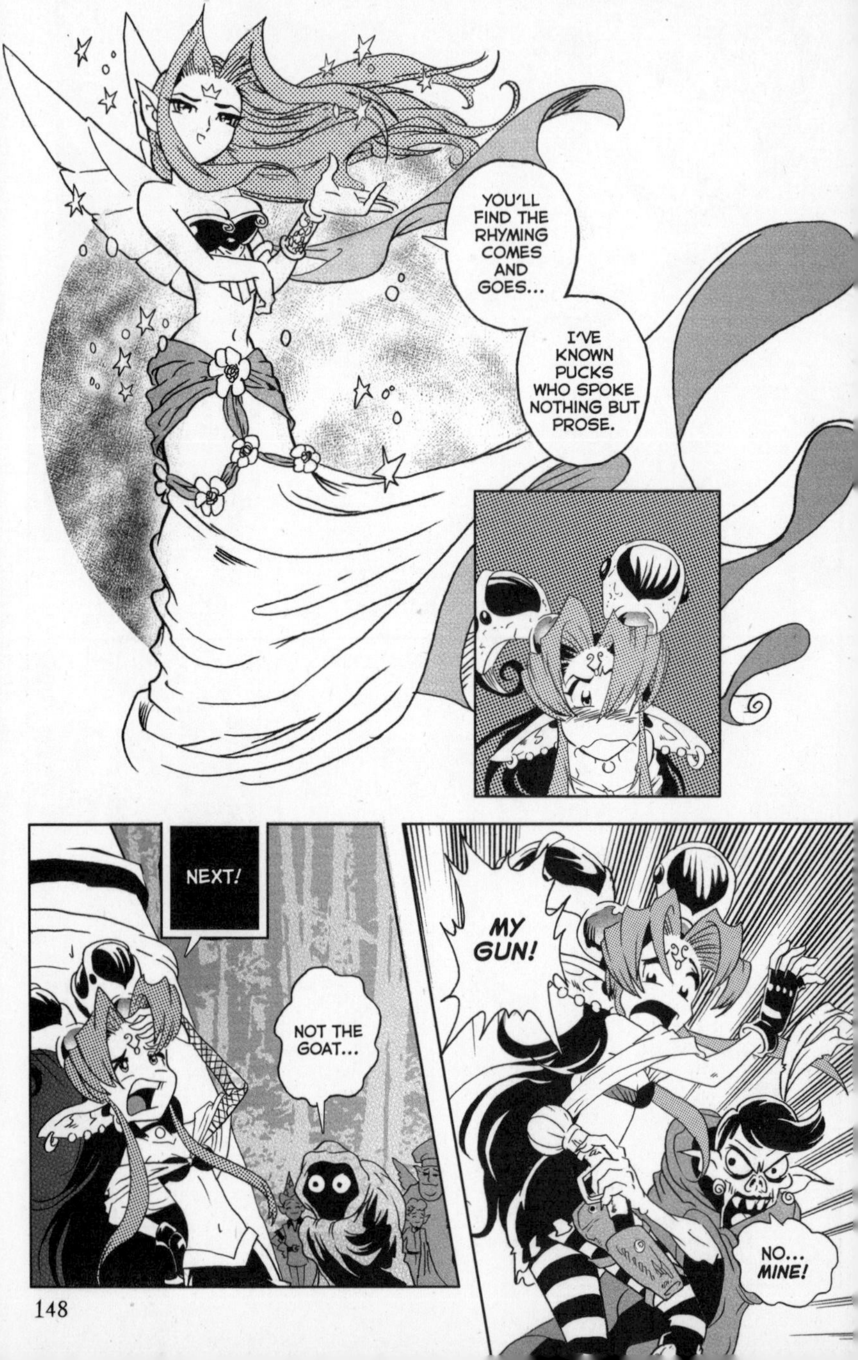
YOU'LL FIND THE RHYMING COMES AND GOES...
I'VE KNOWN PUCKS WHO SPOKE NOTHING BUT PROSE.
NEXT!
NOT THE GOAT...
MY GUN!
NO... MINE!

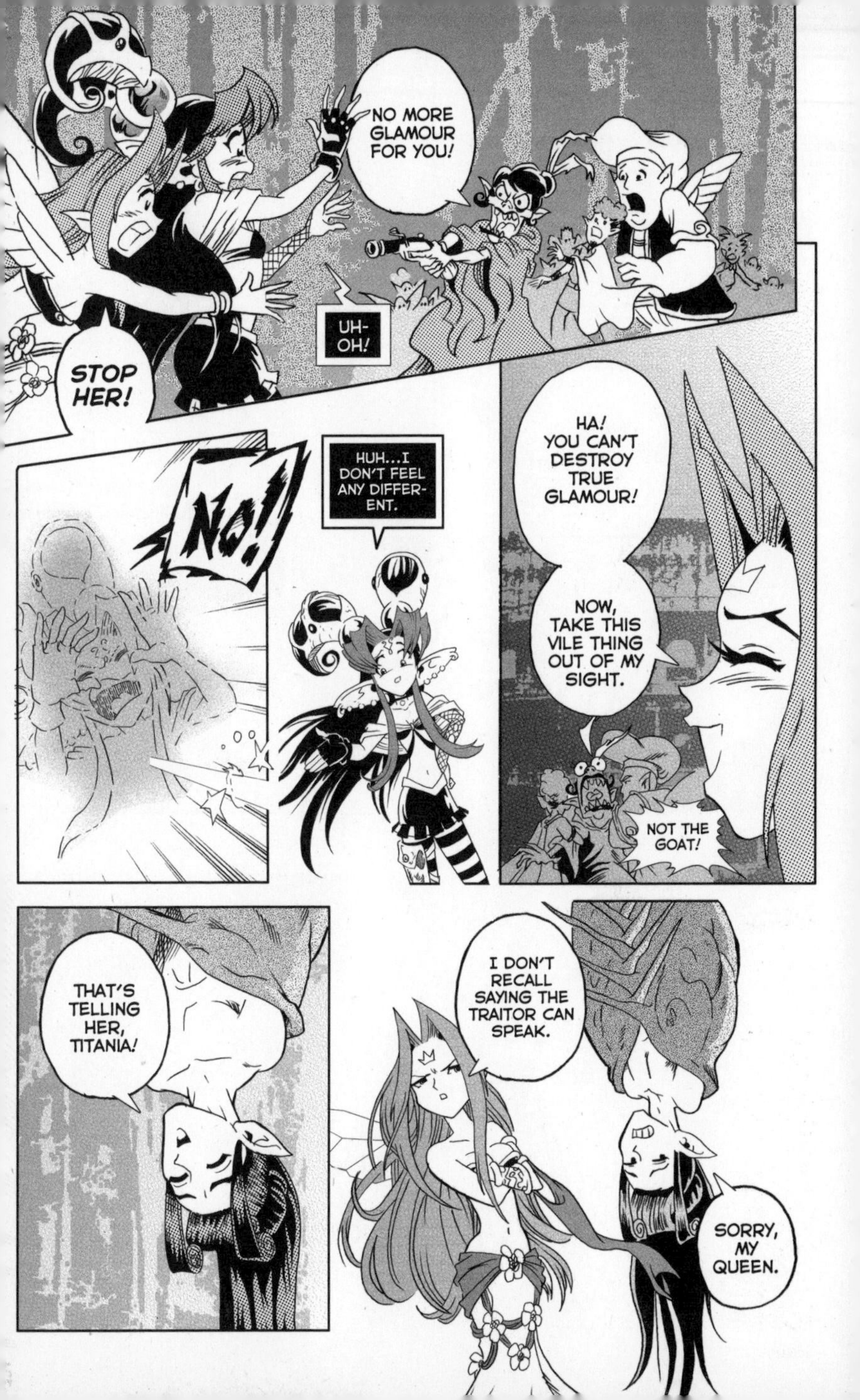
NO MORE GLAMOUR FOR YOU!
UH-OH!
STOP HER!
NO!
HUH...I DON'T FEEL ANY DIFFER-ENT.
HA! YOU CAN'T DESTROY TRUE GLAMOUR!
NOW, TAKE THIS VILE THING OUT OF MY SIGHT.
NOT THE GOAT!
THAT'S TELLING HER, TITANIA!
I DON'T RECALL SAYING THE TRAITOR CAN SPEAK.
SORRY, MY QUEEN.

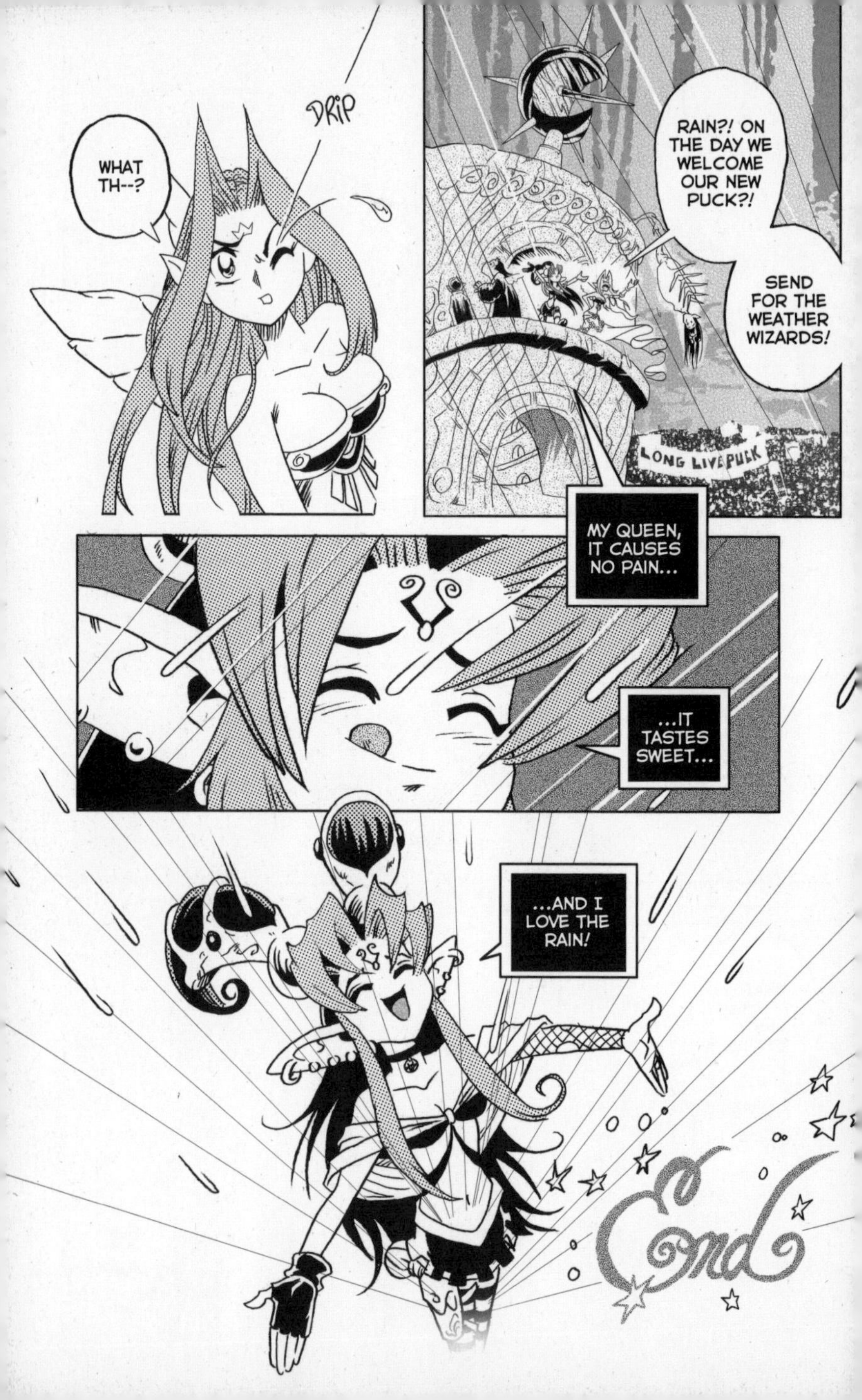
WHAT TH--?
DRIP
RAIN?! ON THE DAY WE WELCOME OUR NEW PUCK?!
SEND FOR THE WEATHER WIZARDS!
LONG LIVE PUCK
MY QUEEN, IT CAUSES NO PAIN...
...IT TASTES SWEET...
...AND I LOVE THE RAIN!
End

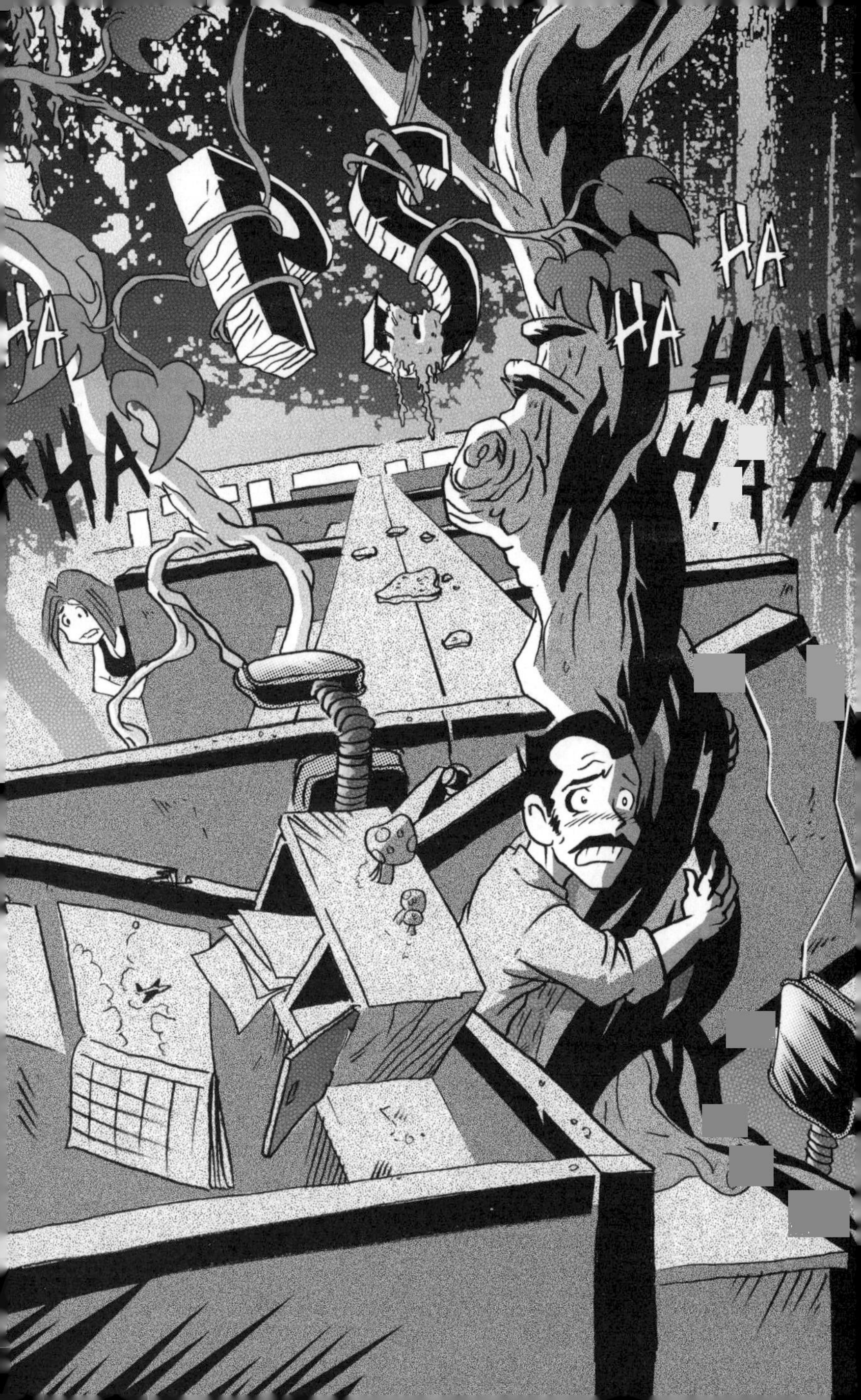
HA
HA
HA
HA
HA HA
HA HA

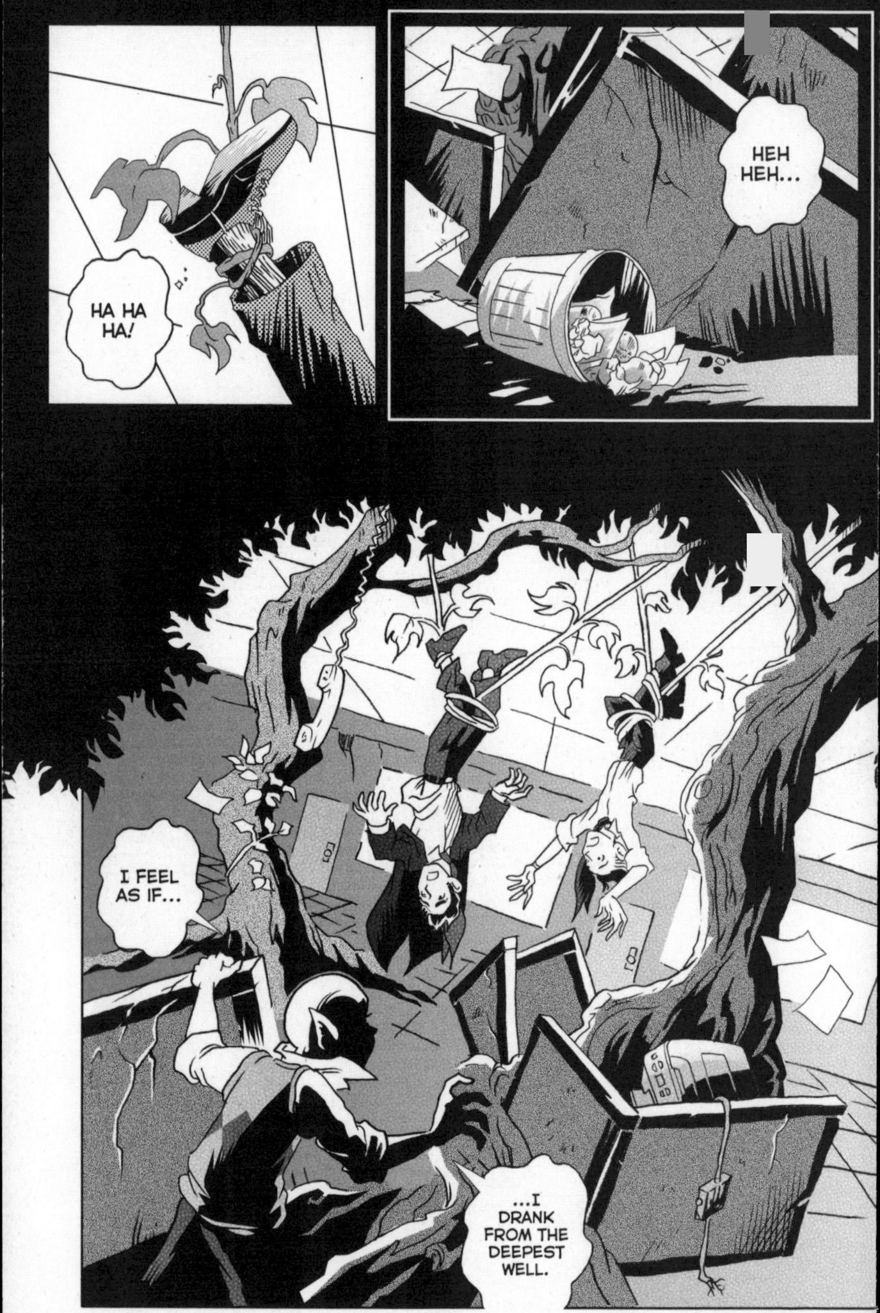
HA HA HA!
HEH HEH...
I FEEL AS IF...
...I DRANK FROM THE DEEPEST WELL.

HA HA HA HA HA HA HA

GARY...

...MR. THOMPSON...

...I'LL SEE YOU IN HELL!

AHHH!!

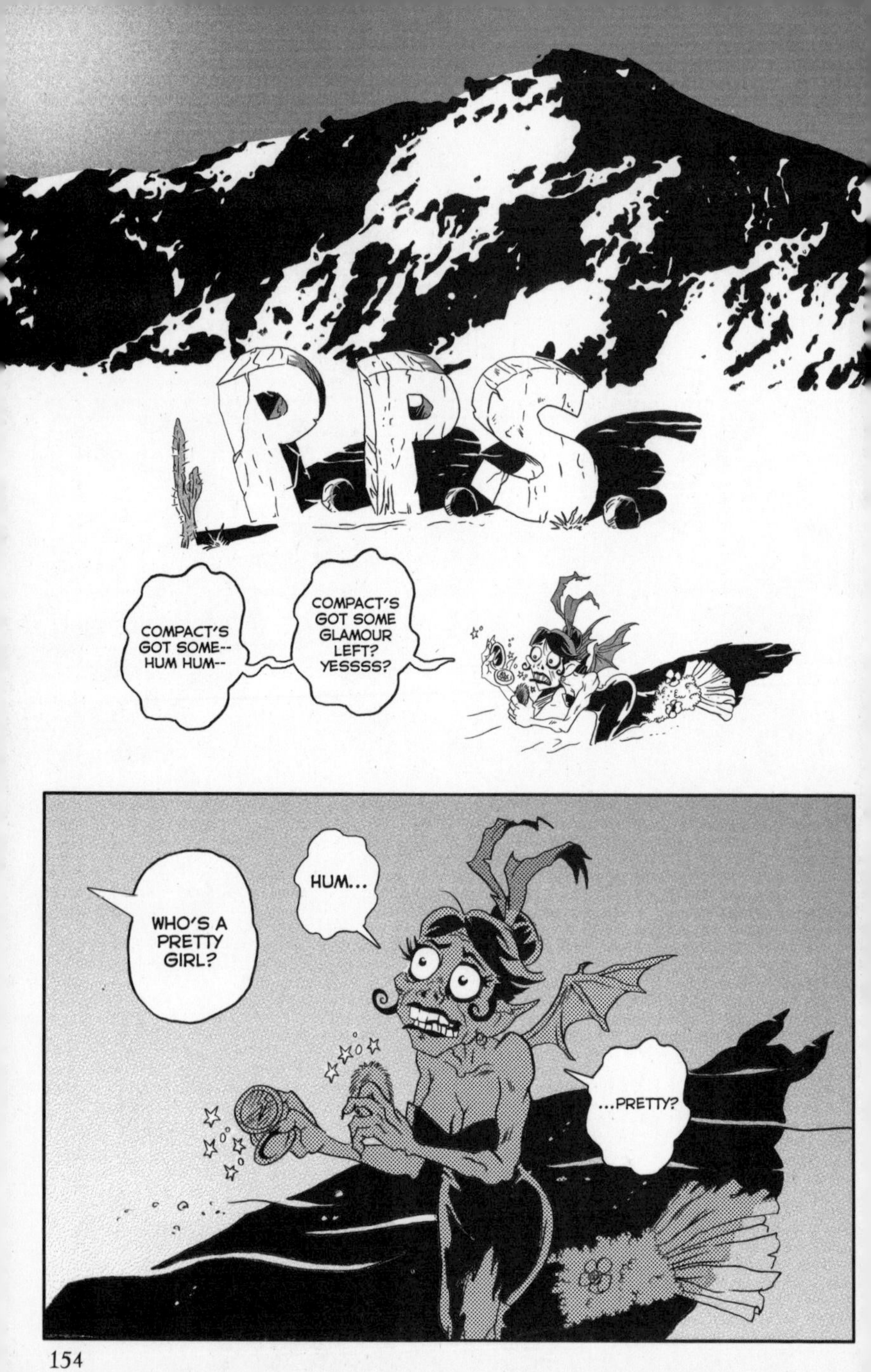
P.P.S.
COMPACT'S GOT SOME-- HUM HUM--
COMPACT'S GOT SOME GLAMOUR LEFT? YESSSS?
WHO'S A PRETTY GIRL?
HUM...
...PRETTY?

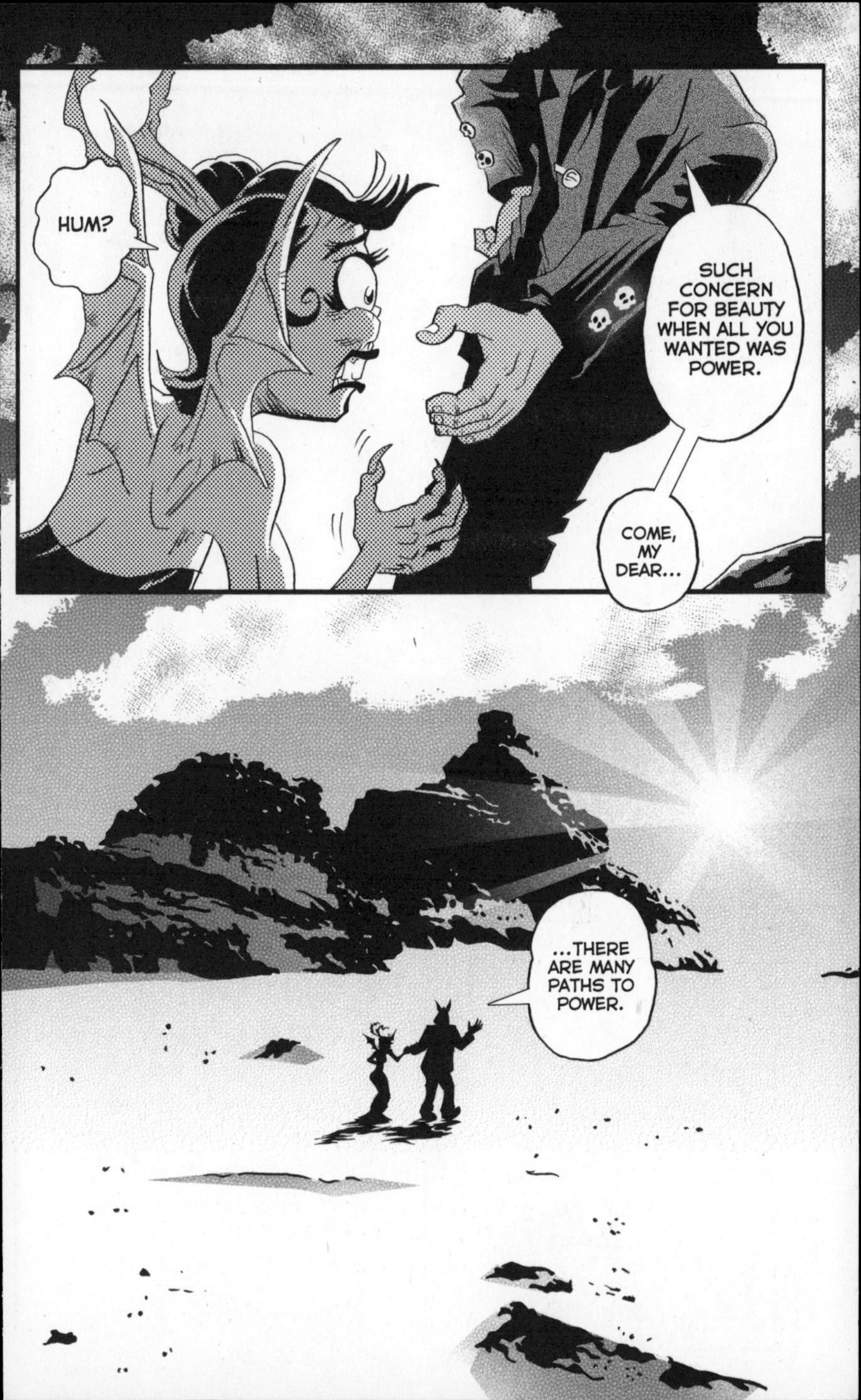
HUM?
SUCH CONCERN FOR BEAUTY WHEN ALL YOU WANTED WAS POWER.
COME, MY DEAR...
...THERE ARE MANY PATHS TO POWER.

Vol. 2 Preview

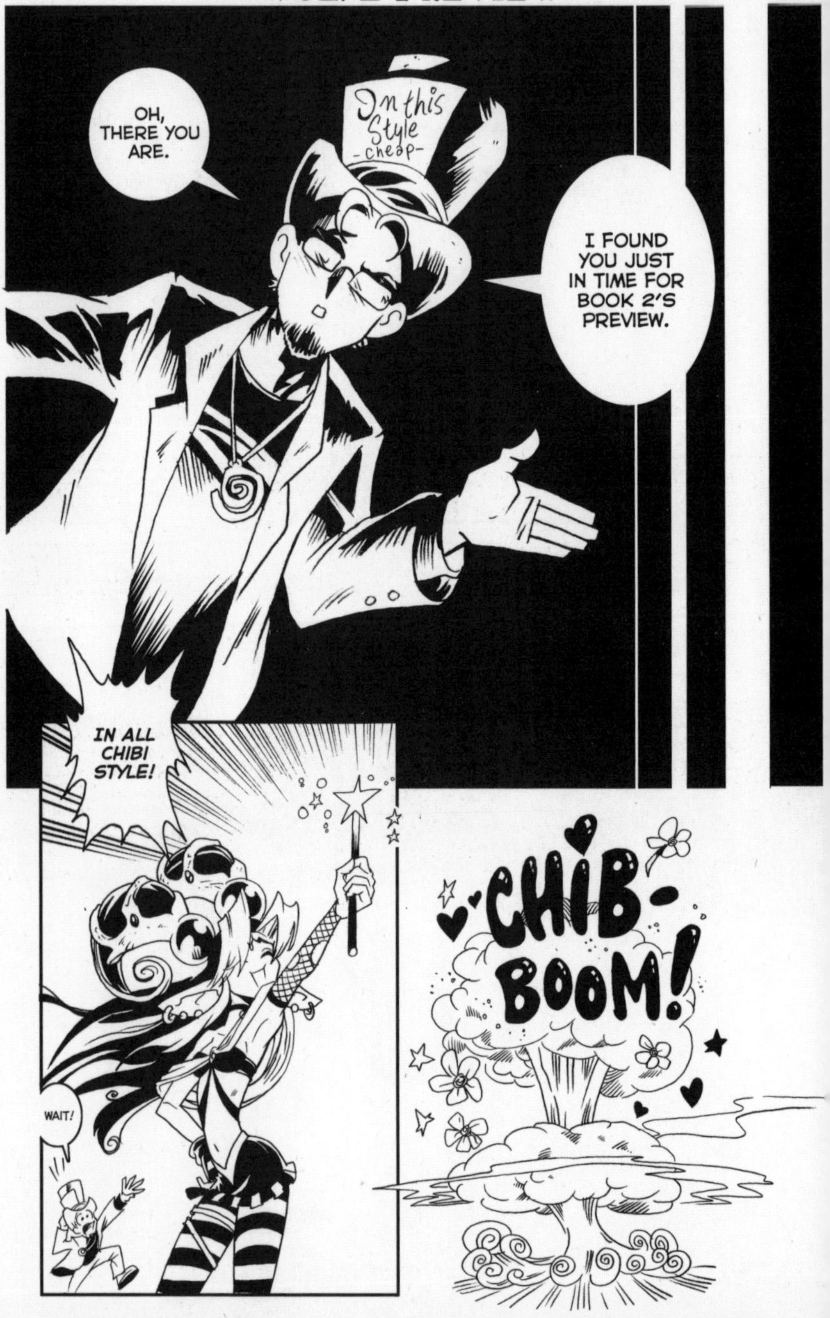

OH, THERE YOU ARE.
In this Style -cheap-
I FOUND YOU JUST IN TIME FOR BOOK 2'S PREVIEW.
IN ALL CHIBI STYLE!
WAIT!
CHIB-BOOM!

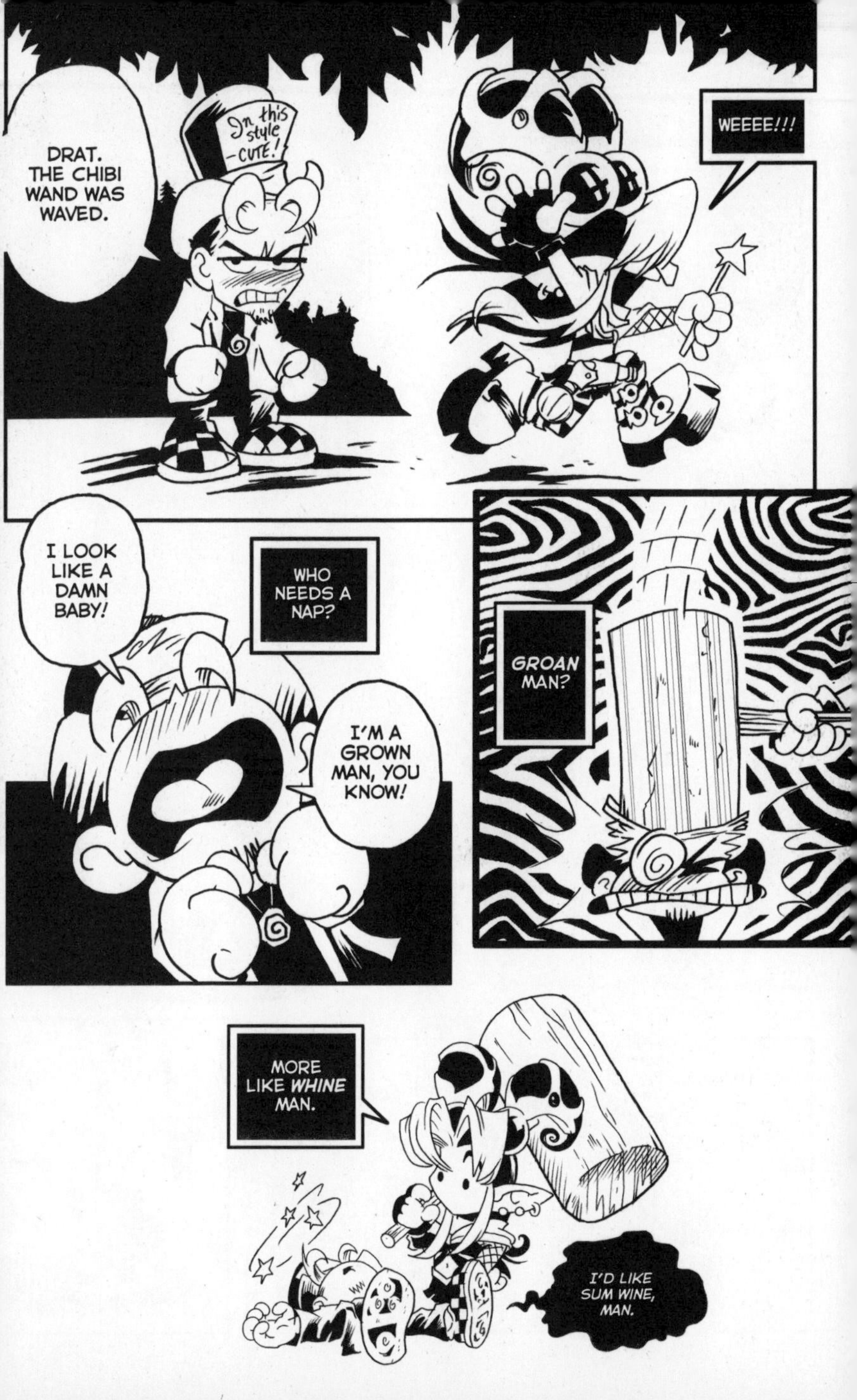
DRAT. THE CHIBI WAND WAS WAVED.
In this style -CUTE!
WEEEE!!!
I LOOK LIKE A DAMN BABY!
WHO NEEDS A NAP?
I'M A GROWN MAN, YOU KNOW!
GROAN MAN?
MORE LIKE WHINE MAN.
I'D LIKE SUM WINE, MAN.

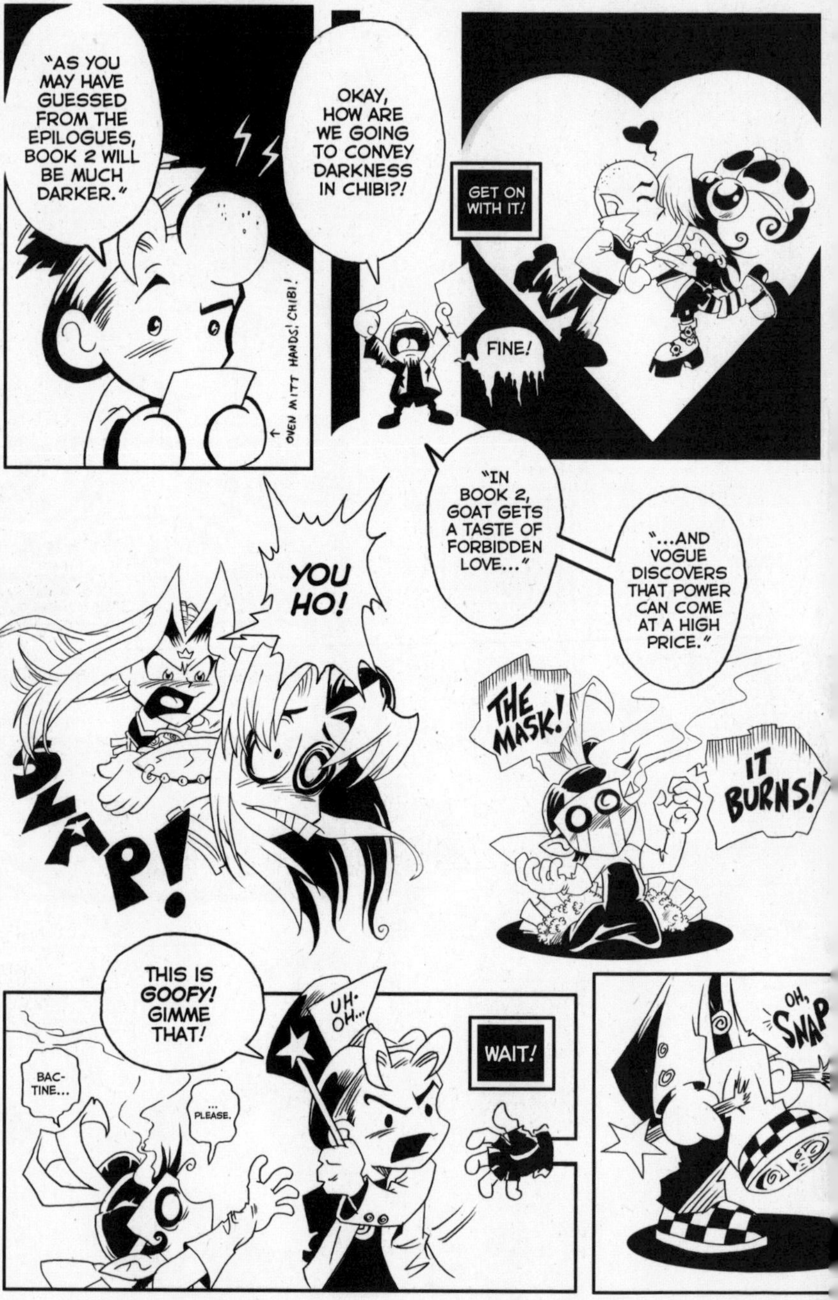
"AS YOU MAY HAVE GUESSED FROM THE EPILOGUES, BOOK 2 WILL BE MUCH DARKER."
OVEN MITT HANDS! CHIBI!
OKAY, HOW ARE WE GOING TO CONVEY DARKNESS IN CHIBI?!
FINE!
GET ON WITH IT!
"IN BOOK 2, GOAT GETS A TASTE OF FORBIDDEN LOVE..."
YOU HO!
SNAP!
"...AND VOGUE DISCOVERS THAT POWER CAN COME AT A HIGH PRICE."
THE MASK!
IT BURNS!
THIS IS GOOFY! GIMME THAT!
BAC-TINE...
... PLEASE.
UH-OH...
WAIT!
OH, SNAP

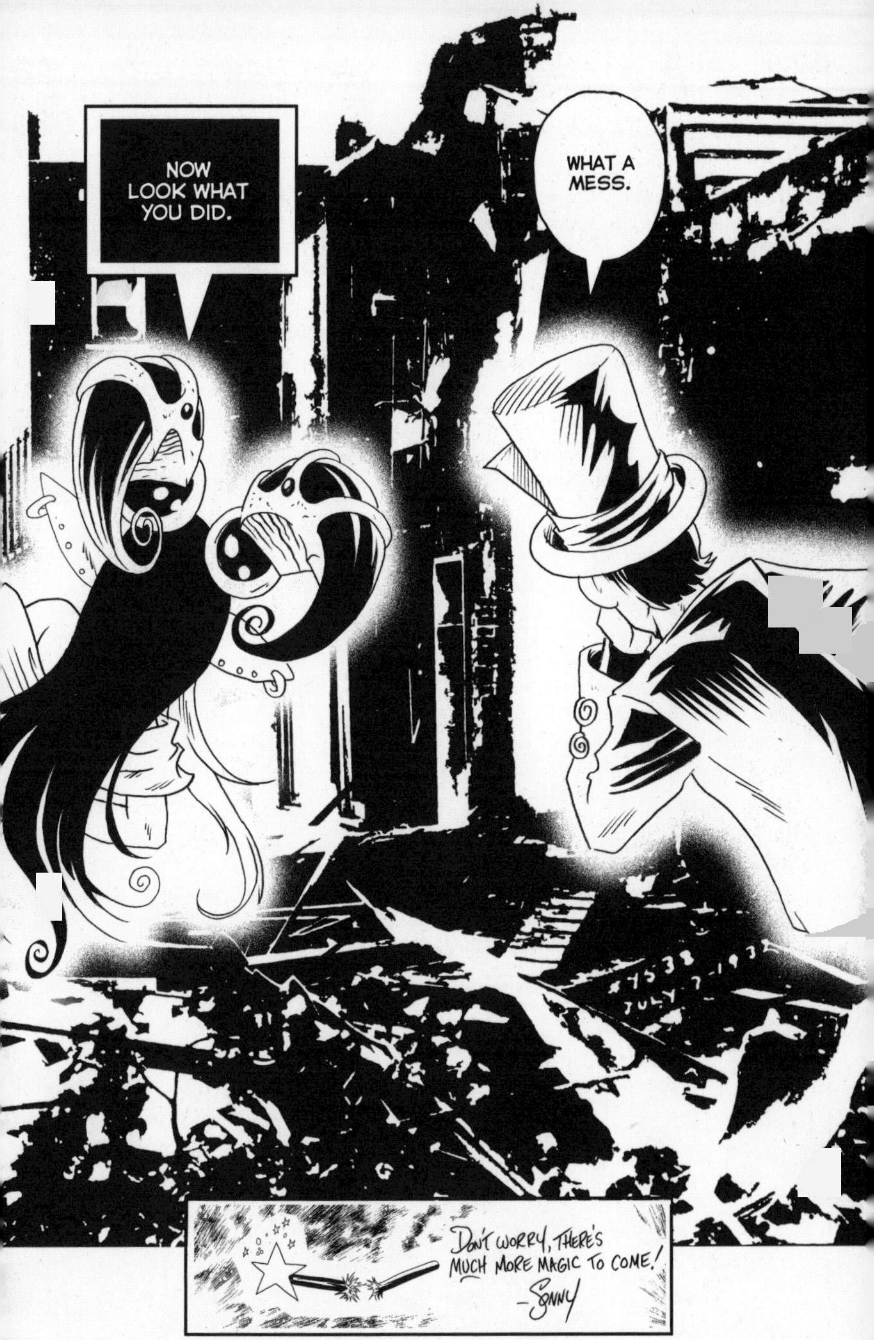
NOW LOOK WHAT YOU DID.
WHAT A MESS.
DON'T WORRY, THERE'S MUCH MORE MAGIC TO COME!
-SONNY

My 24 Hour Comic

By Sonny

THE DARE:

"To create a complete 24 page comic book in 24 continuous hours.
That means everything: Story, finished art, lettering, colors (if you want 'em), paste-up, everything! Once pen hits paper, the clock starts ticking. 24 hours later, the pen lifts off the paper, never to descend again. Even proofreading has to occur in the 24 hour period."

These are the words and challenge from maverick cartoonist Scott McCloud. During the course of illustrating this volume of We Shadows, I took a hiatus to be one of the many cartoonists to brave Mr. McCloud's dare. It was an amazing experience and I encourage any artist to try it.

One thing that you have to understand before beginning...it's not a beauty contest. I can not stress this enough. You have 24 hours to draw 24 pages. The math is very simple...

1 hour = 1 page

Seems uncomplicated yet so many people failed to grasp it. In the comic shop I participated we had over twenty attendees. Out of those only three finished. Three! This wasn't because they lacked the endurance. Many had several false starts, chucking ideas trying to find "the right one." Others spent far too much time trying to make their art presentable. Hour four rolled around and I asked people how they were faring. Some were still trying to come up with an idea. Others were drawing page one for the fourth time. I remember thinking "How are they going to make it?" Of course, they didn't. What happened was toward the final hours the math started kicking in and the realization that they were never going to finish in time caused them to quit.

1 hour = 1 page

So here are the fruits of my twisted labor. I hope you like "Pre-shrink" and that you forgive the rough edges. Speaking of forgiveness, I pray to the gods of Comicdom that Mr. McCloud overlooks my little jab at him on the last page. I was genuinely punch-drunk after climbing this Everest of Comics and I have nothing but the highest regards for him and his contributions to the medium I love so much.

I've explained my process for those who are interested after the story.
Enjoy!

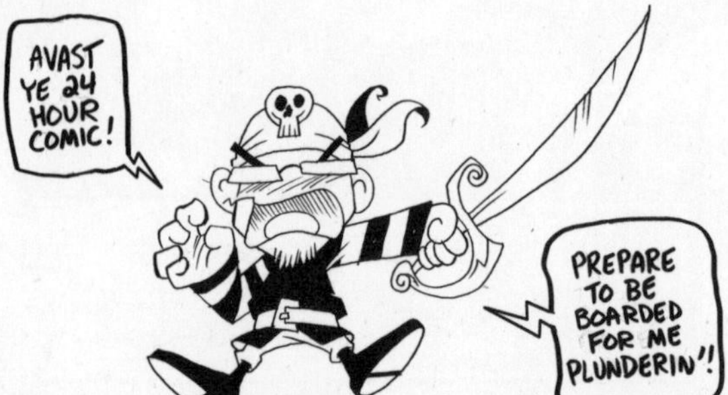
AVAST YE 24 HOUR COMIC!
PREPARE TO BE BOARDED FOR ME PLUNDERIN'!!

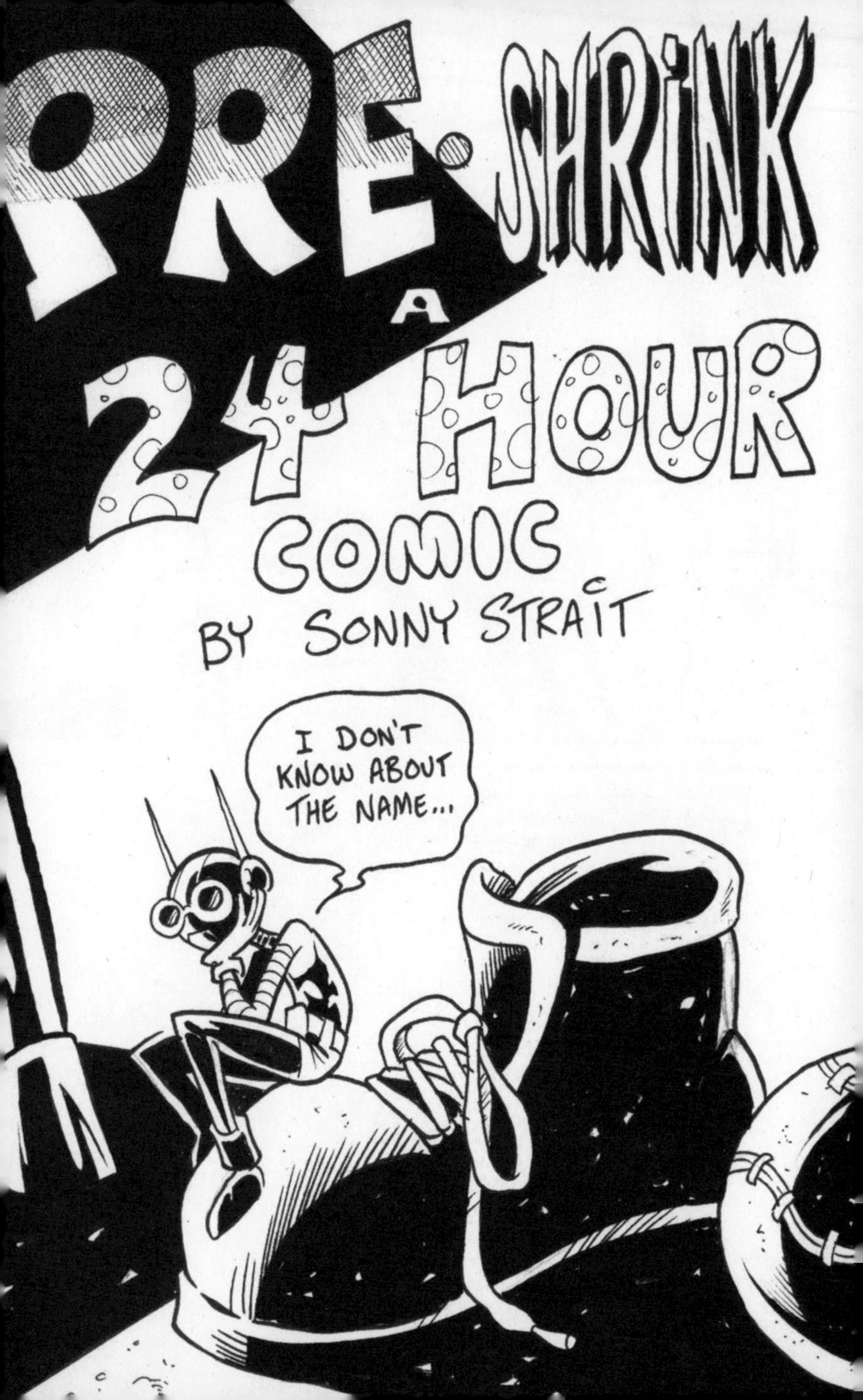
PRE-SHRINK
A
24 HOUR
COMIC
BY SONNY STRAIT
I DON'T KNOW ABOUT THE NAME...

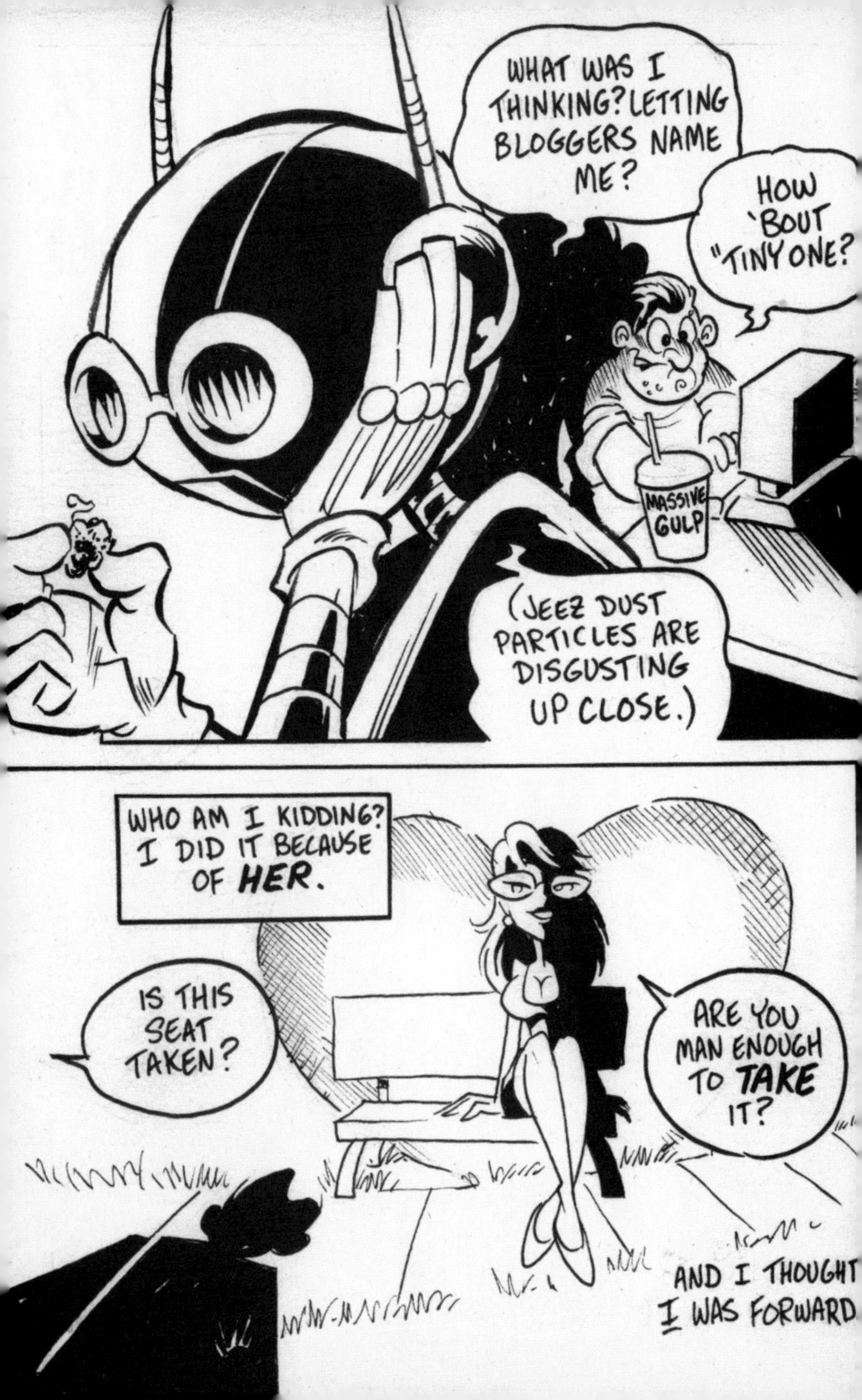
WHAT WAS I THINKING? LETTING BLOGGERS NAME ME?
HOW 'BOUT "TINY ONE?
MASSIVE GULP
(JEEZ DUST PARTICLES ARE DISGUSTING UP CLOSE.)
WHO AM I KIDDING? I DID IT BECAUSE OF **HER**.
IS THIS SEAT TAKEN?
ARE YOU MAN ENOUGH TO **TAKE** IT?
AND I THOUGHT I WAS FORWARD

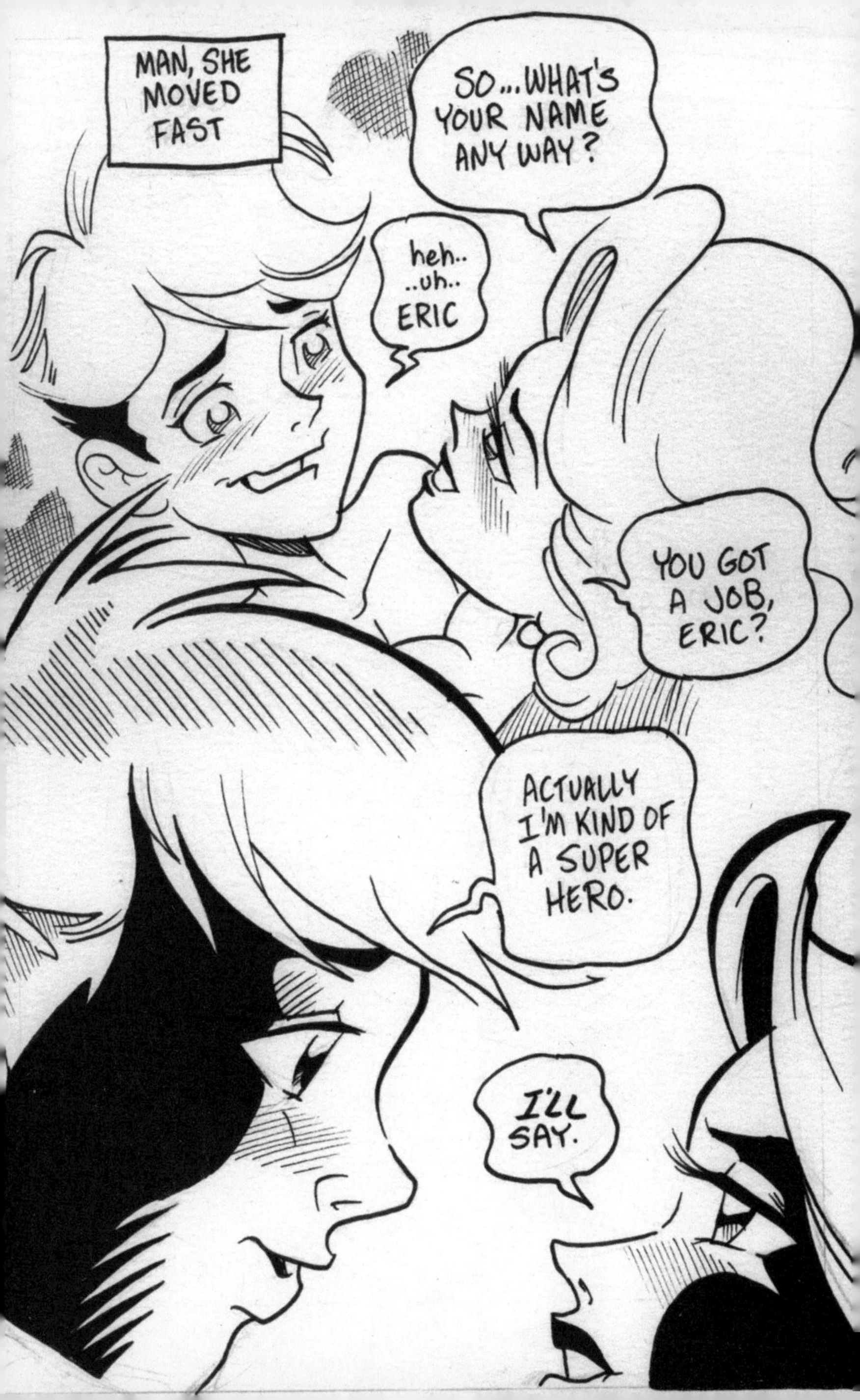
MAN, SHE MOVED FAST
SO...WHAT'S YOUR NAME ANY WAY?
heh.. ..uh.. ERIC
YOU GOT A JOB, ERIC?
ACTUALLY I'M KIND OF A SUPER HERO.
I'LL SAY.

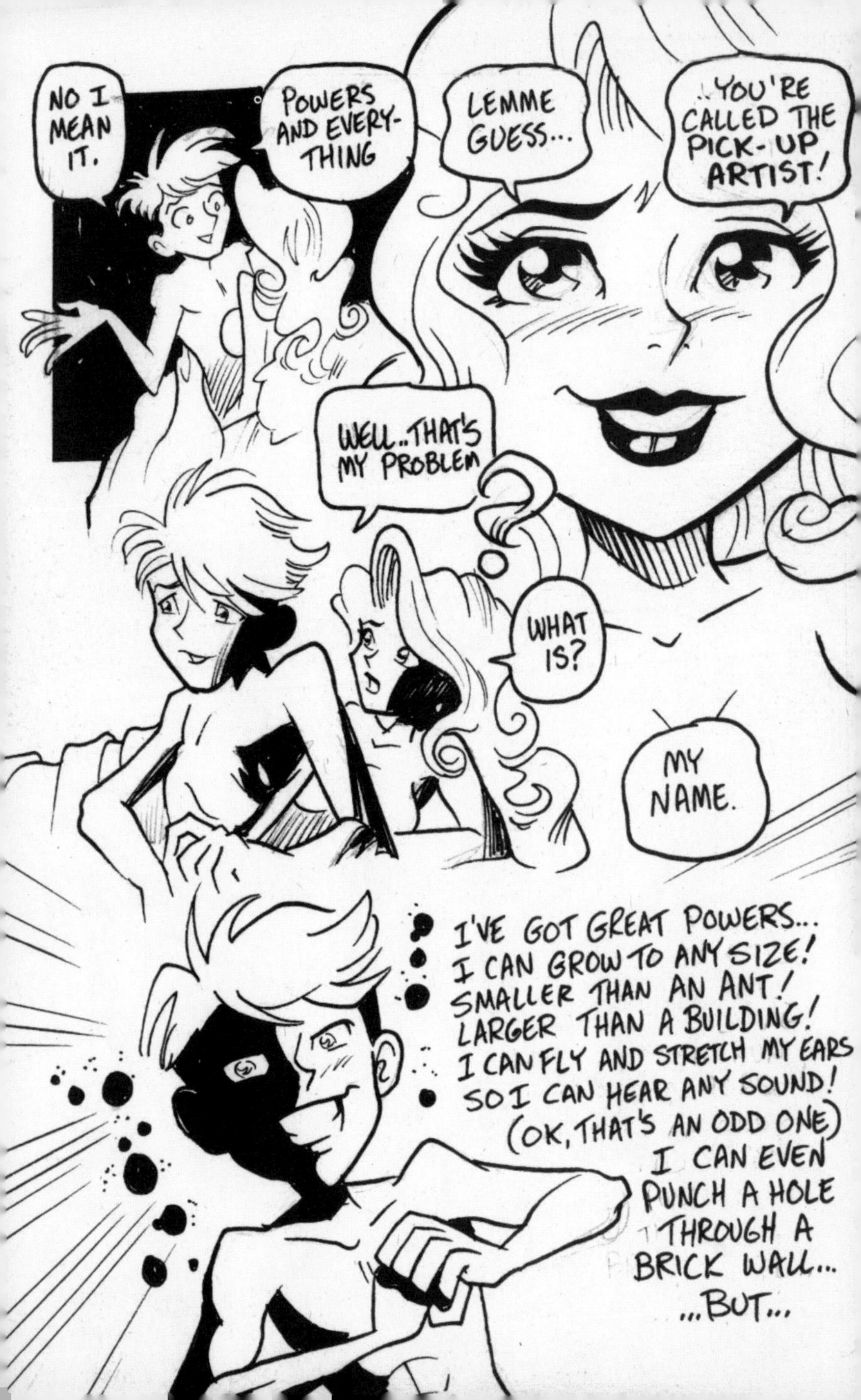
NO I MEAN IT.
POWERS AND EVERY-THING
LEMME GUESS...
...YOU'RE CALLED THE PICK-UP ARTIST!
WELL..THAT'S MY PROBLEM
WHAT IS?
MY NAME.
I'VE GOT GREAT POWERS... I CAN GROW TO ANY SIZE! SMALLER THAN AN ANT! LARGER THAN A BUILDING! I CAN FLY AND STRETCH MY EARS SO I CAN HEAR ANY SOUND! (OK, THAT'S AN ODD ONE) I CAN EVEN PUNCH A HOLE THROUGH A BRICK WALL... ...BUT...

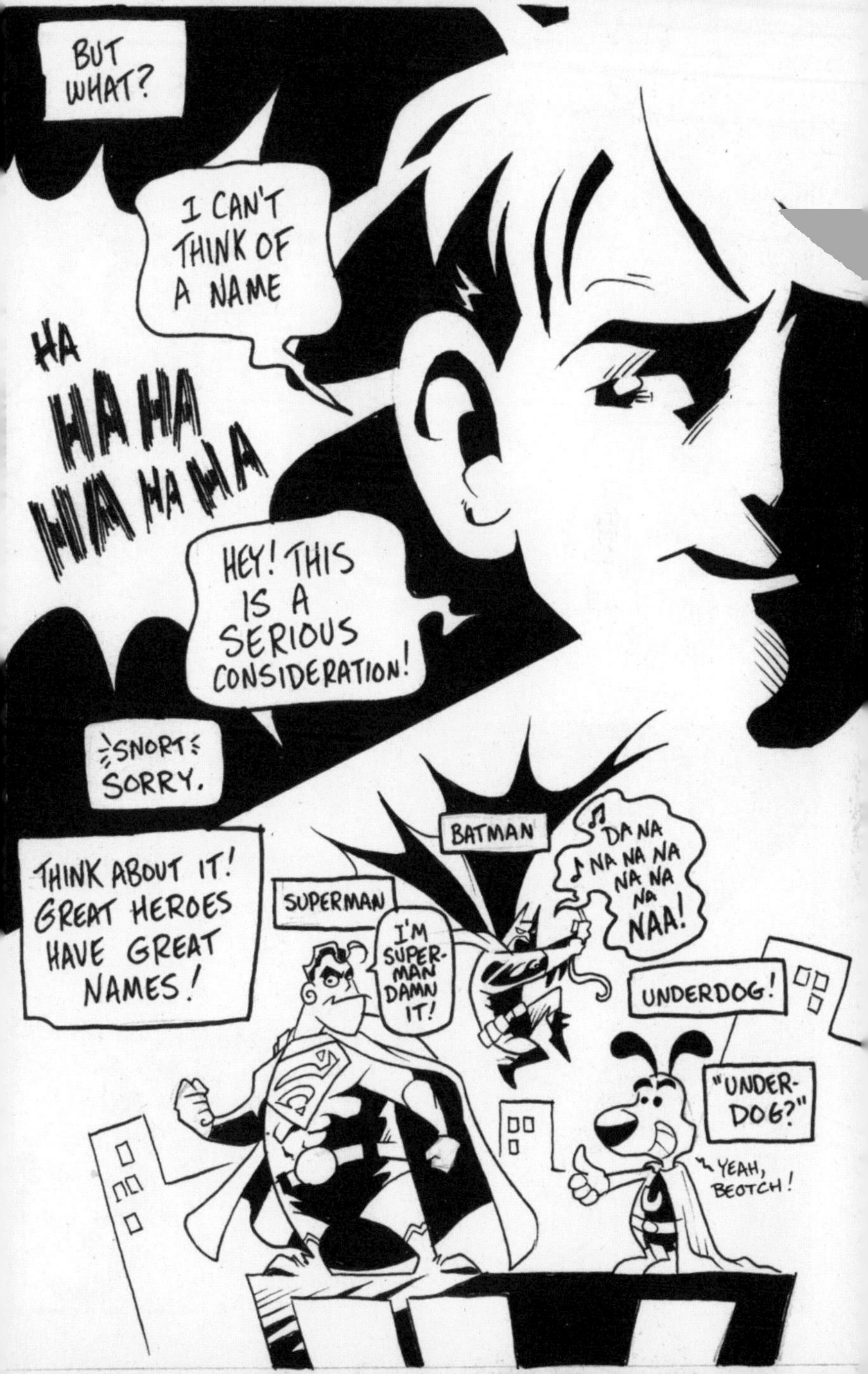
BUT WHAT?
I CAN'T THINK OF A NAME
HA HA HA HA HA HA HA
HEY! THIS IS A SERIOUS CONSIDERATION!
SNORT SORRY.
THINK ABOUT IT! GREAT HEROES HAVE GREAT NAMES!
BATMAN
DA NA NA NA NA NA NA NA NAA!
SUPERMAN
I'M SUPER-MAN DAMN IT!
UNDERDOG!
"UNDER-DOG?"
YEAH, BEOTCH!

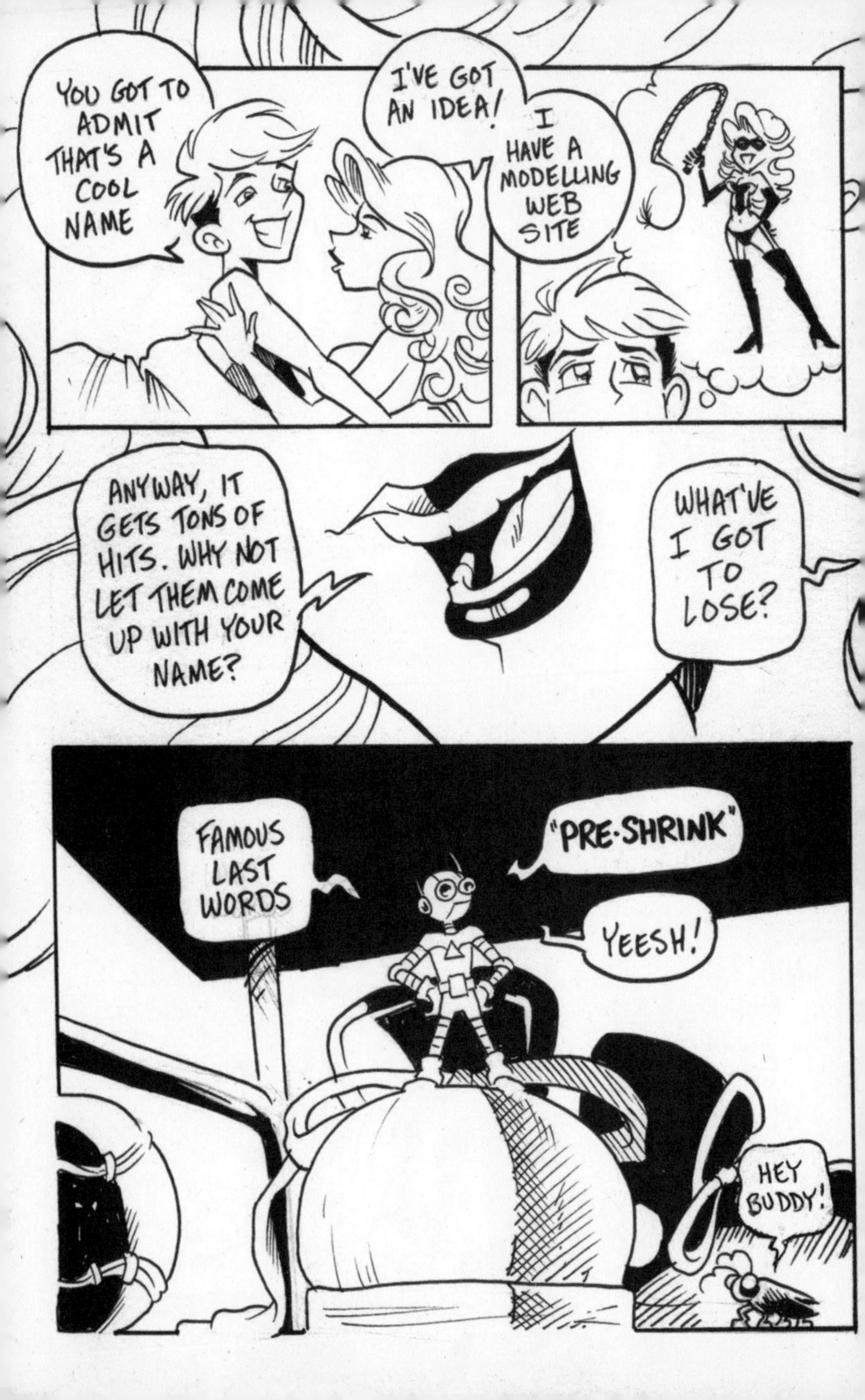
YOU GOT TO ADMIT THAT'S A COOL NAME
I'VE GOT AN IDEA!
I HAVE A MODELLING WEB SITE
ANYWAY, IT GETS TONS OF HITS. WHY NOT LET THEM COME UP WITH YOUR NAME?
WHAT'VE I GOT TO LOSE?
FAMOUS LAST WORDS
"PRE-SHRINK"
YEESH!
HEY BUDDY!

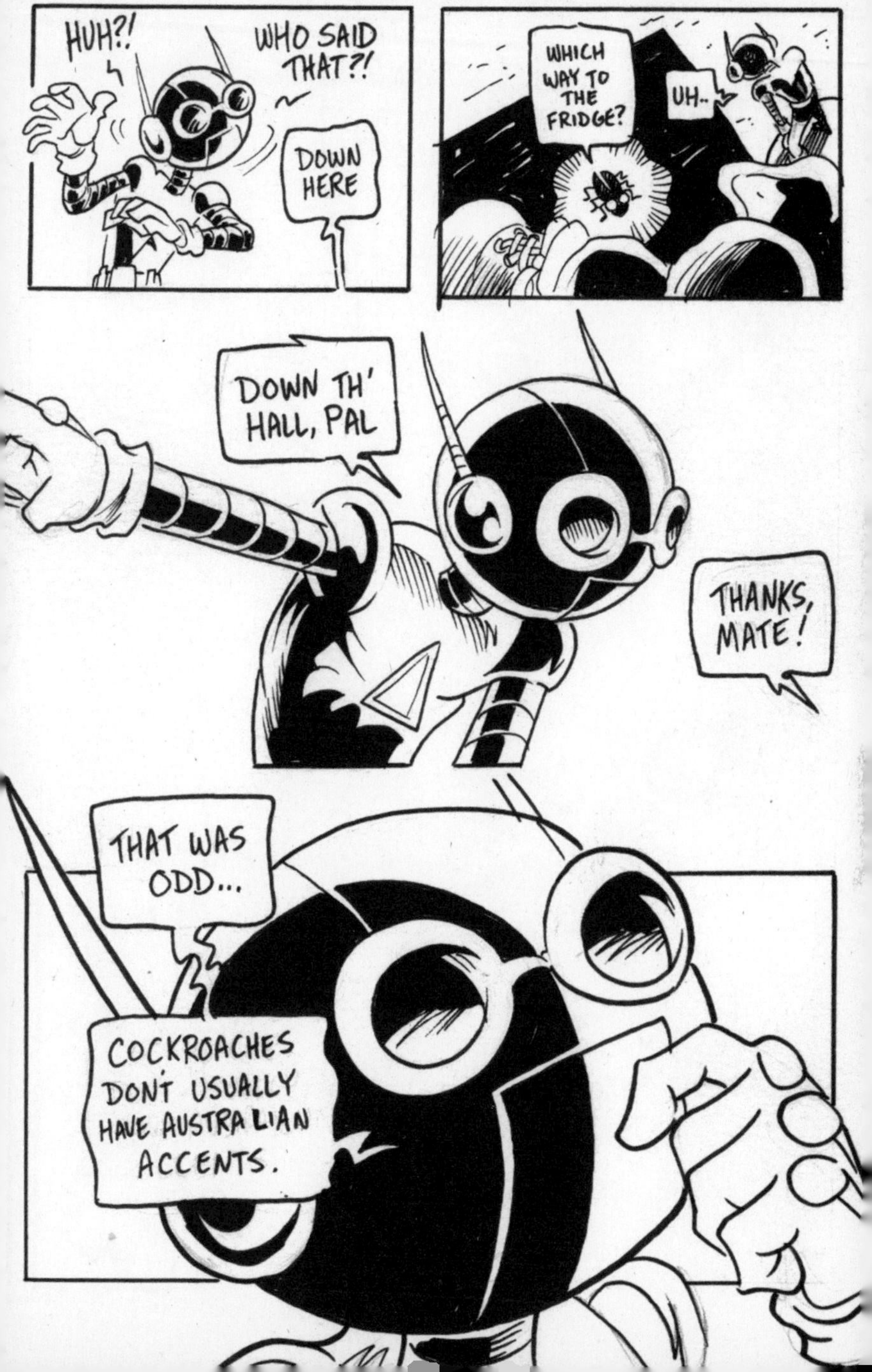
HUH?!
WHO SAID THAT?!
DOWN HERE
WHICH WAY TO THE FRIDGE?
UH..
DOWN TH' HALL, PAL
THANKS, MATE!
THAT WAS ODD...
COCKROACHES DON'T USUALLY HAVE AUSTRALIAN ACCENTS.

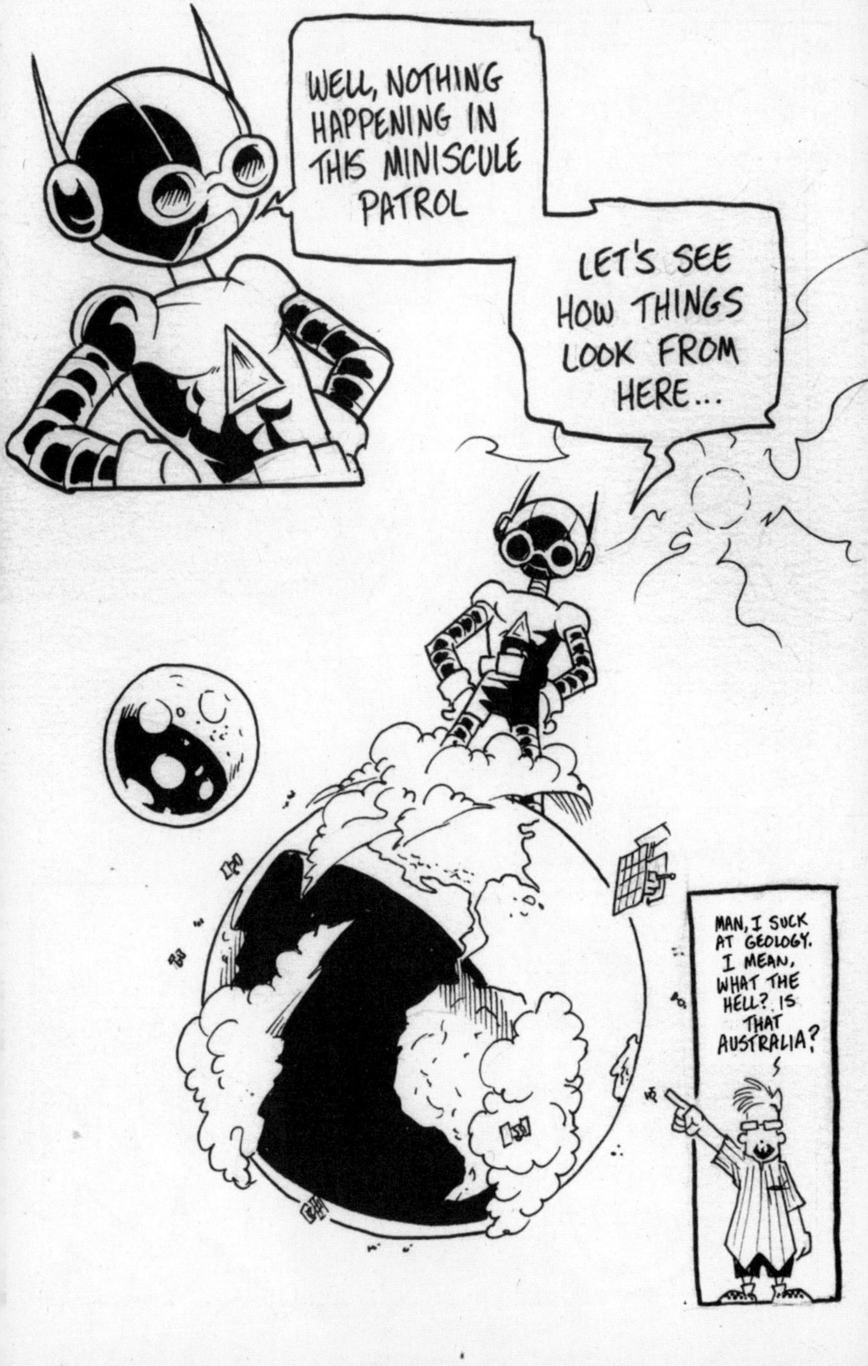
WELL, NOTHING HAPPENING IN THIS MINISCULE PATROL
LET'S SEE HOW THINGS LOOK FROM HERE...
MAN, I SUCK AT GEOLOGY. I MEAN, WHAT THE HELL? IS THAT AUSTRALIA?

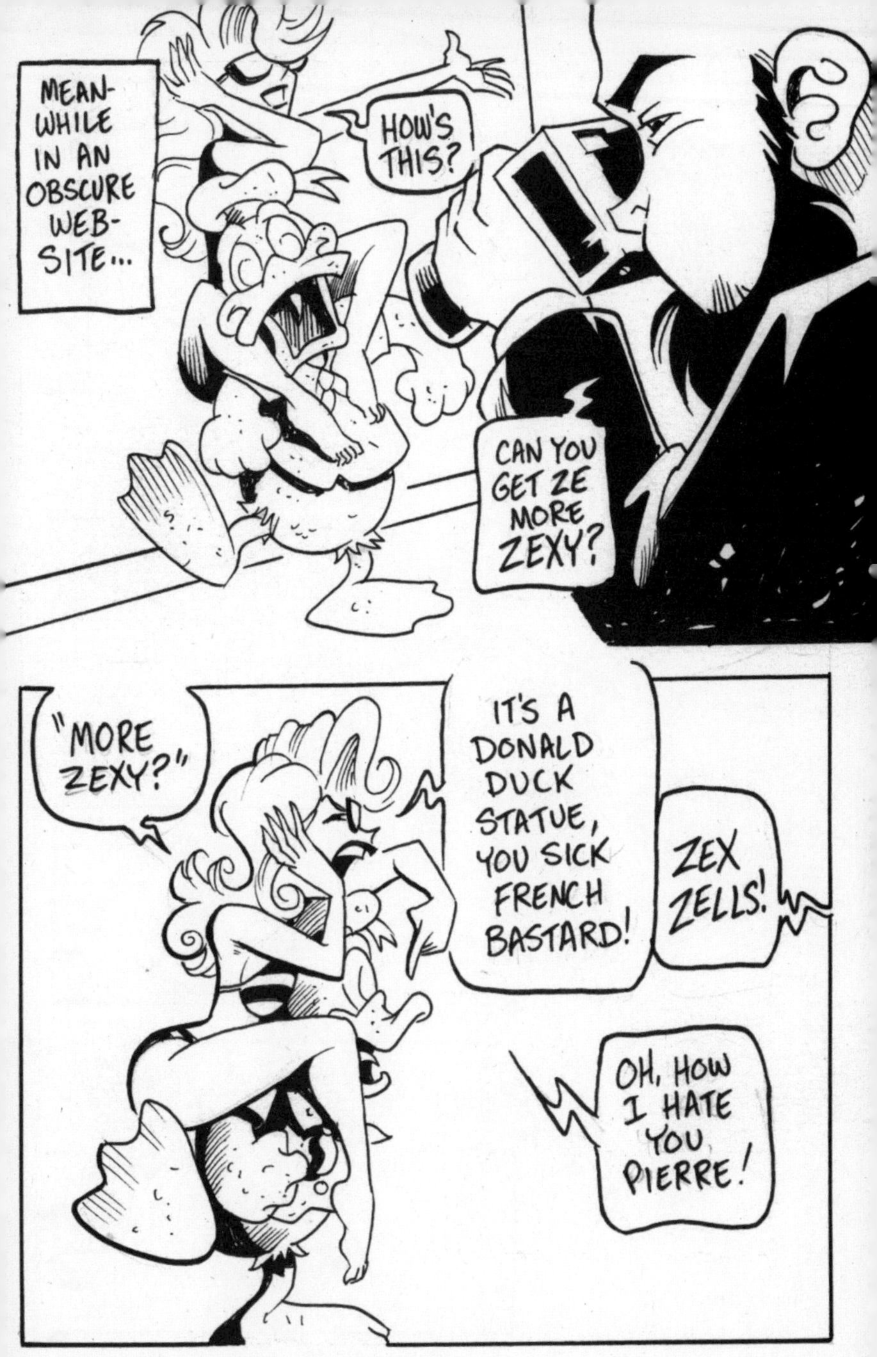
MEAN-WHILE IN AN OBSCURE WEB-SITE...
HOW'S THIS?
CAN YOU GET ZE MORE ZEXY?
"MORE ZEXY?"
IT'S A DONALD DUCK STATUE, YOU SICK FRENCH BASTARD!
ZEX ZELLS!
OH, HOW I HATE YOU PIERRE!

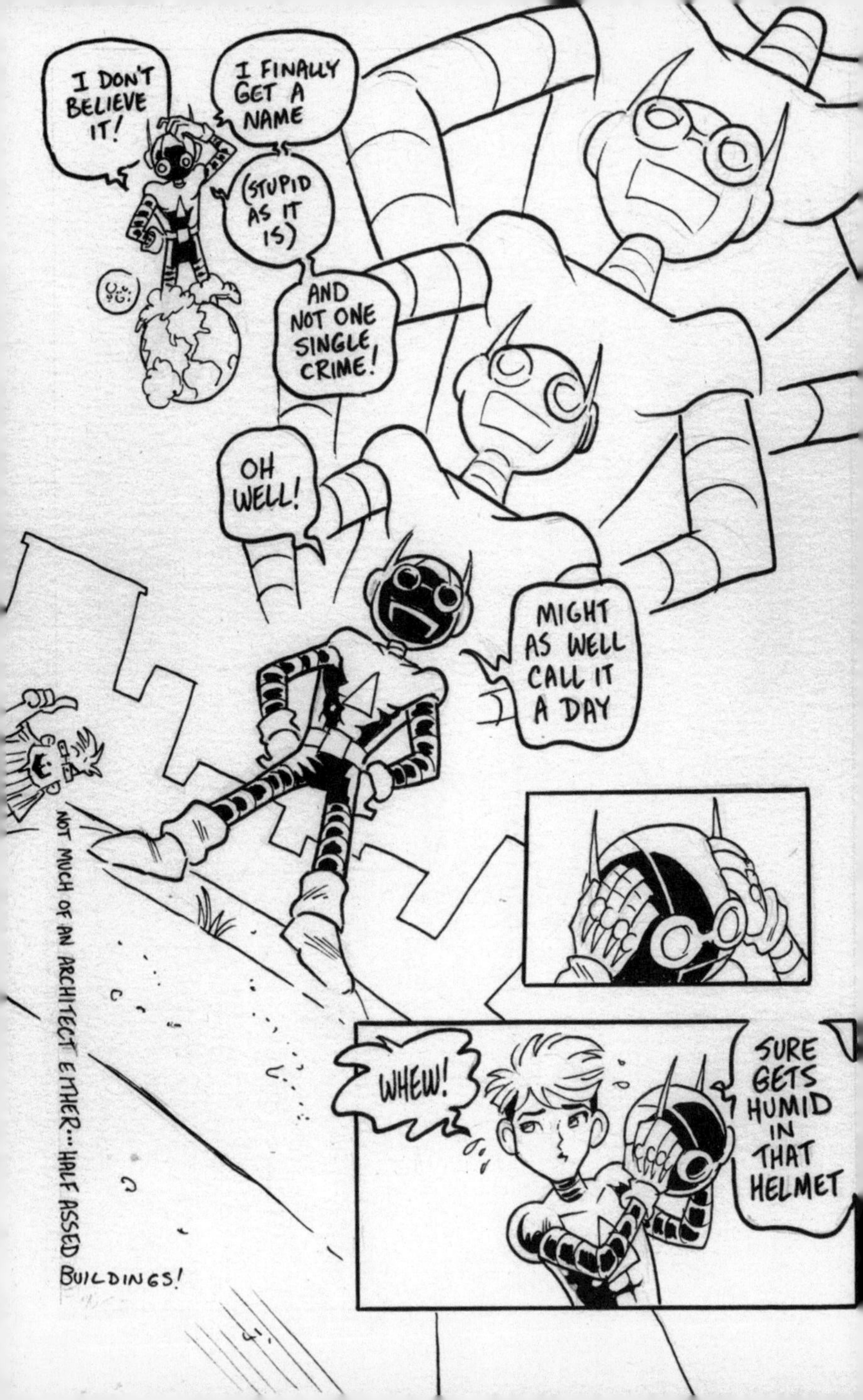
I DON'T BELIEVE IT!
I FINALLY GET A NAME
(STUPID AS IT IS)
AND NOT ONE SINGLE CRIME!
OH WELL!
MIGHT AS WELL CALL IT A DAY
NOT MUCH OF AN ARCHITECT EITHER... HALF ASSED BUILDINGS!
WHEW!
SURE GETS HUMID IN THAT HELMET

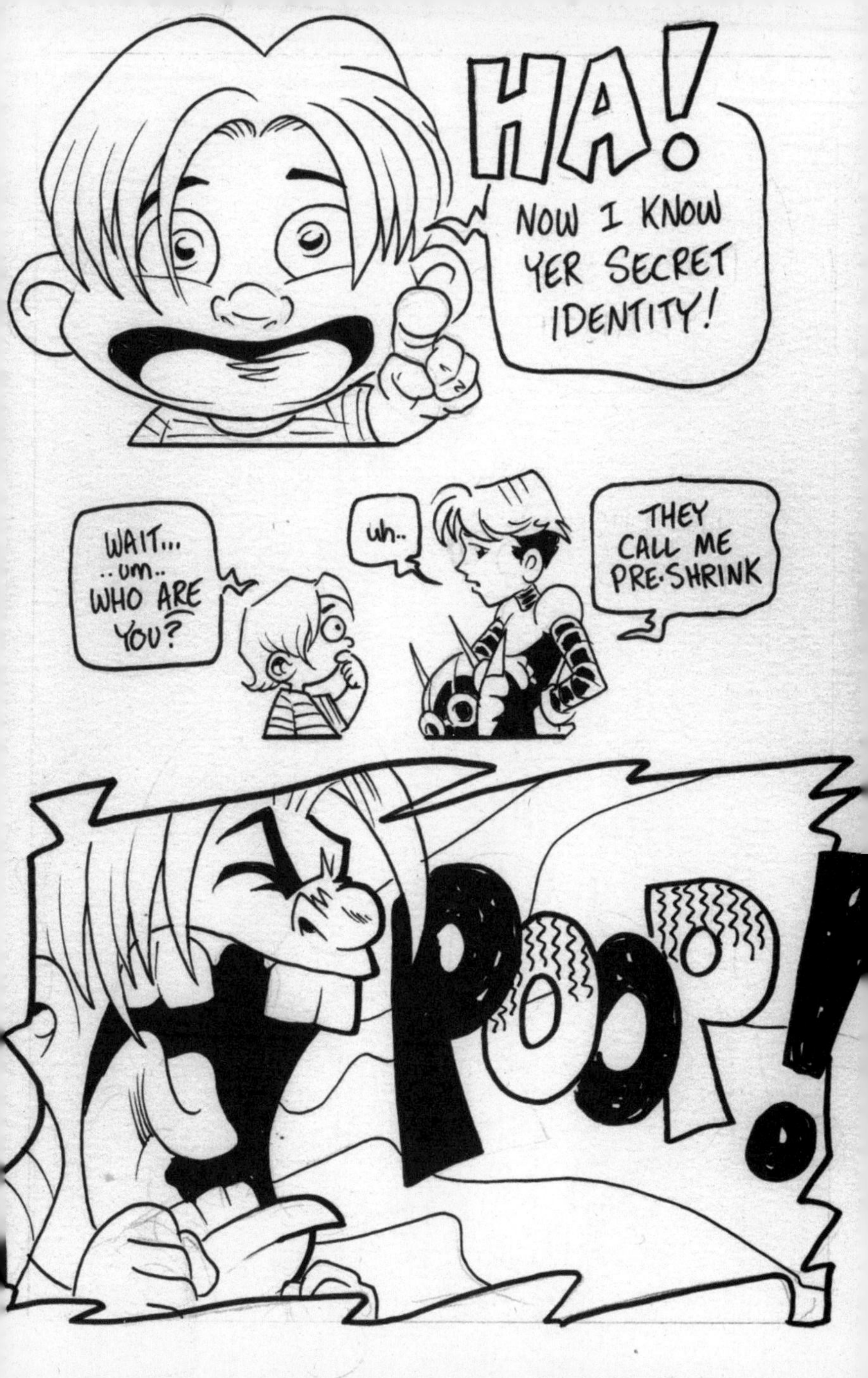
HA!
NOW I KNOW YER SECRET IDENTITY!
WAIT... ..um.. WHO ARE YOU?
uh..
THEY CALL ME PRE·SHRINK
POOP!

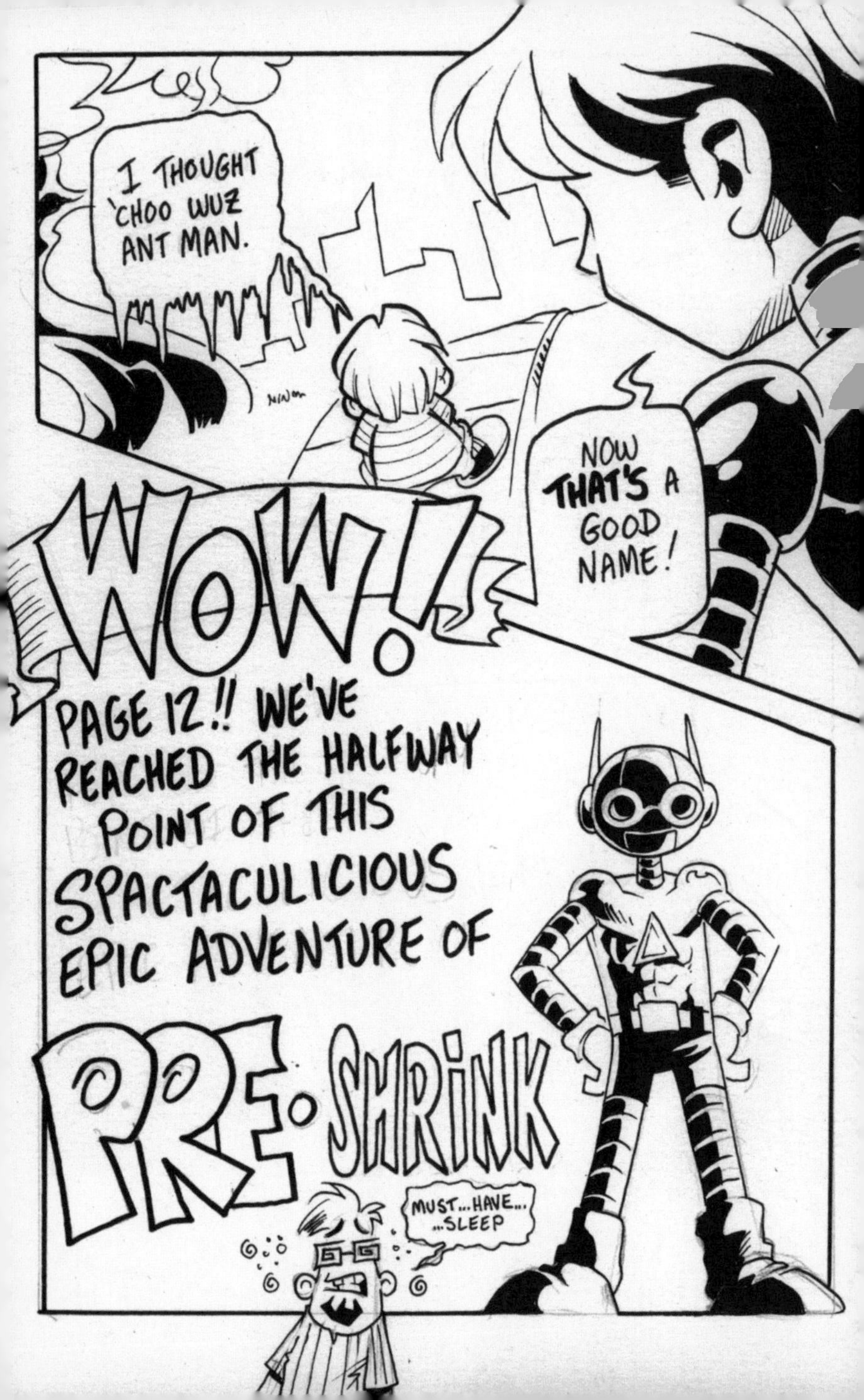
I THOUGHT 'CHOO WUZ ANT MAN.
NOW THAT'S A GOOD NAME!
WOW!!
PAGE 12!! WE'VE REACHED THE HALFWAY POINT OF THIS SPACTACULICIOUS EPIC ADVENTURE OF
PRE-SHRINK
MUST...HAVE... ...SLEEP

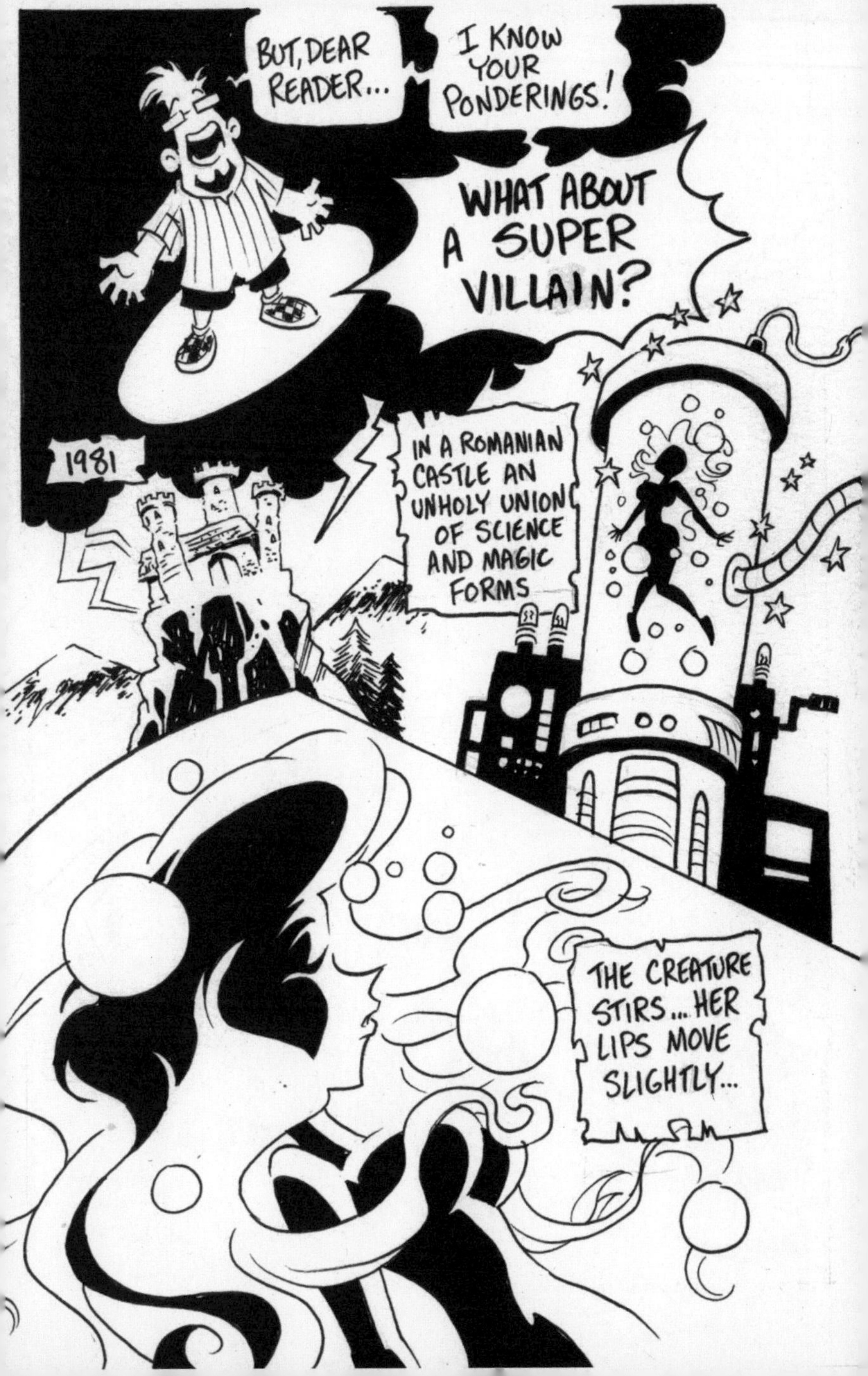
BUT, DEAR READER...
I KNOW YOUR PONDERINGS!
WHAT ABOUT A SUPER VILLAIN?
1981
IN A ROMANIAN CASTLE AN UNHOLY UNION OF SCIENCE AND MAGIC FORMS
THE CREATURE STIRS... HER LIPS MOVE SLIGHTLY...

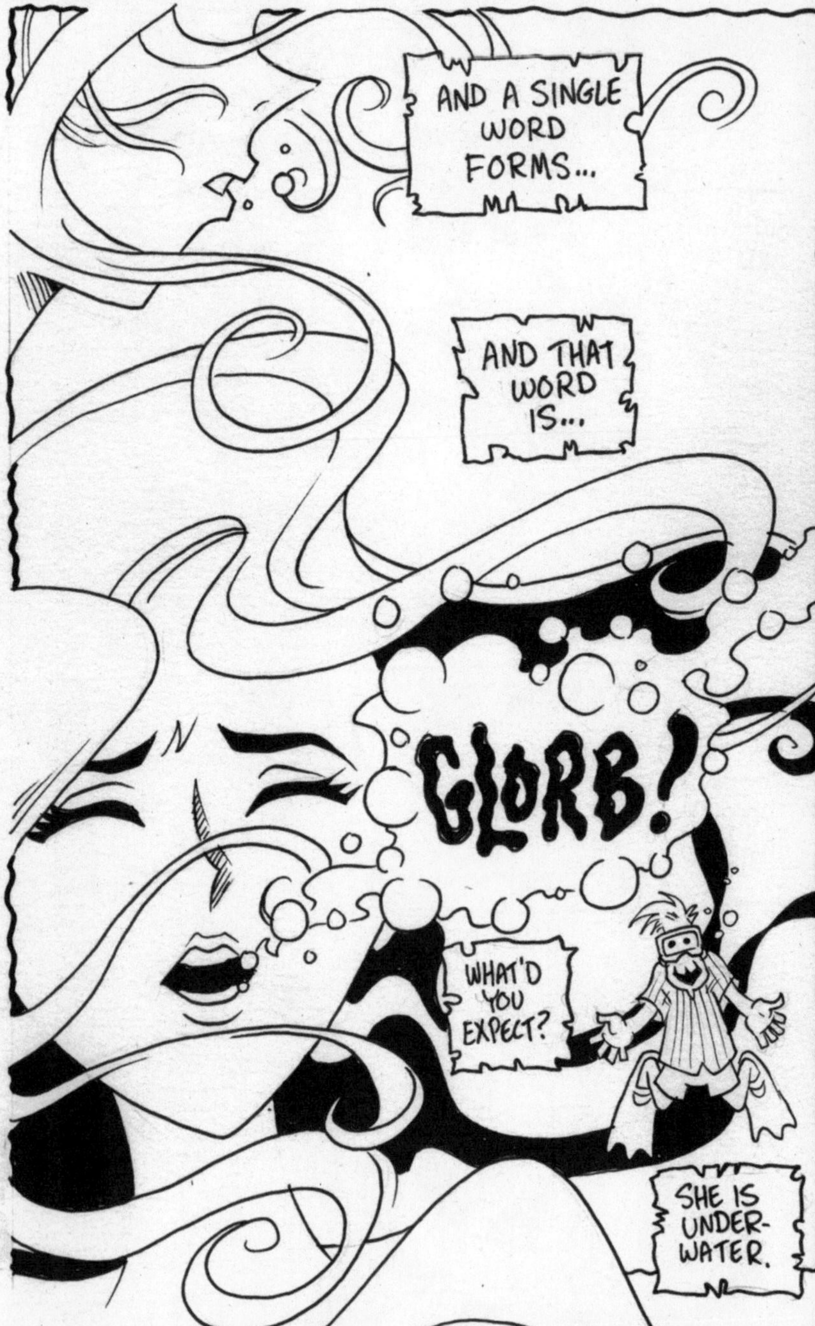
AND A SINGLE WORD FORMS...
AND THAT WORD IS...
GLORB!
WHAT'D YOU EXPECT?
SHE IS UNDER-WATER.

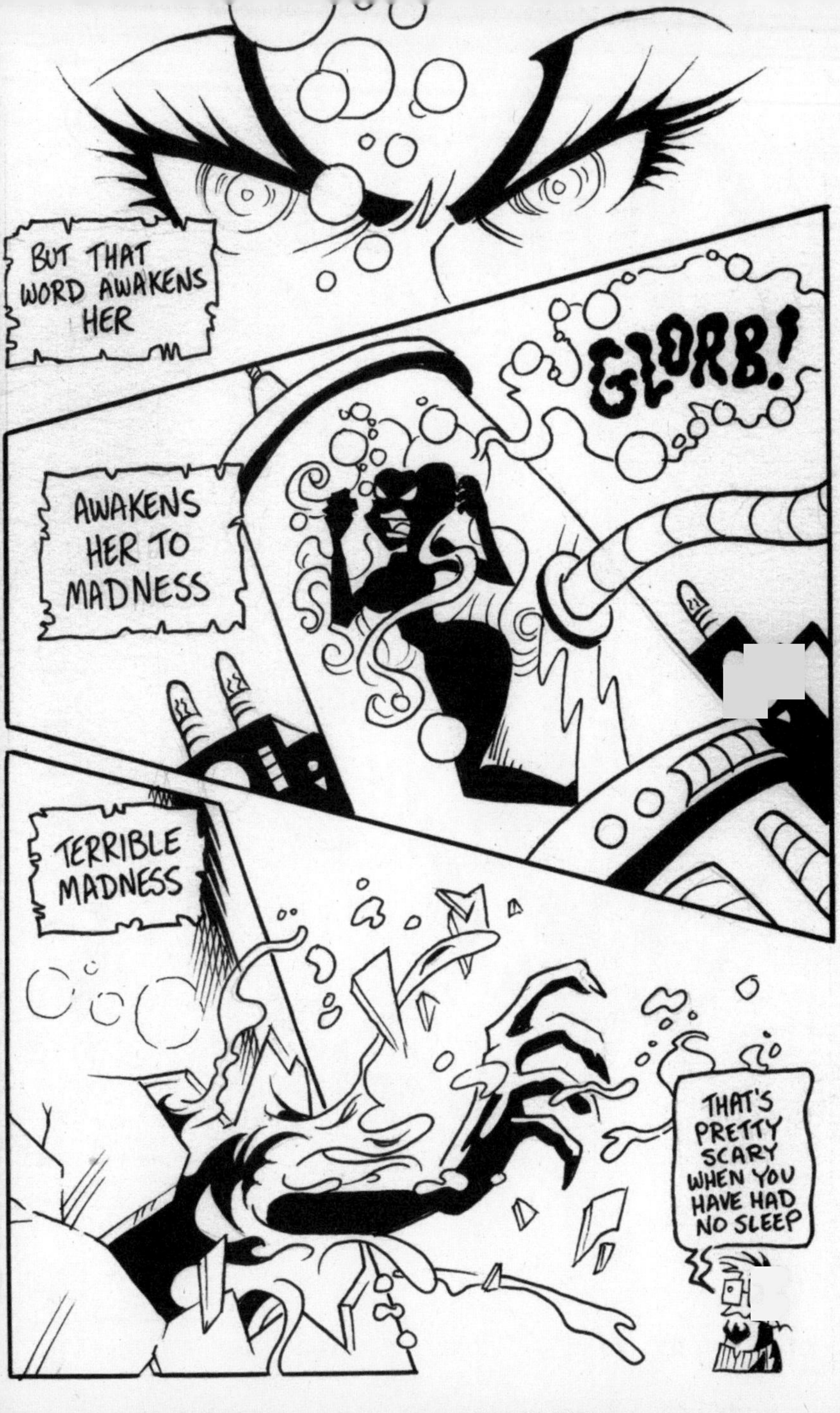
BUT THAT WORD AWAKENS HER
GLORB!
AWAKENS HER TO MADNESS
TERRIBLE MADNESS
THAT'S PRETTY SCARY WHEN YOU HAVE HAD NO SLEEP

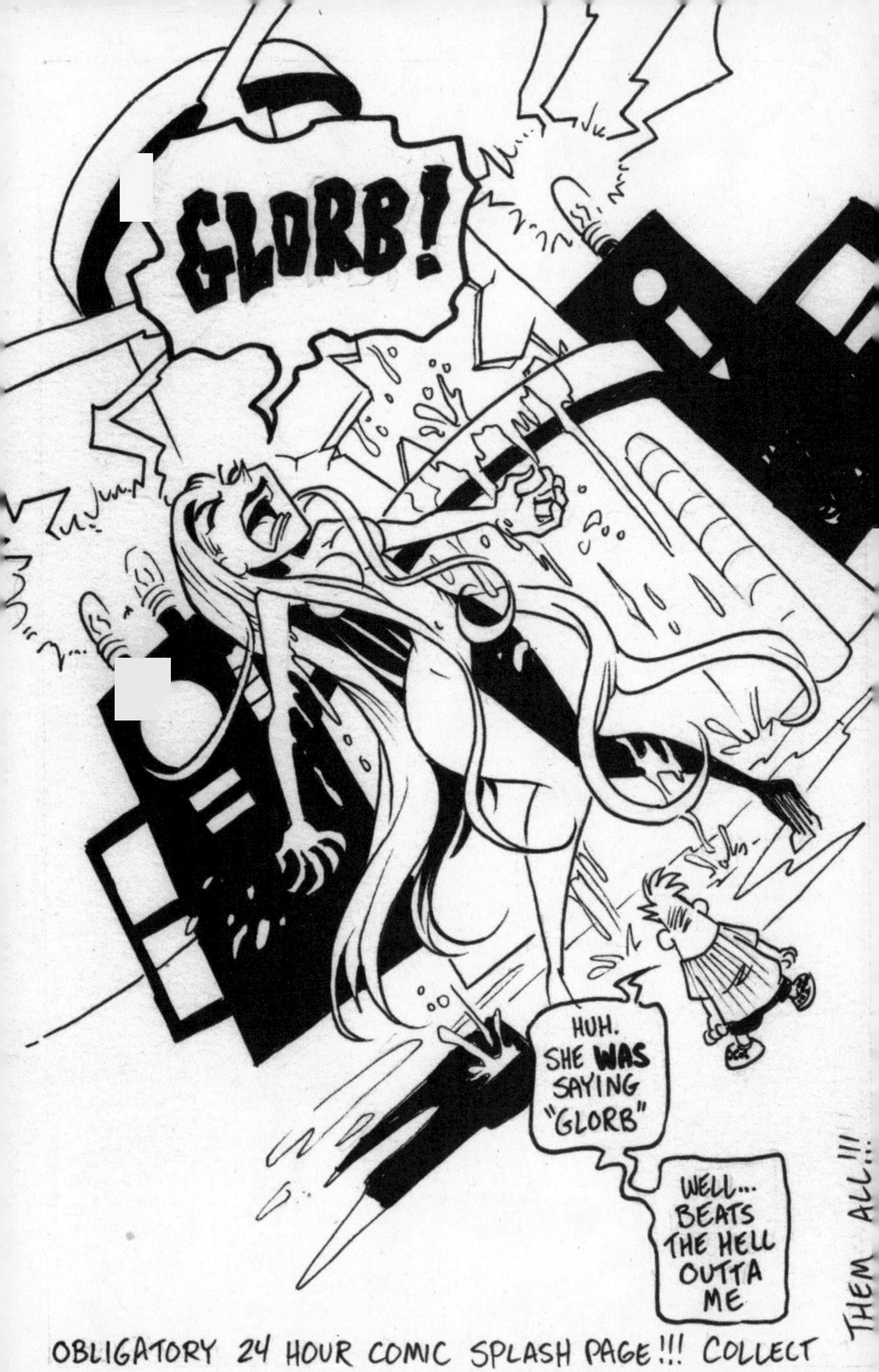
GLORB!
HUH. SHE **WAS** SAYING "GLORB"
WELL... BEATS THE HELL OUTTA ME

OBLIGATORY 24 HOUR COMIC SPLASH PAGE!!! COLLECT THEM ALL!!!

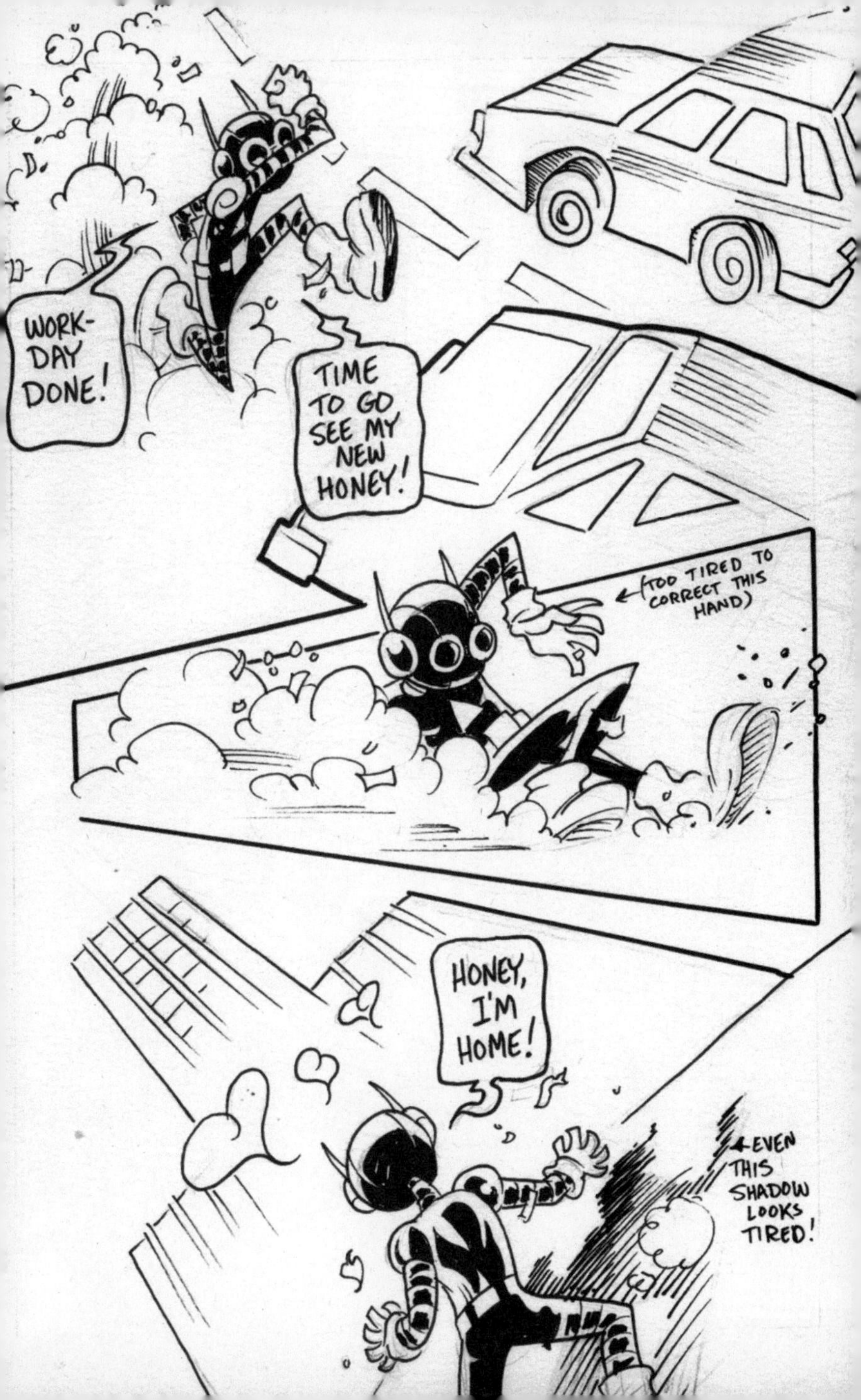
WORK-DAY DONE!
TIME TO GO SEE MY NEW HONEY!
(TOO TIRED TO CORRECT THIS HAND)
HONEY, I'M HOME!
EVEN THIS SHADOW LOOKS TIRED!

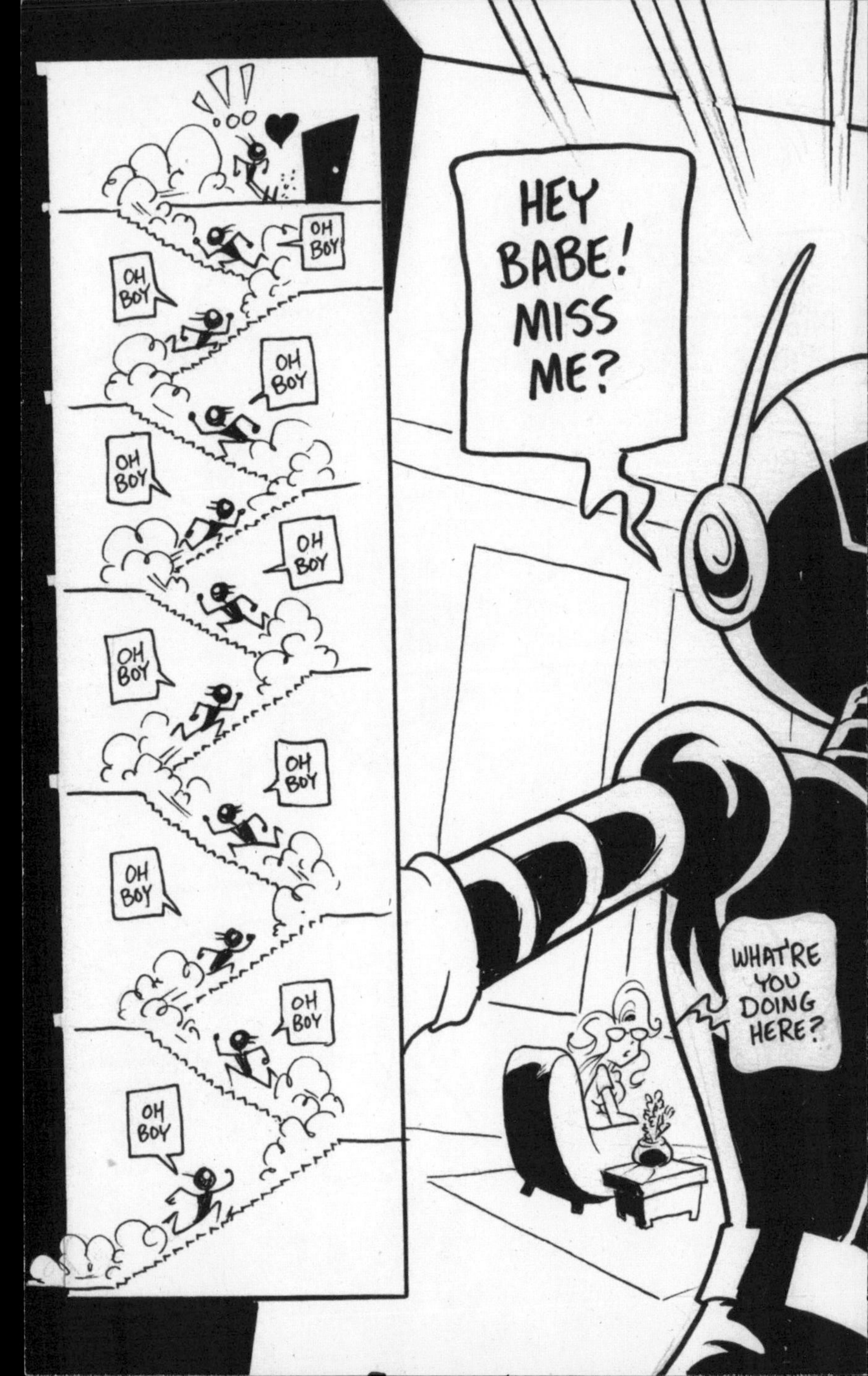
OH BOY
OH BOY
OH BOY
OH BOY
OH BOY
OH BOY
OH BOY
OH BOY
OH BOY
OH BOY
HEY BABE! MISS ME?
WHAT'RE YOU DOING HERE?

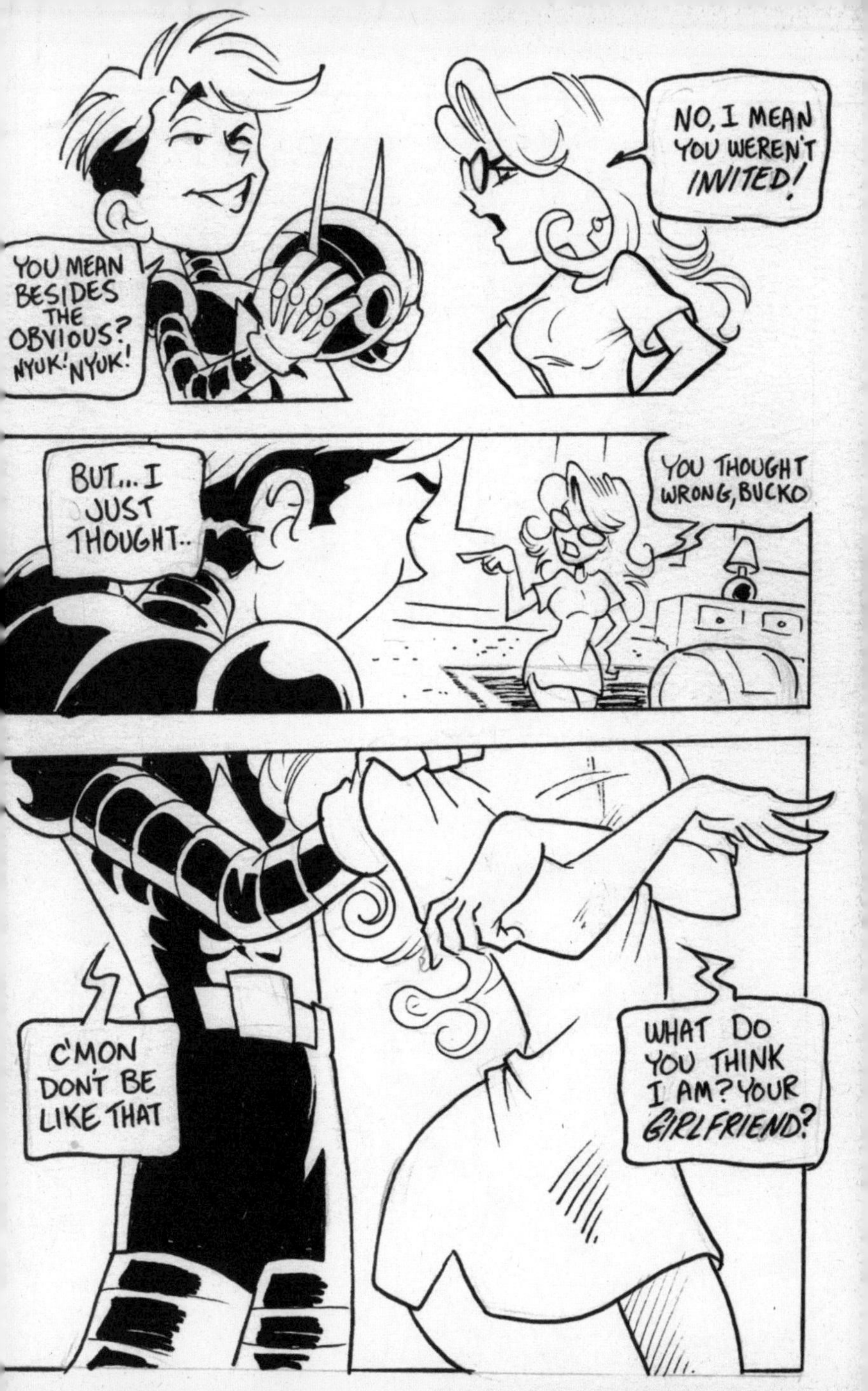
YOU MEAN BESIDES THE OBVIOUS? NYUK! NYUK!
NO, I MEAN YOU WEREN'T INVITED!
BUT... I JUST THOUGHT..
YOU THOUGHT WRONG, BUCKO
C'MON DON'T BE LIKE THAT
WHAT DO YOU THINK I AM? YOUR GIRLFRIEND?

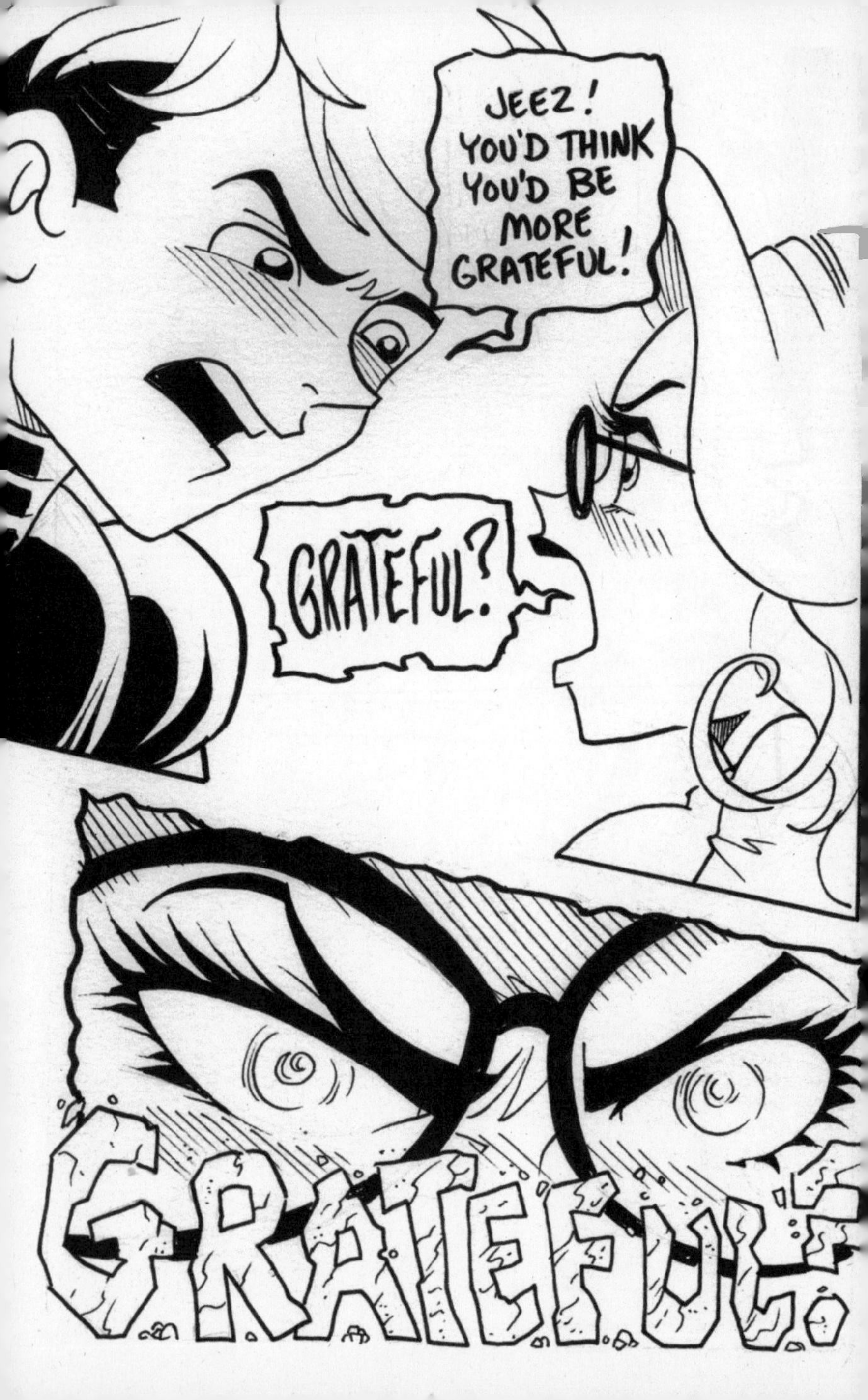
JEEZ! YOU'D THINK YOU'D BE MORE GRATEFUL!
GRATEFUL?
GRATEFUL?

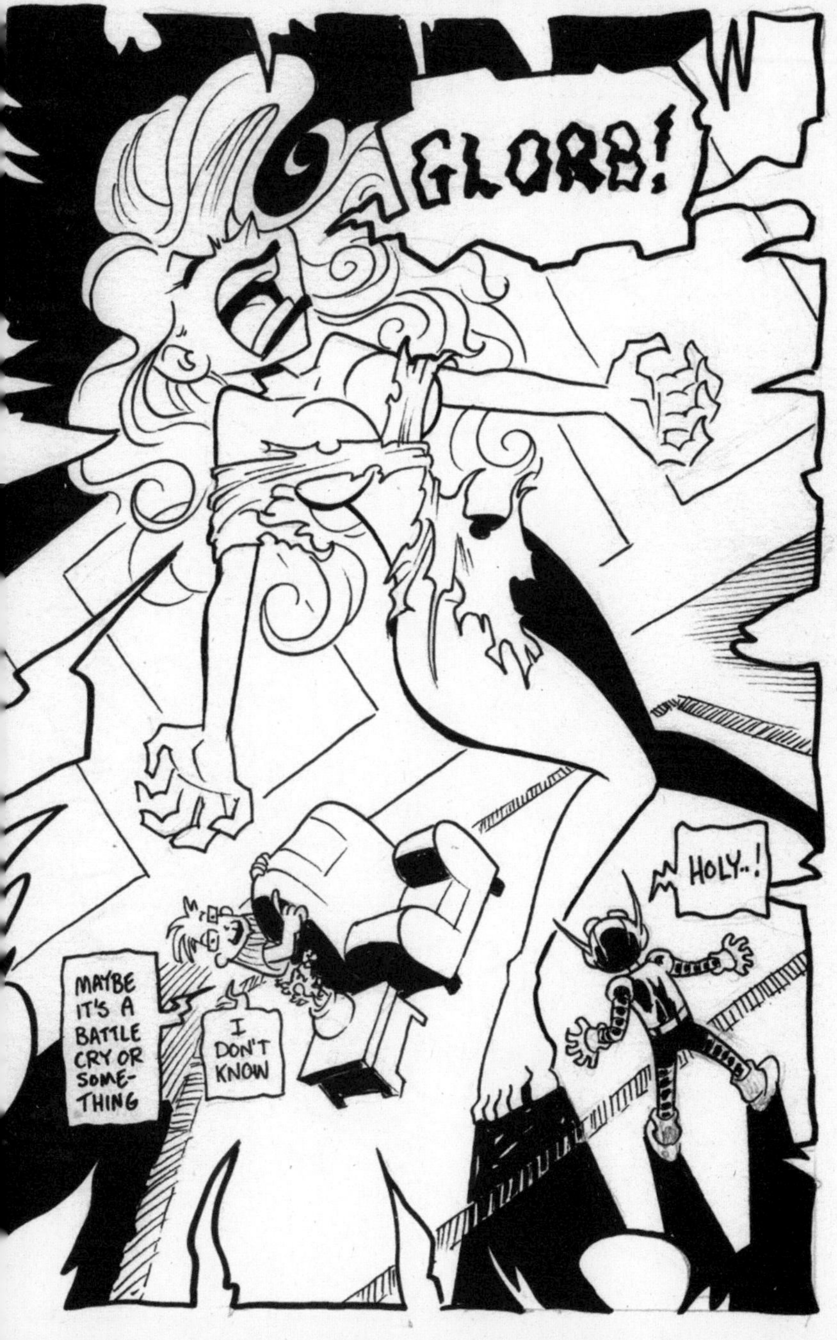
GLORB!
MAYBE IT'S A BATTLE CRY OR SOME-THING
I DON'T KNOW
HOLY..!

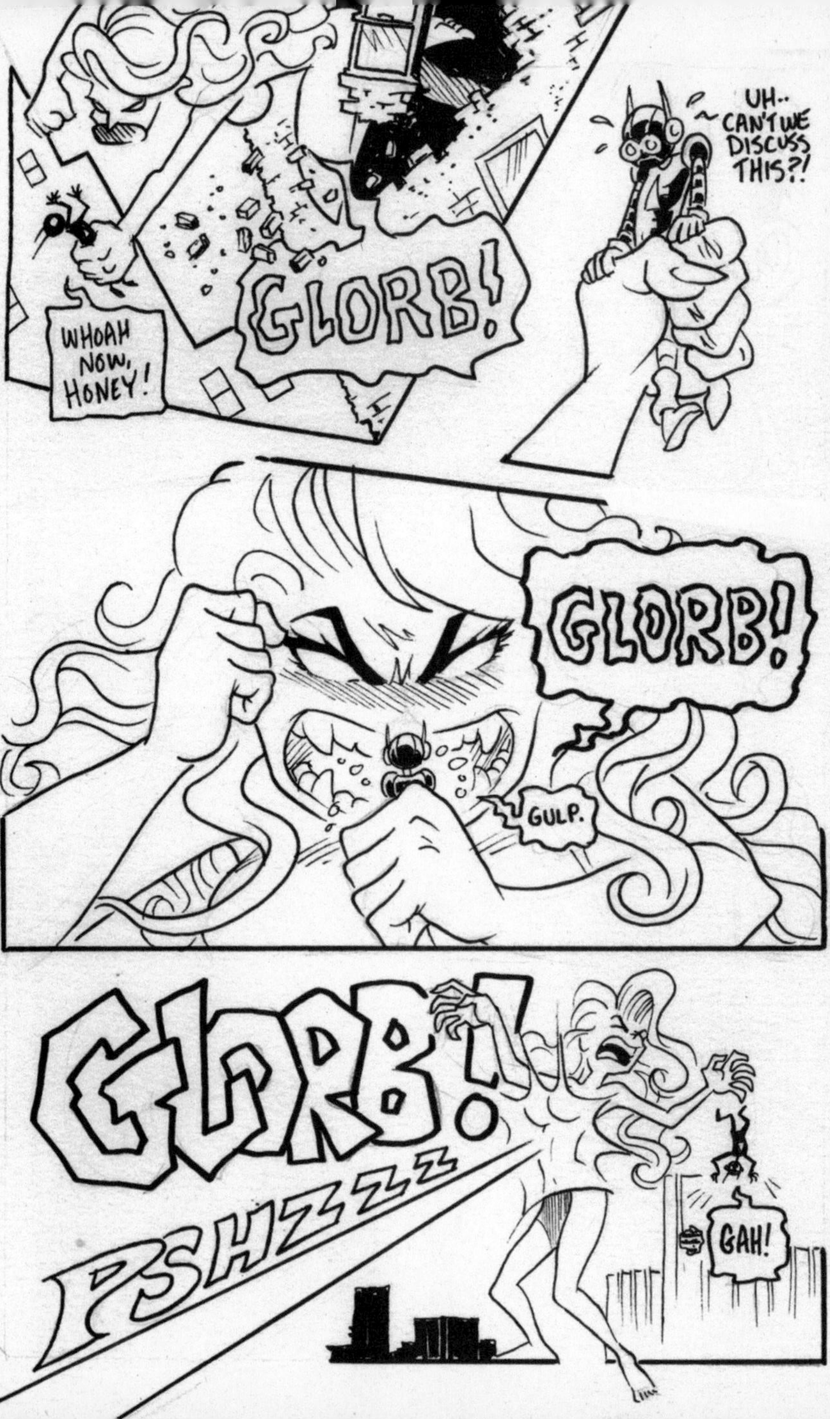
GLORB!
WHOAH NOW, HONEY!
UH.. CAN'T WE DISCUSS THIS?!
GLORB!
GULP.
GLORB!
PSHZZZZ
GAH!

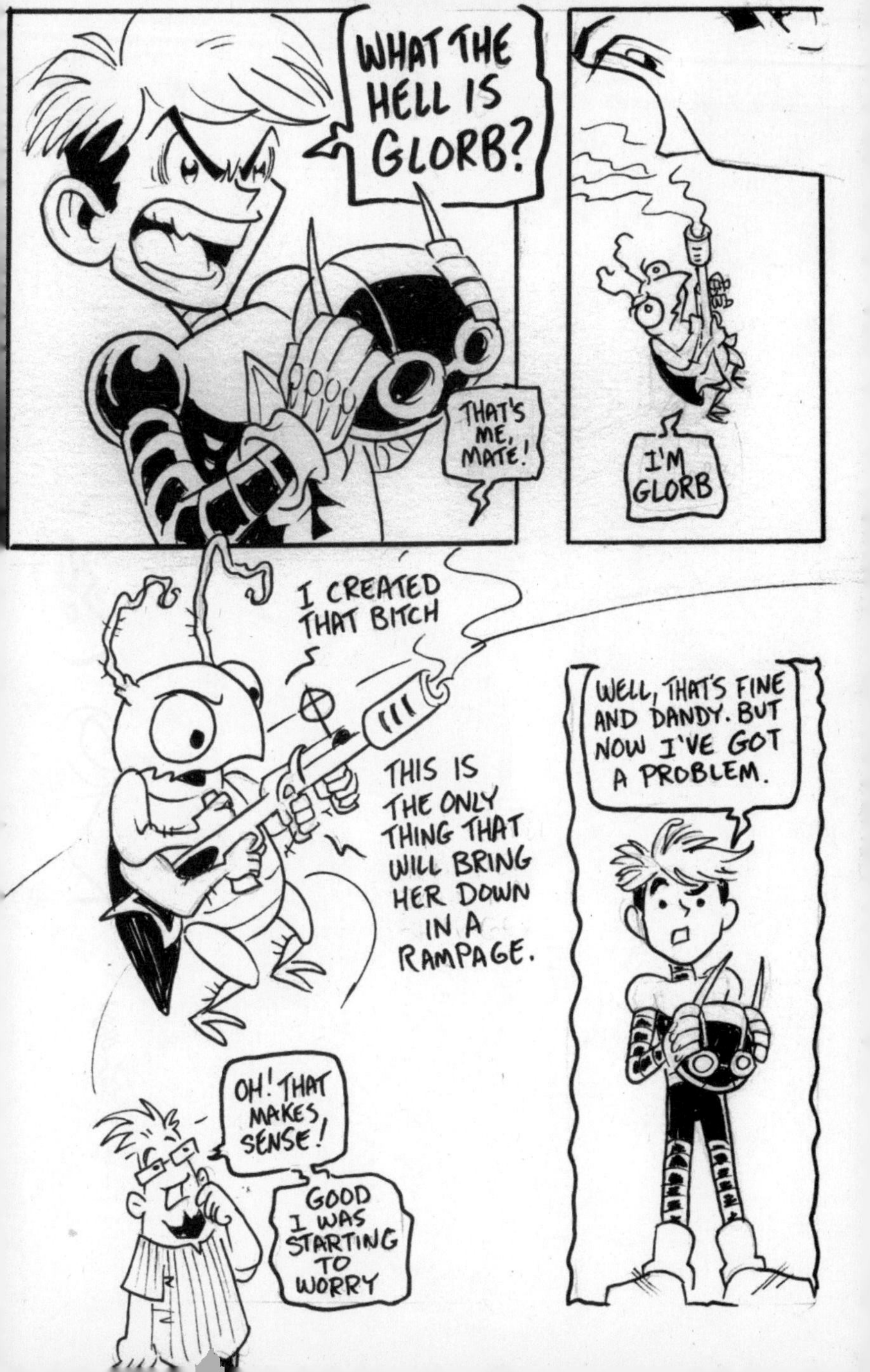
WHAT THE HELL IS GLORB?
THAT'S ME, MATE!
I'M GLORB
I CREATED THAT BITCH
THIS IS THE ONLY THING THAT WILL BRING HER DOWN IN A RAMPAGE.
OH! THAT MAKES SENSE!
GOOD I WAS STARTING TO WORRY
WELL, THAT'S FINE AND DANDY. BUT NOW I'VE GOT A PROBLEM.

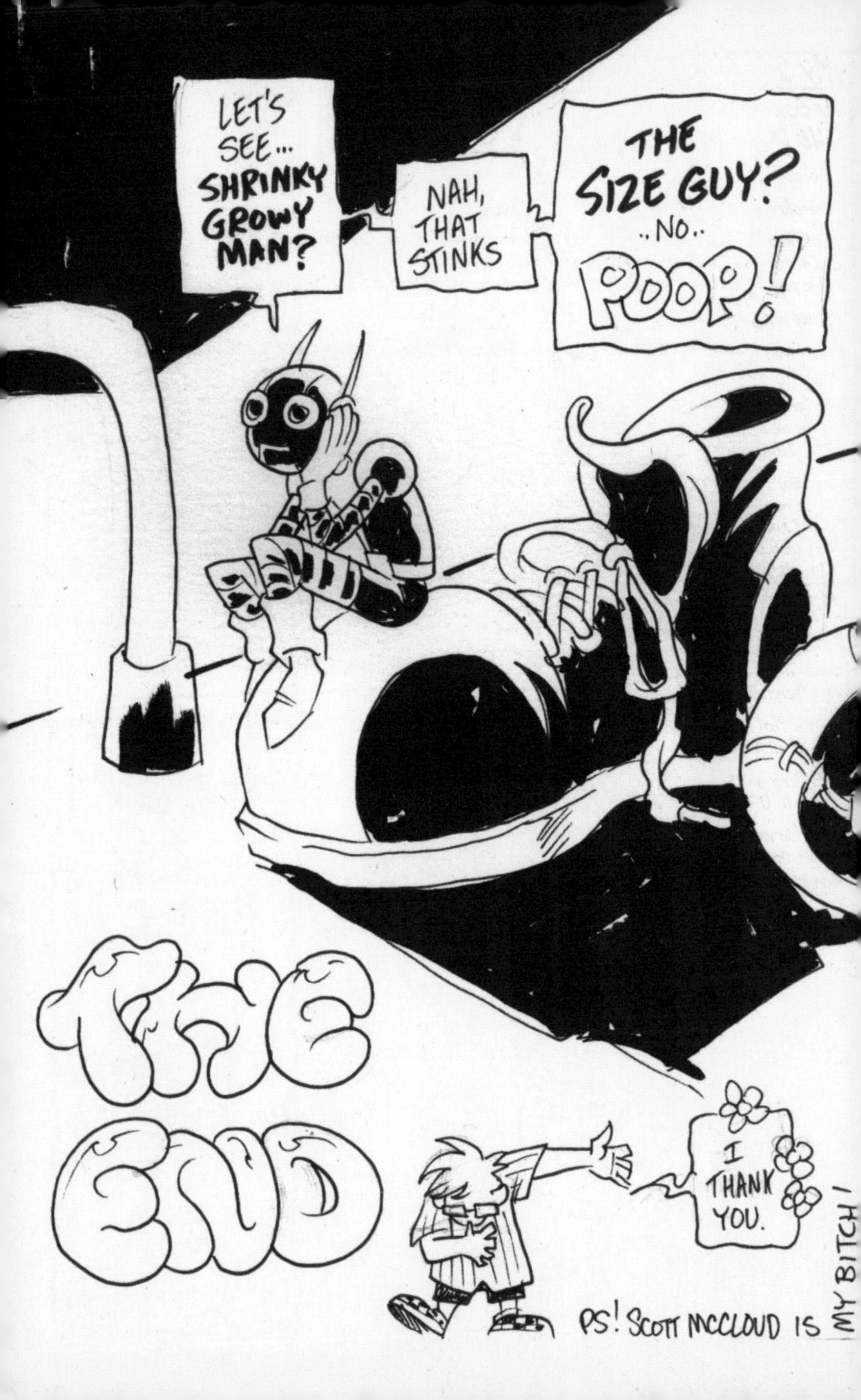
LET'S SEE... SHRINKY GROWY MAN?
NAH, THAT STINKS
THE SIZE GUY? ..NO.. POOP!
THE END
I THANK YOU.
PS! SCOTT MCCLOUD IS MY BITCH!

My 24 Hour Comic

By Sonny (Continued)!

THE DARE:

Eyes closed... flip-flip-flip...point... Okay, what's the word?

"Pre-shrink."

What the hell? How am I going to make a comic book out of that? Is that even a word? It's hyphenated for God's sake! Oh, just pick another word, Sonny. Who's going to know? You could even pick a word on the same page. "Previous" is looking damned good (I could make it a time-traveling adventure or something).

No one would have any idea.

Well, I would. I quickly came to the conclusion that was the point. It wasn't a race. It's a challenge to creativity.

All righty sir, "Pre-shrink" it is. Okay...um...he's...he's a superhero who can adjust his size. Not bad. Okay... um...he wears body armor that kind of looks like an ant. Oh, that'll be fun to draw. Okay...um...
STOP THINKING ABOUT IT, SONNY, AND JUST DRAW THE DAMNED THING!

And away I went. I gave myself an hour per page. I had a pocket watch, given by a dear friend, on the table beside me. When each hour started closing I wrapped it up and moved on to the next. Page by page. Hour by hour. I knew they were rough but that didn't matter. I assumed that as I went on (and became exhausted) the pages would just get worse. I was surprised that the opposite happened. I got into a zone. I began to involuntarily develop a style based on speed. I soon found there was a lot I could do in an hour. I got more inventive. Around hour 13 I was giddy. I never had so much fun drawing comics. It was amazing.

Sure, the results are rough, but as I mentioned, it's not a beauty contest. That being said, I later ran into Scott McCloud at a local signing and showed him my efforts. He said, "This is really tight for a 24 hour comic. It's unbelievable this was done in 24 hours." I immediately stuck that giant feather in my proverbial cap. Then I noticed the look on his face.

What's that look? Does he think I'm lying? When he said "unbelievable" did he mean he didn't believe me? Well of all the...Why would someone lie about this?

I suddenly got a flash of hordes of attention seeking cartoonists accosting Scott with their false inflated claims to (I don't know) undeservedly bask in the holy cartoonist glow of Scott McCloud.

I tried in vain not to look guilty (even though I knew I was innocent) but I was obviously in one of those existential Kafka moments. A giant chibi sweat drop hovered over my head. Luckily my wife Gayla (and more important...my witness) was also at Scott's signing. She piped up, "Actually, he finished it two hours early." She said it with such pride and conviction the look on Scott's face vanished.

Thanks, babe, and in your face...um...Scott's face.

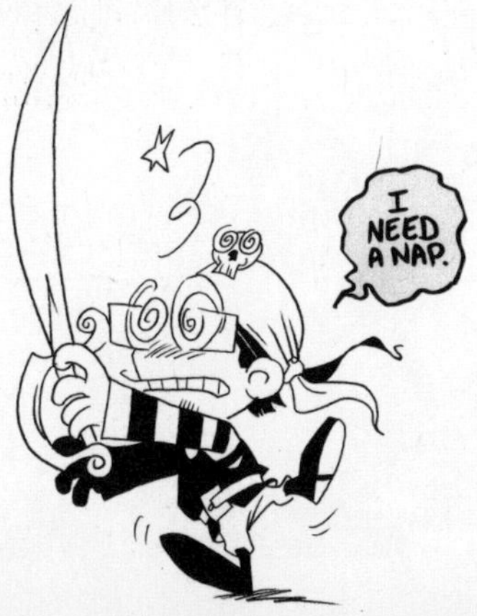
I NEED A NAP.

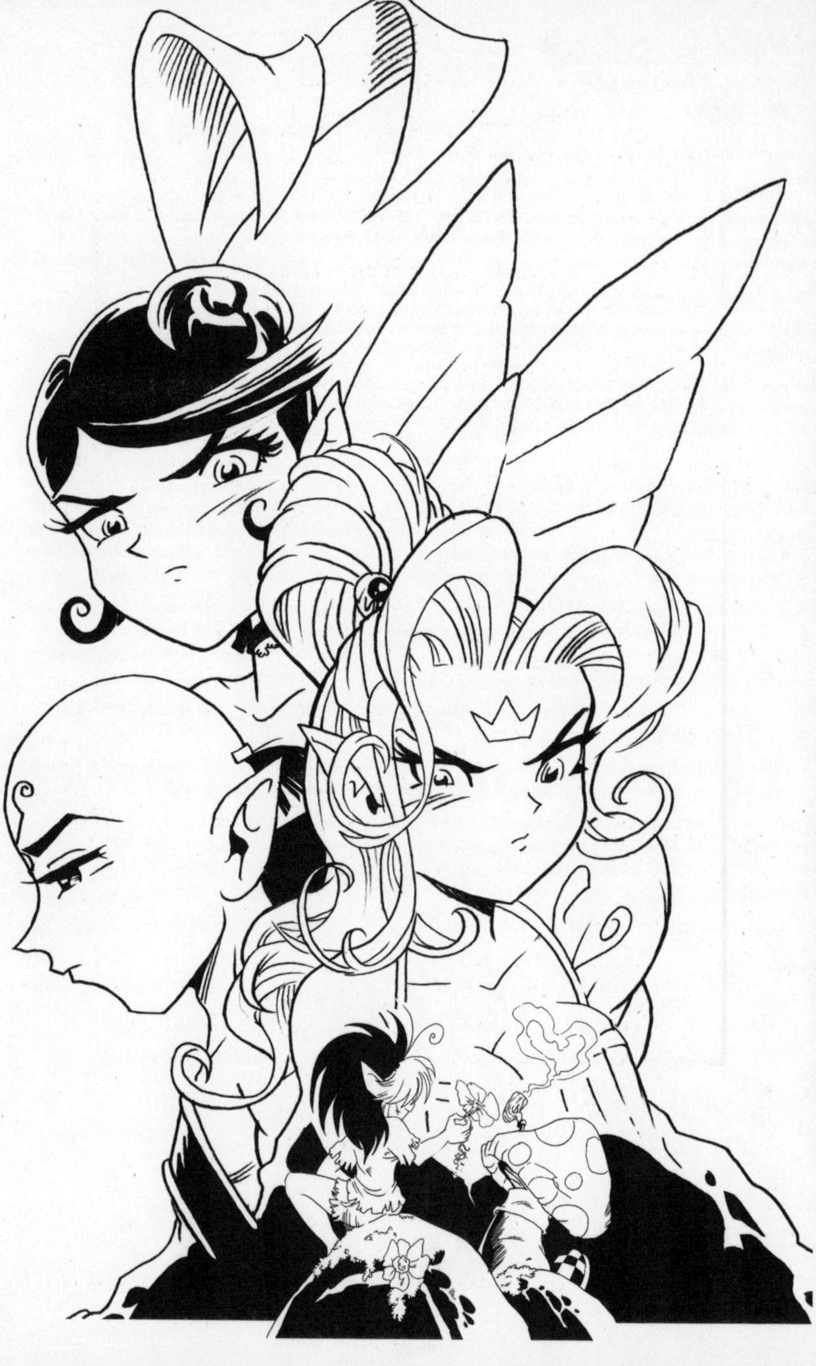

ABOUT THE AUTHOR...

HERO TO MILLIONS OF CONFUSED CHILDREN, SONNY STRAIT WAS ONCE WORSHIPED AS A DISTANT COUSIN TO WAKKA WAKKA WAKKA, THE HAWAIIAN GOD OF POLITE LAUGHTER. HE NOW USES HIS POWERS STRANGE TO PIRATE THE OCEANS OF THE GEEK ARTS... *ALL* OF THE GEEK ARTS.

AS A VOICE ACTOR, DIRECTOR, WRITER AND ILLUSTRATOR, THERE ISN'T A GEEK GENRE THAT HASN'T BEEN WARPED BY HIS PLUNDERING TAINT. MOST NOTABLY HE WAS THE VOICE OF *DRAGONBALL Z'S* KRILLIN, *FULLMETAL ALCHEMIST'S* MAES HUGHES AND THE ORIGINAL TOONAMI TOM FOR THE CARTOON NETWORK. HE HAS ALSO WORKED AS A WRITER AND DIRECTOR FOR MANY FAVORED ANIME PRODUCTIONS INCLUDING *DRAGONBALL, LUPIN III, CASE CLOSED, KODOCHA* AND *KIDDY GRADE.* CURRENTLY HE PORTRAYS SEIJI ON *MOONPHASE,* KUZOU ON *SAMURAI SEVEN* AND ZENJIRO ON *KODOCHA.*

IN THE HIGH SEAS OF ILLUSTRATION HIS EFFORTS HAVE BEEN WITNESSED AS A COMIC BOOK ARTIST AND WRITER FOR DC'S *ELFQUEST* SERIES, AN ILLUSTRATOR FOR PVP CARD GAMES (MOST RECENTLY FOR THE *CHAMPIONS OF THE GALAXY* PRO WRESTLER CARD GAME) AND DEVELOPED PRODUCT ILLUSTRATIONS FOR *ULTRA-PRO* DECK BOXES AND CARD SLEEVES.

SONNY HOPES YOU ENJOY HIS SOJOURN INTO THE MURKY WATERS OF MANGA AND WARNS IF YOU ARE GEEK COUNTRY, UNMARRED BY HIS CAMPAIGN; KNOW THAT YOU ARE SO NEXT!

NOT JOHNNY DEPP

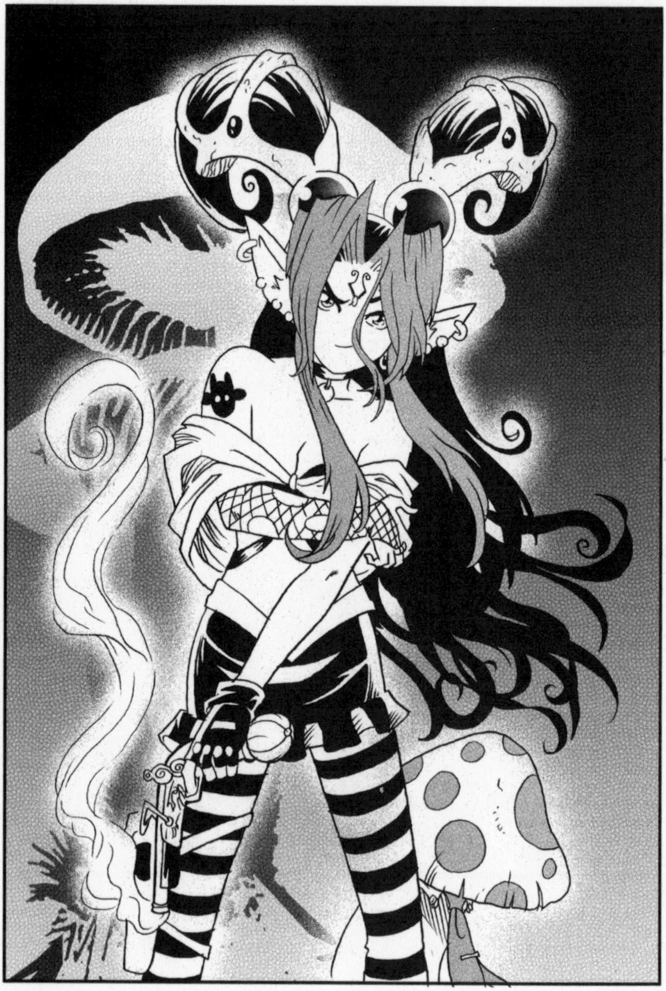

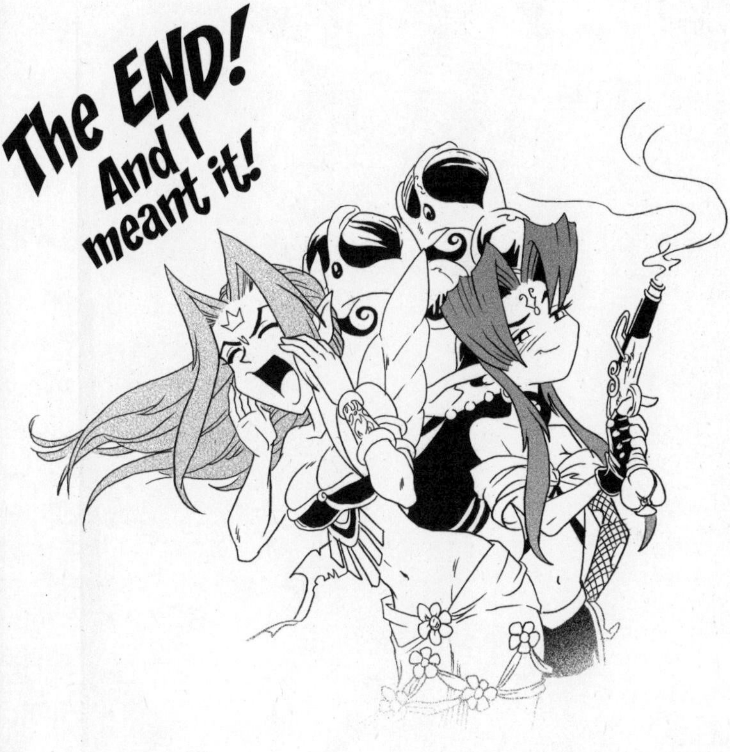
The END!
And I
meant it!

DARK MOON DIARY ™

After losing her parents in a tragic accident, Priscilla goes to live in a new town with her aunt's family. As if adjusting to a new family wouldn't be tough enough, her relatives turn out to be vampires who live in the ghoul-filled town of Nachtwald! Priscilla tries hard to assimilate, but with a ghost for a teacher, a witch as a friend, and food that winks at you, can she ever adapt to life in her new town? Or will she pack her garlic and head back to normal-ville?

FOR MORE INFORMATION VISIT: WWW.TOKYOPOP.COM